2023年第四季度
Fourth Quarter, 2023

中国货币政策执行报告
CHINA MONETARY POLICY REPORT

中国人民银行货币政策分析小组

Monetary Policy Analysis Group of
the People's Bank of China

中国金融出版社

责任编辑：黄海清　童祎薇

责任校对：孙　蕊

责任印制：丁淮宾

图书在版编目（CIP）数据

2023年第四季度中国货币政策执行报告/中国人民银行货币政策分析小组编. —北京：中国金融出版社，2024.6

ISBN 978-7-5220-2426-4

Ⅰ.①2…　Ⅱ.①中…　Ⅲ.①货币政策—工作报告—中国—2023　Ⅳ.①F822.0

中国国家版本馆CIP数据核字（2024）第099093号

2023年第四季度中国货币政策执行报告

2023 NIAN DI-SI JIDU ZHONGGUO HUOBI ZHENGCE ZHIXING BAOGAO

出版
发行　中国金融出版社

社址　北京市丰台区益泽路2号

市场开发部　（010）66024766，63805472，63439533（传真）

网 上 书 店　www.cfph.cn

　　　　　　（010）66024766，63372837（传真）

读者服务部　（010）66070833，62568380

邮编　100071

经销　新华书店

印刷　天津市银博印刷集团有限公司

尺寸　210毫米×285毫米

印张　12.25

字数　246千

版次　2024年6月第1版

印次　2024年6月第1次印刷

定价　108.00元

ISBN 978-7-5220-2426-4

如出现印装错误本社负责调换　联系电话（010）63263947

本书执笔人

总　纂：宣昌能　　邹　澜

审　稿：吕　政　　李　斌　　高　飞　　孙天琦　　张文红

　　　　金中夏　　张雪春　　丁志杰

统　稿：邱潮斌

执　笔：

第一部分：李　磊　　陈　涛　　曾冬青　　胡智慧　　王海纳

第二部分：刘　婕　　蔡春春　　宁　可　　张　昆　　周泽宇

　　　　　蔡思颖　　罗嗣源　　谢　峰　　邱文凯　　刘　珍

　　　　　张尔聪　　王　宁

第三部分：毛奇正　　尹曌天　　张原劼　　梁　爽

第四部分：张筱钰　　单敬雯　　张　琪　　陈　俊　　刘　旸

　　　　　王宜天

第五部分：魏辰皓　　程艳芬　　时昱旻

提供材料：李文喆　　刘生福　　李　航　　李思佳　　王西贝

　　　　　付　童　　陈宇春　　关孟杰　　陈　琳　　潘　璐

英文总纂：张丽红

英文审稿：张　勤　　陈苏燕　　以及前述审稿人、执笔人

　　　　　Nancy Hearst（美国哈佛大学费正清东亚研究中心）

英文翻译：蔡　筠　　陈　松　　陈苏燕　　丁　韡　　付　颖

　　　　　何君玲　　金　怡　　乐嘉旸　　李旷然　　刘翔宇

　　　　　刘孜群　　吴玉南　　张　勤　　章　曦　　郑朝亮

　　　　　钟　文　　周璐珍

Contributors to This Report

CHIEF EDITORS:

XUAN Changneng　　ZOU Lan

READERS:

LÜ Zheng　　LI Bin　　GAO Fei　　SUN Tianqi　　ZHANG Wenhong　　JIN Zhongxia
ZHANG Xuechun　　DING Zhijie

EDITORS:

QIU Chaobin

AUTHORS:

PART ONE: LI Lei　　CHEN Tao　　ZENG Dongqing　　HU Zhihui　　WANG Haina

PART TWO: LIU Jie　　CAI Chunchun　　Ning Ke　　ZHANG Kun　　ZHOU Zeyu
　　　　　　CAI Siying　　LUO Siyuan　　XIE Feng　　QIU Wenkai　　LIU Zhen
　　　　　　ZHANG Ercong　　WANG Ning

PART THREE: MAO Qizheng　　YIN Zhaotian　　ZHANG Yuanjie　　LIANG Shuang

PART FOUR: ZHANG Xiaoyu　　SHAN Jingwen　　ZHANG Qi　　CHEN Jun　　LIU Yang
　　　　　　WANG Yitian

PART FIVE: WEI Chenhao　　CHENG Yanfen　　SHI Yumin

OTHER CONTRIBUTORS: LI Wenzhe　　LIU Shengfu　　LI Hang　　LI Sijia　　WANG Xibei
　　　　　　　　　　FU Tong　　CHEN Yuchun　　GUAN Mengjie　　CHEN Lin
　　　　　　　　　　PAN Lu

ENGLISH EDITION

CHIEF EDITORS: ZHANG Lihong

EDITORS: ZHANG Qin　　CHEN Suyan　　above-mentioned readers and authors
　　　　Nancy Hearst (Fairbank Center for East Asian Research, Harvard University)

TRANSLATORS: CAI Yun　　CHEN Song　　CHEN Suyan　　DING Wei　　FU Ying
　　　　　　HE Junling　　JIN Yi　　YUE Jiayang　　LI Kuangran　　LIU Xiangyu
　　　　　　LIU Ziqun　　WU Yunan　　ZHANG Qin　　ZHANG Xi
　　　　　　ZHENG Zhaoliang　　ZHONG Wen　　ZHOU Luzhen

内容摘要

2023年是三年新冠疫情防控转段后经济恢复发展的一年，也是新一届政府的开局之年，在以习近平同志为核心的党中央坚强领导下，我国顶住外部压力、克服内部困难，加大宏观调控力度，国民经济回升向好，全年国内生产总值（GDP）同比增长5.2%，转型升级成效显著，高质量发展扎实推进。中国人民银行坚持以习近平新时代中国特色社会主义思想为指导，全面贯彻党的二十大精神，认真落实党中央、国务院决策部署，稳健的货币政策精准有力，适时强化逆周期调节，统筹把握总量与结构、数量与价格、内部与外部均衡，有效支持了实体经济发展。

一是加大货币信贷支持经济力度。全年两次降准释放长期资金超1万亿元，中期借贷便利（MLF）超额续作2.5万亿元，灵活开展公开市场操作，保持流动性合理充裕。多次召开金融机构座谈会，引导信贷总量适度、节奏平稳，增强贷款增长的稳定性和可持续性。二是降低融资成本激发有效需求。两次下调政策利率，带动贷款市场报价利率（LPR）等市场利率下行。发挥存款利率市场化调整机制作用，稳定银行负债成本。调整优化住房信贷政策，引导商业银行有序降低存量首套房贷利率。三是优化资金供给推动结构转型。出台金融支持民企的指导性文件，落实支持科技型企业融资行动方案；增加支农支小再贷款额度2 500亿元，延续实施普惠小微贷款支持工具、碳减排支持工具，增加抵押补充贷款（PSL）额度5 000亿元，引导金融资源更多流向重大战略、重点领域和薄弱环节。四是稳定汇率兼顾内外均衡。深化汇率市场化改革，适时上调跨境融资宏观审慎调节参数、下调外汇存款准备金率，发挥外汇自律机制作用，强化预期引导，调节外汇市场供求，保持人民币汇率在合理均衡水平上的基本稳定。五是处置重点领域风险保障金融稳定。加强金融风险监测评估，稳妥处置重点区域和重点机构风险。有序推进金融支持融资平台债务风险化解。强化金融稳定保障体系建设。

总体来看，2023年货币政策坚持稳字当头、稳中求进，为经济回升向好营造了良好的货币金融环境。货币信贷保持合理增长，年末人民币贷款余额达237.6万亿元，广义货币（M2）、社会融资规模存量同比分别增长9.7%和9.5%；全年新增贷款22.7万亿元，同比多增1.3万亿元。信贷结构持续优化，年末普惠小微贷款和制造业中长期贷款余额同比分别增长23.5%和31.9%；民营企业贷款同比增长12.6%，较上年末高1.6个百分点。社会融资成本稳中有降，12月新发放企业贷款加权平均利率为3.75%，较上年同期低0.22个百分点，持续创有统计以来新低；新发放个人住房贷款加权平均利率为3.97%，较上年同期低0.29个百分点，超过23万亿元存量首套房贷款利率平均下调0.73个百分点，每年减少借款人利息支出约1 700亿元。人民币汇率双向浮动、预期收敛，保持基本稳定，年末人民币对美元汇率收盘价为7.0920，较本轮低点升值逾3%。

我国发展仍处于重要的战略机遇期，市场空间广阔、产业体系完备、物质技术基础雄厚、人才红利不断增强，经济发展具有良好支撑，但也要看到，当前全球经济复苏动能分化，发达经济体政策调整、地缘政治冲突等不确定性上升，国内进一步推动经济回升向好需要克服一些困难挑战。综合来看，我国发展面临的有利条件强于不利因素，经济长期向好的基本趋势没有改变，要增强信心和底气。下一阶段，中国人民银行将坚持以习近平新时代中国特色社会主义思想为指导，完整、准确、全面贯彻新发展理念，坚持稳中求进、以进促稳、先立后破，加快建设金融强国，优化金融服务，坚定不移走中国特色金融发展之路，推动金融高质量发展。建设现代中央银行制度，强化宏观政策逆周期和跨周期调节，坚持把金融服务实体经济作为根本宗旨，始终保持货币政策的稳健性，增强宏观政策取向一致性，持续推动经济实现质的有效提升和量的合理增长。

稳健的货币政策要灵活适度、精准有效。合理把握债券与信贷两个最大融资市场的关系，准确把握货币信贷供需规律和新特点，引导信贷合理增长、均衡投放，保持流动性合理充裕，保持社会融资规模、货币供应量同经济增长和价格水平预期目标相匹配。加强政策协调配合，有效支持促消费、稳投资、扩内需，保持物价在合理水平。持续深化利率市场化改革，进一步完善贷款市场报价利率形成机制，发挥存款利率市场化调整机制作用，促进社会综合融资成本稳中有降。发挥好货币政策工具总量和结构双重功能。支持采取债务重组等方式盘活信贷存量，提升存量贷款使用效率。坚持聚焦重点、合理适度、有进有退，做好科技金融、绿色金融、普惠金融、养老金融、数字金融五篇大文章，抓好金融支持民营经济25条举措落实，加大对保障性住房建设、"平急两用"公共基础设施建设、城中村改造的金融支持力度。坚持以市场供求为基础、参考一篮子货币进行调节、有管理的浮动汇率制度，综合施策、稳定预期，防范汇率超调风险，防止形成单边一致性预期并自我强化，保持人民币汇率在合理均衡水平上的基本稳定。持续有效防范化解重点领域风险，坚决守住不发生系统性风险的底线。

Executive Summary

The year 2023 marked a turning point in economic recovery and development following three years of COVID-19 prevention and control, and it was also the first year of the new administration. Under the strong leadership of the CPC Central Committee with Comrade Xi Jinping at its core, China strengthened macroeconomic regulation and control against external pressures and internal difficulties. The national economy showed signs of recovery, with GDP growing 5.2 percent year on year. The year also witnessed remarkable achievements in transformation and upgrading as well as solid progress in high-quality development. Following the guidance of Xi Jinping Thought on Socialism with Chinese Characteristics for a New Era, the People's Bank of China (PBOC) fully implemented the spirit of the 20th CPC National Congress and conscientiously implemented the decisions and arrangements of the CPC Central Committee and the State Council. It pursued a prudent monetary policy in a targeted and effective manner, strengthened counter-cyclical adjustments as appropriate, and coordinated the relationships between aggregate and structure, quantity and price, as well as internal and external equilibria, thereby providing solid support for development of the real economy.

First, money and credit support was strengthened to bolster the economy. The required reserve ratio (RRR) was cut twice in 2023, releasing over RMB 1 trillion of long-term funds. The maturing medium-term lending facility (MLF) loans were rolled over with a higher injection of liquidity, and the operations injected a total of RMB 2.5 trillion into the market. With flexible open market operations (OMOs), the PBOC kept a reasonable and sufficient liquidity level. It also held meetings with financial institutions to guide them in maintaining a moderate credit aggregate and a steady pace of credit disbursement so as to enhance the stability and the sustainability of credit growth. Second, financing costs were lowered to stimulate effective demand. The policy rate was lowered twice, and the cuts brought down market rates such as the loan prime rate (LPR). The mechanism for market-oriented adjustments of deposit rates continued to play a role, and bank liability costs were stabilized. Housing credit policies were adjusted and improved, and commercial banks were guided to lower rates on existing first-home loans in an orderly manner. Third, the supply of funds was improved to promote a structural transformation. The PBOC rolled out guidance documents to encourage financial support for private enterprises and it also implemented the action plan to support the financing of technology-based enterprises. In addition, it increased central bank lending quotas for agricultural development and for micro and small businesses (MSBs) by RMB 250 billion, continued implementation of inclusive MSB loan facilities and the carbon emission reduction facility (CERF), and increased the quotas for pledged supplementary lending (PSL) by RMB 500 billion, thereby channeling more financial resources into major strategies, key areas, and weak links. Fourth, the RMB exchange rate was stabilized while internal and external equilibria were maintained. While deepening the market-oriented reform of the exchange rate, the PBOC raised the macro-prudential adjustment parameter for cross-border financing and cut the RRR for foreign currency deposits as appropriate. Giving play to the role of the foreign exchange market self-disciplinary mechanism, it strengthened expectation guidance and adjusted supply and demand in the foreign exchange market, thus keeping the RMB exchange rate basically stable at a reasonable and balanced level. Fifth, financial risks in key areas were handled to safeguard financial stability. The PBOC intensified financial risk monitoring and assessment and appropriately handled risks in key areas and with key institutions. The work of providing financial support to help resolve the debt risks of financing platforms was promoted in an orderly way, and development of a financial stability guarantee system was stepped up.

Overall, pursuing the principle of seeking progress while giving top priority to stability, the monetary policy created a prudent monetary and financial environment for economic recovery in 2023. Money and credit maintained reasonable growth. At end-2023, outstanding RMB loans reached RMB 237.6 trillion, and broad money (M2) and outstanding aggregate financing to the real economy (AFRE) recorded year-on-year growth of 9.7 percent and 9.5 percent, respectively. In 2023, new RMB loans registered RMB 22.7 trillion, RMB 1.3 trillion more than the amount in 2022. The credit structure continued to improve. At end-2023, inclusive MSB loans and medium and long-term (MLT) loans to the manufacturing sector grew by 23.5 percent and 31.9 percent year on year, respectively. Loans to private enterprises grew by 12.6 percent year on year, an acceleration of 1.6 percentage points from end-2022. Social financing costs were stable with a downward trend. In December, the weighted average rate on new corporate loans registered 3.75 percent, down 0.22 percentage points year on year and continuing to hit a record low; the weighted average rate on personal housing loans registered 3.97 percent, down 0.29 percentage points year on year.

Over RMB 23 trillion of existing first-home mortgages witnessed a rate decline averaging 0.73 percentage points, which resulted in a reduction in interest payments by RMB 170 billion for borrowers. Floating in both directions with more convergent expectations, the RMB exchange rate remained basically stable. It closed at 7.0920 against the US dollar at end-2023, an appreciation of over 3 percent from the trough during this round of fluctuations.

China is still in an important period of strategic opportunity for development. Economic development is well underpinned by a broad market, a fairly complete industrial system, a strong material and technological foundation, and increasing dividends from talent. However, it should also be noted that further economic recovery will require efforts to overcome some difficulties and challenges, in light of the uneven global economic recovery momentum as well as the rising uncertainties, such as the policy adjustments in the developed economies and geopolitical conflicts. From a holistic perspective, the favorable conditions for China's development outweigh the unfavorable ones, and the overall trend of economic recovery and long-term improvement remains unchanged. Confidence and determination must be boosted. During the next stage, under the guidance of Xi Jinping Thought on Socialism with Chinese Characteristics for a New Era, the PBOC will apply the new development philosophy fully, faithfully, and comprehensively, and it will adhere to the general principle of seeking progress while maintaining stability, promoting stability through progress, and establishing the new before abolishing the old. It will speed up efforts to build China into a financial powerhouse, improve financial services, firmly follow the path of financial development with Chinese characteristics, and promote high-quality development of the financial sector. The PBOC will develop a modern central banking system and strengthen counter-cyclical and inter-temporal adjustments to macro policies, with serving the real economy as the fundamental purpose of the financial sector. Maintaining prudence of monetary policies and enhancing consistency in the macroeconomic policy orientation, it will continue to effectively upgrade and appropriately expand economic output.

Prudent monetary policies will be flexible,moderate, precise, and effective. Based on a rational understanding of the relationship between the two largest financing markets, namely, the bond market and the credit market, as well as an appropriate grasp of the patterns and new features of money and credit supply and demand, the PBOC will guide a reasonable growth and a balanced provision of credit. By doing so, it will keep a reasonable and sufficient liquidity level that matches the growth of AFRE and the money supply with the expected targets for economic growth and price levels. It will enhance policy coordination and effectively support the initiative to boost consumption, stabilize investment, and expand domestic demand so as to keep prices at a reasonable level. By continuing to deepen the market-oriented interest rate reform, further improving the LPR formation mechanism, and leveraging the role of the mechanism for market-oriented deposit rate adjustments, it will promote overall social financing costs to remain stable with a downward trend. The PBOC will give play to the role of the monetary policy toolkit in adjusting both the aggregate and the structure. It will support the use of debt restructuring and other methods to activate existing stocks so as to improve efficiency in using existing loans. Implementing policies in a targeted, appropriate, and flexible way, the PBOC will work to develop technology finance, green finance, inclusive finance, pension finance, and digital finance. The 25 measures encouraging financial support for the private economy will continue to be implemented, and more financial support will be provided for the development of government-subsidized housing projects, the construction of public infrastructures for both daily and emergency uses, and the rebuilding of run-down urban areas. Pursuing a managed floating exchange rate regime based on market supply and demand with reference to a basket of currencies, the PBOC will take a holistic approach in policy implementation and stabilize expectations, and it will prevent risks arising from exchange rate overshooting and prevent expectations from becoming unanimously one-sided and self-reinforced so as to keep the RMB exchange rate basically stable at a reasonable and balanced level. The PBOC will continue its efforts to effectively prevent and resolve risks in key areas, thereby firmly defending the bottom line whereby no systemic financial risks will occur.

目　录

Contents

第一部分　货币信贷概况

2023年是全面贯彻党的二十大精神的开局之年，是三年新冠疫情防控平稳转段后经济恢复发展的一年。人民银行以习近平新时代中国特色社会主义思想为指导，全面贯彻落实党的二十大、中央经济工作会议、中央金融工作会议精神，按照《政府工作报告》部署，坚持稳字当头、稳中求进，稳健的货币政策精准有力，强化逆周期和跨周期调节，货币信贷和社会融资规模合理增长，综合融资成本稳中有降，信贷结构不断优化，人民币汇率在合理均衡水平上保持基本稳定，为经济回升向好营造了良好的货币金融环境。

一、银行体系流动性合理充裕

2023年，人民银行坚持稳健的货币政策，综合运用降准、再贷款再贴现、中期借贷便利（MLF）和公开市场操作等多种方式精准有力投放流动性，3月、9月两次降准各0.25个百分点，合计释放长期流动性超1万亿元。持续引导货币市场利率围绕央行公开市场逆回购操作利率平稳运行，为推动金融支持实体经济高质量发展提供了适宜的流动性环境，也为第四季度增发国债和地方政府再融资债券顺利发行提供了有力保障。2023年末，金融机构超额准备金率为2.1%，比上年末高0.1个百分点，银行体系流动性合理充裕。

二、金融机构贷款合理增长，贷款利率处于历史低位

信贷总量合理增长。2023年第一季度，受疫情防控进入新阶段及季节性规律等因素影响，信贷投放有所加快，人民银行着力引导金融机构贷款投放总量适度、节奏平稳。进入第二季度，市场信心和预期偏弱、信贷有效需求不足，人民银行加强逆周期调节，着力引导金融机构保持信贷均衡投放，增强

图1　货币市场利率走势

（数据来源：中国货币网）

表 1　2023 年人民币贷款结构

单位：亿元、%

贷款种类	12 月末余额	同比增速	当年新增额
人民币各项贷款	2 375 905	10.6	227 463
住户贷款	800 921	5.7	43 261
企（事）业单位贷款	1 554 232	13.0	179 074
非银行业金融机构贷款	7 748	40.1	1 928
境外贷款	13 005	32.8	3 200

数据来源：中国人民银行。

注：企（事）业单位贷款是指非金融企业及机关团体贷款。

表 2　2023 年分机构新增人民币贷款情况

单位：亿元

机构类型	当年新增额
中资大型银行①	129 274
中资中小型银行②	98 218
小型农村金融机构③	26 363
外资金融机构	−244

数据来源：中国人民银行。

注：①中资大型银行是指本外币资产总量大于等于2万亿元的银行（以2008年末各金融机构本外币资产总额为参考标准）。

②中资中小型银行是指本外币资产总量小于2万亿元的银行（以2008年末各金融机构本外币资产总额为参考标准）。

③小型农村金融机构包括农村商业银行、农村合作银行、农村信用社。

金融支持实体经济的可持续性。第四季度，人民银行统筹考虑岁末年初信贷投放节奏，及时召开金融机构座谈会，平滑贷款增长，当季信贷投放好于市场预期。2023年末，金融机构本外币贷款余额为242.2万亿元，同比增长10.1%，比年初增加22.2万亿元，同比多增1.5万亿元。人民币贷款余额为237.6万亿元，同比增长10.6%，比年初增加22.7万亿元，同比多增1.3万亿元。

信贷结构持续优化。2023年末，企（事）业单位中长期贷款比年初增加13.6万亿元，在全部企业贷款中占比为75.8%。制造业中长期贷款余额同比增长31.9%，比全部贷款增速高21.3个百分点。普惠小微贷款余额同比增长23.5%，比全部贷款增速高12.9个百分点；普惠小微授信户数6 166万户，同比增长9.1%。

专栏 1　准确把握货币信贷供需规律和新特点

中央金融工作会议明确提出要"准确把握货币信贷供需规律和新特点"。在高质量发展阶段，我们要不断深化对金融工作的规律性认识，切实提升金融服务实体经济的理念、能力和质效。

我国经济结构转型加快推进，要求信贷高质量投放。一方面，新动能贷款持续较快增长，占比稳步提升。2018年以来，普惠小微贷款、制造业中长期贷款、绿色贷款等增速持续高于全部贷款增速。目前，我国各项再贷款工具已实现对"五篇大文章"领域的基本覆盖，将持续引导金融机构加大对重大战略、重点领域和薄弱环节的支持力度，满足经济高质量发展合理的融资需求。另一方面，房地产、地方融资平台等传统动能贷款增势趋缓，占比逐渐下降。过去几年，我国每年20万亿元新增贷款中，房地产和地方融资平台占了很大比重。随着我国房地产发展模式重大转型、地方债务风险防范化解，这两部分贷款需求明显下降。上述两个方面合在一起，虽然总的增速可能较过去有所回落，但金融服务实体经济的质效是显著提升的。

存量和增量的关系也在发生变化，要更多注重盘活低效存量金融资源。目前，我国人民币贷款余额超过230万亿元，是每年增量的10倍，需要更加注重处理好总量与结构、存量与增量的关系，盘活低效存量、不良贷款核销、在社会融资总量中持续提升直接融资占比等，这些因素也会对今后信贷和融资增长带来积极影响。例如，盘活低效占用的金融资源，虽然不体现为贷款增量，但使用金融资源的主体效率提高，能为经济高质量发展注入新动力。再如，为维持商业银行稳健经营而加大不良贷款核销力度，会给贷款增长施加压力，但核销的贷款资金仍对实体经济有

支持作用，且已纳入社会融资规模的统计。又如，先进制造、科技创新、绿色低碳、数字经济等新兴产业蓬勃发展，这些新动能领域与直接融资的金融支持模式更为适配，也会对贷款形成良性替代。

要减少对月度货币信贷高频数据的过度关注。我国贷款增量存在比较明显的季节特征。从历年统计数据看，第一季度尤其是1月新增贷款会多一些，4月、7月、10月则是贷款小月，这些季节性规律主要与银行内外部考核以及融资需求特征有关，要客观看待。比如，我国俗语常说"一年之计在于春"，不少经营主体都会追求"开门红"，大的项目一般也在年初开工建设，还有年初的春耕备耕，春节前的工资发放，这些都会有季节性影响。为应对疫情冲击，近几年宏观政策"靠前发力"，第一季度贷款也进一步增多。由此可见，经济回升向好需要稳定、持续的信贷支持，关键是把握好"度"，平抑不正当竞争、"冲时点"等不合理的信贷投放，而不是改变金融机构信贷投放正常的季节规律，更好地促进信贷投放节奏与实体经济发展的实际需要相匹配。

总体来看，准确把握货币信贷供需规律和新特点，合理评价金融支持的力度，要解决好"看什么"的问题。高质量发展阶段，评判经济发展不只是看经济增速，评判金融支持也不能"唯信贷增量"。要多看利率下降的成效，社会融资成本稳中有降，说明实体经济信贷需求被合理满足；要多看科技创新、绿色发展、中小微企业等重点领域的金融支持力度，更好

反映金融资源对实体经济有效需求的满足程度；要多看涵盖直接融资的社会融资规模，或者拉长时间观察累计增量、余额增速等，更全面看待货币金融条件。下一步，稳健的货币政策将灵活适度、精准有效，强化逆周期和跨周期调节，继续推进

贷款加权平均利率持续处于历史低位。利率市场化改革不断深化，贷款市场报价利率（LPR）改革效能和存款利率市场化调整

存款利率市场化带动整体利率水平下行，保持信贷合理增长、均衡投放，同时，着力提升贷款使用效率，通过部分贷款到期回收后转投更高效率的经营主体、优化新增贷款投向、推动必要的市场化出清，为经济可持续发展提供更好支撑。

机制作用有效发挥，实际贷款利率稳中有降。2023年12月，1年期和5年期以上LPR分别为3.45%和4.20%，分别较上年12月下降0.2

表3　2023 年 12 月新发放贷款加权平均利率情况

项目	12 月（%）	比 9 月变化（个百分点）	同比变化（个百分点）
新发放贷款加权平均利率	3.83	−0.31	−0.31
一般贷款加权平均利率	4.35	−0.16	−0.22
其中：企业贷款加权平均利率	3.75	−0.07	−0.22
票据融资加权平均利率	1.47	−0.33	−0.13
个人住房贷款加权平均利率	3.97	−0.05	−0.29

数据来源：中国人民银行。

表4　2023 年 1～12 月金融机构人民币贷款利率区间占比

单位：%

月份	减点	LPR	加点					
			小计	(LPR，LPR+0.5%)	[LPR+0.5%，LPR+1.5%)	[LPR+1.5%，LPR+3%)	[LPR+3%，LPR+5%)	LPR+5%及以上
1 月	37.38	6.28	56.34	16.65	19.06	10.22	5.70	4.72
2 月	37.60	6.02	56.38	16.32	16.84	10.28	6.54	6.40
3 月	36.96	6.88	56.16	17.10	17.57	10.57	6.18	4.74
4 月	36.62	6.20	57.18	15.54	17.18	11.14	7.08	6.24
5 月	36.28	5.52	58.20	13.98	16.79	11.71	7.98	7.74
6 月	37.74	5.59	56.67	17.79	17.31	10.81	6.09	4.68
7 月	37.05	5.13	57.82	16.60	16.43	10.44	7.12	7.23
8 月	35.76	4.92	59.32	17.08	16.40	10.75	7.57	7.51
9 月	37.37	5.62	57.11	16.70	16.88	10.62	6.71	6.19
10 月	37.34	5.15	57.51	14.92	15.83	11.43	7.43	7.90
11 月	38.43	5.77	55.80	14.60	16.39	11.37	7.01	6.44
12 月	41.89	5.64	52.48	13.70	16.15	10.97	6.34	5.33

数据来源：中国人民银行。

个和0.1个百分点。12月，贷款加权平均利率为3.83%，同比下降0.31个百分点。其中，一般贷款加权平均利率为4.35%，同比下降0.22个百分点，企业贷款加权平均利率为3.75%，同比下降0.22个百分点，金融对实体经济的支持力度持续提升。12月，一般贷款中利率高于LPR的贷款占比为52.48%，利率等于LPR的贷款占比为5.64%，利率低于LPR的贷款占比为41.89%。

外币存款利率和贷款利率均有所上升。2023年12月，活期、3个月以内大额美元存款加权平均利率分别为2.23%和4.70%，分别较上年12月上升1.03个和1.04个百分点；3个月以内、3（含）~6个月美元贷款加权平均利率分别为5.81%和5.80%，分别较上年12月上升0.78个和0.81个百分点。

存款增加较多。2023年末，金融机构本外币存款余额为289.9万亿元，同比增长

表5　2023年1~12月大额美元存款与美元贷款平均利率

单位：%

月份	大额美元存款						美元贷款				
	活期	3个月以内	3（含）~6个月	6（含）~12个月	1年	1年以上	3个月以内	3（含）~6个月	6（含）~12个月	1年	1年以上
1月	1.25	3.99	4.62	5.34	5.46	4.96	4.91	5.12	5.10	5.53	5.99
2月	1.42	4.18	5.10	5.51	5.50	5.44	5.08	5.23	5.39	5.46	5.58
3月	1.64	4.23	5.02	5.53	5.67	5.54	5.25	5.33	5.11	5.34	5.86
4月	1.76	4.50	5.29	5.49	4.91	5.72	5.39	5.47	5.49	5.64	5.62
5月	1.78	4.63	4.65	5.68	5.63	5.64	5.55	5.46	5.52	5.39	5.98
6月	1.65	4.46	5.29	5.63	5.47	5.75	5.68	5.63	5.46	5.41	5.71
7月	2.13	4.44	5.12	5.50	5.52	5.28	5.68	5.66	5.59	5.31	5.65
8月	2.19	4.37	4.57	5.45	5.45	5.25	5.72	5.14	5.30	5.34	5.46
9月	2.26	4.50	5.20	5.34	5.58	5.39	5.88	5.49	5.45	5.42	6.34
10月	2.29	4.56	5.34	5.42	4.76	5.46	5.99	5.73	5.60	5.44	5.79
11月	2.19	4.61	4.69	4.75	4.85	5.37	5.85	5.80	5.59	5.51	6.34
12月	2.23	4.70	5.33	5.49	5.39	5.30	5.81	5.80	5.51	5.82	6.36

数据来源：中国人民银行。

表6　2023年人民币存款结构情况

单位：亿元、%

项目	12月末余额	同比增速	当年新增额
人民币各项存款	2 842 623	10.0	257 416
住户存款	1 369 895	13.8	166 655
非金融企业存款	787 756	5.5	42 235
机关团体存款	35 3261	7.1	22 836
财政性存款	57 937	15.8	7 924
非银行业金融机构存款	255 244	7.2	16 386
境外存款	18 531	9.1	1 380

数据来源：中国人民银行。

9.6%，比年初增加25.4万亿元，同比少增3 978亿元。人民币存款余额为284.3万亿元，同比增长10.0%，比年初增加25.7万亿元，同比少增5 101亿元。外币存款余额为7 978亿美元。比年初减少561亿美元，同比少减869亿美元。

三、货币供应量与社会融资规模合理增长

货币总量合理增长。2023年末，广义货币供应量（M2）余额为292.3万亿元，同比增长9.7%。狭义货币供应量（M1）余额为68.1万亿元，同比增长1.3%。流通中货币（M0）余额为11.3万亿元，同比增长8.3%。全年现金净投放8 815亿元，同比少投放5 047亿元。

社会融资规模平稳增长。初步统计，2023年末社会融资规模存量为378.1万亿元，同比增长9.5%。2023年社会融资规模增量累计为35.6万亿元，比上年同期多3.4万亿元。主要有以下特点：一是人民币贷款保持合理增长。2023年金融机构对实体经济发放的人民币贷款增加22.2万亿元，比上年同期多增1.2万亿元，占同期社会融资规模增量的62.4%。二是政府债券融资同比多增，企业债券融资和非金融企业境内股票融资均同比少增。2023年政府债券净融资9.6万亿元，企业债券净融资和非金融企业境内股票融资分别为1.6万亿元、7 931亿元。三是表外融资有所恢复。2023年委托贷款同比少增3 380亿元，信托贷款同比多增7 579亿元，未贴现银行承兑汇票同比少减1 627亿元。四是贷款核销力度较大。2023年贷款核销增加1.1万亿元，同比多增291亿元。

图2　广义货币（M2）和社会融资规模存量同比增速

（数据来源：中国人民银行）

表 7　2023 年社会融资规模

项目	2023 年 12 月末		2023 年	
	存量（万亿元）	同比增速（%）	增量（亿元）	同比增减（亿元）
社会融资规模	378.09	9.5	355 875	34 080
其中：人民币贷款	235.48	10.4	222 240	11 803
外币贷款（折合人民币）	1.66	−10.2	−2 206	3 048
委托贷款	11.27	0.2	199	−3 380
信托贷款	3.9	4.2	1 576	7 579
未贴现银行承兑汇票	2.49	−6.7	−1 784	1 627
企业债券	31.11	0.3	16 254	−4 254
政府债券	69.79	16	96 045	24 817
非金融企业境内股票融资	11.43	7.5	7 931	−3 826
其他融资	10.73	3.1	3 211	−5 257
其中：存款类金融机构资产支持证券	1.36	−31.6	−6 277	−4 415
贷款核销	8.61	14.6	10 967	291

数据来源：中国人民银行、国家金融监督管理总局、中国证券监督管理委员会、中央国债登记结算有限责任公司、银行间市场交易商协会等部门。

注：①社会融资规模存量是指一定时期末实体经济从金融体系获得的资金余额。社会融资规模增量是指一定时期内实体经济从金融体系获得的资金额。

②自2023年1月起，人民银行将消费金融公司、理财公司和金融资产投资公司三类银行业非存款类金融机构纳入金融统计范围。由此，对社会融资规模中"实体经济发放的人民币贷款"和"贷款核销"数据进行调整。

③表中同比数据按可比口径计算。

四、人民币汇率在合理均衡水平上保持基本稳定

2023年，跨境资本流动平稳有序，外汇市场供求基本平衡，人民币汇率预期总体稳定。国际形势复杂严峻，主要发达经济体利率维持高位，人民币汇率在全球主要货币中表现相对稳健，呈现双向波动特征，发挥了宏观经济和国际收支自动稳定器功能。全年人民币汇率以市场供求为基础，对一篮子货币汇率基本稳定。2023年末，中国外汇交易中心（CFETS）人民币汇率指数报97.42，较6月末升值0.7%，较上年末贬值1.3%。2005年人民币汇率形成机制改革以来至2023年末，国际清算银行测算的人民币名义和实际有效汇率分别升值42.3%和37.5%。2023年末，人民币对美元汇率中间价为7.0827元，较6月末升值2%，较上年末贬值1.7%，2005年人民币汇率形成机制改革以来累计升值16.9%。2023年，人民币对美元汇率年化波动率为4.9%。

跨境人民币业务保持增长，收支基本平衡。2023年，跨境人民币收付金额合计52.3万亿元，同比增长24%，在同期本外币跨境收付总额中的占比达58%，其中，实收25.4万亿元，实付26.9万亿元。经常项目下跨境人民币收付金额合计14万亿元，同比增长33%，其中，货物贸易收付金额10.7万亿元，服务贸易及其他经常项目下收付金额3.3万亿元；资本项目下人民币收付金额合计38.3万亿元，同比增长21%。2023年，货物贸易项下人民币跨境收付金额占同期本外币跨境收付比重为25%。

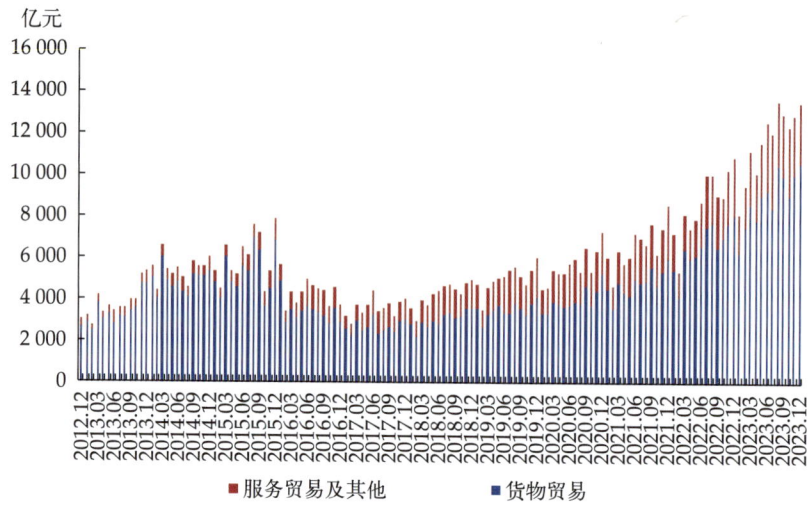

图3　经常项目人民币收付金额按月情况

（数据来源：中国人民银行）

第二部分　货币政策操作

2023年，人民银行坚决贯彻党中央、国务院决策部署，稳健的货币政策精准有力，综合运用降准、中期借贷便利、公开市场操作等工具，保持流动性合理充裕，引导金融机构信贷增长总量适度、节奏平稳；调整优化住房信贷利率政策，推动企业融资和居民信贷成本稳中有降；用好存续的专项再贷款工具，出台金融支持民营经济的指导性文件，加大对普惠金融、科技创新、绿色发展等重点领域和薄弱环节的支持，持续巩固经济回升向好势头。

一、灵活开展公开市场操作

全年公开市场逆回购操作利率两次下行。2023年6月和8月，公开市场7天期逆回购操作中标利率各下行10个基点，年末为1.8%，较上年末下降20个基点，通过金融市场传导带动降低企业融资成本，促进金融支持实体经济发展提质增效。第四季度，影响银行体系流动性供求的短期因素有所增多，人民银行密切关注经济金融运行情况，加强流动性监测分析，前瞻灵活开展公开市场逆回购操作，适时适度加大操作力度，保持银行体系流动性合理充裕，引导货币市场利率围绕公开市场操作利率平稳运行。

支持政府债券集中大量发行。第四季度，地方政府债券发行加快，新增1万亿元国债也集中发行，政府债券净融资额创历史新高。人民银行进一步加强货币政策与财政政策的协调配合，积极与财政部门沟通，及时加大公开市场逆回购等政策工具的操作力度，精准对冲财政发债因素的短期影响，维护流动性和市场利率平稳运行，也为政府债券顺利发行提供了有力支持。

前瞻稳定年底资金面。人民银行于12月18日即启动14天期逆回购操作，并视市场需求逐步加大操作力度，保持年末市场流动性合理充裕，保障各类市场机构平稳跨年。2023年末，公开市场逆回购操作余额为2.8万亿元，比上年末增加1.1万亿元；年末最后一个工作日，银行间市场存款类机构7天期回购加权平均利率（DR007）为1.91%，比上年同期低45个基点。

此外，第四季度人民银行继续每月开展央行票据互换（CBS）操作，助力提升银行永续债的二级市场流动性。同时，坚持常态化在香港发行人民币央行票据，并结合全球投资者需求增加了部分品种的发行规模。2023年，人民银行累计在香港发行12期共1 600亿元人民币央行票据，较上年增加400亿元，对于促进离岸人民币货币市场和债券市场健康发展发挥了积极作用。

二、超额续作中期借贷便利

持续超额续作中期借贷便利（MLF）。2023年12个月MLF均超额续作，其中12月操作量较到期量多8 000亿元，创历史新高。全年四个季度操作量分别为17 590亿元、5 320亿元、10 950亿元和36 890亿元，期限均为1年，年末余额为70 750亿元，比年初增加25 250亿元。MLF中标利率6月、8月分别下行10个和15个基点，年末利率为2.50%。MLF

连续超额续作，有效保障了中长期流动性合理供给。

及时开展常备借贷便利（SLF）操作。2023年，累计开展常备借贷便利操作共456亿元，四个季度操作量分别为77亿元、43亿元、69亿元和267亿元，年末余额为157亿元。年末，隔夜、7天、1个月常备借贷便利利率分别为2.65%、2.80%和3.15%。SLF操作为地方法人金融机构按需足额提供短期流动性支持，稳定了市场预期，增强了银行体系流动性的稳定性。

三、下调金融机构存款准备金率

下调金融机构人民币存款准备金率。2023年3月27日和9月15日，人民银行两次下调金融机构人民币存款准备金率各0.25个百分点，释放中长期流动性超过1万亿元。2024年2月5日，人民银行再次下调金融机构人民币存款准备金率0.5个百分点，释放中长期流动性超过1万亿元，有利于保障春节前资金供应，也有利于传递加大宏观政策调控力度的政策信号，增强社会信心和底气，还有利于优化央行向银行体系供给流动性的结构，降低银行体系资金成本。本次降准后，金融机构加权平均存款准备金率从7.4%降至7.0%。

下调金融机构外汇存款准备金率。自1993年建立外汇存款准备金制度以来，我国金融机构外汇存款准备金率保持相对稳定。近年来，为更有效地应对发达经济体货币政策调整带来的外部冲击，金融机构外汇存款准备金率多次调整。2022年以来，人民银行三次下调金融机构外汇存款准备金率，累计5个百分点，有效提升金融机构外汇资金运用能力，维护外汇市场平稳运行。其中，2023年9月15日，金融机构外汇存款准备金率下调2个百分点，由6%降至4%，释放外汇流动性约150亿美元。

四、继续完善宏观审慎制度和管理框架

发挥好宏观审慎评估（MPA）的导向作用。2023年，进一步优化MPA考核框架，引导金融机构适当平滑大小月信贷波动，保持信贷总量适度、节奏平稳；保持对普惠小微、制造业中长期融资的信贷支持力度。

完善系统重要性金融机构监管框架。9月22日，人民银行、金融监管总局发布2023年我国系统重要性银行名单。基于2022年数据评估认定的国内系统重要性银行共20家，较上年新增1家，包括6家国有商业银行、9家股份制商业银行和5家城市商业银行。第四季度，人民银行会同金融监管总局、财政部审查系统重要性银行提交的2023年恢复计划和处置计划建议，督促系统重要性银行提升风险应对能力。10月20日，人民银行、金融监管总局发布《系统重要性保险公司评估办法》，将系统重要性金融机构认定范围从银行业拓展到保险业，宏观审慎管理迈出新步伐。根据评估办法，对资产规模排名前10位的保险集团公司、人身保险公司、财产保险公司和再保险公司，主要从规模、关联度、资产变现和可替代性四个维度评估，得分达到或超过1 000分的保险公司将被认定为系统重要性保险公司。

调整跨境融资宏观审慎调节参数。7月20日，为进一步完善全口径跨境融资宏观审慎管理，继续增加企业和金融机构跨境资金来源，引导其优化资产负债结构，人民银行、外汇局决定将企业和金融机构的跨境融资宏观审慎调节参数从1.25上调至1.5。

五、发挥货币政策的结构优化作用

聚焦"五篇大文章",发挥货币政策工具总量和结构双重功能。普惠金融方面,运用支农支小再贷款、再贴现引导地方法人金融机构扩大对涉农、小微和民营企业的信贷投放,2024年1月25日下调支农支小再贷款、再贴现各期限档次利率0.25个百分点;扶贫再贷款按照现行规定进行展期,巩固脱贫攻坚成果,支持乡村振兴;继续引导10个省份地方法人金融机构运用好再贷款等工具,促进区域协调发展。2023年末,全国支农再贷款余额为6 562亿元,支小再贷款余额为1.7万亿元,扶贫再贷款余额为1 222亿元,再贴现余额为5 920亿元。继续实施普惠小微贷款支持工具。2023年末,工具累计提供激励资金554亿元,比年初增加279亿元,支持地方法人金融机构累计增加普惠小微贷款33 222亿元,比年初增加17 168亿元。绿色金融方面,碳减排支持工具延续实施至2024年末,将部分地方法人金融机构和外资金融机构纳入工具支持范围;支持煤炭清洁高效利用专项再贷款延续实施至2023年末。截至2023年末,两个工具余额分别为5 410亿元和2 748亿元,分别比年初增加2 314亿元和1 937亿元。科技金融方面,科技创新再贷款、设备更新改造专项再贷款等到期退出,存量资金继续发挥作用。2023年末,两个工具余额分别为2 556亿元和1 567亿元,分别比年初增加556亿元和758亿元。养老金融方面,继续在浙江、江苏等5个试点省份实施普惠养老专项再贷款。2023年末,工具余额为18亿元,比年初增加11亿元。

支持化解房地产风险,构建房地产发展新模式。继续实施保交楼贷款支持计划、租赁住房贷款支持计划、房企纾困专项再贷款等工具。2023年末,保交楼贷款支持计划余额为56亿元,比年初增加56亿元。12月增加抵押补充贷款额度5 000亿元,支持政策性开发性金融机构为保障性住房建设、城中村改造、"平急两用"公共基础设施建设提供信贷支持。2023年末,抵押补充贷款余额为3.3万亿元,比年初增加994亿元。

六、提升信贷政策的结构引导效能

持续优化民营和小微企业金融服务。2023年11月,人民银行牵头印发《关于强化金融支持举措 助力民营经济发展壮大的通知》,从持续加大信贷资源投入、深化债券市场体系建设、发挥多层次资本市场作用、加大外汇便利化政策和服务供给等方面,对金融支持民营经济发展提出具体要求。持续开展中小微企业金融服务能力提升工程,指导金融机构完善内部资金转移定价、绩效考核、尽职免责等政策安排,加快建立敢贷愿贷能贷会贷长效机制。截至2023年末,普惠小微贷款余额为29.4万亿元,同比增长23.5%;普惠小微授信户数为6 166万户,同比增长9.1%;12月新发放的普惠小微贷款加权平均利率为4.68%。

加大对乡村振兴领域的金融支持。持续推动《关于金融支持全面推进乡村振兴 加快建设农业强国的指导意见》落实落细,指导金融机构优化资源配置,持续加大对粮食和重要农产品稳产保供、农业科技装备和绿色发展、乡村产业高质量发展等重点领域金融资源投入。截至2023年末,全国涉农贷款余额为56.6万亿元,同比增长14.9%。

统筹抓好绿色发展和能源转型信贷支持。强化宏观信贷政策指导,发挥信贷资金对清洁能源、节能减排等绿色发展重点领域的精准支持作用；坚持"先立后破"，指导银行平稳保障好传统能源领域合理融资需求；按照"速度服从质量"的原则，推动绿色信贷规模高质量增长。截至2023年末，我国绿色信贷余额约为30.1万亿元，同比增长36.5%。

加大金融对养老领域支持力度。鼓励金融机构创新养老金融组织和产品体系，加大对养老机构和养老产业等信贷投放，做好金融适老化服务升级，助力应对人口老龄化国家战略。2023年末，开发银行、农业发展银行、工商银行、农业银行、中国银行、建设银行、交通银行七家银行各类养老产业贷款余额合计约1 000亿元，同比增长26.4%。

做好交通物流领域金融支持与服务。持续推动《关于进一步做好交通物流领域金融支持与服务的通知》落地见效，鼓励银行聚焦交通强国建设目标和经营主体需求，加大信贷支持力度。截至2023年末，交通运输、仓储和邮政业中长期贷款余额为18.0万亿元，同比增长12.1%。

持续做好制造业和科技创新金融服务。完善金融支持科技创新的政策框架，构建多元化接力式科创金融服务体系，开展科创金融服务能力提升专项行动。联合产业主管部门完善制造业和科技创新重点投资项目和企业融资对接机制，缓解银企信息不对称问题。定期开展全国性银行制造业和科技创新贷款通报，激励引导金融机构加大对制造业和科技创新信贷支持力度。截至2023年末，制造业中长期贷款余额为12.5万亿元，同比增长31.9%；高技术制造业中长期贷款余额为2.7万亿元，同比增长34.0%；科技型中小企业贷款、"专精特新"企业贷款同比分别

增长21.9%和18.6%，均明显超过全部贷款增速。

七、健全市场化利率形成和传导机制

深化利率市场化改革。持续释放贷款市场报价利率（LPR）改革效能，推动实际贷款利率明显下降。2023年，引导1年期LPR和5年期以上LPR分别下降0.2个和0.1个百分点。通过市场化的利率传导机制，引导实际贷款利率更大幅度下行。2023年，企业贷款加权平均利率为3.88%，同比下降0.29个百分点，为历史最低水平。发挥存款利率市场化调整机制作用，引导存款利率下降。2023年6月、9月和12月，主要银行根据自身经营需要和市场供求状况，主动下调存款利率，其中，中长期存款利率降幅更大，进一步优化了存款利率期限结构，提高了存款利率市场化程度，增强了金融支持实体经济的能力和可持续性，有效促进了投资和消费。

调整优化个人住房信贷利率政策。降低存量首套房贷利率。8月31日，与金融监管总局联合发布《关于降低存量首套住房贷款利率有关事项的通知》，引导借贷双方有序降低存量首套房贷利率，切实减轻居民利息负担，支持扩大消费。同时，督促主要银行第一时间将存量房贷利率下调到位，减少居民操作成本。已有超过23万亿元存量房贷的利率完成下调，调整后加权平均利率为4.27%，平均降幅为73个基点，每年减少借款人利息支出约1 700亿元，惠及5 325万户约1.6亿人，受到各方普遍好评。引导新发放房贷利率持续下降。降低二套房贷利率政策下限至LPR加20个基点，发挥新发放首套房贷利率政策动态调整机制作用，引导新发放房贷利

率下行。截至2023年12月，全国343个城市（地级及以上）中，101个下调了首套房贷利率下限，26个取消了下限。2023年，新发放个人住房贷款利率为4.1%，同比下降0.75个百分点。

专栏2 利率自律机制十年：市场化改革的重要保障

自2013年成立以来，利率自律机制坚持市场化改革方向，切实服务宏观调控和金融管理要求，通过务实精干的组织架构和高效有序的工作机制，对合计超过400万亿元的存贷款利率定价进行有效的自律管理，以有限资源撬动了较大规模的管理实效，成为走好中国特色金融发展之路的生动实践。

利率自律机制是深化利率市场化改革的重要制度安排。党的十八大以来，人民银行持续深化利率市场化改革。2012年，允许存款利率适当上浮；2013年7月，贷款利率管制完全放开，改革进入深水区和攻坚期。当时我国金融机构自身和市场环境条件还有待完善，如果不能有效维护市场竞争秩序，就无法实现"放得开，形得成，调得了"的改革目标。2013年9月，人民银行充分借鉴美国、德国等成熟市场通过市场自律方式维护竞争秩序的经验，并结合我国利率市场化改革的实际情况，构建了利率自律机制。

通过加强自律促进市场规范健康发展。组织架构上，利率自律机制由定价能力较强的商业银行牵头，充分体现市场化特征。议事机制上，通过不定期召开工作会议，加强行业自律和协调，维护市场竞争秩序，有序推进利率市场化改革。利率自律机制赋予成员单位更多市场定价权和产品创新权，推动金融机构完善公司治理和提升服务水平，促进形成市场化环境下的合理均衡利率，引导金融资源优化配置，支持经济高质量发展，提升广大人民群众福祉。

利率自律机制工作取得显著成效。一是协助推进贷款市场报价利率（LPR）改革。2019年8月，人民银行推动LPR改革，LPR报价行均为利率自律机制成员。利率自律机制受权承担组织LPR报价工作，督促报价行合理报价，有效反映市场利率走势，传达货币政策意图。同时，推动各类放贷机构明示贷款年化利率，保护金融消费者合法权益。二是促进存款利率市场化程度进一步提高。2015年10月，人民银行放开了银行存款利率的行政性管制。利率自律机制加强高息揽储等非理性定价行为的自律管理，协助清理整顿不规范存款创新产品。2021年6月，将存款利率自律上限改为在基准利率上加点形成，消除杠杆效应。2022年4月，建立存款利率市场化调整机制，引导成员单位参照市场利率变化合理调整存款利率水平。三是有效发挥合格审慎评估作用。通过评估，把具有较好公司治理和较强定价能力的金融机构遴选出来，夯实利率市场化改革的微观基础。持续优化评估指标体系，完善激励约束机制。2023年，利率自律机制成员已有2 055

家，占商业银行数量的一半左右。四是指导省级利率自律机制高效履职。人民银行各省级分行组织建立了省级利率自律机制，目前已初步形成全国—省级利率自律机制协调联动格局，确保第一时间将利率自律要求传达至各层级金融机构，形成工作合力。此外，利率自律机制还在保障存单市场高效运行、参与国际基准利率改革方面发挥了重要作用。

下一步，人民银行将指导利率自律机制完善利率自律管理方式，为健全市场化利率形成、调控和传导机制，推动金融更好服务实体经济作出新贡献。一是加强对LPR报价的监督管理和考核评估，提高报价质量，为促进社会综合融资成本稳中有降提供有力支持。引导成员单位根据市场利率变化合理调整存款利率水平。二是督促银行持续健全存贷款利率定价机制，坚持风险定价原则，切实理顺信贷市场和债券市场、大银行和中小银行之间的利率关系。三是建立健全自律约谈和通报机制，提升利率自律的严肃性和权威性，完善利率自律机制组织架构，促进高效履职。

八、深化人民币汇率市场化改革

完善以市场供求为基础、参考一篮子货币进行调节、有管理的浮动汇率制度。坚持市场在汇率形成中起决定性作用，人民币对国际主要货币汇率有升有贬、双向浮动，发挥汇率调节宏观经济、国际收支的自动稳定器和减震器功能。针对2023年年中人民币汇率外部压力较大的情况，综合采取措施，加强预期管理，防范大起大落。7月上调跨境融资宏观审慎调节参数，9月下调外汇存款准备金率，并召开外汇市场自律机制专题会议，增发离岸央票，平衡外汇市场供求，防范汇率超调风险，保持人民币汇率在合理均衡水平上的基本稳定。2023年，人民币对美元汇率中间价最强为6.7130元，最弱为7.2258元，242个交易日中142个交易日升值、98个交易日贬值、2个交易日持平。最大单日升值幅度为1.0%（654点），最大单日贬值幅度为0.9%（630点）。2023年末，人民币对美元、欧元、英镑、日元汇率中间价分别较6月末升值2%、0.2%、1.1%和贬值0.2%。2005年人民币汇率形成机制改革以来至2023年末，人民币对美元汇率累计升值16.9%，对欧元汇率累计升值27.4%，对英镑汇率累计升值59.4%，对日元汇率累计升值45.5%。银行间外汇市场人民币直接交易成交较为活跃，流动性平稳，降低了企业汇兑成本，促进了双边贸易和投资。

九、防范化解处置金融风险

加强系统性风险监测评估。不断加强系统性金融风险监测和评估，健全金融稳定监测评估框架。持续跟进银行业、证券业、保险业、金融市场风险监测。组织银行业金融机构进行压力测试，及时进行风险提示，引导金融机构稳健运行。

防范化解金融风险取得新成效。进一步完善金融风险监测、评估与防控体系，对新增高风险银行机构建立具有硬约束的早期纠正制度，提升早期纠正的标准化和权威性。定期完成央行金融机构评级工作，对全国4 000多家银行业金融机构开展评级，不断压降高风险机构数量。对预警银行苗头性问题及时纠偏,实现风险"早识别、早预警、早暴露、早处置"。

金融支持融资平台债务风险化解有序推进。推动地方政府和融资平台通过盘活或出售资产等方式,筹措资源偿还债务。引导金融机构按照市场化、法治化原则,与融资平台平等协商,通过展期、借新还旧、置换等方式,分类施策化解存量债务风险、严控增量债务,并建立常态化的融资平台金融债务监测机制。支持地方政府通过并购重组、注入资产等方式,逐步剥离融资平台政府融资功能。

十、提升跨境贸易和投融资服务能力

推进跨境贸易便利化政策优化扩围。持续推动跨境贸易领域改革,出台提升跨境贸易结算便利化的相关措施,进一步优化贸易外汇收支结算业务流程、支持特殊业务办理,推动高水平开放试点政策扩容升级,帮助企业降本增效、防范汇率风险。

不断优化外汇服务。便捷境外来华人员移动支付服务,为杭州亚运会、成都大运会提供优质外汇保障服务,深化跨境金融服务平台建设,拓展多样化应用场景。

深化外汇市场建设。优化企业汇率避险服务,对全国性银行汇率风险管理工作开展专项评估。指导外汇交易中心免收2023年中小微企业外汇套保手续费,并延长外币货币市场和外币对市场交易时间。发布2023—2024年度做市商名单,优化做市商结构。做好新增澳门元挂牌工作。

支持区域开放创新。在横琴粤澳、前海深港、雄安新区等重点区域先行先试外汇管理创新政策,服务国家重大区域发展战略。在上海、江苏、广东(含深圳)、北京、浙江(含宁波)、海南全域扩大实施跨境贸易投资高水平开放政策试点,便利经营主体合规办理外汇业务。

深化对外货币金融合作。稳步推进双边本币互换,优化本币互换框架,发挥互换对支持离岸人民币市场发展和促进贸易投资便利化的作用。以周边及共建"一带一路"国家为重点,加强央行间本币结算合作,优化境外人民币使用环境。2023年末,在人民银

表8 2023年银行间外汇即期市场人民币对各币种交易量

单位:亿元人民币

币种	美元	欧元	日元	港元	英镑	澳大利亚元	新西兰元
交易量	600 511.35	8 320.50	4 994.78	2 082.93	364.38	557.25	123.97
币种	新加坡元	瑞士法郎	加拿大元	马来西亚林吉特	俄罗斯卢布	南非兰特	韩元
交易量	131.31	159.88	448.76	22.97	85.68	5.57	47.51
币种	阿联酋迪拉姆	沙特里亚尔	匈牙利福林	波兰兹罗提	丹麦克朗	瑞典克朗	挪威克朗
交易量	7.16	28.48	5.60	4.53	8.83	53.01	6.19
币种	土耳其里拉	墨西哥比索	泰铢	柬埔寨瑞尔	哈萨克斯坦坚戈	蒙古图格里克	印度尼西亚卢比
交易量	1.38	24.34	57.60	0	0.06	0	26.19

数据来源:中国外汇交易中心。

行与境外货币当局签署的双边本币互换协议下，境外货币当局动用人民币余额1 148.86亿

元，人民银行动用外币余额折合2.46亿美元，对促进双边贸易投资发挥了积极作用。

专栏3　稳步推进央行间双边本币互换

央行间双边本币互换是一种融资安排，一国央行可以用自己的货币置换另一国货币，以此获得对方货币流动性，一般用于维护金融市场稳定等目的，到期后再换回。中央银行之间签署双边本币互换协议是国际上的成熟做法。20世纪60年代，美联储开始与欧洲部分国家央行开展本币互换合作。目前，美联储、加拿大银行、英格兰银行、欧洲中央银行、日本银行、瑞士国家银行6家央行间互相签署有互换协议。在与中国人民银行签署本币互换协议外，欧洲中央银行还与丹麦国家银行、瑞典银行、波兰国家银行签署有本币互换协议，日本银行还与泰国银行、新加坡金融管理局、澳大利亚银行签署有本币互换协议。另外，在次贷危机和新冠疫情期间，美联储与其他一些国家央行也建立了临时性本币互换安排。

2008年国际金融危机后，中国人民银行与境外央行或货币当局开始签署本币互换协议。当时主要国际货币流动性较为紧张，部分国家之间使用本币进行结算的需求上升。中国人民银行累计与超过40家境外央行或货币当局签署了双边本币互换协议。2022年以来，中国人民银行将与香港金融管理局的本币互换协议升级为常备互换安排，与沙特阿拉伯中央银行签署本币互换协议，与印度尼西亚银行、新加坡金融管理局、欧洲中央银行、阿联酋中

央银行等央行或货币当局续签本币互换协议。目前有效双边本币互换协议共31份，基本覆盖了全球六大洲重点地区的主要经济体，互换协议总规模合计约4.16万亿元人民币。互换协议规模是可使用互换资金的上限，并不等同于资金实际使用规模。2023年末，境外央行或货币当局实际使用人民币互换资金余额为1 149亿元人民币，实际使用余额占双边本币互换签约总规模不到3%。为防范汇率变化可能产生的影响，本币互换协议设置了汇率保障机制，互换资金使用期间，双方货币汇率波动超过一定幅度后，会及时按新汇价调整互换货币数量。

双边本币互换在多方面发挥着积极作用。一是人民币双边本币互换已成为全球金融安全网的重要组成部分，在增强市场信心、维护区域和全球金融稳定方面发挥了积极作用。例如，新冠疫情期间，中国人民银行与多个国家和地区央行或货币当局新签、续签双边本币互换协议或扩大互换规模，增强了相关国家和地区应对疫情冲击、保持金融稳定的能力。二是互换资金可用于支持双边贸易投资活动，帮助市场主体节约汇兑成本、降低汇率风险。例如，有的外国企业进口货物希望使用人民币支付时，可申请使用本币互换来获得人民币资金，满足双边贸易支付需求。三是为离岸市场提供必要流动性，优化货币使

用环境。例如，与香港金融管理局签署常备互换协议，可以为香港市场提供更加稳定、长期限的流动性支持，更好发挥香港离岸人民币业务枢纽的功能，促进香港金融业发展。

下一步，中国人民银行将继续聚焦人民币双边本币互换提供流动性支持、维护金融稳定等功能，持续优化本币互换网络布局，更好发挥双边本币互换全球金融安全网组成部分的作用。同时，进一步完善互换交易的操作管理机制，提高互换资金使用效率，维护互换资金安全，支持对方央行合理使用人民币互换资金，便利双边贸易和投资。

第三部分　金融市场运行

2023年金融市场整体平稳运行。货币市场利率小幅下行，市场交易活跃，银行间衍生品市场成交量保持增长。债券市场规模稳定增长，利率水平总体下行。证券市场、保险市场运行总体稳健。

一、金融市场运行概况

（一）货币市场利率小幅回落，市场交易活跃

货币市场利率回落。2023年12月，同业拆借月加权平均利率为1.78%，质押式回购月加权平均利率为1.9%，比9月分别低9个和6个基点。银行业存款类金融机构间利率债质押式回购月加权平均利率为1.64%，低于质押式回购月加权平均利率26个基点。2023年末，隔夜和7天期Shibor分别为1.75%和1.87%，同比分别下降21个和36个基点。

货币市场回购交易活跃。2023年，银行间市场债券回购累计成交1 674.2万亿元，日均成交6.7万亿元，同比增长21.3%；同业拆借累计成交143万亿元，日均成交5 719亿元，同比减少2.6%。从期限结构看，隔夜回购成交量占回购总量的87.5%，比重较上年同期上升1.1个百分点；隔夜拆借成交量占拆借总量的89.5%，比重较上年同期上升0.3个百分点。交易所债券回购累计成交457.6万亿元，同比上升13.4%。

表9　2023年金融机构回购、同业拆借资金净融出、净融入情况

单位：亿元

机构类型	回购市场		同业拆借	
	2023 年	2022 年	2023 年	2022 年
中资大型银行①	−7 547 504	−5 159 892	−559 860	−461 874
中资中型银行②	−1 080 044	−1 505 272	−33 055	−173 370
中资小型银行③	605 794	156 731	101 333	86 211
证券业机构④	2 282 209	1 754 480	424 875	443 887
保险业机构⑤	249 533	229 671	1 952	2 803
外资银行	63 531	55 363	−14 810	−20 464
其他金融机构及产品⑥	5 426 481	4 468 919	79 566	122 807

数据来源：中国外汇交易中心。

注：①中资大型银行包括工商银行、农业银行、中国银行、建设银行、国家开发银行、交通银行、邮政储蓄银行。
②中资中型银行包括政策性银行、招商银行等9家股份制商业银行、北京银行、上海银行、江苏银行。
③中资小型银行包括恒丰银行、浙商银行、渤海银行、其他城市商业银行、农村商业银行和合作银行、民营银行、村镇银行。
④证券业机构包括证券公司、基金公司和期货公司。
⑤保险业机构包括保险公司和企业年金。
⑥其他金融机构及产品包括城市信用社、农村信用社、财务公司、信托投资公司、金融租赁公司、资产管理公司、社保基金、基金、理财产品、信托计划、其他投资产品等，其中部分金融机构和产品未参与同业拆借市场。
⑦负号表示净融出，正号表示净融入。

同业存单和大额存单业务有序发展。2023年，银行间市场发行同业存单2.7万期，发行总量为25.7万亿元，二级市场交易总量为253.6万亿元，年末同业存单余额为14.8万亿元；3个月期同业存单发行加权平均利率为2.4%，较同期限Shibor高8个基点。全年金融机构发行大额存单6.3万期，发行总量为14.2万亿元，同比增加1.6万亿元。

利率互换市场平稳运行。2023年，人民币利率互换市场达成交易35.2万笔，同比增长44.1%；名义本金总额为31.7万亿元，同比增长50.8%。从期限结构看，1年期及1年期以下交易最为活跃，名义本金总额达21.7万亿元，占总量的68.5%。人民币利率互换交易的浮动端参考利率主要包括7天期回购定盘利率和Shibor，与之挂钩的利率互换交易名义本金占比分别为91.5%和7.4%。以LPR为标的的利率互换全年成交1 256笔，名义本金为2 319.3亿元。

利率期权业务平稳发展。2023年利率期权交易共计成交1 007笔、1 606.8亿元，均为挂钩LPR的利率期权产品，其中利率上/下限期权成交1 586.8亿元，利率互换期权成交20亿元。

（二）债券利率整体回落，市场规模稳定增长

债券发行利率回落。2023年12月，财政部发行的10年期国债收益率为2.59%，较9月下降5个基点，较上年同期下降24个基点；主体评级AAA级的企业发行的1年期短期融资券平均利率为3.09%，较上年同期下降76个基点。国家开发银行12月未安排发行，11月发行的10年期金融债收益率为2.66%，较9月下降3个基点。

国债收益率整体下行，期限利差小幅收窄。2023年末，1年期、3年期、5年期、

表 10　2023 年利率互换交易情况

年度	交易笔数（笔）	交易量（亿元）
2023	352 279	317 071.9
2022	244 397	210 295.6

数据来源：中国外汇交易中心。

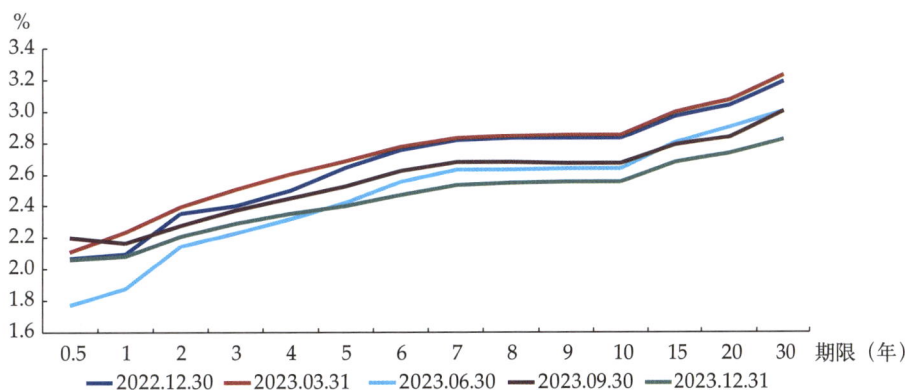

图4　银行间市场国债收益率曲线变化情况

（数据来源：中央国债登记结算有限责任公司）

7年期、10年期国债收益率分别为2.08%、2.29%、2.40%、2.53%和2.56%，较9月末分别下行9个、8个、13个、14个和12个基点；1年期和10年期国债利差为48个基点，较9月末收窄3个基点。

债券发行同比增长。2023年累计发行各类债券70.8万亿元，同比增长15.3%，比上年增加9.4万亿元，主要是国债及地方政府债、同业存单增加较多。年末，国内各类债券托管余额为157.9万亿元，同比增长9.1%。其中，境外机构持有境内债券余额为3.7万亿元，占全部托管量的2.4%，占比与上年末持平。

现券交易量增长。2023年债券市场现券总成交353.9万亿元，同比增长14.5%，其中银行间债券市场现券交易307.3万亿元，同比增长13.3%。交易所债券现券成交46.6万亿元，同比增长23%。

（三）票据融资稳中有升，票据市场利率有所下降

票据承兑业务稳中有升。2023年，企业累计签发商业汇票31.4万亿元，同比上升14.5%；期末商业汇票未到期金额17.1万亿元，同比下降1.4%。票据承兑余额有所上升，年末余额较第三季度末增加4 940亿元，较上年末减少2 381亿元。由中小微企业签发的银行承兑汇票占比为69.6%，较上年上升1.3个百分点。

票据融资稳中有升，利率有所下降。2023年，金融机构累计贴现62.6万亿元，同比上升16.2%。年末票据融资余额为13.2万亿元，同比上升2.7%；占全部贷款的比重为5.5%，同比下降0.5个百分点。2023年末票据市场利率较上年末下降，全年呈先升后降趋势。

表 11　2023 年各类债券发行情况

单位：亿元

债券品种	发行额	较上年同期增减
国债	110 956	13 793
地方政府债券	93 254	19 698
中央银行票据	0	0
金融债券①	364 417	58 222
其中：国家开发银行及政策性金融债	58 760	327
同业存单	257 815	52 694
公司信用类债券②	138 206	1 487
其中：非金融企业债务融资工具	86 979	−4 355
企业债券	3 808	−2 384
公司债	36 458	8 248
国际机构债券	1 430	605
合计	708 263	93 804

数据来源：中国人民银行、中国证券监督管理委员会、中央国债登记结算有限责任公司，根据提供方最新数据更新。

注：①金融债券包括国家开发银行金融债、政策性金融债、商业银行普通债、商业银行次级债、商业银行资本混合债、证券公司债、同业存单等。

②公司信用类债券包括非金融企业债务融资工具、企业债券以及公司债、可转债、可分离债、中小企业私募债，非金融企业发行的交易所资产支持证券等。

（四）股票市场成交量和筹资额同比减少

2023年末，上证综合指数收于2 975点，较上年末回落3.7%；深证成分指数收于9 525点，较上年末回落13.5%。分板块看，通信行业涨幅超20%，电子、汽车等也涨幅居前；商贸零售、房地产等表现较弱。股票市场成交量和筹资额同比减少。全年沪、深股市累计成交212.2万亿元，日均成交8 769亿元，同比减少5.5%。北向资金全年仍保持流入态势，连续第10年实现净买入。全年沪、深股市累计筹资9 170亿元，同比减少30.4%。

（五）保险业保费收入同比增加，资产增长加快

2023年，保险业累计实现保费收入5.1万亿元，同比增长9.1%，比上年高4.5个百分点；累计赔款、给付1.9万亿元，同比增长21.9%，其中，财产险赔付同比增长18.2%，人身险赔付同比增长25.7%。

保险业资产增长加快。2023年末，保险业总资产30万亿元，同比增长10.4%，比上年末高1.3个百分点。其中，银行存款同比下降3.9%，投资类资产同比增长12.3%。

（六）外汇即期、掉期交易量同比增加，远期交易量减少

2023年，人民币外汇即期交易累计成交金额折合8.7万亿美元，同比增长4.8%；人民币外汇掉期交易累计成交金额折合20.6万亿美元，同比增长6.8%，其中隔夜美元掉期交易累计成交金额13.9万亿美元，占总成交金额的67.5%；人民币外汇远期交易累计成交金额折合1 200亿美元，同比减少7.7%。"外币对"累计成交金额折合1.8万亿美元，同比增长18.9%，其中成交最多的产品为美元对日元，市场份额为37.3%。

（七）黄金价格上涨，成交量增加

2023年末，国际黄金价格收于2 078.4美元/盎司，较上年末上涨14.6%；上海黄金交易所Au99.99收于479.59元/克，较上年末上涨16.8%。2023年，上海黄金交易所黄金成交量4.15万吨，同比增长7.1%；成交额18.6万亿元，同比增长22.3%。

二、金融市场制度建设

（一）货币市场制度建设

强化重要货币市场基金监管。2023年2月，证监会联合人民银行共同发布《重要货币市场基金监管暂行规定》，明确了定义及评估条件、标准、程序，对重要货币市场基金的基金管理人、托管人和销售机构提出更为严格审慎的要求，进一步提升重要货币市场基金产品的安全性和流动性，有效防范风险。

表12　2023年末主要保险资金运用余额及占比情况

单位：亿元、%

项目	余额		占资产总额比重	
	2023年末	2022年末	2023年末	2022年末
资产总额	299 573	271 467	100.0	100.0
其中：银行存款	27 243	28 348	9.1	10.4
投资	249 495	222 161	83.3	81.8

数据来源：国家金融监督管理总局。

规范经纪报价及数据展示行为。8月，金融监管总局联合人民银行、证监会、外汇管理局发布《关于规范货币经纪公司数据服务有关事项的通知》，规范货币经纪公司提供数据服务，鼓励数据依法合理使用，确保数据安全，提升市场信息透明度，促进市场公平竞争。

（二）债券市场制度建设

规范银行间债券市场债券估值业务。12月，人民银行发布《银行间债券市场债券估值业务管理办法》，明确了估值机构内部治理、估值基本原则、估值方法、信息披露、利益冲突等要求，提高债券估值业务的中立性、公允性、专业性、透明性，提升债券市场定价的有效性和市场功能，防范市场风险。

稳步扩大债券市场高水平对外开放。指导有关金融基础设施机构落地便利投资一揽子措施。一是拓展在华外资机构作为"北向通"做市商，借助外资做市商在区域境外客户资源、跨境服务能力等方面的较强优势，更好服务境外投资者群体。二是提供一篮子债券组合交易功能，更好满足指数类投资者需求，降低多只债券调仓时的询价成本，提升交易效率。三是优化"北向通"结算失败报备流程，通过基础设施系统改造，实现线上化、一站式报备，较大改善了投资的操作便利度。四是推动内地与香港利率互换市场互联互通合作，通过两地基础设施互联互通，为境外投资者提供更加便利的利率风险管理渠道。

专栏4　进一步深化内地与香港金融合作

近年来，人民银行认真贯彻落实党中央决策部署，按照"一国两制"方针，积极与香港金管局等金融管理部门沟通，推动两地金融合作，支持香港巩固国际金融中心地位，取得了积极成效。

香港全球离岸人民币业务枢纽地位不断强化。自2018年起，人民银行在香港常态化发行人民币央行票据，为香港离岸人民币市场提供高信用等级资产，截至2023年末，累计发行央票7 250亿元。同时，人民银行大力支持内地政府部门、金融机构和非金融企业赴港发行债券，不断完善香港人民币收益率曲线。自2021年10月起，深圳市政府连续三年在香港发行离岸人民币地方政府债券。此外，人民银行与香港金管局签署的本币互换协议已升级为常备互换安排，规模扩大至8 000亿元人民币，为香港离岸人民币业务发展提供中长期流动性支持。目前，香港已成为全球最重要的离岸人民币业务枢纽，跨境人民币结算量在境外国家（地区）中排名始终保持第一，全球约75%的离岸人民币支付通过香港结算。同时，香港的离岸人民币资金池规模、人民币存款规模、人民币债券发行规模以及人民币外汇交易量均在全球主要离岸人民币市场中位居第一。

内地与香港金融市场互联互通持续深化。香港作为连接内地与国际市场的桥梁，一直是国际投资者进入内地投资的重要渠道。为强化香港国际资产管理中心地位，自2014年起，人民银行与两地金融监管部门密切合作，相继推出"沪深港通""债券通""跨境理财通""互换通"等机制。目前，国际投资者持有的A股约七成通过"沪深港通"投资，交易的内地债券超过一半通过"债券通"北向通完成。在此基础上，2024年1月，人民银行和香港金管局等共同推出多项互联互通优化举措，发布优化粤港澳大湾区"跨境理财通"业务试点的实施细则，将"债券通"项下债券纳入香港金管局人民币流动资金安排的合格抵押品，并计划进一步开放境外投资者参与境内债券回购业务，支持包括"债券通"渠道在内的所有已进入银行间债券市场的境外机构参与债券回购。

香港参与粤港澳大湾区建设更加深入。近年来，人民银行会同有关部门先后出台金融支持粤港澳大湾区和前海深港合作区建设的意见，支持香港充分发挥先行先试的政策优势，陆续在粤港澳大湾区内启动合格境内有限合伙人（QDLP）和合格境外有限合伙人（QFLP）试点，扩大港澳居民代理见证开立内地个人Ⅱ类、Ⅲ类银行账户试点银行范围，并支持港澳版"云闪付"钱包、支付宝（香港）电子钱包和微信（香港）电子钱包扩大在全国的适用范围。2024年1月，人民银行还出台文件，更好满足港澳居民在粤港澳大湾区的置业需求，并宣布扩大深港跨境征信合作试点范围，便利两地企业跨境融资。

两地绿色和可持续金融合作有序推进。近年来，两地在绿色金融合作平台建设、绿色债券发行等领域开展了多项合作。2020年9月，粤港澳大湾区绿色金融联盟成立，为两地深化绿色金融合作搭建平台。2022年7月，人民银行推动发布内地首个企业赴香港发行绿色债券的流程参考，支持地方政府和企业主体赴港发行绿色债券。目前，深圳市已连续三年赴港发行绿色和可持续发展债券。香港已成为亚洲绿色投融资的重要市场，累计发行绿色债券超过800亿美元，可持续发展基金（ESG基金）管理的总资产达1 600亿美元。

两地金融科技合作成果丰硕。长期以来，两地在央行数字货币、金融科技监管等领域积极开展务实合作。数字货币方面，自2020年起，人民银行与香港金管局启动数字人民币跨境支付试点项目，并在2024年初进一步深化，为香港和内地居民企业带来更多便利。同时，人民银行与香港金管局共同参与的多边央行数字货币桥项目进展顺利，已完成国际首例基于真实交易场景的试点测试。金融科创方面，2021年10月，人民银行与香港金管局签署金融科技创新监管合作备忘录，稳妥有序推进金融科技创新合作，并于2023年11月与香港金管局、澳门金管局在此基础上签署一项合作备忘录，将人民银行金融科技创新监管工具、香港金管局金融科技监管沙盒、澳门金管局创新金融科技试行项目联网对接。

下一步，人民银行将进一步深化内地和香港金融合作，支持香港国际金融中心建设，推动香港加快融入国家发展大局。继续在港常态化发行人民币央行票据，支持具备条件的地方政府、金融机构和企业赴港发行离岸人民币债券，巩固香港全球离岸人民币业务枢纽地位。深化两地金融市场互联互通，继续优化"债券通""跨境理财通""互换通"等机制，支持香港巩固国际资产管理中心地位。加快推动金融支持粤港澳大湾区建设的各项政策落地，为香港居民在粤港澳大湾区工作、

生活提供便利的金融环境。加强与香港在绿色金融领域的业务合作和规则衔接，支持内地金融机构赴港发行各类绿色金融产品，支持香港发展成为绿色和可持续金融中心。与香港金管局加强金融科技领域合作，共同深化金融科技创新监管协同，不断深化数字人民币跨境试点，支持香港打造亚太地区金融科技枢纽。

（三）证券市场改革和制度建设

稳步推进全市场注册制改革。2023年2月，证监会宣布正式启动全面实行股票发行注册制改革，并发布相关制度规则。本次改革覆盖各类公开发行股票行为，对完善资本市场功能、落实创新驱动发展战略、更好服务高质量发展具有重要意义。4月10日，首批主板注册制企业上市。

加强基金行业制度体系建设。7月，证监会发布《私募投资基金监督管理条例》，全面规范资金募集和备案要求、投资业务活动和市场化退出机制。同月，证监会印发《公募基金行业费率改革工作方案》，分阶段全面优化公募基金费率模式。12月8日，证监会就《关于加强公开募集证券投资基金证券交易管理的规定》公开征求意见，推进公募基金行业第二阶段费率改革。同日，证监会发布《私募投资基金监督管理办法（征求意见稿）》，促进私募基金行业规范健康发展。

完善证券公司及上市公司监管制度体系。11月3日，证监会就修订《证券公司风险控制指标计算标准规定》公开征求意见，进一步完善证券公司风控指标体系。11月17日，证监会发布《上市公司向特定对象发行

可转换公司债券购买资产规则》，支持上市公司以定向可转债为支付工具实施重组，置入优质资产、提高上市公司质量。12月，证监会修订发布《上市公司股份回购规则》，增强回购制度包容度和便利性，推动上市公司重视回购、实施回购、规范回购。

完善资本市场制度建设。2月，证监会发布《境内企业境外发行证券和上市管理试行办法》和5项配套指引，更好支持企业依法合规赴境外上市，推进资本市场双向开放。10月，证监会发布通知健全融券及战略投资者出借配售股份制度，强化融券业务监管。同月，证监会发布《公司债券发行与交易管理办法》及配套文件，完善公司债券的发行、交易或转让行为，保护投资者的合法权益和社会公共利益。

（四）保险市场制度建设

提升人身保险、财产保险服务质量。2023年1月，银保监会发布《一年期以上人身保险产品信息披露规则》，要求充分揭示产品的长期属性和各类风险特征，并明示交费方式、退保损失等产品关键内容。同月，发布《关于财产保险业积极开展风险减量服务

的意见》，要求各财产保险公司扩展风险减量服务内容，增加服务供给，做好消费者权益保护。当月还发布《关于扩大商业车险自主定价系数浮动范围等有关事项的通知》，优化和保障车险产品供给。7月，金融监管总局发布《关于适用商业健康保险个人所得税优惠政策产品有关事项的通知》，扩大所得税优惠政策适用范围，降低医疗费用负担。

加强保险公司监管。9月，金融监管总局发布《保险销售行为管理办法》，分阶段对保险销售行为加以规制，更好维护保险消费权益。同月，金融监管总局发布《关于优化保险公司偿付能力监管标准的通知》，对不同险种、不同规模保险公司实施差异化资本监管，优化资本计量标准和风险因子，引导保险公司支持服务实体经济和科技创新。10月，人民银行和金融监管总局联合印发

《系统重要性保险公司评估办法》，将每两年根据参评保险公司评估指标数据认定系统重要性保险公司，该办法自2024年1月1日起施行。

完善养老保险制度。9月，金融监管总局发布《关于个人税收递延型商业养老保险试点与个人养老金衔接有关事项的通知》，明确衔接过程中的业务调整、产品管理、保单转移等，保障各项工作有序开展。10月，金融监管总局印发《促进专属商业养老保险发展有关事项的通知》，进一步扩大经营专属商业养老保险业务的机构范围。11月，印发《养老保险公司监督管理暂行办法》，对养老保险公司机构管理、公司治理、风险管理等多个方面提出具体要求，弥补养老保险公司缺乏专门监管规定的制度短板。

第四部分　宏观经济分析

一、世界经济金融形势

2023年全球经济增长呈现韧性，但动能趋于弱化。发达经济体通胀压力总体缓解，第四季度以来普遍暂缓加息，劳动力市场保持强劲。展望未来，全球贸易延续低迷、发达经济体宏观政策不确定性、地缘政治风险等对经济增长的影响仍需关注。

（一）主要经济体经济和金融市场概况

全球经济复苏进一步分化。美国经济运行总体平稳，2023年第四季度GDP环比折年率为3.3%，较第三季度的4.9%有所回落，但仍高于市场预期，经济实现软着陆的概率上升。欧洲经济表现疲软，第四季度欧元区GDP同比增长0.1%，环比持平。日本经济增长放缓，第三季度GDP环比折年率萎缩2.9%，与上半年回暖态势形成强烈反差。主要发达经济体制造业PMI普遍位于收缩区间；服务业PMI表现相对较强，美国、日本维持在荣枯线上方，欧元区自8月起跌至荣枯线下方，也显示了经济增长动能分化。

美欧通胀压力较快回落，年末有所反复。12月，美国CPI同比上涨3.4%，较年初回落3个百分点，但较11月小幅走高，核心CPI延续回落态势。12月欧元区HICP同比上涨2.9%，较11月有所回弹，结束此前8个月连续回落态势。12月英国CPI同比上涨4.0%，较上月小幅反弹0.1个百分点，但明显低于年初10%以上的水平。

劳动力市场依然强劲。12月，美国新增非农就业21.6万人，连续2个月回升；美国失业率为3.7%，与11月持平，较10月下降0.1个百分点；劳动参与率为62.5%，较11月下降0.3个百分点；非农就业时薪同比上涨4.1%，较11月的4%略有反弹。12月，职位空缺数从11月的892.5万个反弹至902.6万个。

国际金融市场大幅波动。全球股市总体上涨。2023年，美国标普500指数、欧元区STOXX50指数和日经225指数分别累计上涨24.2%、19.2%和28.2%。8~10月，全球股市曾大幅波动，上述三大股指均显著回调，但10月底后恢复涨势。债市收益率震荡下行。11月以来，全球通胀压力趋缓，经济活动趋弱，市场对主要央行的降息预期升温，主要发达经济体10年期国债收益率大幅下行。年末，美国10年期国债收益率收报3.88%，较10月中旬高点下降110个基点，与上年末基本持平。德国、英国10年期国债收益率分别收报2.02%和3.62%，比上年末分别低49个和18个基点。美元指数波动下行。2023年前三季度总体震荡走强，第四季度以来大幅回落，年末收报101.38，较9月末下跌4.5%，较上年末下跌2.0%。

（二）主要经济体货币政策

主要发达经济体加息周期接近尾声。2023年，美联储全年加息4次，累计加息100个基点，联邦基金利率目标区间由年初的4.25%~4.5%上调至5.25%~5.5%，9月至年末连续三次暂停加息。同时，美联储继续按计划进行缩表，缩表速度为每月上限600亿美元国债、350亿美元抵押贷款支持证券

表 13　主要发达经济体宏观经济金融指标

经济体	指标	2022 年第四季度			2023 年第一季度			2023 年第二季度			2023 年第三季度			2023 年第四季度		
		10 月	11 月	12 月	1 月	2 月	3 月	4 月	5 月	6 月	7 月	8 月	9 月	10 月	11 月	12 月
美国	实际 GDP 增速（环比折年率，%）	2.6			2.2			2.1			4.9			3.3		
	失业率（%）	3.6	3.6	3.5	3.4	3.6	3.5	3.4	3.7	3.6	3.5	3.8	3.8	3.8	3.7	3.7
	CPI（同比，%）	7.7	7.1	6.5	6.4	6.0	5.0	4.9	4.0	3.0	3.2	3.7	3.7	3.2	3.1	3.4
	DJ 工业平均指数（期末）	32 733	34 590	33 147	34 086	32 657	33 274	34 098	32 908	34 408	35 559	34 722	33 508	33 053	35 951	37 690
欧元区	实际 GDP 增速（同比，%）	1.8			1.3			0.6			0.0			0.1		
	失业率（%）	6.6	6.7	6.7	6.7	6.6	6.5	6.5	6.5	6.4	6.5	6.5	6.5	6.5	6.4	6.4
	HICP（同比，%）	10.6	10.1	9.2	8.6	8.5	6.9	7.0	6.1	5.5	5.3	5.2	4.3	2.9	2.4	2.9
	EURO STOXX 50（期末）	3 618	3 964	3 793	4 163	4 238	4 315	4 359	4 218	4 399	4 471	4 297	4 175	4 061	4 382	4 522
英国	实际 GDP 增速（同比，%）	0.6			0.4			0.3			0.3			—		
	失业率（%）	3.7	3.7	3.7	3.8	3.9	3.8	4.0	4.2	4.2	4.2	4.2	4.2	4.2	—	—
	CPI（同比，%）	11.1	10.7	10.5	10.1	10.4	10.1	8.7	8.7	7.9	6.8	6.7	6.7	4.6	3.9	4.0
	富时 100 指数（期末）	7 095	7 573	7 452	7 772	7 876	7 632	7 871	7 446	7 532	7 699	7 439	7 608	7 322	7 454	7 733
日本	实际 GDP 增速（环比折年率，%）	1.0			5.0			3.6			-2.9			—		
	失业率（%）	2.6	2.5	2.5	2.4	2.6	2.8	2.6	2.6	2.5	2.7	2.7	2.6	2.5	2.5	2.4
	CPI（同比，%）	3.7	3.8	4.0	4.3	3.3	3.2	3.5	3.2	3.3	3.3	3.2	3.0	3.3	2.8	2.6
	日经 225 指数（期末）	27 587	27 969	26 095	27 327	27 446	28 041	28 856	30 888	33 189	33 172	32 619	31 857	30 859	33 487	33 464

数据来源：各经济体相关统计部门及中央银行。

（MBS）。欧央行2023年加息6次，累计加息200个基点，主要再融资操作利率、边际贷款便利利率和存款便利利率分别上调至4.5%、4.75%和4%，第四季度连续两次暂停加息。此外，欧央行自3月起开始缩表，6月底前平均每月减持150亿欧元，7月起停止资产购买计划（APP）下的到期证券本金再投资，并计划从2024年下半年起降低抗疫紧急购债计划（PEPP）下的资产规模，平均每月减持75亿欧元，2024年底停止到期证券本金再投资。英格兰银行2023年加息5次，累计加息175个基点至5.25%，第四季度连续两次暂停加息。英格兰银行计划于2023年10月至2024年9月期间减持1 000亿英镑英国国债至6 580亿英镑。日本银行维持短期政策利率在-0.1%、10年期国债收益率目标在0附近，但提高了收益率曲线控制（YCC）的灵活性，以1%作为收益率浮动的参考上限。此外，2023年澳大利亚、新西兰、加拿大、韩国央行分别加息5次、3次、3次和1次，累计加息幅度分别为125个、125个、75个和25个基点。

新兴市场经济体货币政策分化。俄罗斯、南非、墨西哥、印度尼西亚、印度、马来西亚央行2023年分别加息5次、3次、2次、2次、1次和1次，累计加息幅度分别为850个、125个、75个、50个、25个和25个基点。智利、巴西央行均降息4次，累计降息幅度分别为300个和200个基点。

（三）值得关注的问题和趋势

经济增长动能趋缓。2023年全球经济表现出一定韧性，一个重要原因是前期刺激政策的累积效应。随着政策效应不断消退，而加息的滞后影响逐渐显现，全球经济未来增长动能可能进一步弱化。国际货币基金组织（IMF）预测，2024年全球经济增速为3.1%，与2023年持平，世界银行、经济合作与发展组织（OECD）对2024年全球经济增速的预测分别为2.4%和2.9%，但都低于2000年至2019年3.8%的年均水平。

通胀将延续缓慢下行态势。发达经济体通胀已由高点的9%以上大幅回落至3%左右。目前，全球供应链已基本恢复，消费需求也有所降温，发达经济体通胀大概率延续回落势头。但考虑到服务项目通胀仍具黏性，地缘政治冲突还可能引发大宗商品价格波动，通胀回落仍是一个相对缓慢的过程。IMF预测，全球通胀水平将从2023年的6.9%稳步降至2024年的5.8%，多数经济体的通胀要到2025年才能回落至目标区间。

主要发达经济体央行何时启动降息有较大不确定性。2023年第四季度，美联储、欧央行和英格兰银行均暂缓加息，但三家央行表态出现分化。美联储政策重心从控通胀转向在稳增长和控通胀之间寻求平衡，欧央行和英格兰银行仍坚持"鹰派"表态。美联储在2024年1月议息会议声明中表示，在对通胀持续向2%回落更有信心前不宜降低利率，市场对美联储3月降息预期有所降温。

政治和地缘政治风险上升制约经济增长。美国、俄罗斯、印度、巴西等70余个国家和地区将于2024年进行大选，不仅选举结果将对全球政治经济格局产生影响，选举过程的不确定性也会对全球经济运行造成扰动。地缘政治冲突一波未平一波又起。俄乌冲突已持续近两年，双方战事仍处于胶着状态，冲突正向长期化演进；巴以冲突再度爆发，中东地区局势更趋复杂，也会增加全球经济发展的不确定性。

二、中国宏观经济形势

2023年，面对复杂严峻的国际环境和艰巨繁重的国内改革发展稳定任务，各地区各部门坚决贯彻落实党中央、国务院决策部署，加大宏观调控力度，国民经济回升向好，供给需求稳步改善，转型升级积极推进，就业物价总体稳定，民生保障有力有效，高质量发展扎实推进。初步核算，全年国内生产总值126.1万亿元，按不变价格计算，同比增长5.2%。其中，第四季度同比增长5.2%，环比增长1.0%。

（一）消费恢复较快，投资规模继续扩大，进出口总体平稳

居民收入持续增加，市场销售恢复较快。2023年，全国居民人均可支配收入39 218元，同比名义增长6.3%，扣除价格因素实际增长6.1%，较前三季度加快0.2个百分点。收入分配结构持续改善，农村居民人均可支配收入名义增速和实际增速分别快于城镇居民2.6个和2.8个百分点。2023年，最终消费支出

对经济增长的贡献率达到82.5%。全年社会消费品零售总额同比增长7.2%。基本生活类消费稳定增长,限额以上单位服装鞋帽针纺织品类、粮油食品类商品零售额同比分别增长12.9%和5.2%;升级类商品销售增长较快,限额以上单位金银珠宝类,体育、娱乐用品类,通信器材类商品零售额同比分别增长13.3%、11.2%和7.0%。消费者信心指数企稳回升,12月为87.6,较年中低点回升1.3个百分点。

投资规模继续扩大,高技术产业投资增势较好。2023年,资本形成总额对经济增长的贡献率为28.9%。全年全国固定资产投资(不含农户)503 036亿元,同比增长3.0%。分领域看,制造业投资增长6.5%,高于全部投资3.5个百分点;基础设施投资增长5.9%;房地产开发投资下降9.6%。高技术产业投资增长10.3%,快于全部投资7.3个百分点。其中,高技术制造业、高技术服务业投资分别增长9.9%和11.4%。高技术制造业中,航空、航天器及设备制造业,计算机及办公设备制造业,电子及通信设备制造业投资分别增长18.4%、14.5%和11.1%;高技术服务业中,科技成果转化服务业、电子商务服务业投资分别增长31.8%和29.2%。

货物进出口总体平稳,贸易结构持续优化。2023年,货物进出口总额417 568亿元,同比增长0.2%。其中,出口增长0.6%,进口下降0.3%,贸易顺差57 884亿元。民营企业进出口增长6.3%,占进出口总额的比重为53.5%,比上年提高3.1个百分点。对"一带一路"共建国家进出口增长2.8%,占进出口总额的比重为46.6%,比上年提高1.2个百分点。机电产品出口增长2.9%,占出口总额的比重为58.6%。

外商直接投资基本稳定,引资质量持续提升。2023年,全国实际使用外资金额11 339.1亿元,同比下降8%。引资质量持续提升,高技术制造业实际使用外资增长6.5%,其中电子及通信设备制造业、医疗仪器设备及仪器仪表制造业分别增长12.2%和32.1%。建筑业和科学成果转化服务领域实际使用外资分别增长43.7%和8.9%。

(二)农业生产形势总体良好,工业生产稳步回升,服务业增长较快

2023年,第一产业增加值89 755亿元,同比增长4.1%;第二产业增加值482 589亿元,同比增长4.7%;第三产业增加值688 238亿元,同比增长5.8%。

农业生产形势总体良好,畜牧业生产稳定增长。2023年,农林牧渔业增加值同比增长4.2%。全年全国粮食总产量69 541万吨,比上年增加888万吨,增长1.3%。全年猪牛羊禽肉产量9 641万吨,比上年增长4.5%,其中猪肉产量5 794万吨,增长4.6%。年末,生猪存栏下降4.1%。全年生猪出栏增长3.8%。

工业生产稳步回升,装备制造业增长较快。2023年,全国规模以上工业增加值同比增长4.6%,比前三季度加快0.6个百分点。从三大门类看,采矿业增加值增长2.3%,制造业增长5.0%,电力、热力、燃气及水生产和供应业增长4.3%。装备制造业增加值增长6.8%,增速比规模以上工业快2.2个百分点。分经济类型看,国有控股企业增加值增长5.0%,私营企业增长3.1%。分产品看,太阳能电池、新能源汽车、发电机组(发电设备)产品产量分别增长54.0%、30.3%和28.5%。

服务业增长较快,接触型聚集型服务业

明显改善。2023 年，服务业增加值同比增长 5.8%。其中，住宿和餐饮业，信息传输、软件和信息技术服务业，金融业增加值同比分别增长 14.5%、11.9% 和 6.8%。12 月，服务业生产指数同比增长 8.5%。其中，住宿和餐饮业，信息传输、软件和信息技术服务业生产指数分别增长 34.8% 和 13.8%。1~11 月，规模以上服务业企业营业收入同比增长 8.5%。其中，文化、体育和娱乐业，信息传输、软件和信息技术服务业营业收入分别增长 18.9% 和 12.8%。

（三）居民消费价格小幅上涨，核心 CPI 总体平稳

居民消费价格温和上涨。2023 年，居民消费价格指数（CPI）同比上涨 0.2%，总体呈前高后低、逐步放缓态势，第四季度同比平均下跌 0.3%。从供给看，国内产能充足且恢复较快，第四季度工业产能利用率为 75.9%，较第一季度回升 1.6 个百分点。从需求看，消费恢复动能边际减弱，第四季度社会消费品零售总额的季调环比约为 0.3%，低于上半年的 0.8%。此外，猪肉等食品价格的基数影响加大，第四季度猪肉价格下拉 CPI 超过 0.5 个百分点，果蔬等其他食品价格涨幅也低于历史同期均值。全年食品价格同比下降 0.3%，非食品价格同比上涨 0.4%，涨幅分别比上年回落 3.2 个和 1.4 个百分点；不包括食品和能源的核心 CPI 同比上涨 0.7%，涨幅比上年低 0.2 个百分点。

生产价格降幅收窄。受国际大宗商品价格震荡回落、需求偏弱、供给充足和上年高基数等因素影响，2023 年工业生产者出厂价格指数（PPI）同比持续下降，全年下降 3.0%，比上年低 7.3 个百分点。总体来看，PPI 呈 "V 形" 走势，年中 6 月降至最低点 -5.4%，12 月降幅收窄至 -2.7%。全年工业生产者购进价格指数（PPIRM）同比下降 3.6%，比上年低 9.9 个百分点。人民银行监测的企业商品价格指数（CGPI）同比下降 2.1%，比上年同期低 5.6 个百分点。

（四）财政收入平稳增长，财政支出保持稳定

2023 年，全国一般公共预算收入 21.7 万亿元，同比增长 6.4%。其中，中央和地方本级财政收入分别增长 4.9% 和 7.8%。全国税收收入 18.1 万亿元，同比增长 8.7%。其中，国内增值税增长 42.3%，主要是由于上年同期留抵退税较多、基数较低。

2023 年，全国一般公共预算支出 27.5 万亿元，同比增长 5.4%。其中，中央一般公共预算本级支出和地方一般公共预算支出分别增长 7.4% 和 5.1%。从支出结构看，社会保障和就业支出、科学技术支出和教育支出增长较快，同比分别增长 8.9%、7.9% 和 4.5%。

（五）就业形势总体平稳

城镇调查失业率下降。2023 年，全国城镇调查失业率平均值为 5.2%，比上年下降 0.4 个百分点。12 月，全国城镇调查失业率为 5.1%，同比回落 0.4 个百分点。重点群体就业持续改善，2023 年农民工总量达到 2.98 亿人，比上年增加 191 万人，外来农业户籍人口城镇调查失业率全年均值比上年下降 0.7 个百分点。

（六）国际收支及外债

2023 年前三季度，我国经常账户顺差 2 090 亿美元，与同期国内生产总值（GDP）

之比为1.6%。其中，国际收支口径的货物贸易顺差4 544亿美元；服务贸易逆差1 684亿美元，国内居民跨境旅游、留学等有序恢复，目前仍低于疫情前水平。从初步统计情况看，全年经常账户顺差继续处于相对高位，并保持在合理均衡区间。资本项下跨境投资活动有序开展，总体呈现趋稳向好态势。其中，外商股权性质直接投资保持净流入，第四季度明显回升；我国对外股权性质直接投资稳定增长。证券投资逐步恢复净流入，第四季度境外投资者净增持境内债券超过620亿美元。2023年末，我国外汇储备余额32 380亿美元，较上年末增加1 103亿美元，主要受汇率折算和资产价格变化等因素综合影响。截至2023年9月末，我国全口径（含本外币）外债余额23 829亿美元。

（七）行业分析

1. 机械工业

机械工业是为国民经济发展提供技术装备支撑的基础性和战略性行业。2023年，机械工业整体呈现回暖态势，高质量发展稳步推进。一是行业运行平稳，盈利状况提升。机械工业营业收入与利润总额在规模以上工业中的占比均在两成以上，2023年同比分别增长6.8%和4.1%，都明显高于规模以上工业总体增速。二是创新发展引领固定资产投资保持增长。全年汽车、电气机械行业投资增速分别达19.4%和32.2%，为拉动制造业投资提供重要支撑。三是出口产品结构升级趋势明显。电动载人汽车、锂电池和太阳能电池"新三样"产品全年出口破万亿元大关，同比增长29.9%。

也要看到，我国机械工业回升向好的基础尚不牢固。一是需求压力较为突出，近年来机械工业中低端产品需求明显放缓，加之钢铁、煤炭等下游传统行业处于产业转型期，机械工业行业经营压力加大。二是转型升级任重道远，我国机械工业门类齐全、规模优势突出，但产业链韧性不强，部分关键零部件依赖进口，一些基础材料也落后于国际先进水平。三是行业内部存在分化，虽然机械工业行业总体稳定向好，汽车等行业增长较快，但也有部分行业面临较大下行压力。

展望未来，我国机械工业高质量发展将扎实推进。一是更加聚焦自主创新能力。加快发展战略性新兴产业，充分发挥企业技术创新主体作用，加强梯次衔接的多层次人才队伍建设，进一步建立完善产业技术创新体系，培育优质品牌产品。二是不断坚实产业基础。以制造业绿色低碳化改造为契机，持续推动产业优化升级，推进设备更新、工艺优化、产品升级改造，带动制造业投资，促进模式创新和发展方式转变。三是持续保障产业链供应链安全。集中行业优势力量解决"卡脖子"问题，加快关键性前沿技术赶超，改变高端供给"不充分"局面，助力产业链上下游协同发展。

2. 养老产业

党的二十大报告指出，要实施积极应对人口老龄化国家战略，发展养老事业和养老产业。当前，我国已进入深度老龄化社会，2023年末全国60岁及以上人口、65岁及以上人口占总人口比例分别达到21.1%和15.4%，较10年前都提高了5个百分点以上。近年来，中央和各地区、各部门出台了一系列支持养老产业发展的政策，内容涵盖土地、税收、财政、金融、人才等多个方面，带动了我国养老产业的加速发展。截至2023年9月底，全国各类养老服务机构和设施总数达40万个、床位820.6万张，床位数10年来接近翻番。据市场机构测算，2023年我国养老产业规模约10万亿元，预计2030年将达到20万亿元，届时将占到GDP的一成。

金融部门主动作为，积极采取多种措施支持养老产业高质量发展。2022年4月，普惠养老专项再贷款工具适时推出，支持金融机构向普惠养老服务机构提供优惠利率贷款，推动增加普惠养老服务供给。政策实施以来，累计带动金融机构向浙江、江苏等5个试点省份的69个普惠养老服务项目提供融资支持21.6亿元，有力支持了普惠养老项目的建设。国务院办公厅印发《关于发展银发经济增进老年人福祉的意见》，强调用好普惠养老专项再贷款，支持公益型普惠型养老机构运营、居家社区养老体系建设、老年产品制造企业等。此外，人民银行还积极引导金融机构推出养老产业专属信贷产品，并通过加强与政府产业基金、融资担保机构等合作的方式，为养老产业提供针对性的金融服务。

未来，在老龄化程度不断加深的背景下，以养老金融、养老服务和养老用品等为核心的养老产业还存在巨大的发展潜力。也要看到，当前我国养老产业高质量发展依然存在养老机构数量不足、质量参差不齐、养老服务费用高昂等挑战，金融支持养老产业发展客观上也面临低收益、长周期、高风险等难题，亟须进一步完善支持养老产业发展的政策体系。2023年中央金融工作会议将养老金融纳入五篇大文章，下一阶段要更有针对性地丰富养老金融产品供给，拓宽养老服务机构融资渠道，更好满足日益多元化的养老金融需求，并加强财税、产业等政策协调配合，充分调动社会力量参与积极性，推动构建面向社会大众的养老服务体系，更好满足普通老年群体的养老需求。

第五部分 货币政策趋势

一、中国宏观经济金融展望

2023年，我国经济回升向好，高质量发展扎实推进。全年国内生产总值（GDP）同比增长5.2%，顺利完成年初制定目标，对世界经济增长的贡献率有望超过30%；居民人均可支配收入实际同比增长6.1%，城乡收入差异继续收窄，人民生活水平不断提高。

展望2024年，我国经济有望进一步回升向好。一是投资继续加力。2023年第四季度增发的1万亿元国债结转使用，以及新增的5 000亿元抵押补充贷款（PSL）额度，将有效拉动防汛抗灾项目以及保障性住房、"平急两用"公共基础设施建设、城中村改造投资，激发带动更多民间投资。二是消费稳步改善。随着疫情影响消退，企业营收、居民收入逐步恢复，消费意愿持续回升。当前我国汽车、家电保有量巨大，更新换代的需求和潜力很足；我国还有约3亿新市民，完善配套制度安排、优化消费金融服务也有助于拓展教育、医疗、养老等领域的市场深度，加快培育新型消费。三是外贸韧性较强。中美新一轮经贸对话启动，有助于推动双边经贸关系健康稳定发展；我国与"一带一路"共建国家经贸往来日益紧密，不断拓宽外贸发展空间。中央经济工作会议明确要求"聚焦经济建设这一中心工作和高质量发展这一首要任务"，也将有力调动各方积极性。

经济持续回升向好也需要克服一些困难和挑战。从国际看，发达经济体本轮加息周期或已结束，但高利率的滞后影响还将持续显现。2024年还是全球选举大年，世界政治经济形势的不确定性可能增大。从国内看，经济大循环也存在堵点，消费者信心指数和民间投资增速仍处于低位，需求不足与产能过剩的矛盾较为突出；制造业PMI连续4个月位于收缩区间，社会预期依然偏弱。对此，既要正视困难，也要增强信心和底气，我国经济长期向好的基本趋势没有改变，有利条件强于不利因素，要坚持稳中求进、以进促稳、先立后破，扎实推动高质量发展，在发展中解决问题。

物价有望温和回升。2023年第四季度以来，CPI同比持续在负值区间运行，除了受猪肉等食品价格高基数影响，耐用品和服务价格涨幅也偏弱，核心CPI同比由此前的0.8%降至0.6%。通胀根本上取决于实体经济供需的平衡情况，目前物价水平较低背后反映的是经济有效需求不足、总供求恢复不同步。未来随着基数效应逐步减弱，以及商品和服务需求的持续恢复，预计物价总体呈温和回升态势。PPI降幅预计也将持续收敛。从中长期看，我国处于经济恢复和产业转型升级的关键期，供需条件有望持续改善，货币条件合理适度，居民预期稳定，不存在长期通缩或通胀的基础。

二、下一阶段货币政策主要思路

中国人民银行将坚持以习近平新时代中国特色社会主义思想为指导，全面贯彻落实党的二十大精神，完整、准确、全面贯彻新发展理念，坚持稳中求进、以进促稳、先立后破，加快建设金融强国，优化金融服务，坚定不移走中国特色金融发展之路，推动金融高质量发展。建设现代中央银行制度，强化宏观政策逆周期和跨周期调节，坚持把金融服务实体经济作为根本宗旨，始终保持货币政策的稳健性，增强宏观政策取向一致性，持续推动经济实现质的有效提升和量的合理增长。

稳健的货币政策要灵活适度、精准有效。合理把握债券与信贷两个最大融资市场的关系，准确把握货币信贷供需规律和新特点，引导信贷合理增长、均衡投放，保持流动性合理充裕，保持社会融资规模、货币供应量同经济增长和价格水平预期目标相匹配。加强政策协调配合，有效支持促消费、稳投资、扩内需，保持物价在合理水平。持续深化利率市场化改革，进一步完善贷款市场报价利率形成机制，发挥存款利率市场化调整机制作用，促进社会综合融资成本稳中有降。发挥好货币政策工具总量和结构双重功能。支持采取债务重组等方式盘活信贷存量，提升存量贷款使用效率。坚持聚焦重点、合理适度、有进有退，做好科技金融、绿色金融、普惠金融、养老金融、数字金融五篇大文章，抓好金融支持民营经济25条举措落实，加大对保障性住房建设、"平急两用"公共基础设施建设、城中村改造的金融支持力度。坚持以市场供求为基础、参考一篮子货币进行调节、有管理的浮动汇率制度，综合施策、稳定预期，防范汇率超调风险，防止形成单边一致性预期并自我强化，保持人民币汇率在合理均衡水平上的基本稳定。持续有效防范化解中小金融机构、地方债务、房地产等重点领域风险，坚决守住不发生系统性风险的底线。

一是保持融资和货币总量合理增长。按照大力发展直接融资的要求，合理把握债券与信贷两个最大融资市场的关系。继续推动公司信用类债券和金融债券市场发展。持续加强对银行体系流动性供求和金融市场变化的分析监测，密切关注主要央行货币政策变化，灵活有效开展公开市场操作，搭配运用多种货币政策工具，保障政府债券顺利发行，引导金融机构加强流动性风险管理，保持银行体系流动性合理充裕和货币市场利率平稳运行。支持金融机构积极挖掘信贷需求和项目储备，促进贷款合理增长，加强信贷均衡投放，增强贷款增长的稳定性和可持续性，保持社会融资规模、货币供应量同经济增长和价格水平预期目标相匹配。着力提升贷款使用效率，通过部分贷款到期回收后转投更高效率的经营主体、优化新增贷款投向、推动必要的市场化出清，为经济可持续发展提供更好支撑。

二是充分发挥货币信贷政策导向作用。坚持"聚焦重点、合理适度、有进有退"，保持再贷款、再贴现政策稳定性，用好普惠小微贷款支持工具，实施好存续的各类专项再贷款工具，整合支持科技创新和数字金融领域的工具方案，继续加大对普惠小微、制造业、绿色发展、科技创新等重点领域和薄弱环节的支持。推动《关于强化金融支持举措 助力民营经济发展壮大的通知》落实落细，继续开展中小微企业金融服务能力提升工程，提高民营和小微企业融资可得性和便利性。指导金融机构持续加大金融支持乡村振兴力度，更好地满足涉农领域多样化融资需求。因城施策精准实施差别化住房信贷政策，更好地支持刚性和改善性住房需求，一视同仁满足不同所有制房地产企业合理融资需求，促进房地产市场平稳健康发展。用好新增的抵押补充再贷款工具，加大对保障性住房建设、"平急两用"公共基础设施建设、城中村改造的金融支持力度，推动加快构建房地产发展新模式。

三是把握好利率、汇率内外均衡。深入推进利率市场化改革，畅通货币政策传导渠道。健全市场化利率形成和传导机制，完善央行政策利率体系，引导市场利率围绕政策利率波动。落实存款利率市场化调整机制，着力稳定银行负债成本。发挥贷款市场报价利率改革效能，加强行业自律协调和管理，督促金融机构坚持风险定价原则，理顺贷款利率与债券收益率等市场利率的关系，维护市场竞争秩序，推动社会综合融资成本稳中有降。稳步深化汇率市场化改革，完善以市场供求为基础、参考一篮子货币进行调节、有管理的浮动汇率制度，坚持市场在汇率形成中起决定性作用，发挥汇率调节宏观经济和国际收支自动稳定器功能。加强预期管理，做好跨境资金流动的监测分析，坚持底线思维，防范汇率超调风险，防止形成单边一致性预期并自我强化，保持人民币汇率在合理均衡水平上的基本稳定。加强外汇市场管理，引导企业和金融机构树立"风险中性"理念，指导金融机构基于实需原则和风险中性原则积极为中小微企业提供汇率避险服务，维护外汇市场平稳健康发展。

四是不断深化金融改革和对外开放。完善债券市场法制体系，夯实公司信用类债券的法制基础。建立做市商与公开市场业务一级交易商联动机制，完善债券承销、估值、做市等业务管理，提升债券市场定价功能和

市场稳健性。推动柜台债券业务扩容，提高个人、企业、中小金融机构通过柜台渠道投资政府债券的便利性和效率。加强货币市场宏观审慎管理，完善货币市场流动性监测机制。坚持市场化、法治化原则，继续贯彻"零容忍"理念，加大对债券市场违法违规行为查处力度。坚定不移推动债券市场对外开放。有序推进人民币国际化，进一步扩大人民币在跨境贸易和投资中的使用，深化对外货币合作，发展离岸人民币市场。开展跨境贸易投资高水平开放试点，提升跨境贸易投资自由化、便利化水平，稳步推进人民币资本项目可兑换。

五是积极稳妥防范化解金融风险。进一步完善宏观审慎政策框架，提高系统性风险监测、评估与预警能力，丰富宏观审慎政策工具箱。完善系统重要性金融机构监管，推动系统重要性银行按时满足附加监管要求，加快推动我国全球系统重要性银行建立健全总损失吸收能力，切实提高风险抵御能力。积极推动重点区域、重点机构和重点领域风险处置和改革化险工作。指导金融机构按照市场化、法治化原则，合理运用债务重组、置换等手段，支持地方融资平台债务风险化解。加强对房地产市场运行情况的监测分析。推动化解中小金融机构风险，健全具有硬约束的早期纠正机制。推动金融稳定法尽快出台。健全权责一致、激励约束相容的风险处置责任机制，发挥好存款保险专业化风险处置职能，强化金融稳定保障体系建设，防止金融风险累积扩散，牢牢守住不发生系统性风险的底线。

Part 1 Money and Credit Analysis

The year 2023 marked the beginning of full implementation of the guidelines of the 20th National Congress of the Communist Party of China (CPC), and it was also the year for economic recovery and development during the new stage of the COVID-19 response after three years of prevention and control. The People's Bank of China (PBOC) has followed the guidance of Xi Jinping Thought on Socialism with Chinese Characteristics for a New Era and has fully implemented the guiding principles of the 20th CPC National Congress, the Central Economic Work Conference, the Central Financial Work Conference, as well as the requirements set forth in the *Report on the Work of the Government*. Taking stability as its top priority and pursuing progress while ensuring stability, the PBOC has implemented a sound monetary policy in a targeted and effective manner and it has strengthened counter-cyclical and inter-temporal adjustments. Money, credit and aggregate financing to the real economy (AFRE) have witnessed reasonable growth, overall financing costs have declined steadily, the credit structure has improved continuously, and the RMB exchange rate has remained basically stable at a reasonable and equilibrium level, thereby creating a favorable monetary and financial environment for the economic recovery.

I. Liquidity in the banking system was adequate and at a reasonable level

Since the beginning of 2023, adhering to

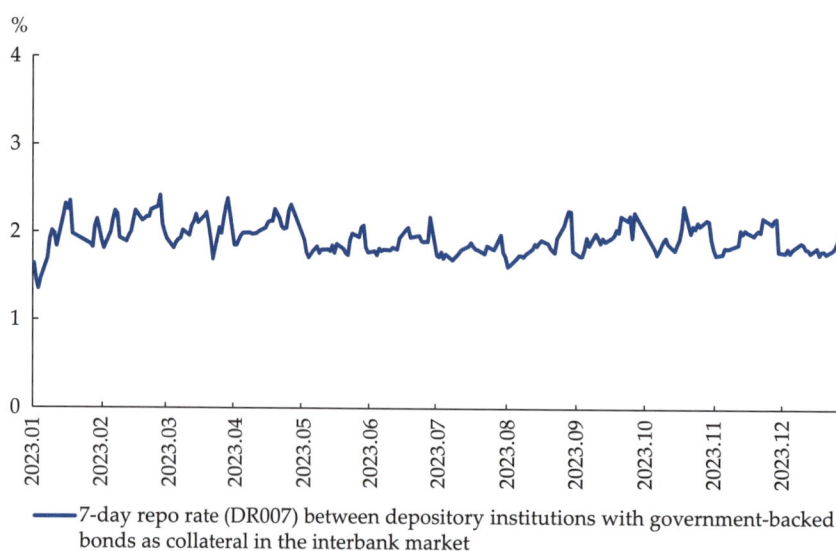

——7-day repo rate (DR007) between depository institutions with government-backed bonds as collateral in the interbank market

Figure 1 Movement of Money Market Interest Rates

(Source: www.chinamoney.com.cn)

a sound monetary policy, the PBOC has employed a mix of instruments, such as a cut in the required reserve ratio (RRR), central bank lending and discounts, the medium-term lending facility (MLF), and open market operations (OMOs), to inject liquidity into the economy in a targeted and effective manner. In March and September respectively, the RRR was cut by 0.25 percentage points, releasing a total of over RMB 1 trillion in long-term liquidity. It has continued to guide money market rates to move smoothly around the central bank's open market reverse repo rates, thereby creating a favorable liquidity environment for promoting financial support for high-quality development of the real economy and providing a strong guarantee for the smooth issuance of additional government bonds and local government refinancing bonds in the fourth quarter. At end-2023, the excess reserve ratio for financial institutions registered 2.1 percent, 0.1 percentage point higher than that at the end of 2022, indicating that liquidity in the banking system was adequate and at a reasonable level.

II. Lending by financial institutions grew reasonably, and lending rates remained at historic lows

Credit aggregates grew reasonably. In the first quarter of 2023, the supply of credit picked up pace due to factors such as the smooth shift in the COVID-19 response and the growing demand for credit at the beginning of the year. The PBOC made efforts to guide financial institutions to supply loans in a moderate and steady manner. In the second quarter, market confidence and expectations were weak, and effective demand for credit was insufficient. The PBOC strengthened counter-cyclical adjustments and placed an emphasis on guiding financial institutions to maintain a balanced supply of loans so as to enhance the sustainability of financial support for the real economy. In the fourth quarter, in a bid to maintain a well-paced supply of credit at the turn of the year, the PBOC held a symposium with financial institutions in a timely manner to smooth out loan growth. The supply of credit in the quarter was better than market expectations. At end-2023, outstanding loans issued by financial institutions in domestic and foreign currencies grew 10.1 percent year on year to RMB 242.2 trillion, RMB 22.2 trillion more than that at the beginning of 2023 or a year-on-year (YOY) acceleration of RMB 1.5 trillion. Outstanding RMB loans grew 10.6 percent year on year to RMB 237.6 trillion, RMB 22.7 trillion more than that at the beginning of 2023 or a YOY acceleration of RMB 1.3 trillion.

The credit structure has been improving. At end-2023, medium and long-term (MLT) loans to enterprises and public entities grew by RMB 13.6 trillion from the beginning of 2023, accounting for 75.8 percent of total corporate loans. The YOY growth of MLT loans to the manufacturing sector registered 31.9 percent, 21.3 percentage points higher than the growth of total loans. Outstanding inclusive loans to MSBs grew 23.5 percent year on year, 12.9 percentage points higher than the growth of total loans. A total of 61.66 million MSBs were supported, representing a rise of 9.1 percent year on year.

Table 1 The Structure of RMB Loans in 2023

Unit: RMB 100 million, %

Type of loan	Outstanding amount at end-December	YOY growth	Increase from the beginning of the year
RMB loans to	2,375,905	10.6	227,463
Households	800,921	5.7	43,261
Enterprises and public entities	1,554,232	13.0	179,074
Non-banking financial institutions	7,748	40.1	1,928
Overseas	13,005	32.8	3,200

Source: The People's Bank of China.
Note: Loans to enterprises and public entities refer to loans to non-financial enterprises, government departments, and organizations.

Table 2 New RMB Loans from Financial Institutions in 2023

Unit: RMB 100 million

Type of institution	Increase from the beginning of the year
Chinese-funded large-sized banks[1]	129,274
Chinese-funded small and medium-sized banks[2]	98,218
Small-sized rural financial institutions[3]	26,363
Foreign-funded financial institutions	−244

Source: The People's Bank of China.
Notes: 1. Chinese-funded large-sized banks refer to banks with assets (in both domestic and foreign currencies) of RMB 2 trillion or more (according to the amount of total assets in both domestic and foreign currencies at end-2008).
2. Chinese-funded small and medium-sized banks refer to banks with total assets (in both domestic and foreign currencies) of less than RMB 2 trillion (according to the amount of total assets in both domestic and foreign currencies at end-2008).
3. Small-sized rural financial institutions include rural commercial banks, rural cooperative banks, and rural credit cooperatives.

Box 1 An Accurate Assessment of the Patterns and New Features of Money and Credit Supply and Demand

The Central Financial Work Conference clearly stated the requirement that there be an accurate assessment of the patterns and new features in the supply and demand of money and credit. During the stage of high-quality development, we should continuously deepen our understanding of the regular pattern in financial work so as to enhance the awareness, capacity, quality and efficiency of providing financial services for the real economy.

China's economic restructuring is accelerating, requiring a high-quality supply of credit. On the one hand, loans for new economic drivers continue to grow rapidly, and their proportion to total loans is rising stably. Since the beginning of 2018, the growth rates of inclusive MSB loans, of MLT loans to the manufacturing sector, and of green loans have been outpacing the growth of total loans. Currently, central bank lending instruments *have covered almost all areas of sci-tech finance, green finance, inclusive finance, digital finance, and pension finance. The PBOC will continuously guide financial institutions to ramp up support for major strategies, major areas, and weak links and it will meet the proper financing demands for high-quality economic development. On the other hand, the growth rates of loans for traditional economic drivers, such as the real estate sector and local financing platforms, have decelerated, and their proportions in the amount of total loans have gradually decreased. Over the past few years, a very large proportion of the RMB 20 trillion in new loans was channeled to the real estate sector and local financing platforms. However, with the real estate sector development mode undergoing a major transition and the risks of local debts being prevented and defused, demand from these two areas has obviously plunged. Due to the combined aforementioned two factors, the quality and efficiency of providing financial services for the real economy have been remarkably enhanced, although growth on the whole has somewhat declined.*

As the relationship between outstanding and new loans is witnessing changes, we should focus on activating financial resources that are not being used efficiently. Currently, outstanding RMB loans topped RMB 230 trillion, 10 times the amount of new loans in each year. Therefore, we should be more attentive to the relationship between the aggregate and the structure as well as to the relationship between outstanding and new

loans. To be more specific, we should mobilize outstanding loans that are inefficiently used, write off non-performing loans (NPL), and continuously increase the proportion of direct financing in the AFRE, which will have a positive impact on credit and financing growth. For instance, activating financial resources that are inefficiently used will enhance the efficiency of entities in utilizing financial resources and will help inject a new impetus for the high-quality development of the economy, even though these resources will not be counted as new loans. Writing off more NPLs to maintain the sound functioning of commercial banks will exert downward pressures on the growth of loans. However, written-off loans which can still provide support for the real economy have been included into the AFRE statistics. In addition, emerging industries such as advanced manufacturing, sci-tech innovation, green and low-carbon industries, and the digital economy have prospered. Direct financing is more suitable for these new economic drivers in terms of financial support modes and it serves as a virtuous alternative to loans.

We should refrain from paying too much attention to high-frequency monthly money and credit data. China's loan increment is remarkably seasonal. According to statistics over the past years, more new loans are issued in the first quarter, especially in January, compared with a trough in April, July, and October. These seasonal changes are mainly attributable to internal and external assessments by banks as well as to the variations in financing demand, which should be objectively treated. For instance, as a Chinese saying goes, "The whole year's work depends on a good start in the spring." Therefore, many business entities embark on a good start, and the construction of most major projects also kicks off at the beginning of the year. These, coupled with spring farming and preparations at the beginning of the year as well as salary payments prior to the Spring Festival, all have an impact on the seasonal variations in loan increments. Furthermore, in response to the shock of COVID-19, macro policies in recent years adopt quick measures at an early stage, contributing to a further increase in loans during the first quarter. It should be noted that economic recovery needs stable and sustained credit support, the key of which lies in managing the "intensity". Instead of changing the regular pattern of a seasonal credit supply by financial institutions, we should moderate unreasonable credit supplies resulting from illicit competition and the rush to increase loan issuance at month ends, quarter ends, or at other crucial timings to accomplish assessment goals so as to better match the pace of credit supply with actual demand for developing the real economy.

On the whole, to accurately assess the pattern and new features in the supply and demand of money and credit and to properly evaluate the intensity of financial support, we should address the problem of locating a focus. In the stage of high-quality development, economic growth

should not be the only index for evaluating economic development, and credit growth should not be the only index for evaluating financial support. First, we should focus more on the effects of interest rate cuts. Social financing costs remain stable with a slight decline, indicating that the credit demands of the real economy are reasonably met. Second, we should focus more on financial support for major areas, such as sci-tech innovation, green development, and MSMEs, which better reflect how much effective demand of the real economy has been met by financial resources. Third, we should focus more on the AFRE which covers direct financing and observe the cumulative increment/balance in the growth of credit over a longer term so as to have a comprehensive view of monetary and financial conditions. Going forward, we will pursue the sound monetary policy in a flexible, appropriate, targeted, and effective manner, enhance counter-cyclical and inter-temporal adjustments, and continue to press ahead with the market-based reform of deposit rates so as to bring down the overall interest rates and maintain the reasonable growth and balanced supply of credit. Meanwhile, we will focus on enhancing the efficiency of utilizing loans, channeling funds from maturing loans to more efficient business entities, improving the allocation of new loans, and promoting necessary market-based clearances so as to provide stronger support for sustainable economic development.

The weighted average interest rate on loans remained at a historic low. The PBOC has continuously advanced the market-oriented reform of interest rates, effectively tapping into the loan prime rate (LPR) reform and bringing into play the key role of the market-based adjustment mechanism for deposit interest rates so as to promote a steady decline in actual lending rates. In December 2023, the one-year LPR and the over-five-year LPR stood at 3.45 percent and 4.20 percent, respectively, down 0.2 percentage points and 0.1 percentage point from December 2022, respectively. In December, the weighted average interest rate on loans recorded 3.83 percent, down 0.31 percentage points year on year. In particular, the weighted average interest rate on ordinary loans registered 4.35 percent, down 0.22 percentage points year on year, and the weighted average interest rate on corporate loans was 3.75 percent, down 0.22 percentage points year on year, both of which represent a continuous increase in financial support for the real economy. In

Table 3 Weighted Average Interest Rates on New Loans Issued in December 2023

Item	December (%)	Change from September (Percentage point)	YOY Change (Percentage point)
Weighted average interest rate on new loans	3.83	−0.31	−0.31
On ordinary loans	4.35	−0.16	−0.22
Of which: on corporate loans	3.75	−0.07	−0.22
On bill financing	1.47	−0.33	−0.13
On mortgage loans	3.97	−0.05	−0.29

Source: The People's Bank of China.

Table 4 Shares of RMB Lending Rates at Different Levels, from January to December 2023

Unit: %

Month	LPR−bps	LPR	LPR+bps					
			Subtotal	(LPR, LPR+0.5%)	[LPR+0.5%, LPR+1.5%)	[LPR+1.5%, LPR+3%)	[LPR+3%, LPR+5%)	LPR+5% and above
January	37.38	6.28	56.34	16.65	19.06	10.22	5.70	4.72
February	37.60	6.02	56.38	16.32	16.84	10.28	6.54	6.40
March	36.96	6.88	56.16	17.10	17.57	10.57	6.18	4.74
April	36.62	6.20	57.18	15.54	17.18	11.14	7.08	6.24
May	36.28	5.52	58.20	13.98	16.79	11.71	7.98	7.74
June	37.74	5.59	56.67	17.79	17.31	10.81	6.09	4.68
July	37.05	5.13	57.82	16.60	16.43	10.44	7.12	7.23
August	35.76	4.92	59.32	17.08	16.40	10.75	7.57	7.51
September	37.37	5.62	57.11	16.70	16.88	10.62	6.71	6.19
October	37.34	5.15	57.51	14.92	15.83	11.43	7.43	7.90
November	38.43	5.77	55.80	14.60	16.39	11.37	7.01	6.44
December	41.89	5.64	52.48	13.70	16.15	10.97	6.34	5.33

Source: The People's Bank of China.

December, the share of ordinary loans with rates above, at, or below the LPR registered 52.48 percent, 5.64 percent and 41.89 percent, respectively.

Interest rates on foreign-currency deposits and loans edged up. In December 2023, the weighted average interest rates on demand large-value USD-denominated deposits and on large-value USD-denominated deposits with maturities within three months registered 2.23 percent and 4.70 percent, respectively, up 1.03 and 1.04 percentage points from December 2022, respectively. The weighted average interest rates on USD-denominated loans with maturities within three months and with maturities between three months (including three months) and six months registered 5.81 percent and 5.80 percent, up 0.78 and

0.81 percentage points from December 2022, respectively.

Deposits grew significantly. At end-2023, outstanding deposits in domestic and foreign currencies at all financial institutions had increased 9.6 percent year on year to RMB 289.9 trillion, up RMB 25.4 trillion from the beginning of 2023 and a deceleration of RMB 397.8 billion year on year. Outstanding RMB deposits grew 10.0 percent year on year to RMB 284.3 trillion, an increase of RMB 25.7 trillion from the beginning of 2023 and a deceleration of RMB 510.1 billion year on year. Outstanding deposits in foreign currencies stood at USD 797.8 billion, USD 56.1 billion less than that at the beginning of 2023. The decrease was USD 86.9 billion less than that in the previous year.

Table 5 Average Interest Rates on Large-value USD-denominated Deposits and Loans, from January to December 2023

Unit: %

Month	Large-value deposits						Loans				
	Demand deposits	Within 3 months	3–6 months (including 3 months)	6–12 months (including 6 months)	1 year	Over 1 year	Within 3 months	3–6 months (including 3 months)	6–12 months (including 6 months)	1 year	Over 1 year
January	1.25	3.99	4.62	5.34	5.46	4.96	4.91	5.12	5.10	5.53	5.99
February	1.42	4.18	5.10	5.51	5.50	5.44	5.08	5.23	5.39	5.46	5.58
March	1.64	4.23	5.02	5.53	5.67	5.54	5.25	5.33	5.11	5.34	5.86
April	1.76	4.50	5.29	5.49	4.91	5.72	5.39	5.47	5.49	5.64	5.62
May	1.78	4.63	4.65	5.68	5.63	5.64	5.55	5.46	5.52	5.39	5.98
June	1.65	4.46	5.29	5.63	5.47	5.75	5.68	5.63	5.46	5.41	5.71
July	2.13	4.44	5.12	5.50	5.52	5.28	5.68	5.66	5.59	5.31	5.65
August	2.19	4.37	4.57	5.45	5.45	5.25	5.72	5.14	5.30	5.34	5.46
September	2.26	4.50	5.20	5.34	5.58	5.39	5.88	5.49	5.45	5.42	6.34
October	2.29	4.56	5.34	5.42	4.76	5.46	5.99	5.73	5.60	5.44	5.79
November	2.19	4.61	4.69	4.75	4.85	5.37	5.85	5.80	5.59	5.51	6.34
December	2.23	4.70	5.33	5.49	5.39	5.30	5.81	5.80	5.51	5.82	6.36

Source: The People's Bank of China.

III. Money supply and the AFRE grew at a reasonable pace

The monetary aggregate grew at a reasonable pace. At end-2023, outstanding broad money M2 registered RMB 292.3 trillion, up 9.7 percent year on year; narrow money M1 and currency in circulation M0 registered RMB 68.1 trillion and RMB 11.3 trillion, respectively, up 1.3 percent and 8.3 percent year on year, respectively. In total, 2023 witnessed a net cash injection of RMB 881.5

billion, down RMB 504.7 billion year on year. The AFRE grew stably. According to preliminary statistics, the outstanding AFRE reached RMB 378.1 trillion at end-2023 and its YOY growth registered 9.5 percent. In 2023, the AFRE increment totaled RMB 35.6 trillion, RMB 3.4 trillion more than that during the same period in 2022. The AFRE was characterized by the following features: first, RMB loans maintained reasonable growth. In 2023, new RMB loans issued by financial institutions to the real economy

Table 6 The Structure of RMB Deposits in 2023

Unit: RMB 100 million, %

Item	Outstanding deposits at end-December	YOY growth	Increase from the beginning of the year
RMB deposits	2,842,623	10.0	257,416
Households	1,369,895	13.8	166,655
Non-financial enterprises	787,756	5.5	42,235
Public entities	353,261	7.1	22,836
Fiscal entities	57,937	15.8	7,924
Non-banking financial institutions	255,244	7.2	16,386
Overseas	18,531	9.1	1,380

Source: The People's Bank of China.

Figure 2 YOY Growth of Outstanding Broad Money (M2) and the AFRE

(Source: The People's Bank of China)

grew by RMB 1.2 trillion year on year to RMB 22.2 trillion, accounting for 62.4 percent of the AFRE increment during the same period. Second, new government bond financing increased year on year, while new corporate bond financing and domestic equity financing by non-financial enterprises decreased year on year. In 2023, the net financing amount of government bonds and corporate bonds posted RMB 9.6 trillion and RMB 1.6 trillion, respectively, and domestic equity financing by non-financial enterprises reached RMB 793.1 billion. Third, there was a recovery in off-balance-sheet financing. In 2023, new entrusted loans decreased by RMB 338 billion, new trust loans increased by RMB 757.9 billion, and undiscounted bankers' acceptances decreased by a smaller margin of RMB 162.7 billion. Fourth, loans were written off at a relatively rapid pace. In 2023, the increment of written-off loans stood at RMB 1.1 trillion, up RMB 29.1 billion year on year.

Table 7 Aggregate Financing to the Real Economy in 2023

Item	End-December 2023		2023	
	Stock (RMB 1 trillion)	YOY growth (%)	Flow (RMB 100 million)	YOY change (RMB 100 million)
The AFRE	378.09	9.5	355,875	34,080
Of which: RMB loans	235.48	10.4	222,240	11,803
Foreign currency loans (RMB equivalent)	1.66	−10.2	−2,206	3,048
Entrusted loans	11.27	0.2	199	−3,380
Trust loans	3.9	4.2	1,576	7,579
Undiscounted bankers' acceptances	2.49	−6.7	−1,784	1,627
Corporate bonds	31.11	0.3	16,254	−4,254
Government bonds	69.79	16	96,045	24,817
Domestic equity financing by non-financial enterprises	11.43	7.5	7,931	−3,826
Other financing	10.73	3.1	3,211	−5,257
Of which: Asset-backed securities of depository institutions	1.36	−31.6	−6,277	−4,415
Loans written off	8.61	14.6	10,967	291

Sources: The People's Bank of China, National Administration of Financial Regulation, China Securities Regulatory Commission, China Central Depository & Clearing Co., Ltd., National Association of Financial Market Institutional Investors, etc.

Notes: ① The AFRE (stock) refers to outstanding funds provided by the financial system to the real economy at the end of a period. The AFRE (flow) refers to the volume of funds provided by the financial system to the real economy within a certain period of time.

② Since January 2023, the PBOC has included three types of non-deposit financial institutions in the banking industry, namely, consumer finance companies, wealth management companies, and financial asset investment companies, into the scope of the financial statistics. Therefore, adjustments will be made to the data on "RMB loans issued by the real economy" and "loans written off" in the scale of social financing.

③ YOY statistics in the table are on a comparable basis.

IV. The RMB exchange rate remained basically stable at an adaptive and equilibrium level

In 2023, cross-border capital flows were stable and orderly, supply and demand in the foreign exchange market was basically in equilibrium, and RMB exchange rate expectations were generally stable. The international situation has been complex and serious, with interest rates in the major developed economies remaining at a high level. The RMB exchange rate has been relatively sound among the world's major currencies, fluctuating in both directions and playing its role as an auto stabilizer in macroeconomic management and the balance of payments. In 2023, based on market supply and demand, the RMB exchange rate remained basically stable against a basket of currencies. At end-2023, the China Foreign Exchange Trade System (CFETS) RMB Exchange Rate Index closed at 97.42, appreciating 0.7 percent from end-June 2023 and depreciating

1.3 percent from end-2022, respectively. According to calculations by the Bank for International Settlements (BIS), from 2005, when the reform of the RMB exchange-rate formation regime began, to end-2023, the nominal effective exchange rate (NEER) and the real effective exchange rate (REER) of the RMB appreciated 42.3 percent and 37.5 percent, respectively. At end-2023, the central parity of the RMB against the US dollar was 7.0827, appreciating 2 percent from end-June 2023 while depreciating 1.7 percent from end-2022. Since the beginning of the reform of the exchange-rate formation regime in 2005, the central parity of the RMB against the US dollar has appreciated 16.9 percent in total. In 2023, the annualized volatility rate of the RMB against the US dollar was 4.9 percent.

Cross-border RMB businesses have maintained growth, with receipts and payments basically reaching a balance. In 2023, cross-border RMB settlements increased 24 percent year

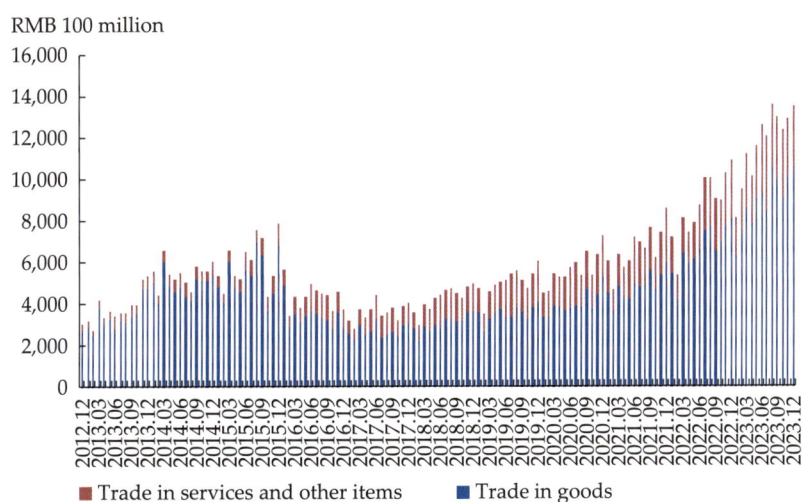

Figure 3 Monthly RMB Settlements under the Current Account

(Source: The People's Bank of China)

on year to RMB 52.3 trillion, accounting for 58 percent of the total cross-border settlements denominated in domestic and foreign currencies over the same period. Specifically, cross-border RMB receipts and payments registered RMB 25.4 trillion and RMB 26.9 trillion, respectively. Cross-border RMB settlements under the current account increased 33 percent year on year to RMB 14 trillion. In particular, RMB settlements under trade in goods registered RMB 10.7 trillion and RMB settlements under trade in services and under other current items registered RMB 3.3 trillion. Cross-border RMB settlements under the capital account grew by 21 percent year on year to RMB 38.3 trillion. In 2023, 25 percent of cross-border receipts and payments under trade in goods were settled in RMB.

Part 2 Monetary Policy Operations

In 2023, with resolute implementation of the decisions and arrangements made by the CPC Central Committee and the State Council, the PBOC pursued a sound monetary policy in a targeted and effective manner. It comprehensively utilized financial tools, such as the reserve requirement ratio (RRR) cut, medium-term lending facility (MLF) operations, and open market operations (OMOs), to keep liquidity adequate and at a reasonable level and to guide financial institutions to maintain appropriate aggregates and a steady pace in the supply of money and credit. Meanwhile, it adjusted and optimized the interest rate policy for home mortgage loans, facilitating a steady decline in corporate financing costs and resident credit. It also made good use of the existing special central bank lending, issued guiding documents on financial support for the private economy, and stepped up support for key areas and weak links, such as financial inclusion, sci-tech innovation, and green development. These efforts continuously consolidated the momentum for the recovery of the national economy.

I. Conducting open market operations in a flexible manner

The interest rates on reverse repo operations declined on two occasions in 2023. In June and in August, the rates on the open market 7-day reverse repos dropped by 10 basis points each time, registering 1.8 percent at end-2023 and down 20 basis points from end-2022.

Corporate financing costs were reduced through financial market transmissions. The quality and efficiency of financial support for the development of the real economy were improved. In Q4, given that the short-term factors affecting liquidity supply and demand in the banking system increased, the PBOC followed closely the economic and financial conditions, strengthened monitoring and analysis of liquidity, conducted reverse repo operations in a flexible and forward-looking manner, and intensified open market operations in a timely and appropriate manner so as to keep liquidity in the banking system adequate and at a reasonable level and to guide money market interest rates to move smoothly around the interest rate on open market operations.

Supporting intensive large-scale issuances of government bonds. In Q4, the issuance of local government bonds accelerated, and newly increased central government bonds were issued in a concentrated manner, so the net financing of government bonds hit a record high. The PBOC further strengthened coordination between monetary and fiscal policies through active communication with fiscal departments and increased the operational intensity of policy instruments, such as reverse repo operations, precisely offsetting the short-term influence of financial issuances, keeping liquidity and market rate movements stable, and providing strong support for the successful issuance of government bonds.

Stabilizing year-end liquidity supply in a forward-looking way. The PBOC conducted 14-day reverse repo operations on December 18 and gradually increased their intensity in light of market demand, with a view to keeping market liquidity adequate at a reasonable level at year-end and ensuring the stable operation of all kinds of market institutions at the turn of the year. At end-2023, outstanding reverse repo operations registered RMB 2.8 trillion, up RMB 1.1 trillion from end-2022. On the last working day of 2023, the weighted average 7-day repo rate between deposit institutions in the interbank market (DR007) was 1.91 percent, a drop of 45 basis points year on year.

In addition, the PBOC continued to conduct central bank bills swap (CBS) operations on a monthly basis in Q4 to improve the liquidity of bank-issued perpetual bonds in the secondary market. Meanwhile, the PBOC has been issuing central bank bills in Hong Kong on a regular basis and has been scaling up some types of central bank bills based on the demand of global investors. In 2023, the PBOC issued in Hong Kong 12 batches of central bank bills worth a total of RMB 160 billion, up RMB 40 billion over the previous year, which was conducive to the sound development of the offshore RMB money market and the bond market.

II. Conducting medium-term lending facility (MLF) operations to roll over maturing loans with a higher injection of liquidity

Boosting liquidity support with MLF Loans. In 2023, the PBOC ramped up liquidity injections as it rolled over maturing MLF loans for the twelfth consecutive month. Among these, the December operations resulted in a net fresh fund injection of RMB 800 billion, booking the biggest monthly increase on record. In particular, the amount of MLF operations posted RMB 1.759 trillion, RMB 0.532 trillion, RMB 1.095 trillion and RMB 3.689 trillion in Q1, Q2, Q3 and Q4, respectively, all of which were with a maturity of one year. At end-2023, outstanding MLFs registered RMB 7.075 trillion, an increase of RMB 2.525 trillion from the beginning of 2023. The MLF rate was lowered by 10 basis points in June and by 15 basis points in August, and it registered 2.50 percent at end-2023. The continuous excess provision of MLF operations effectively ensured a reasonable supply of medium to long-term liquidity.

Conducting standing lending facility (SLF) operations in a timely manner. In 2023, the PBOC conducted a total of RMB 45.6 billion of SLF operations, among which those in the four quarters reached RMB 7.7 billion, RMB 4.3 billion, RMB 6.9 billion and RMB 26.7 billion, respectively. At end-2023, outstanding SLF operations registered RMB 15.7 billion. At end-2023, the overnight, 7-day and 1-month SLF rates stood at 2.65 percent, 2.80 percent and 3.15 percent, respectively. SLF operations provided locally-incorporated financial institutions with a sufficient amount of short-term liquidity support as needed so that market expectations were stabilized and the stability of liquidity in the banking system was strengthened.

III. Lowering the RRR for financial institutions

Lowering the RRR for financial institutions. On March 27 and September 15, 2023, the PBOC reduced the RRR for financial institutions by 0.25 percentage points each time, freeing up over RMB 1 trillion in medium and long-term liquidity. On February 5, 2024, the PBOC again cut the RRR for financial institutions by 0.5 percentage points. This move released over RMB 1 trillion in medium and long-term liquidity, which was conducive to ensuring the supply of money before the Spring Festival, delivering policy signals to strengthen macro-policy adjustments to boost confidence, optimizing the structure of the PBOC's supply of liquidity to the banking system, and reducing fund costs in the banking system. After this RRR cut, the weighted average RRR for financial institutions fell from 7.4 percent to 7 percent.

Lowering the foreign exchange RRR for financial institutions. Since the establishment of the foreign exchange RRR system in 1993, the foreign exchange RRR for financial institutions has remained relatively stable. In recent years, to effectively respond to external shocks brought about by monetary policy adjustments in the advanced economies, the foreign exchange RRR for financial institutions has been adjusted on several occasions. Since 2022, the PBOC has reduced the foreign exchange RRR for financial institutions three times, by a total of 5 percentage points, which has effectively enhanced the capacity of financial institutions to utilize foreign exchange funds and safeguarded smooth operations in the foreign exchange market. Among these cuts, on September 15, 2023, the foreign exchange RRR was cut by 2 percentage points, from 6 percent to 4 percent, freeing up foreign exchange liquidity in the amount of about USD 15 billion.

IV. Further improving the macro-prudential system and the management framework

Giving full play to the guiding role of the macro-prudential assessment (MPA). In 2023, the PBOC further optimized the MPA framework and guided financial institutions to moderately flatten credit fluctuations during "low and peak seasons," thereby maintaining appropriate and well-paced credit supply as well as sustained credit support for inclusive MSB loans and medium and long-term financing to the manufacturing sector.

Refining the regulatory framework for systemically important financial institutions. On September 22, the PBOC and the National Financial Regulatory Administration (NFRA) released a list of China's systemically important banks (SIBs) in 2023. A total of 20 domestic SIBs were identified based on 2022 data assessments, one more than the total in 2022, including 6 state-owned commercial banks, 9 joint-stock commercial banks, and 5 city commercial banks. In Q4, the PBOC, together with the NFRA and the Ministry of Finance, reviewed the 2023 recovery plans and resolution plan proposals submitted by the SIBs and urged them to enhance their risk response capabilities. On October 20, the PBOC and the NFRA jointly issued the *Measures for the Assessment of Systemically Important Insurers*, which expanded the assessment of systemically important financial institutions to cover not only the banking sector but also the insurance industry, marking a new step in macro-prudential management. In accordance with the *Measures*, China's top ten insurance groups, life insurance companies, property and casualty insurance companies, and reinsurance companies in terms of asset size, were mainly evaluated based on four dimensions, namely, size, interconnectedness, asset liquidity, and substitutability, and those with a score of 1,000 or higher are to be identified as systematically important issuers (SIIs).

Adjusting the macro-prudential adjustment parameter for cross-border financing. On July 20, 2023, in order to further improve the macro-prudential management of unified cross-border financing and to continue to expand the sources of cross-border funds for enterprises and financial institutions and to guide them in optimizing their asset-liability structure, the PBOC and the State Administration of Foreign Exchange (SAFE) decided to raise the macro-prudential adjustment parameter for cross-border financing of enterprises and financial institutions from 1.25 to 1.5.

V. Giving full play to the role of monetary policies to optimize the structure

Focusing on technology finance, green finance, inclusive finance, pension finance, and digital finance, and leveraging the role of monetary instruments to adjust both the aggregate and the structure. In terms of inclusive finance,

central bank lending for rural development and for MSBs, as well as central bank discounts, were utilized to guide locally-incorporated financial institutions to expand their credit supply for agro-linked businesses, MSB and private enterprises. On January 25, 2024, the PBOC cut the interest rate on central bank lending for rural development and MSBs and central bank discounts for all terms by 25 basis points. Central bank lending for poverty alleviation was rolled over according to current regulations so as to consolidate the achievements in poverty alleviation and support for rural revitalization. The PBOC promoted coordinated regional development by continuously guiding locally-incorporated financial institutions in ten provinces to effectively use central bank lending and other policy instruments. At end-2023, outstanding central bank lending in support of rural development, in support of MSBs, and for poverty alleviation posted RMB 656.2 billion, RMB 1.7 trillion and RMB 122.2 billion, respectively, and outstanding central bank discounts registered RMB 592.0 billion. The inclusive MSB loan facility continued. At end-2023, RMB 55.4 billion in incentive funding was provided through these instruments, an increase of RMB 27.9 billion from the beginning of the year. With such support, locally-incorporated financial institutions boosted the issuance of inclusive MSB loans by RMB 3.3222 trillion, up RMB 1.7168 trillion from the beginning of the year. Concerning green finance, the carbon emission reduction facility was extended to the end of 2024, and some locally-incorporated and overseas-funded financial institutions were covered by the facility. Special central bank lending for the clean and efficient use of coal was extended to the end of 2023. At end-2023, the outstanding amount of these two instruments registered RMB 541.0 billion and RMB 274.8 billion, respectively, an increase of RMB 231.4 billion and RMB 193.7 billion, respectively, from the beginning of the year. With regard to technology finance, central bank lending for sci-tech innovation and special central bank lending for equipment upgrading and renovation expired, but with the outstanding funds continuing to serve these purposes. At end-2023, the outstanding amount of these two instruments registered RMB 255.6 billion and RMB 156.7 billion, respectively, up RMB 55.6 billion and RMB 75.8 billion, respectively, from the beginning of the year. With respect to pension finance, the PBOC continued to carry out the pilot program of special central bank lending for inclusive elderly care services in five provinces, including Zhejiang and Jiangsu. At end-2023, the outstanding amount of the instrument posted RMB 1.8 billion, an increase of RMB 1.1 billion from the beginning of the year.

Supporting the resolution of risks in the real estate sector and forging a new real estate development model. The PBOC continued to implement instruments, such as the guaranteed residential building delivery loan program, the loan support scheme for rental housing, and the special central bank lending for troubled property developers. At end-2023, the outstanding amount in the guaranteed residential building delivery loan program posted RMB 5.6 billion, up RMB 5.6 billion from the beginning of the year. The quota for the pledged supplementary lending

(PSL) facility increased by RMB 500 billion in December, supporting policy-backed and development-oriented financial institutions to grant loans for the development of government-subsidized housing projects, the rebuilding of run-down urban areas, and the construction of public infrastructure for both daily and emergency uses. At end-2023, the outstanding amount of the PSL posted RMB 3.3 trillion, an increase of RMB 99.4 billion from the beginning of the year.

VI. Enhancing the efficiency and the role of credit policy in structural guidance

Constantly improving financial services for private enterprises and MSBs. In November 2023, the PBOC took the lead in issuing the *Notice on Strengthening Financial Support Measures to Boost the Development and Growth of the Private Economy*. The *Notice* specifies the financial support requirements for development of the private economy, in terms of continuously increasing the input of credit resources, deepening the development of the bond market system, giving full play to the role of the multi-tiered capital market, and increasing the supply of foreign exchange facilitation policies and services. The PBOC continued to carry out the project to enhance financial services for micro, small, and medium-sized enterprises, and it guided financial institutions to improve the implementation of policy arrangements, including funds transfer pricing, performance appraisals, and due diligence exemptions, so as to accelerate the establishment of a long-term mechanism for boosting the confidence, willingness, capacity, and professionalism of financial institutions to issue loans. By the end of 2023, outstanding inclusive MSB loans registered RMB 29.4 trillion, increasing 23.5 percent year on year and benefiting 61.66 million MSBs, an increase of 9.1 percent year on year. The weighted average interest rate on newly issued inclusive MSB loans in December posted 4.68 percent.

Increasing financial support for rural revitalization. The PBOC continuously promoted the implementation of the *Guiding Opinions on Providing Financial Support for Advancing Rural Revitalization Across the Board and Stepping Up Efforts to Build Up China's Strength in Agriculture*. It guided financial institutions to optimize resource allocations by continuously increasing the supply of financial resources for key areas, such as stable production and secure supplies of grain and key agricultural products, sci-tech equipment innovation and green development in agriculture, and the high-quality development of rural industries. By the end of 2023, outstanding agro-related loans had registered a YOY increase of 14.9 percent, reaching RMB 56.6 trillion.

Coordinating credit support for green development and energy transformation. The PBOC strengthened macro credit policy, guiding credit funds to provide targeted support for key areas, such as clean energy, energy conservation, and emission reductions. It adhered to the principle of "establishing before breaking" and guided banks to satisfy the reasonable financing needs of the traditional energy sector in a steady manner. Acting in accordance with the principle that "speed should be subordinate

to quality," the PBOC promoted the high-quality development of green credits. At end-2023, the outstanding amount of green credit in China posted about RMB 30.1 trillion, an increase of 36.5 percent year on year.

Strengthening financial support for the pension sector. The PBOC encouraged financial institutions to innovate the organizations and production systems for pension finance, to increase the supply of credit to elderly-care facilities and industry, and to upgrade financial services that cater to the needs of senior citizens, contributing to the national strategy of responding to the aging population. At end-2023, all types of outstanding loans issued to the pension sector by seven banks, namely, China Development Bank, the Agricultural Development Bank of China, Industrial and Commercial Bank of China, Agricultural Bank of China, Bank of China, China Construction Bank, and Bank of Communications, amounted to a total of about RMB 100 billion, up 26.4 percent year on year.

Improving financial support and services for the transportation and logistics industry. The PBOC continuously executed effective implementation of the *Notice on Further Enhancing Financial Support and Services for the Transportation and Logistics Industries* in a sustained manner. It encouraged banks to focus on the goal of building up China's strength in transportation and responding to the needs of business entities by stepping up credit support. By the end of 2023, the outstanding medium and long-term loans to the transport, logistics, warehousing, and postal industries had registered RMB 18.0 trillion, a YOY increase of 12.1 percent.

Continuously delivering financial services to the manufacturing sector and to sci-tech innovation. The PBOC improved the policy framework for financial support to sci-tech innovation, promoted the establishment of a diversified relay-style financial service system for sci-tech innovation, and organized special actions to improve financial service capabilities for science and technology. Together with the administrative agencies of the relevant industries, the PBOC improved matchmaking between key investment projects and enterprises in need of funds for the manufacturing sector and for sci-tech innovation purposes so as to alleviate the informational asymmetries between banks and enterprises. The PBOC periodically circulated reports on loans issued to the manufacturing sector and for sci-tech innovation by banks licensed to operate nationwide so as to motivate financial institutions to increase credit support in these areas. By the end of 2023, outstanding medium and long-term loans to the manufacturing sector had grown by 31.9 percent year on year to RMB 12.5 trillion, and those to the high-tech manufacturing sector had grown by 34.0 percent year on year to RMB 2.7 trillion. The YOY growth rate of loans granted to sci-tech small and medium enterprises and to "specialized, sophisticated, distinctive, and innovative" enterprises was recorded at 21.9 percent and 18.6 percent, respectively, both significantly outpacing the growth rate of all loans.

VII. Improving the formation and transmission mechanism of the market-based interest rate

Deepening the market-based interest rate reform. The benefits of the LPR reform have been unleashed continuously to significantly drive down actual loan interest rates. In 2023, the PBOC guided the one-year and over-five-year LPR to drop by 0.2 percentage points and 0.1 percentage point, respectively. Actual loans rates were guided to decline more substantially through the market-based interest rate transmission mechanism. In 2023, the weighted average interest rate on corporate loans registered 3.88 percent, the lowest level ever and falling by 0.29 percentage points year on year, The PBOC tapped into the role of the market-based adjustment mechanism for deposit interest rates to guide their decline. In June, September, and December of 2023, major banks voluntarily lowered deposit rates in light of their own operating needs and market supply and demand. Specifically, the medium- and long-term deposit rates fell at a more rapid pace. The above efforts further improved the term structure of deposit rates, made the deposit rates more market-based, enhanced the sustainability and capacity of financial support serving the real economy, and effectively promoted investment and consumption.

Adjusting and refining the interest rate policy for individual mortgage loans. Existing first-home mortgage rates were reduced. On August 31, the PBOC and the National Administration of Financial Regulation jointly released the *Notice on Matters Concerning Lowering the Interest Rates on Existing First-Home Mortgage Loans* to guide both the lenders and the borrowers to reduce existing first-home mortgage rates in an orderly manner, thus effectively reducing the interest burden on residents and boosting consumption. Meanwhile, major banks were urged to place this rate reduction policy in place as soon as possible to reduce the borrowers' operational costs. Existing mortgage loans worth more than RMB 23 trillion have witnessed interest rate reductions. After the adjustment, the weighted average mortgage rate registered 4.27 percent, with the average decline standing at 73 basis points. The annual interest expenses for borrowers dropped by about RMB 170 billion, benefiting 53.25 million households or about 160 million people. This policy has been well received by all parties. The PBOC guided continued interest rate declines for newly issued mortgage loans, lowered the interest rate floor on second-home mortgage loans to the LPR plus 20 basis points, and gave play to the dynamic adjustment mechanism for newly-issued first-home mortgage rates to guide their decline. As of December 2023, of 343 cities at or above the prefectural level across the country, 101 cities had adjusted the first-home interest rate floor and 26 cities had scraped the first-home interest rate floor. In 2023, the interest rate on newly issued individual mortgage loans registered 4.1 percent, a year-on-year decline of 0.75 percentage points.

Box 2 The Ten-year Interest Rate Self-regulatory Mechanism: An Important Guarantee for Market-based Reforms

Since its establishment in 2013, the interest rate self-regulatory mechanism has followed the direction of the market-based reforms, effectively served the requirements of macro regulation and financial management, conducted effective self-regulation on interest rate pricing for deposits and loans worth over RMB 400 trillion in total via a pragmatic and streamlined organizational structure and an efficient and orderly working mechanism, and generated significant effects in management via limited resources, thus providing a vivid practice to pursue a path of financial development with Chinese characteristics.

The interest rate self-regulatory mechanism is an important institutional arrangement for deepening the market-based interest rate reforms. Since the 18th CPC National Congress, the PBOC has made continuous efforts to deepen the market-based interest rate reforms. In 2012, deposit interest rates were allowed to float upward to a certain extent. In July 2013, the controls on loan interest rates were lifted completely, and the reform entered a critical phase fraught with tough challenges. As China's financial institutions and market environment require further improvements, the reform target of a smooth liberalization process, a proper formation mechanism, and an appropriate adjustment system cannot be attained without efficiently safeguarding market competition order. In September 2013, by drawing on the experience of mature markets such as the U.S. and Germany as much as possible, and by safeguarding competition order through market self-regulation, the PBOC established the interest rate self-regulatory mechanism, which also conformed to China's own market-based interest rate reforms.

Promoting the regulated and healthy development of the market through enhanced self-regulation. In terms of the organizational structure, the interest rate self-regulatory mechanism is headed by the commercial banks with strong pricing capabilities, and this arrangement fully reflects the market-oriented feature of this self-regulatory mechanism. As for the consultation mechanism, irregular working meetings are convened to strengthen self-regulation and coordination, safeguard market competition order, and advance the market-oriented reforms in an orderly manner. The self-regulatory mechanism enables its members to have more rights in pricing and product innovation, pushes financial institutions to enhance their corporate governance and improve their services, fosters the formation of reasonable and balanced interest rates in a market-oriented environment, and guides the efficient allocation of financial resources, thus supporting high-quality economic development and enhancing the well-being of the people.

The interest rate self-regulatory mechanism has made remarkable achievements. First, advancing the LPR reform in a coordinated

manner. In August 2019, the PBOC facilitated the LPR reform, with the LPR panel banks all being members of the interest rate self-regulatory mechanism. This mechanism is empowered to organize LPR quotations and to urge panel banks to offer reasonable rates so as to effectively reflect market interest rate movements and the monetary policy stance. Meanwhile, the PBOC also urged various lending institutions to post annualized loan interest rates to safeguard the legitimate rights of financial consumers. Second, fostering more market-based deposit interest rates. In October 2015, the PBOC lifted the administrative controls over bank deposit interest rates. The interest rate self-regulatory mechanism strengthened self-regulation on irrational pricing conduct, which allured depositors with high interest rates and helped to rectify non-compliant innovative deposit products. In June 2021, the self-regulatory ceiling for deposit interest rates was adjusted as the benchmark interest rate plus basis points to combat any leveraging effects. In April 2022, the market-based adjustment mechanism for deposit interest rates was established to guide members to make reasonable adjustments to deposit interest rates with reference to the changes in market interest rates. Third, effectively leveraging the role of conformity and prudential assessments. Financial institutions with better corporate governance and stronger pricing capabilities have been selected through the assessments to reinforce the micro foundations of the market-based interest rate reform. The PBOC continued to optimize the assessment metrics and to improve the incentive and constraint mechanism. As of 2023, 2,055 banks, or about half of the commercial banks, had been members of the interest rate self-regulatory mechanism. Fourth, guiding interest rate self-regulatory mechanisms at the provincial levels to fulfill their responsibilities efficiently. The PBOC branches at the provincial levels have all established corresponding mechanisms for interest rate self-regulation. A preliminary pattern for coordination, consisting of self-regulatory mechanisms at the national and provincial levels, took shape to guarantee prompt transmission of the interest rate self-regulatory requirements to financial institutions at various levels, thus forming a collective force. In addition, the interest rate self-regulatory mechanism played a key role in guaranteeing the efficient operation of the Certificate of Deposit market and in facilitating participation in the reform of international benchmark interest rates.

During the next stage, the PBOC will guide the interest rate self-regulatory mechanism to improve its management methods for interest rate self-regulation, thus making a new contribution to an enhanced mechanism for the formation, adjustment, and transmission of market-based interest rates and for the financial sector to better serve the real economy. First, strengthening regulation and evaluation of LPR quotations to enhance their quality, thus providing strong support for a steady decline in overall social financing costs. Members are guided to make reasonable adjustments to deposit interest rates in light of the changes in market interest rates. Second, urging banks to improve the interest rate pricing mechanism for deposits and loans on a continuous basis. The interest rate relationship between the credit market and the bond market, as well as between large banks and small and medium-sized banks, will be overhauled based on a risk pricing mechanism. Third, establishing and improving the mechanism for regulatory talks and notifications to enhance the seriousness and authority of the interest rate self-regulation, to improve the organizational framework of the interest rate self-regulatory mechanism, and to promote the efficient fulfillment of its responsibilities.

VIII. Deepening the market-based reform of the RMB exchange rate

The PBOC continued to improve the managed floating exchange-rate regime based on market supply and demand with reference to a basket of currencies. It ensured that the market plays a decisive role in determining the exchange rate. The RMB witnessed both appreciations and depreciations against the major international currencies, with two-way fluctuations. The PBOC gave play to the role of the exchange rate as an auto stabilizer and as a shock absorber for macroeconomic management and for the balance of payments. Responding to relatively high external pressures on the RMB exchange rate in 2023, the PBOC took comprehensive measures and strengthened expectation guidance to prevent big ups and downs. In July, the PBOC raised the macro-prudential adjustment parameter for cross-border financing. In September, the PBOC cut the reserve requirement ratio for foreign exchange deposits. In addition, it held a meeting on the foreign exchange market self-regulatory framework, issued additional offshore central bank bills, balanced supply with demand in the foreign exchange market, and prevented the risks of exchange rate overshooting. As a result, the RMB exchange rate remained basically stable at an adaptive and equilibrium level. In 2023, the highest and lowest RMB central parities against the US dollar were 6.7130 and 7.2258, respectively. During the 242 trading days, the RMB appreciated on 142 days, depreciated on 98 days, and remained flat on 2 days. The biggest intraday appreciation and depreciation was 1.0 percent (654 bps) and 0.9 percent (630 bps), respectively. As of end-2023, the central parity of the RMB against the US dollar, the euro, the pound sterling, and the Japanese yen had appreciated 2 percent, 0.2 percent, 1.1 percent, and had depreciated 0.2 percent from end-June, respectively. From the beginning of the reform of the RMB exchange-rate formation regime in 2005 to the end of 2023, the RMB appreciated by a cumulative 16.9 percent, 27.4 percent, 59.4 percent, and 45.5 percent, respectively, against the US dollar, the euro, the pound sterling, and the Japanese yen. Direct RMB trading was rather buoyant in the interbank foreign exchange market with stable liquidity so that the exchange costs for enterprises were reduced and bilateral trade and investment was promoted.

IX. Forestalling and defusing financial risks

Strengthening the monitoring and assessment of systemic risks. The PBOC continued to strengthen its monitoring and assessment of systemic financial risks and to improve its framework for the monitoring and assessment of financial stability. It continued to improve risk monitoring in the banking sector, securities sector, insurance sector, and financial markets. The PBOC also conducted stress tests for banking financial institutions and provided them with timely risk warnings, thus guiding financial institutions to operate in a sound manner.

Making new progress in the prevention and resolution of financial risks. The PBOC further improved the financial risk monitoring, assessment, prevention, and control system, and established an early corrective mechanism with hard constraints on emerging high-risk banking institutions to make an early rectification more normative and authoritative. It conducted Central Bank Ratings on financial institutions on a regular basis, covering over 4,000 banking financial institutions, and it continuously reduced the number of high-risk institutions. The PBOC rectified emerging bank problems through early warnings so as to identify and resolve risks at an early stage.

Providing financial support for defusing debt risks of Local Government Financing Vehicles (LGFV) in an orderly manner. Local governments and LGFV were encouraged to raise resources to repay their debts by revitalizing or selling assets. Financial institutions were guided to consult with LGFV equally based on the marketization principle and the rule of law, to adopt category-based measures to defuse outstanding debts as well as to impose strict controls on incremental debts through extensions, refinancing, restructuring, etc. Regular mechanisms for monitoring the financial debts of LGFV were also set up. Local governments were supported in gradually divesting the government financing function of LGFV through mergers and acquisitions and capital injections.

X. Improving the capability to serve cross-border trade, investment, and financing

Advancing the improvement and coverage of cross-border trade facilitation policies. The PBOC continuously moved forward with the reforms to facilitate cross-border trade, issued relevant measures to further facilitate cross-border trade settlement, streamlined the procedures for foreign exchange payments and settlements, and introduced measures to support special business processing. These actions have upgraded and expanded the coverage of the pilot policies in support of high-quality development, and they have helped enterprises lower costs and hedge risks.

Continuously optimizing foreign exchange services. The PBOC has further facilitated mobile payment services for overseas visitors to China and has provided high-quality foreign exchange services for the Hangzhou Asian Games and the Chengdu Universiade. Work has been done to promote the construction of cross-border financial service platforms and to expand diverse application scenarios.

Promoting construction of the foreign exchange market. The PBOC has improved services for enterprises to hedge against exchange rate risks, and it has conducted a special evaluation of banks licensed for nationwide operations in terms of their management of exchange rate risks. The PBOC guided the China Foreign Exchange Trade System (CFETS) to waive foreign exchange risk hedging fees for micro, small, and medium-sized enterprises (MSMEs) in 2023, and it extended the trading hours of the foreign exchange money market and the currency pair market. The PBOC released a list of market makers for 2023 and 2024 to optimize the structure of market makers. Work has also been done to ensure smooth implementation of the listing of the Macau patacas on the interbank foreign exchange market.

Supporting regional opening-up and innovation. The PBOC introduced innovation policies for foreign exchange management on a trial basis in key areas such as Hengqin-Guangdong-Macau, Qianhai-Shenzhen-Hong Kong, and Xiong'an New Area, so as to serve the country's major regional development strategies. Pilot programs regarding high-level opening-up policies for cross-border trade and investment have also been expanded in Shanghai, Jiangsu, Guangdong (including Shenzhen), Beijing, Zhejiang (including Ningbo), and Hainan, thereby facilitating the conduct of foreign exchange transactions by business entities in compliance with the regulations.

Deepening international monetary and

Table 8 Trading Volume of the RMB Against Other Currencies in the Interbank Foreign Exchange Spot Market in 2023

Unit: RMB 100 million

Currency	USD	EUR	JPY	HKD	GBP	AUD	NZD
Trading volume	600,511.35	8,320.50	4,994.78	2,082.93	364.38	557.25	123.97
Currency	SGD	CHF	CAD	MYR	RUB	ZAR	KRW
Trading volume	131.31	159.88	448.76	22.97	85.68	5.57	47.51
Currency	AED	SAR	HUF	PLN	DKK	SEK	NOK
Trading volume	7.16	28.48	5.60	4.53	8.83	53.01	6.19
Currency	TRY	MXN	THB	KHR	KZT	MNT	IDR
Trading volume	1.38	24.34	57.60	0	0.06	0	26.19

Source: China Foreign Exchange Trade System.

financial cooperation. The PBOC continued to steadily advance its progress in bilateral currency swap arrangements, improved the currency swap framework, and gave play to the role of currency swaps in supporting development of the offshore RMB market and facilitating trade and investment. With a focus on neighboring countries and countries along the Belt and Road, the PBOC strengthened currency settlement cooperation with its counterparts and fostered a better environment for overseas use of the RMB. As of end-2023, based on the bilateral currency swap agreements between the PBOC and overseas monetary authorities, the overseas monetary authorities had drawn RMB 114.886 billion and the PBOC had drawn foreign currencies equivalent to USD 246 million. These operations have played an active role in promoting bilateral trade and investment.

Box 3 Steadily Advancing Bilateral Currency Swaps Between Central Banks

Bilateral currency swaps between central banks (currency swap lines) are a financing arrangement in which a central bank can swap its own currency for the provision of liquidity in the counterparty central bank's currency. It is generally used to maintain financial market stability, and it can be swapped back upon maturity. Entering into currency swap agreements is a mature worldwide central bank practice. In the 1960s, the Federal Reserve began to engage in currency swap cooperations with some European central banks. At present,

bilateral currency swap agreements among six central banks, i.e., the Federal Reserve, the Bank of Canada, the Bank of England, the European Central Bank, the Bank of Japan, and the Swiss National Bank, have been signed. In addition to signing currency swap agreements with the PBOC, the European Central Bank has also signed currency swap agreements with the National Bank of Denmark, the Swedish Central Bank, and the National Bank of Poland. As for the Bank of Japan, it has signed currency swap agreements with the

Bank of Thailand, the Monetary Authority of Singapore, and the Reserve Bank of Australia. In addition, during the subprime crisis and the COVID-19 pandemic, the Federal Reserve also established temporary currency swap lines with some other central banks.

The PBOC began to sign currency swap agreements with overseas central banks or monetary authorities in the wake of the 2008 international financial crisis when the liquidity conditions of the major international currencies were tight, pushing up demand among some countries to use local currencies for settlement. The PBOC has signed bilateral currency swap agreements with over 40 overseas central banks or monetary authorities. Since 2022, the PBOC has upgraded its currency swap agreement with the Hong Kong Monetary Authority to a long-standing arrangement, signed a currency swap agreement with the Central Bank of Saudi Arabia, and renewed its swap agreements with some central banks or monetary authorities, such as the Bank of Indonesia, the Monetary Authority of Singapore, the European Central Bank, and the Central Bank of the United Arab Emirates. At present, a total of 31 currency swap lines are in force, covering the major economies in key regions across six continents worldwide. The total size of the swap lines is approximately RMB 4.16 trillion. The size is the upper limit of funds available to be drawn on the swap lines and it is not equivalent to the actual amount of fund use. At the end of 2023, the balance of the actual draws by overseas central banks or monetary authorities posted RMB 114.9 billion, accounting for less

than 3 percent of the total size of the currency swap lines. To guard against the potential impact of exchange rate fluctuations, an exchange rate protection mechanism has been set up in the swap lines based on which the amount of the swap currencies will be timely adjusted according to a new exchange rate if the fluctuations in the exchange rate exceed a certain range during use of the swap funds.

Bilateral currency swaps play a positive role in various respects. First, the RMB liquidity swap lines have been an important part of the global financial safety net, playing an active part in boosting market confidence and maintaining regional and global financial stability. For instance, in response to COVID-19, the PBOC signed or renewed currency swap agreements, or expanded the size of existing swap lines, with a number of its foreign counterparts, which helped the relevant countries and regions tide over the impact of the pandemic and maintain financial stability. Second, the swap funds can be used to support bilateral trade and investment and they can help to save exchange costs and to reduce exchange rate risks. For example, when a foreign company wants to pay for goods it has imported in RMB, it can apply for currency swaps to obtain RMB funds for the bilateral trade payments. Third, currency swap lines can provide necessary liquidity for the offshore market and help improve the environment for the use of local currencies. For instance, the long-standing swap agreement between the PBOC and the Hong Kong Monetary Authority is expected to provide the Hong Kong market with more stable and long-term liquidity, which will help better leverage the role of Hong Kong as an offshore RMB business hub and promote the development of Hong Kong's financial industry.

Going forward, the PBOC will continue to provide liquidity support and maintain financial stability through RMB liquidity swap lines, and it will improve the layout of the swap network so as to bring into full play the role of bilateral currency swaps as a component in the global financial safety network. In addition, the PBOC will step up efforts to improve the management mechanism for swap transactions, raise the efficiency of swap fund use, safeguard the security of swap funds, and support the counterparty central banks in making reasonable use of RMB swap funds in a bid to further facilitate bilateral trade and investment.

Part 3 Financial Market Conditions

In 2023, the performance of the financial market was generally stable. Money market interest rates edged down, with active market transactions. The trading volume of interbank derivatives market maintained growth. The bond market grew steadily in size with an overall decline in interest rate levels. The securities and insurance markets maintained an overall stable performance.

I. Financial market overview

1. Money market interest rates dropped slightly, with active market transactions

Money market interest rates dropped. In December 2023, the monthly weighted average interest rate for interbank lending was 1.78 percent, and the monthly weighted average interest rate for pledged repos posted 1.9 percent, 9 basis points, and 6 basis points lower than those in September 2023, respectively. The monthly weighted average interest rate for government-backed bond pledged repos among depository institutions posted 1.64 percent, 26 basis points lower than the monthly weighted average interest rate for pledged repos. At end-2023, the overnight and 7-day Shibor posted 1.75 percent and 1.87 percent, respectively, down 21 basis points and 36 basis points from end-2022, respectively.

Repos transactions on the money market were active. In 2023, the cumulative volume of bond repos trading on the interbank market registered RMB 1,674.2 trillion, representing an average daily turnover of RMB 6.7 trillion and an increase of 21.3 percent year on year. The cumulative volume of trading for interbank lending registered RMB 143 trillion, representing an average daily turnover of RMB 571.9 billion and a decrease of 2.6 percent year on year. In terms of the maturity structure, overnight repos accounted for 87.5 percent of the total turnover in bond repos, up 1.1 percentage points year on year; and overnight lending constituted 89.5 percent of the total turnover in interbank lending, up 0.3 percentage points year on year. The volume of bond repos trading on the exchange markets increased 13.4 percent year on year to RMB 457.6 trillion.

Interbank Certificates of Deposits (CDs) and negotiable CD businesses operated in an orderly manner. In 2023, about 27,000 interbank CDs were issued on the interbank market, raising RMB 25.7 trillion. The total volume of trading on the secondary market registered RMB 253.6 trillion. At end-2023, outstanding interbank CDs reached RMB 14.8 trillion. The weighted average interest rate of 3-month interbank CDs was 2.4 percent, 8 basis points higher than that of the 3-month Shibor. About 63,000 negotiable CDs were issued by financial institutions throughout the year, raising RMB 14.2 trillion, an increase of RMB 1.6 trillion year on year.

Interest rate swap transactions remained

stable. In 2023, the RMB interest rate swap market witnessed 352,000 transactions, increasing 44.1 percent year on year, with the volume of the notional principal totaling RMB 31.7 trillion, an increase of 50.8 percent year on year. In terms of the maturity structure, contracts with maturities of up to one year traded most briskly, and the volume of the notional principal posted RMB 21.7 trillion, accounting for 68.5 percent of the principal of all maturities. The 7-day fixing repo rate (FR) and the Shibor served as the main reference

rates for the floating leg of the RMB interest rate swaps, accounting for 91.5 percent and 7.4 percent, respectively, of the total notional principal of the interest rate swaps. Interest rate swaps anchored to the loan prime rate (LPR) witnessed 1,256 transactions, with RMB 231.93 billion of the notional principal.

The interest rate options business developed at a steady pace. In 2023, a total of 1,007 interest rate options transactions were concluded, totaling RMB 160.68 billion, all

Table 9 Fund Flows Among Financial Institutions in 2023

Unit: RMB 100 million

Type of institution	Repos		Interbank lending	
	2023	2022	2023	2022
Chinese-funded large banks[1]	−7,547,504	−5,159,892	−559,860	−461,874
Chinese-funded medium-sized banks[2]	−1,080,044	−1,505,272	−33,055	−173,370
Chinese-funded small-sized banks[3]	605,794	156,731	101,333	86,211
Securities institutions[4]	2,282,209	1,754,480	424,875	443,887
Insurance institutions[5]	249,533	229,671	1,952	2,803
Foreign-funded banks	63,531	55,363	−14,810	−20,464
Other financial institutions and vehicles[6]	5,426,481	4,468,919	79,566	122,807

Source: China Foreign Exchange Trade System.
Notes：1.Chinese-funded large banks include the Industrial and Commercial Bank of China, Agricultural Bank of China, Bank of China, China Construction Bank, China Development Bank, Bank of Communications, and Postal Savings Bank of China.
2.Chinese-funded medium-sized banks refer to policy banks, China Merchants Bank, and eight other joint-equity commercial banks, Bank of Beijing, Bank of Shanghai, and Bank of Jiangsu.
3. Chinese-funded small-sized banks refer to the Hengfeng Bank, China Zheshang Bank, China Bohai Bank, other city commercial banks, rural commercial banks, rural cooperative banks, private banks, and village and township banks.
4. Securities institutions include securities firms, fund management companies, and futures companies.
5. Insurance institutions include insurance firms and corporate annuities.
6. Other financial institutions and vehicles include urban credit cooperatives, rural credit cooperatives, finance companies, trust and investment companies, financial leasing companies, asset management companies, social security funds, mutual funds, wealth management products, trust plans, and other investment vehicles. Some of these financial institutions and vehicles do not participate in the interbank lending market.
7. A negative sign indicates net lending and a positive sign indicates net borrowing.

Table 10 Interest Rate Swap Transactions in 2023

Year	Transactions	Notional principal (RMB 100 million)
2023	352,279	317,071.9
2022	244,397	210,295.6

Source: China Foreign Exchange Trade System.

of which were LPR interest rate options transactions. Specifically, interest rate cap/floor transactions amounted to RMB 158.68 billion, and interest rate swap transactions amounted to RMB 2 billion.

2. The coupon rates of bonds witnessed an overall decline, while its market size maintained stable growth

Bond issuance rates fell. In December 2023, the yield on 10-year government bonds issued by the Ministry of Finance was 2.59 percent, 5 basis points lower than the rate in September and 24 basis points lower than the rate in the same period of the previous year; the average rate of 1-year short-term financing bills issued by AAA-rated enterprises was 3.09 percent, down 76 basis points from the same period of the previous year. China Development Bank (CDB) did not issue bonds in December, and the yield on 10-year financial bonds issued in November was 2.66 percent, 3 basis points lower than the rate in September.

The yields on government bonds marked a downward trend, and the term spreads narrowed slightly. At end-2023, the yields on 1-year, 3-year, 5-year, 7-year and 10-year government bonds were 2.08 percent, 2.29 percent, 2.40 percent, 2.53 percent and 2.56 percent, respectively, down 9 basis points, 8 basis points, 13 basis points, 14 basis points, and 12 basis points, respectively, compared with those of end-September; and the term spread on 1-year and 10-year government bonds was 48 basis points, which narrowed by 3 basis points from end-September.

Bond issuances increased year on year. The cumulative value of bonds issued in 2023 grew by 15.3 percent year on year to RMB 70.8 trillion, RMB 9.4 trillion more than that in the same period of last year mainly due to the large increase in government bonds, local government bonds, and interbank certificates of deposits. At end-2023, outstanding bonds held in custody amounted to RMB 157.9 trillion, representing an increase of 9.1 percent year on year. Specifically, the balance of domestic bonds held by foreign institutions stood at RMB 3.7 trillion, accounting for 2.4 percent of the total volume in custody, on par with that at the end of the previous year.

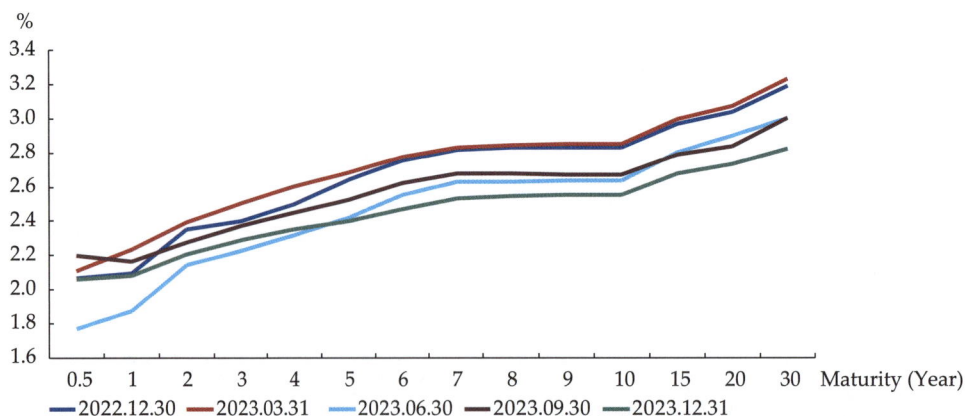

Figure 4 Yield Curves of Government Bonds in the Interbank Market

(Source: China Central Depository & Clearing Co., Ltd)

Table 11 Bond Issuances in 2023

Unit: RMB 100 million

Type of bond	Issuance	YOY change
Government securities	110,956	13,793
Local government bonds	93,254	19,698
Central bank bills	0	0
Financial bonds[1]	364,417	58,222
Of which: Financial bonds issued by the CDB and policy financial bonds	58,760	327
Interbank certificates of deposits	257,815	52,694
Corporate credit bonds[2]	138,206	1,487
Of which: Debt-financing instruments of non-financial enterprises	86,979	−4,355
Enterprise bonds	3,808	−2,384
Corporate bonds	36,458	8,248
Bonds issued by international institutions	1,430	605
Total	708,263	93,804

Sources: The People's Bank of China, China Securities Regulatory Commission (CSRC), and China Central Depository & Clearing Co., Ltd. Updated with the latest data from the providers.

Notes: 1. Including financial bonds issued by the CDB, policy financial bonds, bonds issued by commercial banks (including ordinary bonds, subordinated bonds, and hybrid bonds), bonds issued by securities firms, and interbank certificates of deposit.

2. Including debt-financing instruments issued by non-financial enterprises, enterprise bonds, corporate bonds, convertible bonds, bonds with detachable warrants, privately offered SME bonds, and asset-backed securities on the Shanghai Stock Exchange and the Shenzhen Stock Exchange issued by non-financial enterprises.

The trading volume of spot bonds grew. In 2023, the value of cash bonds traded on the bond market posted RMB 353.9 trillion, registering an increase of 14.5 percent year on year. Specifically, the value of cash bonds traded on the interbank market was RMB 307.3 trillion, representing an increase of 13.3 percent year on year. The value of cash bond transactions on the stock exchanges totaled RMB 46.6 trillion, an increase of 23 percent year on year.

3. The bill financing business witnessed steady growth, with interest rates for bill financing declining slightly

The bill acceptance business registered a steady increase. In 2023, commercial drafts issued by enterprises totaled RMB 31.4 trillion, increasing 14.5 percent year on year. At end-2023, outstanding commercial drafts stood at RMB 17.1 trillion, decreasing by 1.4 percent year on year. Outstanding commercial draft acceptances increased. At end-2023, outstanding commercial draft acceptances increased by RMB 494 billion from the end of Q3, and decreased by RMB 238.1 billion compared to that of end-2022. Of the outstanding bankers' acceptances, 69.6 percent were issued by micro, small, and medium-sized enterprises (MSMEs), up 1.3 percentage points from the previous year.

Bill financing witnessed steady growth, with interest rates declining slightly. In 2023, total discounts by financial institutions amounted to RMB 62.6 trillion, increasing by 16.2 percent year on year. At end-2023, the balance of bill financing was RMB 13.2 trillion, up 2.7 percent year on year. The balance accounted for 5.5 percent of the total outstanding loans, down 0.5 percentage points year on year. At end-2023, the interest rates for bill financing went down year on year, falling after an initial rise in the year.

4. The total turnover and the amount funds raised in the stock market declined year on year

At end-2023, the Shanghai Stock Exchange Composite Index closed at 2,975 points, down 3.7 percent from end-2022. The Shenzhen Stock Exchange Component Index closed at 9,525 points, down 13.5 percent from end-2022. In terms of specific sectors, the communications sector witnessed a growth rate of over 20 percent, with electronics, automobiles, and other sectors ranking among the top performers. Trade and retail, as well as the real estate sector, experienced relatively weak performance. The total turnover and amount of funds raised in the stock market decreased year on year. In 2023, the combined turnover on the Shanghai Stock Exchange and the Shenzhen Stock Exchange reached RMB 212.2 trillion, and the average daily turnover was RMB 876.9 billion, down 5.5 percent year on year. Northbound funds maintained an inflow trend throughout 2023, achieving net buying for the 10th consecutive year. In 2023, cumulative funds in the amount of RMB 917.0 billion were raised through the Shanghai Stock Exchange and the Shenzhen Stock Exchange, a decrease of 30.4 percent year on year.

5. Premium income increased year on year and the growth of assets accelerated

In 2023, total premium income in the insurance sector amounted to RMB 5.1 trillion, up 9.1 percent year on year and an acceleration of 4.5 percentage points compared to that recorded in 2022. Claim and benefit payments totaled RMB 1.9 trillion, representing a year-on-year increase of 21.9 percent. Specifically, total property insurance claims and benefit payments increased by 18.2 percent year on year and total life insurance claims and benefit payments increased by 25.7 percent year on year.

The growth of assets in the insurance sector accelerated. At end-2023, total assets in the insurance sector increased by 10.4 percent year on year to RMB 30 trillion, an acceleration of 1.3 percentage points from end-2022. Specifically, bank deposits decreased by 3.9 percent, while investment-

Table 12 Asset Allocations in the Insurance Sector at end-2023

Unit: RMB 100 million, %

Item	Balance		As a share of total assets	
	End-2023	End-2022	End-2023	End-2022
Total assets	299,573	271,467	100.0	100.0
Of which: Bank deposits	27,243	28,348	9.1	10.4
Investments	249,495	222,161	83.3	81.8

Source: National Administration of Financial Regulation.

linked assets increased by 12.3 percent year on year.

6. The turnover of spot and swap foreign exchange transactions increased year on year, while that of forward transactions declined

In 2023, the cumulative turnover of spot RMB/ foreign exchange transactions registered USD 8.7 trillion, an increase of 4.8 percent year on year. The cumulative turnover of swap RMB/ foreign exchange transactions totaled USD 20.6 trillion, an increase of 6.8 percent year on year. Specifically, cumulative overnight RMB/USD swap transactions posted USD 13.9 trillion, accounting for 67.5 percent of the total swap turnover. The turnover of RMB/ foreign exchange forward transactions totaled USD 120 billion, decreasing by 7.7 percent year on year. The turnover of foreign currency pair transactions totaled USD 1.8 trillion, increasing by 18.9 percent year on year. In particular, the USD/JPY pair registered the largest trading volume, accounting for 37.3 percent of the total market share.

7. Gold prices went up and the volume of gold trading expanded

At end-2023, international gold prices closed at USD 2,078.4 per ounce, representing an increase of 14.6 percent from end-2022. The Au99.99 on the Shanghai Gold Exchange closed at RMB 479.59 per gram, increasing by 16.8 percent from end-2022. In 2023, the volume of gold traded on the Shanghai Gold Exchange was 41,500 tons, an increase of 7.1 percent year on year. The turnover posted RMB 18.6 trillion, up 22.3 percent year on year.

II. Development of institutional arrangements in the financial markets

1. Institutional arrangements in the money market

The regulation of important money market funds was strengthened. In February 2023, China Securities Regulatory Commission (CSRC), together with the PBOC, released the *Interim Provisions on the Regulation of Important Money Market Funds*, improving the safety and liquidity of important fund products in the money market and effectively preventing risks. The interim provisions specified relevant definitions as well as the prerequisites, criteria and procedures for the evaluation of important money market funds. More stringent and prudent requirements were imposed on the managers, trustees, and sales institutions of such funds.

Broker quotes and data displays were regulated. In August, the PBOC, the National Administration of Financial Regulation (NAFR), the CSRC, and the State Administration of Foreign Exchange (SAFE) jointly released the *Notice on Matters Concerning Data Services for Money Brokers*, regulating data services provided by money brokers and encouraging the proper use of data in compliance with the law, so as to ensure data security, enhance the transparency of market information, and promote fair competition.

2. Institutional arrangements in the bond market

The bond evaluation business was regulated in the interbank bond market. In December 2023, the PBOC released the *Measures for the Administration of Bond Valuation Services in the Interbank Bond Market*, specifying the requirements on such aspects as the internal governance of service providers, basic principles and methods for valuation, information disclosure, and conflicts of interest. The measures served to improve the neutrality, fairness, professionalism and transparency of the bond valuation services, rendering the valuation more effective and market-based, and preventing risks.

The opening-up of the bond market at a high level was steadily promoted. Under the guidance of the PBOC, relevant financial infrastructure institutions implemented a package of measures to facilitate investment. First, foreign-funded institutions in China were included in the market makers for the Northbound Bond Connect, which could tap into their advantages in regional overseas client resources and in cross-border service capabilities to provide better services for overseas investors. Second, the function of trading a basket of bond portfolio became available. It better met the needs of index investors, reduced the cost of inquiry when multiple bonds were transferred, and improved trading efficiency. Third, the reporting procedure for settlement failures in the Northbound Bond Connect was improved. After upgrading the infrastructure system, we enabled online one-stop reporting, thus greatly improving the convenience of investments. Fourth, mutual access was enhanced between the interest rate swap markets of the mainland and Hong Kong. With connected infrastructures, overseas investors can enjoy a greater convenience in interest rate risk management.

Box 4 Further Deepening the Financial Cooperation between the Mainland and Hong Kong SAR

In recent years, the PBOC has conscientiously implemented the policy arrangements of the CPC Central Committee. According to the "one country, two systems" policy, it has been actively engaged with the Hong Kong Monetary Authority (HKMA) and other financial regulators, so as to promote financial cooperation between the Mainland and Hong Kong SAR, and to support Hong Kong to consolidate its status as an international financial center. These efforts have produced positive effects.

Hong Kong's status as a global offshore RMB business hub has been continuously strengthened. Since 2018, the PBOC has been regularly issuing RMB-denominated central bank bills in Hong Kong, providing high credit-rating assets for Hong Kong's offshore RMB market. By the end of 2023, the cumulative amount of central bank bill issuance totals RMB 725 billion. Meanwhile, the PBOC has strongly supported Mainland government sector, financial institutions, and non-financial enterprises to issue bonds in Hong Kong, so as to constantly improve Hong Kong's offshore RMB yield curve. Since October 2021, the government of Shenzhen municipality has issued offshore RMB-denominated local government bonds in Hong Kong for three consecutive years. Besides, the bilateral local currency swap arrangement signed between the PBOC and the HKMA has been upgraded into a standing currency swap arrangement, and the size of the swap has been expanded to RMB 800 billion, providing medium- to long-term liquidity support for the development of offshore RMB business in Hong Kong. Currently, Hong Kong has become the most important global offshore RMB business hub, consistently ranking the first in cross-border RMB settlement among offshore RMB markets, with around 75 percent of global offshore RMB payments settled through Hong Kong. In the meantime, the size of offshore RMB cash pool, RMB deposit, and RMB-denominated bond issuance, as well as RMB foreign exchange trading volume in Hong Kong have all ranked the first among major offshore RMB markets.

The connectivity of financial markets between the Mainland and Hong Kong has been constantly deepened. As a bridge that connects the Mainland with international markets, Hong Kong has always been an important channel for global investors to invest in the Mainland. To strengthen Hong Kong's status as an international asset management center, the PBOC has worked closely with financial regulators from both the Mainland and Hong Kong since 2014, and have launched multiple connect programs, such as the Shanghai/Shenzhen-Hong Kong Stock Connect, Bond Connect, Cross-boundary Wealth Management

Connect, and Swap Connect. Currently, around 70 percent of the A-share stocks held by global investors are invested through the Shanghai/Shenzhen-Hong Kong Stock Connect, while over half of the Mainland bonds traded by global investors are executed through the Northbound Trading under the Bond Connect. On the basis of previous progress, the PBOC and the HKMA jointly launched multiple measures to improve connect schemes in January 2024, including the announcement of implementation rules to improve the Cross-boundary Wealth Management Connect pilot program in the Guangdong-Hong Kong-Macao Greater Bay Area (GBA), the inclusion of bonds under the Bond Connect in the list of eligible collateral for the HKMA's RMB liquidity arrangement, and plans to further open up the domestic bond repurchase business to overseas investors, supporting all overseas institutions that have already entered the interbank bond market, including those through the Bond Connect, to participate in bond repurchase business.

Hong Kong's participation in the development of the GBA has been further increased. In recent years, the PBOC and relevant authorities have jointly released opinions on financial support for the development of the GBA and the Qianhai Shenzhen-Hong Kong Cooperation Zone, supporting Hong Kong to give full play to the advantages of pioneer policies and pilot programs. The authorities have successively launched Qualified Domestic Limited Partners (QDLP) and Qualified Foreign Limited Partners (QFLP) pilot programs in the

GBA, expanded the list of banks eligible for the pilot program of Mainland Type II and III personal bank account agency opening witness service for Hong Kong and Macao residents, and supported the Hong Kong- and Macao-version of UnionPay wallet, Alipay (Hong Kong) digital wallet, and WeChat (Hong Kong) digital wallet to expand their application across the country. Recently, the PBOC also released official papers to better serve the demands of Hong Kong and Macao residents to purchase properties in the GBA, and announced the expansion of the scope for the Shenzhen-Hong Kong cross-border credit referencing collaboration pilot program, so as to facilitate cross-border financing activities for both Mainland and Hong Kong enterprises.

Cooperation in green and sustainable finance between the Mainland and Hong Kong has been advanced in an orderly manner. In recent years, multiple collaborations in green finance areas, such as the development of green finance collaboration platform and the issuance of green bonds, have been conducted between the Mainland and Hong Kong. In September 2020, the Green Finance Alliance of the GBA was established, creating a platform for deepening cooperation in green finance between the Mainland and Hong Kong. In July 2022, the PBOC promoted the release of the first process reference for Mainland enterprises to issue green bond in Hong Kong, encouraging local government and enterprise entities to issue green bonds in Hong Kong. Currently, the government of Shenzhen municipality has issued green and sustainable development bonds in Hong Kong for three consecutive years. Hong Kong has become an important market for green financing and investment in Asia, with a cumulative green bond issuance exceeding USD 80 billion, and the total asset under management of sustainable development funds (ESG funds) reaching USD 160 billion.

Cooperation in fintech between the Mainland and Hong Kong has delivered fruitful results. For a long period of time, substantive collaborations in areas such as central bank digital currency and fintech supervision have been conducted between the Mainland and Hong Kong. For digital currency, the PBOC and the HKMA have launched the cross-border e-CNY payment pilot program since 2020, and further enhanced the program at the beginning of 2024, to better serve Hong Kong and Mainland residents and enterprises. Meanwhile, the multiple-central bank digital currency bridge project (Project mBridge), which both the PBOC and the HKMA have participated in, has progressed smoothly and finished the world's first pilot test based on real transaction scenarios. For fintech innovation, the PBOC and the HKMA signed a Memorandum of Understanding (MOU) on fintech innovation supervisory cooperation in October 2021, and promoted cooperation in fintech innovation in a steady and orderly manner. Base on the existing MOU, the PBOC, the HKMA, and the Monetary Authority of Macao (AMCM) jointly signed another MOU in November 2023. Under the new MOU, the three authorities agreed to link up, in the form of a network, the PBOC's Fintech Innovation Regulatory Facility, the HKMA's Fintech Regulatory Sandbox, and *the AMCM's Regulatory Requirements for Innovative Fintech Trials.*

Going forward, the PBOC will further deepen the financial cooperation between the Mainland and Hong Kong, support the development of Hong Kong as an international financial center, and promote Hong Kong to accelerate the integration of its own development into the overall development of the country. It will continue its regular issuance of RMB-denominated central bank bills in Hong Kong, and support eligible Mainland local governments, financial institutions, and enterprises to issue offshore RMB-denominated bonds in Hong Kong, so as to consolidate Hong Kong's status as a global offshore RMB business hub. The PBOC will further enhance the financial market connectivity between the Mainland and Hong Kong, and continue to improve connect schemes such as the Bond Connect, Cross-boundary Wealth Management

Connect, and Swap Connect, supporting Hong Kong to strengthen its status as an international asset management center. It will accelerate the implementation of policies which provide financial support for the development of the GBA, creating a convenient financial environment for Hong Kong residents to live and work in the GBA. In green finance, it will improve business cooperation and alignment of rules with Hong Kong, and support Mainland financial institutions to issue all types of green finance products in Hong Kong, so as to support Hong Kong to develop into a center for green and sustainable finance. In fintech, the PBOC will strengthen its cooperation with the HKMA. The two authorities will jointly increase the synergy of regulatory cooperation on fintech innovation, and constantly improve the pilot for cross-border use of e-CNY, supporting Hong Kong to build a fintech hub for the Asia-Pacific region.

3. Institutional reform and arrangements in the securities market

The reform was advanced towards registration-based IPO systems in all market. In February 2023, the CSRC officially launched the reform towards a fully functional registration-based IPO system, and released relevant provisions and rules. The reform covered all types of public offering of stocks and was of great importance for improving the function of capital markets, implementing the innovation-driven development strategy, and better serving the high-quality development. On April 10, the first batch of registration-based IPOs started

trading on main boards of the Shanghai and Shenzhen stock exchanges.

Institutional arrangements were improved in the fund industry. In July 2023, the CSRC released the *Regulations on the Supervision and Administration of Private Equity Investment Funds*, regulating fund raising, filing, investment activities and market-based withdrawal mechanism in a comprehensive manner. In the same month, the CSRC released the *Work Plan for the Reform of Mutual Fund Fee Rate*, enabling a comprehensive improvement in mutual funds fee rate in a phased manner. On December 8, the CSRC started soliciting public opinion on *Provisions for Strengthening the Administration of the Securities Transactions of Publicly Offered Securities Investment Funds* to promote the second phase of fee rate reform in the mutual fund industry. On the same day, the CSRC released the *Measures for the Supervision and Administration of Private Investments Funds (Exposure Draft)* to facilitate the regulated and sound development of the private fund industry.

The regulatory framework for securities companies and listed companies are refined. On November 3, the CSRC started soliciting public opinion on revising the *Measures for the Calculation Standards for Risk Control Indicators of Securities Companies*, for the purpose of upgrading the system of risk control indicators. On November 17, the CSRC released the *Rules for the Asset Purchase Activities of Listed Companies Using Convertible Corporate Bonds Issued to Specific Objects*, which supported listed companies to restructure using directional convertible bonds as payment tools, so as to acquire high-quality assets and improve the quality of such companies. In December, the CSRC revised and released the *Rules for Share Repurchases by Listed Companies*, enhancing the inclusiveness and convenience of repurchase and encouraging listed companies to put more emphasis on repurchase and execute it in a regulated way.

The institutional arrangements in the capital market were improved. In February, the CSRC released the *Trial Administrative Measures of Overseas Securities Offering and Listing by Domestic Companies*, as well as five other supporting guidelines, to support the lawful and compliant overseas securities offering and listing by domestic companies and promote the two-way opening up of the capital market. In October, the CSRC announced optimizations to the rules of securities lending and strategic investors shares lending, for the purpose of strengthening the regulation of securities lending regulation. In the same month, the CSRC released the *Measures for the Administration of the Issuance and Trading of Corporate Bonds* and supporting documents. The *Measures* regulated the issuance, transaction and transfer of corporate bonds, and protected the legitimate rights and interests of investors as well as public interests.

4. Institutional arrangements in the insurance market

The services were improved in life insurance and property insurance. In January 2023, the China Banking and Insurance Regulatory Commission (CBIRC) released the *Rules for Information Disclosure of Life Insurance Products with Terms of More Than One Year*, which required full disclosure of such products' long-term nature and risk characteristics, as well as other key information such as ways of payment and loss arising from surrender. In the same month, the former CBIRC released the *Opinions on Proactively Providing Risk Reduction Services in Property Insurance Industry* and the *Notice on Expanding the Floating Range of Independent Pricing Coefficients of Commercial Auto Insurance and Other Related Matters*. The former required property insurance companies to enrich the content and increase the supply of risk reduction services, and ensured the protection of consumers' the rights and interest. And the latter improved and guaranteed the supply of auto insurance products. In July, the NAFR released the *Notice on Matters Concerning Products Covered by the Favorable Policy of the Personal Income Tax for Commercial Health Insurance*, expanding the eligibility criteria of the preferential personal income tax and reducing medical expense burdens.

Regulation on insurance companies were strengthened. In September, the NAFR released the *Measures for the Administration of Insurance Sales*, imposing restrictions on insurance sales throughout the entire process to better protect the rights and interests of consumers. In the same month, the NAFR released the *Notice on Improving the Regulatory Standards for the Solvency of Insurance Companies*. The Notice implemented differentiated capital regulation on insurance companies with different sizes and with different product ranges and improved capital measurement standards and risk factors, so as to guide insurance companies to provide support and services for the real economy and sci-tech innovation. In October,

the PBOC and the NAFR jointly released the *Measures for the Assessment of Systemically Important Insurers*, stipulating that the assessment of systemically important insurers will be conducted every two years based on the indicators and data of the insurers to be assessed. The *Measures* took effect on January 1, 2024.

The pension system was improved. In September, the NAFR released the *Notice on Matters Concerning the link-up of the PTDA Pilot Program with the Personal Pension,* clarifying the business adjustments, product management, and policy transfer during the process to ensure orderly link-up. In October, the NAFR released the *Notice on Matters Related to Promoting the Development of Exclusive Commercial Pension Insurance*, further expanding the scope of insurers allowed to engage in the business of exclusive commercial pension insurance. In November, the NAFR released the *Interim Rules on Pension Insurance Companies*. The *Interim Rules* clarified specific requirements on such aspects as institutions management, corporate governance and risk management, so as to fill in the vacuum of exclusive regulatory rules for pension insurance firms.

Part 4 Macroeconomic Overview

I. Global economic and financial developments

The global economy was resilient in 2023, but the growth momentum weakened. As inflationary pressures eased, central banks in the advanced economies have mostly paused rate hikes since the fourth quarter. But the labor market remained tight. Looking ahead, the implications of sluggish global trade, uncertain macroeconomic policies in the advanced economies, and geopolitical risks for the global economy still merit attention.

1. Economic performance and financial markets in the major economies

Economic recovery continued to diverge. The economic performance in the U.S. was broadly stable. In Q4 2023, the quarterly real GDP increased at an annual rate of 3.3 percent, lower than the 4.9 percent in Q3, but still higher than market expectations. The likelihood of a "soft landing" has increased. The economic growth in Europe faltered. The GDP grew by 0.1 percent year on year in Q4 in the euro area, and was flat quarter on quarter. The growth in Japan slowed down. The annual rate of quarterly real GDP growth contracted by 2.9 percent in Q3, a sharp contrast with the upward trend in the first half of 2023. The manufacturing PMI in the major advanced economies was mostly below 50, whereas the services PMI was higher. The services PMI was above 50 in the U.S. and Japan, and has been under 50 in the euro area since August. This has once again pointed to

diverging growth momentum.

Inflation came down quickly in the U.S. and Europe, but went up a bit towards the end of 2023. In the U.S., the year-on-year growth rate of the headline CPI fell by 3 percentage points from earlier this year to 3.4 percent in December, but was slightly higher than that in November, while the core CPI continued to fall. In December, the HICP in the euro area rose by 2.9 percent year on year, a bit higher than that in November, which snapped the eight-month falling streak. In the U.K., the CPI registered a year-on-year increase of 4.0 percent in December, up by 0.1 percentage point compared with the prior month, but it was notably lower than the growth of more than 10 percent earlier this year.

Labor market remained tight. In December, the U.S. nonfarm payrolls increased by 216 thousand, growing for two months in a row. The unemployment rate posted 3.7 percent, on a par with that in November and falling by 0.1 percentage point from October. The labor force participation rate was down by 0.3 percentage points from November to 62.5 percent. Average hourly earnings for nonfarm payrolls rose by 4.1 percent year on year, slightly rebounded from 4 percent in November. Job vacancies increased from 8.925 million in November to 9.026 million in December.

Global financial markets were highly volatile.

Global equity markets increased. In 2023, the S&P 500, the EURO STOXX 50, and the Nikkei 225 jumped by 24.2 percent, 19.2 percent, and 28.2 percent, respectively. From August to October, global equity markets underwent sharp fluctuations, with the three major indices experiencing big corrections. However, they resumed the upward trend at the end of October. Bond yields fluctuated downwards. Market expectations for rate cuts by the major central banks have increased since November amid easing global inflationary pressures and faltering economic activities. Against this backdrop, the yields on 10-year government bonds in the major advanced economies fell sharply. The yield on the 10-year U.S. Treasury closed down by 110 bps from the peak in mid-October at 3.88 percent at the end of 2023, almost flat compared with end-2022. The yield on the 10-year German and U.K. government bonds closed at 2.02 percent and 3.62 percent respectively, down by 49 bps and 18 bps compared with end-2022. The U.S. dollar index also fluctuated downwards. It increased in the first three quarters of 2023, but has fallen significantly since Q4 and closed at 101.38 at the end of 2023, down by 4.5 percent from end-September and 2.0 percent from end-2022.

Table 13 Macroeconomic and Financial Indicators in the Major Advanced Economies

Economy	Indicator	Q4 2022			Q1 2023			Q2 2023			Q3 2023			Q4 2023		
		Oct.	Nov.	Dec.	Jan.	Feb.	Mar.	Apr.	May	Jun.	Jul.	Aug.	Sept.	Oct.	Nov.	Dec.
United States	Real GDP growth (annualized quarterly rate, %)	2.6			2.2			2.1			4.9			3.3		
	Unemployment rate (%)	3.6	3.6	3.5	3.4	3.6	3.5	3.4	3.7	3.6	3.5	3.8	3.8	3.8	3.7	3.7
	CPI (YOY, %)	7.7	7.1	6.5	6.4	6.0	5.0	4.9	4.0	3.0	3.2	3.7	3.7	3.2	3.1	3.4
	DJ Industrial Average (end of the period)	32,733	34,590	33,147	34,086	32,657	332,74	34,098	32,908	34,408	35,559	34,722	33,508	33,053	35,951	37,690
Euro Area	Real GDP growth (YOY, %)	1.8			1.3			0.6			0.0			0.1		
	Unemployment rate (%)	6.6	6.7	6.7	6.7	6.6	6.5	6.5	6.5	6.4	6.5	6.5	6.5	6.5	6.4	6.4
	HICP (YOY, %)	10.6	10.1	9.2	8.6	8.5	6.9	7.0	6.1	5.5	5.3	5.2	4.3	2.9	2.4	2.9
	EURO STOXX 50 (end of the period)	3,618	3,964	3,793	4,163	4,238	4,315	4,359	4,218	4,399	4,471	4,297	4,175	4,061	4,382	4,522
United Kingdom	Real GDP growth (YOY, %)	0.6			0.4			0.3			0.3			—		
	Unemployment rate (%)	3.7	3.7	3.7	3.8	3.9	3.8	4.0	4.2	4.2	4.2	4.2	4.2	4.2	—	—
	CPI (YOY, %)	11.1	10.7	10.5	10.1	10.4	10.1	8.7	8.7	7.9	6.8	6.7	6.7	4.6	3.9	4.0
	FTSE 100 (end of the period)	7,095	7,573	7,452	7,772	7,876	7,632	7,871	7,446	7,532	7,699	7,439	7,608	7,322	7,454	7,733
Japan	Real GDP growth (annualized quarterly rate, %)	1.0			5.0			3.6			−2.9			—		
	Unemployment rate (%)	2.6	2.5	2.5	2.4	2.6	2.8	2.6	2.6	2.5	2.7	2.7	2.6	2.5	2.5	2.4
	CPI (YOY, %)	3.7	3.8	4.0	4.3	3.3	3.2	3.5	3.2	3.3	3.3	3.2	3.0	3.3	2.8	2.6
	NIKKEI 225 (end of the period)	27,587	27,969	26,095	27,327	27,446	28,041	28,856	30,888	33,189	33,172	32,619	31,857	30,859	33,487	33,464

Sources: Statistical Bureaus and Central Banks of the Relevant Economies.

2. Monetary policies of the major economies

This round of rate hikes in the major advanced economies was close to an end. The Fed raised rates on four occasions by a total of 100 bps in 2023, bringing the target range for the federal funds rate to 5.25-5.5 percent from 4.25-4.5 percent earlier this year. It paused rate hikes three times between September and the end of 2023. Meanwhile, the Fed continued to shrink its balance sheet as scheduled, with the monthly cap for Treasury securities set at USD 60 billion and that for agency MBS at USD 35 billion. The ECB raised policy rates six times by a total of 200 bps in 2023, with the interest rate on its main refinancing operations, marginal lending facility, and deposit facility increased to 4.5 percent, 4.75 percent, and 4 percent, respectively. It stood pat on rates twice in Q4. In the mean time, the ECB started to shrink its balance sheet in March by a monthly average amount of EUR 15 billion until the end of June, ended the reinvestment of the principal payments from maturing securities under the asset purchase program (APP) in July, and planned to reduce the pandemic emergency purchase programme (PEPP) portfolio by EUR 7.5 billion per month on average over the second half of 2024 and discontinue reinvestments under the PEPP at the end of 2024. The Bank of England (BOE) raised its policy rate five times by a total of 175 bps to 5.25 percent in 2023, and kept interest rates on hold twice in Q4. The Monetary Policy Committee of the BOE voted to reduce the stock of gilts by GBP 100 billion to GBP 658 billion between October 2023 and September 2024. The Bank of Japan (BOJ) maintained its short-term policy rate at -0.1 percent and its target yield on 10-year Japanese government bond (JGB) at around zero percent, but it increased the flexibility of yield curve control, setting 1 percent as a reference upper bound for 10-year JGB yield fluctuations in its market operations. In 2023, the Reserve Bank of Australia hiked rates five times by a total of 125 bps, the Reserve Bank of New Zealand three times by 125 bps, the Bank of Canada three times by 75 bps, and the Bank of Korea once by 25 bps.

Monetary policies in the emerging market economies diverged. In 2023, the central banks in Russia, South Africa, Mexico, Indonesia, India, and Malaysia raised rates five times, three times, two times, two times, one time, and one time by a total of 850 bps, 125 bps, 75 bps, 50 bps, 25 bps, and 25 bps, respectively, while the central banks of Chile and Brazil both cut rates on four occasions by a total of 300 bps and 200 bps, respectively.

3. Issues and trends that merit attention

The economic growth momentum has weakened. The global economy was resilient in 2023, and one of the major contributing factor is the cumulative effects of earlier stimulus policies. As policy effects perter out and the lagged effects of rate hikes bite, the growth momentum of the global economy may weaken further down the road. The global economy is projected to grow by 3.1 percent in 2024 according to the IMF, the same growth rate as 2023. The 2024 global growth forecasts by the World Bank and the Organization for Economic Cooperation and Development are 2.4 percent and 2.9 percent, respectively, both lower than the average growth rate of 3.8 percent between 2000 and 2019.

Inflation will continue to fall slowly. Inflation has already come down significantly from the high of over 9 percent to around 3 percent in the advanced economies. As global supply chains have normalized and consumer demand has cooled down, inflation is likely to fall further in the advanced economies. However, given that services inflation remains sticky and geopolitical tensions may once again increase the volatility of commodity prices, the fall of inflation will remain a gradual and slow process. The IMF projected the global inflation would fall steadily to 5.8 percent in 2024 from 6.9 percent in 2023 and would not return to target until 2025 in most economies.

The timing for rate cuts by central banks in the major advanced economies is uncertain. In Q4 2023, the Fed, the ECB, and the BOE all paused rate hikes, but their comments on future policy paths diverged. The Fed shifted its policy focus from taming inflation to striking a balance between stabilizing growth and controlling inflation, while the ECB and the BOE remained hawkish. According to the statement released in January 2024, the Federal Open Market Committee does not expect it will be appropriate to reduce the target range until it has gained greater confidence that inflation is moving sustainably toward 2 percent, which has dampened market expectations for a rate cut by the Fed in March.

Rising political and geopolitical risks weigh

on economic growth. Over 70 jurisdictions will hold general elections in 2024, including the U.S., Russia, India, and Brazil. Apart from the implications of election results for global political and economic landscapes, the uncertainties in the election process may also disrupt the global economy. In the meantime, geopolitical tensions keep escalating. The Russia-Ukraine conflict, which has lasted for nearly two years, is still at a stalemate. The conflict may persist. The resurgence of Palestinian-Israeli conflict has complicated the situation in the Middle East, which may also add to the global economic uncertainty.

II. Macroeconomic developments in China

In 2023, faced with the complex and severe international environment and the arduous tasks of domestic development, reform and stability, all regions and departments had earnestly implemented the strategic arrangements of the CPC Central Committee and the State Council, increasing the intensity of macro adjustments. The national economy witnessed a continuous recovery and turned toward high-quality development, with production and supply steadily improving, transformation and upgrading actively advancing, overall employment and prices generally stable, people's livelihood effectively securing, and high-quality development solidly advancing. According to preliminary statistics, GDP in 2023 grew by 5.2 percent year on year to RMB 126.1 trillion on a comparable basis. Specifically, GDP in Q4 grew by 5.2 percent year on year and 1.0 percent quarter on quarter.

1. Consumption recovered rapidly, investments continued to expand, and imports and exports were generally stable

Residents' income continued to increase and market sales recovered rapidly. In 2023, China's per capita disposable income posted RMB 39,218, increasing by 6.3 percent year on year in nominal terms, or 6.1 percent in real terms, 0.2 percentage points higher than the first three quarters. The structure of income distribution has been continuously improved. The nominal and real growth rates of rural residents' per capita disposable income were 2.6 percentage points and 2.8 percentage points higher than those of urban residents, respectively. In 2023, the final consumption expenditure accounted for 82.5 percent of the economic growth. Meanwhile, total retail sales of consumer goods grew by 7.2 percent year on year. Consumption of basic living items saw stable growth, with retail sales of enterprises (units) above the designated size in terms of textile products, such as clothing, shoes, and hats, increasing by 12.9 percent and those in terms of grain, oil, and food increasing by 5.2 percent year on year. Sales of upgraded products increased fairly rapidly, with retail sales of gold/silver/jewelry, sports/entertainment products and communication equipment by enterprises (units) above the designated size increasing by 13.3 percent, 11.2 percent, and 7.0 percent, respectively. The Consumer Confidence Index stabilized and rebounded, reaching 87.6 in December, up 1.3 percentage points from the middle of 2023.

Investments continued to expand and investments in the high-tech sector grew rapidly. In 2023, the total investments accounted for 28.9 percent of the economic growth. The total fixed-asset investments throughout China (those by rural households excluded) increased by 3.0 percent year on year to RMB 50.3036 trillion. In terms of sectors, investments in the manufacturing sector increased by 6.5 percent, 3.5 percentage points higher than the total investment growth. Investments in infrastructure increased by 5.9 percent. Investments in real estate development decreased by 9.6 percent year on year. Investments in the high-tech sector grew by 10.3 percent year on year, 7.3 percentage points higher than the total investment growth. Specifically, investments in the high-tech manufacturing sector and high-tech services sector grew by 9.9 percent and 11.4 percent year on year, respectively. In the high-tech manufacturing sector, investments in the aviation/spacecraft/instrument manufacturing industry, computer/office equipment manufacturing industry, and electronic/communication equipment manufacturing industry increased by 18.4 percent, 14.5 percent and 11.1 percent year on year, respectively. In the high-tech services sector, investments in the service industry of the commercialization of sci-tech achievements and e-commerce service industry increased by 31.8 percent and 29.2 percent year on year, respectively.

Imports and exports were generally stable, with the trade structure continuously improving. In 2023, imports and exports of goods increased by 0.2 percent year on year to RMB 41.7568 trillion. Specifically, exports grew by 0.6 percent year on year and imports fell by 0.3 percent year on year, with the trade surplus in goods posting RMB 5.7884 trillion. Imports and exports of private enterprises increased by 6.3 percent, accounting for 53.5 percent of total imports and exports, an acceleration of 3.1 percentage points year on year. Imports and exports with trading partners countries along the Belt and Road grew by 2.8 percent year on year, increasing by 1.2 percentage points and accounting for 46.6 percent of total imports and exports. Exports of mechanical and electrical products increased by 2.9 percent, accounting for 58.6 percent of total exports.

Foreign direct investment (FDI) was basically stable and the quality of investments continued to improve. In 2023, actually utilized FDI decreased by 8 percent year on year to RMB 1.13391 trillion. The quality of investments continued to improve. Actually utilized FDI in the high-tech manufacturing industries increased by 6.5 percent year on year. Specifically, the electronic and communications equipment manufacturing sector and medical equipment/instrument manufacturing sector grew by 12.2 percent and 32.1 percent year on year, respectively. Actually utilized FDI in construction sector and the service sector of the commercialization of sci-tech achievements increased by 43.7 percent and 8.9 percent year on year, respectively.

2. Agricultural production was generally stable, industrial production rebounded steadily, and the service industry grew rapidly

In 2023, the value-added of the primary industry totaled RMB 8.9755 trillion, up 4.1 percent year on year. The value-added of the secondary industry totaled RMB 48.2589 trillion, up 4.7 percent year on year. The value-added of the tertiary industry totaled RMB 68.8238 trillion, up 5.8 percent year on year.

Agricultural production was generally stable and animal husbandry grew steadily. In 2023, the value-added of agriculture (farming) increased by 4.2 percent year on year. The output of grain totaled 695.41 million tons, an increase of 8.88 million tons or 1.3 percent year on year. In 2023, the output of pork, beef, lamb, and poultry grew by 4.5 percent year on year to 96.41 million tons. Specifically, the output of pork grew by 4.6 percent year on year to 57.94 million tons. At end-2023, the number of hogs in stock decreased by 4.1 percent year on year and the number of hogs for slaughter increased by 3.8 percent year on year.

The industrial production recovered steadily and the equipment manufacturing industry grew rapidly. In 2023, the value-added of Industrial Enterprises Above a Designated Size (IEDS) increased by 4.6 percent year on year, 0.6 percentage points higher than the first three quarters. In terms of sectors, the value-added of the mining sector and of the manufacturing sector increased by 2.3 percent and 5.0 percent year on year, respectively. The value-added of electricity, heat, gas, and water production and supply sector increased by 4.3 percent year on year. The value-added of equipment manufacturing sector increased by 6.8 percent, which was 2.2 percentage points higher than the growth of the value-added of IEDS. In terms of enterprises, the value-added of state-owned enterprises and private enterprises increased by 5.0 percent and 3.1 percent year on year, respectively. In terms of products, the output of solar cells, new energy vehicles and charging stations grew by 54.0 percent, 30.3 percent, and 28.5 percent year on year, respectively.

The service industry grew rapidly, with the contact-intensive service industry improving significantly. In 2023, the value-added of the service industry grew by 5.8 percent year on year. Specifically, the value-added of accommodations and catering, electronic information transmission/software/information technology services, and the financial services sector grew by 14.5 percent, 11.9 percent, and 6.8 percent year on year, respectively. In December, the Index of Service Production (ISP) increased by 8.5 percent year on year. Specifically, the ISP of accommodations and catering and electronic information transmission/software/information technology services increased by 34.8 percent and 13.8 percent year on year, respectively. From January to November, the revenue of enterprises above a designated size in the services industry registered an 8.5 percent year-on-year increase. Specifically, the revenue of culture/sports/entertainment, and information transmission/software/information technology services increased by 18.9 percent and 12.8 percent year on year, respectively.

3. Consumer prices increased slightly, and the core CPI remained generally stable

Consumer prices increased moderately.

In 2023, the Consumer Price Index (CPI) increased by 0.2 percent year on year, showing an overall trend of initial increase followed by decrease and gradual slowdown. In Q4, the CPI decreased on average by 0.3 percent year on year. From the supply side, domestic production capacity was sufficient and recovering quickly. The industrial capacity utilization rate in Q4 was 75.9 percent, up 1.6 percentage points from Q1. From the demand side, the momentum of consumption recovery weakened marginally. The seasonally adjusted quarter-on-quarter growth rate of total retail sales of consumer goods in Q4 was about 0.3 percent, lower than the 0.8 percent growth rate in H1. In addition, the base effect of pork and other food prices has increased. In Q4, the decline in pork prices pulled down CPI by more than 0.5 percentage points, while the price increase of fruits and vegetables and other food items was lower than the historical average for the same period. In 2023, food prices decreased by 0.3 percent year on year, while non-food prices increased by 0.4 percent year on year, with a decrease of 3.2 percentage points and 1.4 percentage points in growth rate compared to the previous year, respectively. The core CPI, excluding food and energy, increased by 0.7 percent year on year, a deceleration of 0.2 percentage points from the previous year.

The decline in production prices has narrowed. Influenced by factors such as the fall of international commodity prices, comparatively weak demand, sufficient supply, and a high base effect from the previous year, the Producer Price Index (PPI) continued to decrease by 3.0 percent year on year in 2023, which was 7.3 percentage points lower than the previous year. Overall, the PPI showed a V-shaped trend, reaching its lowest point of -5.4 percent in June and narrowing down to -2.7 percent in December. The Purchasing Price Index of Raw Material (PPIRM) decreased by 3.6 percent year on year, 9.9 percentage points lower compared to the previous year. The Corporate Goods Price Index (CGPI), monitored by the PBOC, decreased by 2.1 percent year on year, 5.6 percentage points lower from the same period last year.

4. Fiscal revenue rose steadily and fiscal expenditures remained stable

In 2023, revenue in the national general public budget posted RMB 21.7 trillion, increasing by 6.4 percent year on year. Specifically, central and local fiscal revenue increased by 4.9 percent and 7.8 percent, respectively. National tax revenue amounted to RMB 18.1 trillion, increasing by 8.7 percent year on year. Specifically, the domestic value-added tax (VAT) increased by 42.3 percent year on year, mainly due to the large amount of VAT credit refunds and the low base over the same period of 2022.

In 2023, expenditures in the national general public budget posted RMB 27.5 trillion, increasing by 5.4 percent year on year. Specifically, expenditures in the central level general public budget and the local level general public budget increased by 7.4 percent and 5.1 percent year on year, respectively. In terms of the expenditure structure, expenditures related to social security and employment, science and technology, and

education grew rapidly, witnessing a year-on-year increase of 8.9 percent, 7.9 percent, and 4.5 percent, respectively.

5. The employment situation remained generally stable

The surveyed urban unemployment rate decreased. In 2023, the surveyed urban unemployment rate averaged 5.2 percent, decreasing 0.4 percentage points compared to the previous year. In December, the surveyed urban unemployment rate averaged 5.1 percent, decreasing by 0.4 percentage points year on year. The employment situation of key groups continued to improve. In 2023, the total number of migrant workers reached 298 million, increasing 1.91 million compared to the previous year. The annual average of the surveyed urban unemployment rate for rural registered labor force in urban areas decreased by 0.7 percentage points compared to the previous year.

6. The balance of payments and the external debt

In Q1-Q3 2023, China's current account surplus registered USD 209.0 billion, equivalent to 1.6 percent of GDP over the same period. Specifically, according to the balance of payments statistics, trade in goods recorded a surplus of USD 454.4 billion, while trade in services recorded a deficit of USD 168.4 billion. Domestic residents' cross-border tourism and overseas studies have resumed in an orderly manner but are still below pre-pandemic levels. According to preliminary statistics, the annual current account surplus remained relatively high and stayed within a reasonably balanced range. Cross-border investment activities under the capital account were carried out in an orderly manner, showing an overall trend of stability and improvement. Specifically, foreign inbound equity direct investment maintained a net inflow, with a significant rebound in Q4. China's outbound equity direct investment grew stably. Securities investment gradually recovered to net inflows, with foreign investors increasing their holdings of domestic bonds by over USD 62 billion in Q4. As of end-2023, outstanding foreign currency reserves stood at USD 3.238 trillion, increasing USD 110.3 billion from end-2022, mainly influenced by factors such as changes in exchange rates and asset prices. As of end-September 2023, the balance of full-caliber foreign debt (denominated in both domestic and foreign currencies) posted USD 2.3829 trillion.

7. Analysis by sector

7.1 The machinery sector

The machinery sector is a basic and strategic sector that provides technical and equipment support for the national economic development. In 2023, the overall machinery sector showed an overall recovery trend, and steady progress was made in terms of high-quality development. First, the sector operated smoothly with improved profitability. Operating revenue and total profits in the machinery sector accounted for more than 20 percent of those industries above a designated size, increasing by 6.8 percent and 4.1 percent year on year in 2023, respectively, which were significantly higher than the overall growth of industries above a designated size. Second, innovation and development led to the continuous growth of fixed asset investments. Annual investment

growth in the automobile and electric machinery sectors registered 19.4 percent and 32.2 percent, respectively, which played an important role in driving investment in the manufacturing sector. Third, there was an obvious trend of upgrading in the structure of export products. Annual exports of the "new three," namely, electric passenger vehicles, lithium batteries, and solar cells, exceeded the ceiling of RMB 1 trillion, with a year-on-year growth of 29.9 percent.

It should also be noted that the foundation for the recovery of China's machinery sector is yet not solid. First, the pressure on the demand side is rather prominent. In recent years, the demand for medium- and low-end products in the machinery sector has slowed down significantly, and the traditional downstream industries such as steel and coal industries have been undergoing industrial transformation, increasing the operating pressure of the machinery sector. Second, the transformation and upgrading of the machinery sector has a long way to go. China's machinery sector boasts of complete categories and prominent scale advantages. However, the resilience of the industrial chain is not strong, as it relies on imports of some key parts and is lagging behind the international advanced level in terms of some basic materials. Third, differentiation exists within the sector. Although the overall development of the machinery sector is positive and stable, with the automobile sector witnessing fast growth, yet some industries are faced with greater downward pressure.

Looking ahead, the high-quality development of China's machinery sector will be steadily promoted. First, focusing more on the capability of independent innovation. China will accelerate the development of strategic emerging industries, give full play to the role of enterprises in technological innovation, strengthen the build-up of a multi-layered talent team structured with echelons, further establish and improve the industrial technological innovation system, and cultivate premium brand products. Second, continuously strengthening the industrial foundation. Taking the green and low-carbon transformation of the manufacturing sector as an opportunity, China will continuously promote the industrial optimization and upgrading, promote equipment renewal, process optimization, and product upgrading, drive investment in the manufacturing sector, and promote innovation and transformation of the development pattern. Third, continuously ensuring the security of industrial and supply chains. China will concentrate the industry's superior forces on removing the "bottlenecks", accelerate the catching-up of key frontier technologies, change the situation of "insufficient" high-end supply, and help the coordinated development of the upstream and downstream industrial chains.

7.2 The elderly care sector

The report of the 20th CPC National Congress points out that it is necessary to implement the national strategy of actively coping with the aging of the population and to develop the elderly care sector. Currently, China has entered the period of an aged society.

At end-2023, the proportion of people aged 60 and above, and those aged 65 and above, accounted for 21.1 percent and 15.4 percent of the total population, respectively, which were both over 5 percentage points higher than those of a decade ago. In recent years, the central government and various regions and departments have issued a series of policies to support the development of the elderly care sector, covering land, taxation, fiscal support, finance, talents and other aspects, which have driven the accelerated development of the elderly care sector in China. As of end-September 2023, there were a total of 400,000 elderly care service institutions and facilities around the country, with 8.206 million beds which has nearly doubled over the past decade. According to market estimates, the scale of China's elderly care sector in 2023 stood at about RMB 10 trillion, and is expected to reach RMB 20 trillion by 2030, accounting for one-tenth of GDP.

The financial sector has taken proactive measures to support the high-quality development of the elderly care sector. In April 2022, the special central bank lending tool for inclusive elderly care was launched in a timely manner to encourage financial institutions to provide loans to inclusive elderly care service institutions at preferential rates to promote the increase of inclusive elderly care service supply. Since the implementation of the policy, financial institutions have provided a total financing of RMB 2.16 billion to 69 inclusive elderly care service projects in five pilot provinces, including Zhejiang and Jiangsu, effectively supporting the construction of inclusive elderly care projects. Recently, the General Office of the State Council issued *the Opinions on Developing the Silver Economy to Enhance the Well-being of the Elderly*, which also emphasized on effective use of the special central bank lending facility for inclusive elderly care, so as to support the operation of public welfare and inclusive elderly care institutions, the construction of home and community elderly care systems, and the enterprises manufacturing products for the elderly. In addition, the PBOC has been actively guiding financial institutions to launch exclusive credit products for the elderly care sector. Through strengthening cooperation with government industrial funds and financing guarantee institutions, it provides targeted financial services for the elderly care sector.

Going forward, with the continuous deepening of the aging problem, there is huge potential for development of the elderly care sector, with elderly financial services, elderly care services, and elderly care products as the core. It should also be noted that China's high-quality development of the elderly care sector still faces challenges, such as insufficient elderly care institutions, uneven quality, high costs of elderly care services, etc. The financial support for the development of the elderly care sector also faces objective difficulties, such as low returns, long cycles, and high risks. There is an urgent need to further improve the policy system supporting development of the elderly care sector. At the Central Financial Work Conference in 2023, "the elderly care finance" was included in the five key areas. In the next stage, more targeted efforts will be made to enrich the supply of elderly financial products, to broaden the financing channels for elderly care service institutions, so as to better meet the increasingly diverse financial needs for elderly care. Besides, China will strengthen the coordination and cooperation of fiscal, taxation and industrial policies. It is necessary to fully mobilize the social forces to participate in this enterprise, promote the construction of an elderly care service system for the general public, and better meet the elderly care needs of the ordinary elderly people.

Part 5 Monetary Policy Outlook

I. China's macroeconomic and financial outlook

In 2023, China's economy was recovering and it achieved solid progress in pursuing high-quality development. With its full-year GDP registering a year-on-year growth rate of 5.2 percent, China successfully reached the growth target set for 2023 at the beginning of the year, and it is projected to contribute more than 30 percent of global economic growth. Meanwhile, per capita disposable income in China saw a year-on-year increase of 6.1 percent in real terms; the urban-rural income gap continued to narrow; and people's lives were further improved.

Looking ahead to 2024, China's economy is on track for further recovery. First, investment will continue to gain steam. The funds carried over from the additional RMB 1 trillion worth of treasury bonds issued in Q4 2023, together with the newly added quota of RMB 500 billion for pledged supplementary lending (PSL), will play an effective role in boosting investments in flood prevention and disaster relief projects, government-subsidized housing projects, the construction of public infrastructures for both daily and emergency use, and the rebuilding of run-down urban areas, thereby further stimulating private investment. Second, consumption is steadily improving. Amid the waning impact of the pandemic, corporate revenue and household income are picking up, so is people's

willingness to consume. In light of the huge numbers of automobiles and home appliances currently in use in China, both demand and potential demand for upgraded products are sufficient. Moreover, as there are about 300 million new urban residents in China, to improve the supporting institutional arrangements and consumer financial services for them will help enhance market depth in such fields as education, medical care, and elderly care and speed up cultivation of new types of consumption. Third, China's foreign trade is highly resilient. The start of a new round of economic and trade talks between China and the U.S. will contribute to the sound and stable development of bilateral economic and trade relations. In addition, with the strengthening of economic and trade ties between China and the countries participating in the Belt and Road Initiative, China's foreign trade will have increasingly wider space for development. Furthermore, as it has been clearly laid down at the Central Economic Work Conference that we focus on the central task of economic development and the overarching mission of high-quality development, this requirement will give a strong boost to the enthusiasm of all parties.

To sustain the economic recovery, China still has to overcome some difficulties and challenges. Globally, although this cycle of interest rate hikes by the advanced economies may have come to an end, the lag effect of the high interest rates will continue to linger. Moreover, as 2024 is a year of global elections, we will likely see rising uncertainties in political and economic situations around the world. Domestically, there are blockages to economic circulation; the consumer confidence index and the growth rate of private investment remain low; and insufficient demand contrasts with excess capacity. With the manufacturing PMI having remained in contraction territory for four consecutive months, social expectations are still weak. That said, we should not only face up to the difficulties but also strengthen confidence and belief in ourselves. The fundamentals for China's sound economic growth over the long run remain unchanged, and the favorable conditions outweigh the unfavorable ones. It is important to follow the general principle of seeking progress while maintaining stability, promoting stability through progress, and establishing the new before abolishing the old to advance high-quality development with solid efforts and to solve the problems in the process of development.

Prices are expected to rise mildly. China's year-on-year CPI growth remained in negative territory in Q4 2023 due to weak rises in the prices of durable goods and services as well as due to the high base caused by the previous surges in the prices of pork and other food items. Meanwhile, year-on-year core CPI growth slowed from 0.8 percent to 0.6 percent. Given that inflation fundamentally depends on the balance between supply and demand in the real economy, behind the current low prices is the lack of effective demand in the economy and the fact that total supply and total demand are recovering at different paces. With the base effect diminishing and the demand for goods and services continuing to rebound in the future, prices are expected on the whole to see a mild uptick. The decline in the PPI is also expected to narrow further. From a medium- to long-term perspective, as China is undergoing a critical period of economic recovery as well as industrial transformation and upgrading, supply and demand are poised to improve continually, monetary conditions will be appropriate, and people's expectations will remain stable. Therefore, there is no basis for long-term deflation or inflation in China.

II. Outlook for monetary policy in the next stage

Under the guidance of Xi Jinping Thought on Socialism with Chinese Characteristics for a New Era, the PBOC will fully implement the spirit of the 20th CPC National Congress and apply the new development philosophy fully, faithfully, and comprehensively. It will adhere to the general principle of seeking progress while maintaining stability, promoting stability through progress, and establishing the new before abolishing the old. It will speed up efforts to build China into a financial powerhouse, improve financial services, firmly follow the path of financial development with Chinese characteristics, and promote high-quality development of the financial sector. The PBOC will develop a modern central banking system and strengthen counter-cyclical and inter-temporal adjustments to macro policies, with serving the real economy as the fundamental purpose of the financial sector. Maintaining prudence of monetary policies and enhancing consistency in the macroeconomic policy orientation, it will continue to effectively upgrade and appropriately expand economic output.

Prudent monetary policies will be flexible,moderate, precise, and effective. Based on a rational understanding of the relationship between the two largest financing markets, namely, the bond market and the credit market, as well as an appropriate grasp of the patterns and new features of money and credit supply and demand, the PBOC will guide a reasonable growth and a balanced provision of credit. By doing so, it will keep a reasonable and sufficient liquidity level that matches the growth of AFRE and the money supply with the expected targets for economic growth and price levels. It will enhance policy coordination and effectively support the initiative to boost consumption, stabilize investment, and expand domestic demand so as to keep prices at a reasonable level. By continuing to deepen the market-oriented interest rate reform, further improving the LPR formation mechanism, and leveraging the role of the mechanism for market-oriented deposit rate adjustments, it will promote overall social financing costs to remain stable with a downward trend. The PBOC will give play to the role of the monetary policy toolkit in adjusting both the aggregate and the structure. It will support the use of debt restructuring and other methods to activate existing stocks so as to improve efficiency in using existing loans. Implementing policies

in a targeted, appropriate, and flexible way, the PBOC will work to develop technology finance, green finance, inclusive finance, pension finance, and digital finance. The 25 measures encouraging financial support for the private economy will continue to be implemented, and more financial support will be provided for the development of government-subsidized housing projects, the construction of public infrastructures for both daily and emergency uses, and the rebuilding of run-down urban areas. Pursuing a managed floating exchange rate regime based on market supply and demand with reference to a basket of currencies, the PBOC will take a holistic approach in policy implementation and stabilize expectations, and it will prevent risks arising from exchange rate overshooting and prevent expectations from becoming unanimously one-sided and self-reinforced so as to keep the RMB exchange rate basically stable at a reasonable and balanced level. The PBOC will continue its efforts to effectively prevent and resolve risks in key areas including small and medium-sized financial institutions, local debts and the real estate sector, thereby firmly defending the bottom line whereby no systemic financial risks will occur.

First, the PBOC will maintain reasonable growth in financing and monetary aggregates. In line with the requirements to promote direct financing with vigorous efforts, the PBOC will appropriately manage the relationship between the two largest financing markets, i.e., the bond market and the credit market. Further work will be done to develop the corporate credit bond and financial bond markets. Continuing to strengthen monitoring and analysis of financial market movements as well as liquidity supply and demand in the banking system, the PBOC will keep a close watch on the monetary policy shifts of the major central banks. It will conduct open market operations (OMOs) in a flexible and effective manner while using a mix of monetary policy tools. It will also do its part to ensure successful issuance of government bonds. Guiding financial institutions to enhance liquidity risk management, it will keep liquidity in the banking system at a reasonable and sufficient level and it will maintain the stable movement of money market rates. Moreover, the PBOC will support efforts by financial institutions to actively explore credit demand and tap into the projects in reserve, working to promote reasonable loan growth, to reinforce a balanced supply of loans, and to make the growth of loans more stable and sustainable. By doing so, it will ensure that the AFRE and the money supply are aligned with economic growth and the expected target level of prices. The PBOC will put efforts into improving the efficiency of loan utilization. It will channel funds from maturing loans to entities operating with higher efficiency, optimize the use of new loans, and promote market clearing as necessary, thereby providing better support for sustainable development of the economy.

Second, the PBOC will give full play to the guiding role of monetary and credit policies. Conducting the policies in a targeted, appropriate, and flexible manner, the PBOC will keep central bank lending and discount policies stable, make effective use of the inclusive lending facility for micro and small businesses (MSBs), and duly implement the different types of special central bank lending facilities still in effect. It will integrate the schemes for facilities supporting sci-tech innovation and those in the digital financial field, and it will further step up support for key fields and weak links, such as inclusive services for MSBs, the manufacturing sector, green development, and sci-tech innovation. The PBOC will move ahead with solid implementation of the *Notice on Strengthening Financial Support Measures to Boost the Development and Growth of the Private Economy*. It will continue the project for improving the capacity of providing financial services for micro, small, and medium-sized enterprises (MSMEs) in order to increase the availability of financing to private enterprises and MSBs and to make the process more convenient. Moreover, it will guide financial institutions to continue stepping up financial support for rural revitalization to better meet the diverse financing needs of the agro-related sectors. The PBOC will adopt city-specific measures to implement differentiated housing credit policies in a targeted manner, providing better support for people's rigid demands for housing and their needs to improve living conditions. It will meet the reasonable financing needs of property enterprises, regardless of their ownership types, to promote the stable and sound development of the real estate market. In addition, it will make effective use of the newly added PSL quota to intensify financial support for the development of affordable housing, the construction of public infrastructure for both normal and emergency use, and the renovation of urban villages. These efforts are aimed at accelerating the establishment of a new development model for the real estate sector.

Third, the PBOC will properly manage internal and external equilibria regarding the interest rate and the exchange rate. Continuing to advance the market-oriented interest rate reform, the PBOC will smooth the channels for monetary policy transmission. It will improve the market-oriented interest rate formation and transmission mechanism, optimize the central bank policy rate system, and guide market rates to move around the policy rates. It will implement the mechanism for market-oriented deposit rate adjustments in an effort to stabilize bank liability costs. At the same time, it will tap into the LPR reform and enhance self-regulatory coordination and management in the industry. Urging financial institutions to adhere to risk-based pricing and to straighten out the relationship between loan rates and market rates such as bond yields, it will maintain a level playing field in the market so as to stabilize and bring down overall social financing costs. Taking steady steps to deepen the market-oriented exchange rate reform, the PBOC will improve the managed floating exchange rate regime that is based on market supply and demand with reference to a basket of currencies. Letting the market play a decisive role in the formation of exchange rates, it will give play to the role of the exchange rate as an automatic stabilizer for the macro economy and the balance of payments. Furthermore, it will strengthen expectation management, duly

conduct monitoring and analysis of cross-border capital flows, and uphold bottom-line thinking to prevent the risks of exchange rate overshooting. Additionally, it will prevent the formation and self-reinforcement of one-sided, unanimous expectations to keep the RMB exchange rate basically stable at a reasonable and balanced level. Meanwhile, the PBOC will strengthen management of the foreign exchange market. Guiding both enterprises and financial institutions to be risk-neutral, it will offer guidance to financial institutions on providing services of exchange rate risk hedging for MSMEs with authentic needs based on a risk-neutral concept, thereby maintaining the stable and sound development of the foreign exchange market.

Fourth, the PBOC will make continued efforts to deepen the financial reforms and opening-up. It will improve the legal system for the bond market and consolidate the legal basis for corporate credit bonds. By establishing a mechanism linking up market-makers and OMO primary dealers, it will improve management of businesses, such as bond underwriting, valuation, and market-making, in order to enhance the pricing function and robustness of the bond market. It will also expand the over-the-counter (OTC) bond business and make OTC investments in government bonds more convenient and efficient for individuals, businesses, and small and medium-sized financial institutions. At the same time, the PBOC will strengthen macro-prudential management of the money market and improve the mechanism for money market liquidity monitoring. Adhering to market principles and the rule of law, it will continue to adopt a zero-tolerance approach and step up efforts to crack down on illegal and irregular conduct in the bond market. It will remain firmly committed to advancing the opening-up of the bond market. Moreover, the PBOC will advance the internationalization of the RMB in an orderly manner. It will further expand use of the RMB in cross-border trade and investment, deepen international monetary cooperation, and develop offshore RMB markets. It will further liberalize and facilitate cross-border trade and investment by carrying out pilot programs for high-standard opening-up in the field, and it will steadily move ahead with the convertibility of the RMB under the capital account.

Fifth, the PBOC will work proactively and prudently to forestall and defuse financial risks. Further steps will be taken to improve the macro-prudential policy framework as well as the capacity for systemic risk monitoring, assessment, and early warning and to enrich the macro-prudential policy tools. The PBOC will improve regulation of systemically important financial institutions. It will urge systemically important banks to meet the additional regulatory requirements as scheduled. Meanwhile, it will pick up pace in pushing China's global systemically important banks to establish and improve

their total loss-absorbing capacity so as to effectively enhance their risk prevention ability. Moreover, the PBOC will actively advance the resolution of risks in key regions, key institutions, and key fields and it will push ahead with reforms to defuse their risks. It will guide financial institutions to support, based on market principles and the rule of law, the mitigation of the debt risks of local financing platforms through reasonable use of such means as debt restructuring and replacement. It will also strengthen monitoring and analysis of real estate market movements. The PBOC will advance the mitigation of risks in small and medium-sized financial institutions and it will improve the mechanism that presses for early rectification with hard constraints. It will work to accelerate the launch of the *Law on Financial Stability*. In addition, the PBOC will improve the accountability mechanism for risk resolution that matches power with responsibility and ensures compatibility between incentives and constraints. It will leverage the role of deposit insurance in resolving risks professionally, reinforce the building of the financial stability guarantee system, and prevent the buildup and spread of financial risks, thereby firmly defending the bottom line whereby no systemic financial risks will occur.

附录一　2023年中国货币政策大事记

1月16日，人民银行开展中期借贷便利（MLF）操作，操作金额为7 790亿元，利率为2.75%，与前次持平。

1月18日，人民银行印发《关于向全国性金融资产管理公司发放再贷款支持房地产纾困的通知》，向全国性金融资产管理公司提供低成本资金，支持其并购受困房地产企业存量房地产项目。

1月19日，人民银行印发《关于延续实施碳减排支持工具有关事宜的通知》，明确碳减排支持工具延续实施两年至2024年，并将部分外资银行和地方法人银行纳入碳减排支持工具金融机构范围。

1月20日，人民银行授权全国银行间同业拆借中心公布贷款市场报价利率（LPR），1年期LPR为3.65%，5年期以上LPR为4.30%，均与前次持平。

2月1日，人民银行向全国人大财经委员会汇报2022年货币政策执行情况。

2月7日，人民银行与巴西中央银行签署了在巴西建立人民币清算安排的合作备忘录；21日，授权中国工商银行（巴西）股份有限公司担任巴西人民币业务清算行。

2月10日，人民银行印发《关于开展租赁住房贷款支持计划试点有关事宜的通知》，引导金融机构在自主决策、自担风险的前提下，向试点城市专业化住房租赁经营主体发放长期限租赁住房购房贷款。

2月15日，人民银行开展中期借贷便利（MLF）操作，操作金额为4 990亿元，利率为2.75%，与前次持平。

2月20日，人民银行授权全国银行间同业拆借中心公布贷款市场报价利率（LPR），1年期LPR为3.65%，5年期以上LPR为4.30%，均与前次持平。

2月20日，人民银行与埃及中央银行续签规模为180亿元人民币/807亿埃及镑的双边本币互换协议。

2月24日，人民银行发布《2022年第四季度中国货币政策执行报告》。

3月15日，人民银行开展中期借贷便利（MLF）操作，操作金额为4 810亿元，利率为2.75%，与前次持平。

3月20日，人民银行授权全国银行间同业拆借中心公布贷款市场报价利率（LPR），1年期LPR为3.65%，5年期以上LPR为4.30%，均与前次持平。

3月27日，人民银行下调金融机构存款准备金率0.25个百分点（不含已执行5%存款准备金率的金融机构）。

4月7日，人民银行货币政策委员会召开2023年第一季度例会。

4月14日，人民银行向全国人大财经委员会汇报2023年第一季度货币政策执行情况。

4月17日，人民银行开展中期借贷便利（MLF）操作，操作金额为1 700亿元，利率为2.75%，与前次持平。

4月20日，人民银行授权全国银行间同业拆借中心公布贷款市场报价利率（LPR），1年期LPR为3.65%，5年期以上LPR为4.30%，均与前次持平。

4月28日，人民银行发布《内地与香港

利率互换市场互联互通合作管理暂行办法》（中国人民银行公告〔2023〕第8号）。

5月15日，人民银行发布《2023年第一季度中国货币政策执行报告》。

5月15日，人民银行开展中期借贷便利（MLF）操作，操作金额为1 250亿元，利率为2.75%，与前次持平。

5月15日，内地与香港利率互换市场互联互通合作正式上线运行。

5月22日，人民银行授权全国银行间同业拆借中心公布贷款市场报价利率（LPR），1年期LPR为3.65%，5年期以上LPR为4.30%，均与前次持平。

6月9日，人民银行就《银行间债券市场债券估值业务管理办法（征求意见稿）》向社会公开征求意见。

6月9日，人民银行与阿根廷中央银行续签规模为1 300亿元人民币/4.5万亿比索的双边本币互换协议。

6月13日，人民银行下调常备借贷便利（SLF）利率。其中，隔夜利率从2.85%下调至2.75%，7天利率从3%下调至2.9%，1个月利率从3.35%下调至3.25%。

6月15日，人民银行开展中期借贷便利（MLF）操作，操作金额为2 370亿元，利率为2.65%，较前次下降10个基点。

6月16日，人民银行会同金融监管总局、证监会、财政部、农业农村部印发《关于金融支持全面推进乡村振兴 加快建设农业强国的指导意见》，聚焦建立完善多层次、广覆盖、可持续的现代农村金融服务体系，增强金融服务能力。

6月20日，人民银行授权全国银行间同业拆借中心公布贷款市场报价利率（LPR），1年期LPR为3.55%，5年期以上LPR为4.20%，均较前次下降10个基点。

6月28日，人民银行货币政策委员会召开2023年第二季度例会。

7月12日，人民银行与老挝中央银行续签规模为60亿元人民币/158 000亿老挝基普的双边本币互换协议。

7月17日，人民银行向全国人大财经委员会汇报2023年上半年货币政策执行情况。

7月17日，人民银行开展中期借贷便利（MLF）操作，操作金额为1 030亿元，利率为2.65%，与前次持平。

7月20日，人民银行授权全国银行间同业拆借中心公布贷款市场报价利率（LPR），1年期LPR为3.55%，5年期以上LPR为4.20%，均与前次持平。

7月20日，人民银行、外汇管理局决定将企业和金融机构的跨境融资宏观审慎调节参数从1.25上调至1.5。

7月31日，人民银行与蒙古国中央银行续签规模为150亿元人民币/72 500亿蒙古图格里克的双边本币互换协议。

8月3日，人民银行召开金融支持民营企业发展座谈会。

8月4日，人民银行就《关于银行间债券市场柜台业务有关事项的通知（征求意见稿）》向社会公开征求意见。

8月15日，人民银行下调常备借贷便利（SLF）利率。其中，隔夜利率从2.75%下调至2.65%，7天利率从2.9%下调至2.8%，1个月利率从3.25%下调至3.15%。

8月15日，人民银行开展中期借贷便利（MLF）操作，操作金额为4 010亿元，利率为2.50%，较前次下降15个基点。

8月17日，人民银行发布《2023年第二季度中国货币政策执行报告》。

8月18日，人民银行印发《关于延长保交楼贷款支持计划政策实施期限有关事宜的通知》，明确将保交楼贷款支持计划政策实施期限延长至2024年5月末。

8月21日，人民银行授权全国银行间同业拆借中心公布贷款市场报价利率（LPR），1年期LPR为3.45%，5年期以上LPR为4.20%，分别较前次下降10个基点和持平。

8月30日，人民银行、金融监管总局、证监会联合全国工商联召开金融支持民营企业发展工作推进会。

8月31日，人民银行、金融监管总局发布《关于调整优化差别化住住房款信贷政策的通知》，商业性个人住房贷款最低首付款比例统一为首套住房不低于20%、二套住房不低于30%，二套住房商业性个人住房贷款利率政策下限调整为不低于相应期限贷款市场报价利率加20个基点。

8月31日，人民银行、金融监管总局发布《关于降低存量首套住房贷款利率有关事项的通知》，自2023年9月25日起，存量首套住房商业性个人住房贷款的借款人可向承贷金融机构申请，由金融机构新发放贷款置换存量首套住房商业性个人住房贷款，或协商变更合同约定的利率水平。

8月31日，人民银行、金融监管总局印发《关于做好金融支持防汛抗洪救灾和灾后恢复重建工作的通知》，对加大重点领域信贷投放、提升灾后恢复重建信贷服务效率、积极发挥保险风险分散功能、多渠道拓展灾后重建资金来源、全面提升灾区金融保障功能五个方面提出具体要求。

9月15日，人民银行下调金融机构存款准备金率0.25个百分点（不含已执行5%存款准备金率的金融机构）。

9月15日，人民银行下调金融机构外汇存款准备金率2个百分点，由6%下调至4%。

9月15日，人民银行开展中期借贷便利（MLF）操作，操作金额为5 910亿元，利率为2.50%，与前次持平。

9月15日，人民银行印发《关于延长租赁住房贷款支持计划政策实施期限有关事宜的通知》，明确将租赁住房贷款支持计划政策实施期限延长至2024年末。

9月20日，人民银行授权全国银行间同业拆借中心公布贷款市场报价利率（LPR），1年期LPR为3.45%，5年期以上LPR为4.20%，均与前次持平。

9月22日，人民银行、金融监管总局发布2023年我国系统重要性银行名单。

9月25日，人民银行货币政策委员会召开2023年第三季度例会。

9月28日，人民银行、金融监管总局、证监会、外汇管理局、香港金管局、香港证监会、澳门金管局决定进一步优化粤港澳大湾区"跨境理财通"业务试点，推进大湾区金融市场互联互通。

10月16日，人民银行开展中期借贷便利（MLF）操作，操作金额为7 890亿元，利率为2.50%，与前次持平。

10月18日，人民银行向全国人大财经委员会汇报2023年前三季度货币政策执行情况。

10月20日，人民银行会同金融监管总局发布《系统重要性保险公司评估办法》，将系统重要性金融机构认定范围从银行业拓展到保险业，加强系统重要性金融机构监管，增强金融体系稳健性。

10月20日，人民银行授权全国银行间同业拆借中心公布贷款市场报价利率

（LPR），1 年期 LPR 为 3.45%，5 年期以上 LPR 为 4.20%，均与前次持平。

11 月 9 日，人民银行发布《中国区域金融运行报告（2023）》。

11 月 15 日，人民银行开展中期借贷便利（MLF）操作，操作金额为 14 500 亿元，利率为 2.50%，与前次持平。

11 月 20 日，人民银行授权全国银行间同业拆借中心公布贷款市场报价利率（LPR），1 年期 LPR 为 3.45%，5 年期以上 LPR 为 4.20%，均与前次持平。

11 月 27 日，人民银行发布《2023 年第三季度中国货币政策执行报告》。

11 月 27 日，人民银行会同金融监管总局、证监会、外汇管理局、发展改革委、工信部、财政部、全国工商联发布《关于强化金融支持举措 助力民营经济发展壮大的通知》，引导金融机构树立"一视同仁"理念，持续加强民营企业金融服务，助力民营经济发展壮大。

11 月 28 日，人民银行与阿联酋中央银行续签规模为 350 亿元人民币/180 亿阿联酋迪拉姆的双边本币互换协议。

12 月 1 日，人民银行发布《银行间债券市场债券估值业务管理办法》（中国人民银行公告〔2023〕第 19 号），规范银行间债券市场债券估值业务，保护投资者合法权益，促进债券市场平稳健康发展。

12 月 1 日，人民银行与沙特中央银行签署规模为 500 亿元人民币/260 亿沙特里亚尔的双边本币互换协议。

12 月 5 日，人民银行与柬埔寨国家银行签署了在柬埔寨建立人民币清算安排的合作备忘录；11 日，授权中国银行金边分行担任柬埔寨人民币业务清算行。

12 月 15 日，人民银行开展中期借贷便利（MLF）操作，操作金额为 14 500 亿元，利率为 2.50%，与前次持平。

12 月 20 日，人民银行授权全国银行间同业拆借中心公布贷款市场报价利率（LPR），1 年期 LPR 为 3.45%，5 年期以上 LPR 为 4.20%，均与前次持平。

12 月 25 日，人民银行与塞尔维亚国家银行签署了在塞尔维亚建立人民币清算安排的合作备忘录；29 日，授权中国银行（塞尔维亚）有限公司担任塞尔维亚人民币业务清算行。

12 月 27 日，人民银行货币政策委员会召开 2023 年第四季度例会。

Appendix 1 Highlights of Monetary Policies in 2023

On January 16, the People's Bank of China (PBOC) conducted medium-term lending facility (MLF) operations in the amount of RMB 779 billion, with an interest rate of 2.75 percent, unchanged from the previous operations.

On January 18, the PBOC issued the *Notice on the Issuance of Central Bank Lending to National Financial Asset Management Companies to Ease the Financial Burdens on Real Estate,* providing low cost funds to national financial asset management companies to support them in the acquisition of existing projects of distressed real estate enterprises.

On January 19, the PBOC issued the *Notice on Matters Relating to Extending the Carbon Emissions Reduction Facility,* clarifying that the facility will be extended for two additional years until 2024 and it will include some foreign banks and local corporate banks.

On January 20, with the authorization of the PBOC, the National Interbank Funding Center (NIFC) announced the Loan Prime Rate (LPR) as follows: the one-year and the over-five-year LPR would be 3.65 percent and 4.30 percent, respectively, unchanged from the previous announcement.

On February 1, the PBOC reported to the Financial and Economic Affairs Committee of the National People's Congress (NPC) on monetary policy implementation in 2022.

On February 7, the PBOC signed a Memorandum of Understanding (MOU) with Banco Central do Brasil (BCB) to establish Renminbi (RMB) clearing arrangements in Brazil. On February 21, the PBOC authorized the Industrial and Commercial Bank of China (Brazil) Co., Ltd. (ICBC Brazil) to function as the clearing bank for RMB business in Brazil.

On February 10, the PBOC issued the *Notice on Matters Regarding the Pilot Support Scheme for Rental Housing Loans,* guiding financial institutions to issue long-term loans, at their own discretion and at their own risk, for rental housing purchases by specialized rental housing operators in pilot cities.

On February 15, the PBOC conducted MLF operations in the amount of RMB 499 billion, with an interest rate of 2.75 percent, unchanged from previous operations.

On February 20, with the authorization of the PBOC, the NIFC announced the LPR as follows: the one-year and the over-five-year LPR would be 3.65 percent and 4.30 percent, respectively, unchanged from the previous announcement.

On February 20, the PBOC and the Central Bank of Egypt (CBE) renewed their bilateral currency swap agreement. The size of the agreement is RMB 18 billion/EGP 80.7 billion.

On February 24, the PBOC released *China*

Monetary Policy Report (Q4 2022).

On March 15, the PBOC conducted MLF operations in the amount of RMB 481 billion, with an interest rate of 2.75 percent, unchanged from previous operations.

On March 20, with the authorization of the PBOC, the NIFC announced the LPR as follows: the one-year and the over-five-year LPR would be 3.65 percent and 4.30 percent, respectively, unchanged from the previous announcement.

On March 27, the PBOC lowered the required reserve ratio (RRR) for financial institutions by 0.25 percentage points (excluding those that had already implemented an RRR of 5 percent).

On April 7, the PBOC Monetary Policy Committee held its first quarterly meeting of 2023.

On April 14, the PBOC reported to the Financial and Economic Affairs Committee of the NPC on monetary policy implementation in Q1 2023.

On April 17, the PBOC conducted MLF operations in the amount of RMB 170 billion, with an interest rate of 2.75 percent, unchanged from previous operations.

On April 20, with the authorization of the PBOC, the NIFC announced the LPR as follows: the one-year and the over-five-year LPR would be 3.65 percent and 4.30 percent, respectively, unchanged from the previous announcement.

On April 28, the PBOC issued the *Interim Measures for the Administration of Cooperation on Mutual Access Between Chinese Mainland and Hong Kong Interest Rate Swap Markets* (Announcement No. 8 [2023] of the PBOC).

On May 15, the PBOC released *China Monetary Policy Report (Q1 2023).*

On May 15, the PBOC conducted MLF operations in the amount of RMB 125 billion, with an interest rate of 2.75 percent, unchanged from previous operations.

On May 15, mutual access between the Chinese Mainland and Hong Kong interest rate swap markets (Swap Connect) was officially launched.

On May 22, with the authorization of the PBOC, the NIFC announced the LPR as follows: the one-year and the over-five-year LPR would be 3.65 percent and 4.30 percent, respectively, unchanged from the previous announcement.

On June 9, the PBOC solicited public opinions on the *Measures for Administration of the Bond Valuation Business in the Interbank Bond Market (Exposure Draft).*

On June 9, the PBOC and the Central Bank of Argentina (BCRA) renewed their bilateral currency swap agreement. The size of the agreement is RMB 130 billion/ ARS4.5 trillion.

On June 13, the PBOC lowered the standing lending facility (SLF) interest rates, among which, the overnight rate was lowered from 2.85 percent to 2.75 percent, the 7-day rate was lowered from 3 percent to 2.9 percent, and the 1-month rate was lowered from 3.35 percent to 3.25 percent.

On June 15, the PBOC conducted MLF operations in the amount of RMB 237 billion, with an interest rate of 2.65 percent, down 10 basis points from previous operations.

On June 16, the PBOC, together with the National Financial Regulatory Administration (NFRA), China Securities Regulatory Commission (CSRC), the Ministry of Finance (MOF), and the Ministry of Agriculture and Rural Affairs (MOA), issued the *Guiding Opinions on Providing Financial Support for Advancing Rural Revitalization Across the Board and Stepping Up Efforts to Build Up China's Strength in Agriculture,* focusing on the establishment and improvement of a multi-level, wide-coverage, sustainable, and modern financial service system for rural areas and the enhancement of its capacity for financial services.

On June 20, with the authorization of the PBOC, the NIFC announced the LPR as follows: the one-year and the over-five-year LPR would be 3.55 percent and 4.20 percent, respectively, down 10 basis points from the previous announcement.

On June 28, the PBOC Monetary Policy Committee held its second quarterly meeting of 2023.

On July 12, the PBOC and the Central Bank of Laos (CBL) renewed their bilateral currency swap agreement. The size of the agreement is RMB 6 billion/LAK15.8 trillion.

On July 17, the PBOC reported to the Financial and Economic Affairs Committee of the NPC on monetary policy implementation in H1 2023.

On July 17, the PBOC conducted MLF operations in the amount of RMB 103 billion, with an interest rate of 2.65 percent, remaining unchanged from previous operations.

On July 20, with the authorization of the PBOC, the NIFC announced the LPR as follows: the one-year and over-five-year LPR would be 3.55 percent and 4.20 percent, respectively, unchanged from the previous announcement.

On July 20, the PBOC and the SAFE decided to raise the macro-prudential adjustment parameter for cross-border financing of enterprises and financial institutions from 1.25 to 1.5.

On July 31, the PBOC and the Bank of Mongolia (BOM) renewed the bilateral currency swap agreement. The size of the agreement is RMB 15 billion/MNT7.25 trillion.

On August 3, the PBOC held a meeting on providing financial support to promote development of private enterprises.

On August 4, the PBOC solicited public opinions on the *Notice on Matters Relating to Over-the-Counter Businesses in the Interbank*

Bond Market (Exposure Draft).

On August 15, the PBOC lowered the standing lending facility (SLF) interest rates, among which the overnight rate was lowered from 2.75 percent to 2.65 percent, the 7-day rate was lowered from 2.9 percent to 2.8 percent, and the 1-month rate was lowered from 3.25 percent to 3.15 percent.

On August 15, the PBOC conducted MLF operations in the amount of RMB 401 billion, with an interest rate of 2.50 percent, down 15 basis points from previous operations.

On August 17, the PBOC released *China Monetary Policy Report (Q2 2023).*

On August 18, the PBOC issued the *Notice on Matters Relating to Extension of the Policy Implementation Period for the Loan Support Scheme to Ensure Deliveries of Presold Housing Projects,* explicitly extending the implementation period to the end of May 2024.

On August 21, with the authorization of the PBOC, the NIFC announced the LPR as follows: the one-year LPR would be 3.45 percent, a lowering of 10 basis points from the previous announcement, and the over-five-year LPR would be 4.20 percent, unchanged from the previous announcement.

On August 30, the PBOC, together with the NFRA, the SAFE, and the All-China Federation of Industry and Commerce (ACFIC) held a meeting to provide financial support to promote the development of private enterprises.

On August 31, the PBOC and the NFRA issued the *Notice on Adjusting and Optimizing Differentiated Housing Credit Policies.* For households that take loans to buy units of commercial housing, the minimum downpayment ratios shall be uniformly set at no lower than 20 percent for commercial personal mortgage loans issued to first-time homebuyers and at no lower than 30 percent for loans to second-time homebuyers; the interest rate floors on commercial personal mortgage loans to second-time homebuyers shall be adjusted to levels no lower than the loan prime rates (LPRs) with the corresponding maturities plus 20 basis points.

On August 31, the PBOC and the NFRA issued the *Notice on Matters Concerning Lowering the Interest Rates on Existing First-Home Mortgage Loans.* Starting from September 25, 2023, borrowers of existing first-home mortgage loans may apply to their financial lending institutions to replace their loans with new loans. The interest rate of their new loans is to be independently determined by the financial institution and the borrower through negotiation.

On August 31, the PBOC and the NFRA issued the *Notice on Ensuring Financial Support for Flood and Disaster Prevention and Relief and Post-Disaster Recovery and Reconstruction,* containing specific directions for increasing the supply of credit in key sectors, raising the efficiency of credit services during post-disaster recovery and reconstruction, tapping into the risk dispersion function of insurance, widening the source of funding for post-disaster reconstruction, and generally improving financial security in the disaster-hit areas.

On September 15, the PBOC cut the RRR for financial institutions by 0.25 percentage points (excluding those that had already implemented an RRR of 5 percent).

On September 15, the PBOC lowered the RRR for foreign currency deposits of financial institutions by 2 percentage points, from 6 percent to 4 percent.

On September 15, the PBOC conducted MLF operations in the amount of RMB 591 billion, with an interest rate of 2.50 percent, remaining unchanged from previous operations.

On September 15, the PBOC issued the *Notice on Matters Relating to Extension of the Policy Implementation Period of the Loan Support Scheme for Rental Housing*, explicitly extending the implementation period to the end of 2024.

On September 20, with the authorization of the PBOC, the NIFC announced the LPR as follows: the one-year and over-five-year LPR would be 3.45 percent and 4.20 percent, respectively, remaining unchanged from the previous announcement.

On September 22, the PBOC and the NFRA released the list of China's Systemically Important Banks of 2023.

On September 25, the PBOC Monetary Policy

Committee held its third quarterly meeting of 2023.

On September 28, the PBOC, the NAFR, the CSRC, the SAFE, the Hong Kong Monetary Authority (HKMA), the Securities and Futures Commission (SFC) of Hong Kong, and the Monetary Authority of Macao (AMCM) decided to further enhance the Cross-boundary Wealth Management Connect Pilot Scheme in the Guangdong-Hong Kong-Macao Greater Bay Area (GBA), with the aim of promoting the interconnection of financial markets within the GBA.

On October 16, the PBOC conducted MLF operations in the amount of RMB 789 billion, with an interest rate of 2.50 percent, remaining unchanged from previous operations.

On October 18, the PBOC reported to the Financial and Economic Affairs Committee of the NPC on monetary policy implementation in Q1–Q3 2023.

On October 20, the PBOC formulated the *Measures for the Assessment of Systemically Important Insurers* in collaboration with the NFRA, expanding the scope of systemically important financial institutions from the banking industry to the insurance industry, thus strengthening the supervision of systemically important financial institutions and enhancing the robustness of the financial system.

On October 20, with the authorization of the PBOC, the NIFC announced the LPR as follows: the one-year and over-five-year

LPR would be 3.45 percent and 4.20 percent, respectively, remaining unchanged from the previous announcement.

On November 9, the PBOC released *China Regional Financial Operations Report (2023)*.

On November 15, the PBOC conducted MLF operations in the amount of RMB 1.45 trillion, with an interest rate of 2.50 percent, remaining unchanged from previous operations.

On November 20, with the authorization of the PBOC, the NIFC announced the LPR as follows: the one-year and over-five-year LPR would be 3.45 percent and 4.20 percent, respectively, remaining unchanged from the previous announcement.

On November 27, the PBOC released *China Monetary Policy Report (Q3 2023)*.

On November 27, the PBOC, the NFRA, the CSRC, the SAFE, the National Development and Reform Commission (NDRC), the Ministry of Industry and Information Technology (MIIT), the MOF, and the All-China Federation of Industry and Commerce (ACFIC) issued the *Notice on Strengthening Financial Support Measures to Boost the Development and Growth of the Private Economy*, guiding financial institutions to provide equal treatment to public and private enterprises, to continuously strengthen financial services for private enterprises, and to boost the development and growth of the private economy.

On November 28 , the PBOC and the Central Bank of the UAE (CBUAE) renewed their bilateral currency swap agreement. The size of the agreement is RMB 35 billion/AED 18 billion.

On December 1, the PBOC released the *Measures for the Administration of Bond Valuation Services in the Interbank Bond Market* (Announcement No. 19 [2023] of the PBOC) to further regulate bond valuation services in the interbank bond market, to protect the legitimate rights of investors, and to promote the smooth and healthy development of the bond market.

On December 1, the PBOC and Saudi Central Bank (SCB) signed a bilateral currency swap agreement. The size of the agreement is RMB 50 billion/SAR 26 billion.

On December 5, the PBOC signed an MOU with the National Bank of Cambodia (NBC) to establish RMB clearing arrangements in Cambodia. On December 11, the PBOC authorized the Bank of China Ltd., Phnom Penh Branch, to function as the clearing bank for RMB business in Cambodia.

On December 15, the PBOC conducted MLF operations in the amount of RMB 1.45 trillion, with an interest rate of 2.50 percent, remaining unchanged from previous operations.

On December 20, with the authorization of the PBOC, the NIFC announced the LPR as follows: the one-year and over-five-year LPR would be 3.45 percent and 4.20 percent, respectively, remaining unchanged from the previous announcement.

On December 25, the PBOC and the National Bank of Serbia (NBS) signed an MOU on establishing RMB clearing arrangements in Serbia. On December 29, the PBOC authorized the Bank of China, Serbia, to function as the clearing bank for RMB business in Serbia.

On December 27, the PBOC Monetary Policy Committee held its fourth quarterly meeting of 2023.

附录二　2023年主要经济体中央银行货币政策

一、美联储

美联储加息周期接近尾声。2023年，美联储共加息4次，累计加息100个基点，联邦基金利率目标区间由年初的4.25%~4.5%上调至5.25%~5.5%，9月至年末连续三次暂停加息。自2022年3月启动本轮加息周期以来，美联储已加息11次，累计加息525个基点，达到2001年以来最高水平。12月议息会议纪要显示，美联储将在一段时间内保持限制性立场，直至通胀明显下降，并预计未来一年可能降息。12月议息会议公布的季度经济预测概要（Summary of Economic Projections）点阵图显示，18名与会委员对2024年末联邦基金利率目标区间的预测中值为4.5%~4.75%，对应全年降息75个基点。同时，美联储按计划减持国债和抵押贷款支持证券（MBS）规模，缩表速度保持在每月上限600亿美元国债、350亿美元MBS，未来仍将维持当前缩表节奏。截至2023年末，美联储资产规模7.7万亿美元，较2022年3月峰值下降近14%。

二、欧央行

欧央行紧缩步伐放缓。2023年，欧央行加息6次，累计加息200个基点，其中2月、3月各加息50个基点，5月、6月、7月、9月各加息25个基点，10月起暂停加息。年末主要再融资操作利率、边际贷款便利利率、存款便利利率分别为4.5%、4.75%和4%。同时，欧央行自2023年3月起开始缩表，6月底前平均每月减持150亿欧元，7月起停止对资产购买计划（APP）下的到期证券本金再投资，并计划从2024年下半年起降低抗疫紧急购债计划（PEPP）下的资产规模，平均每月减持75亿欧元，2024年底停止到期证券本金再投资。此外，欧央行自2023年5月1日起将欧元区政府存款利率的上限由存款便利利率与欧元短期利率（€STR）中较低者调降为€STR减20个基点，自9月20日起将最低法定存款准备金利率水平由存款便利利率下调至0，提高货币政策传导效率。

三、日本银行

日本银行维持宽松货币政策。2023年，日本银行维持短期政策利率在-0.1%不变；将交易所交易基金（ETF）和房地产投资信托基金（J-REITs）年度购买上限维持在12万亿日元和1 800亿日元不变。此外，日本银行继续不设上限购买日本国债，维持10年期日本国债收益率在0附近，浮动区间为±0.5%不变，但在7月议息会议上提高了收益率曲线控制（YCC）的灵活性，区间上下限将作为参考而不再是严格限制，允许10年期国债收益率在0.5%至1%之间波动，每日将按1%的固定利率购买10年期国债。

四、英格兰银行

英格兰银行暂缓加息。2023年，英格兰银行共加息5次，累计加息175个基点，2月、3月、5月各加息25个基点，6月超预期加息50个基点，8月再次收窄至25个基点，并于9月起暂停加息。年末基准利率为5.25%，为15年来最高水平。此外，英格兰银行计划于2023年10月至2024年9月期间逐步减持1 000亿英镑政府债券，最终将资产购买规模降至6 580亿英镑。

Appendix 2 Monetary Policies of Major Economies in 2023

I. The US Federal Reserve

The rate hike cycle of the Federal Reserve draws to a close. In 2023, the Fed raised interest rates four times by a total of 100 basis points (bps), bringing the target range for the federal funds rate to 5.25-5.5 percent from 4.25-4.5 percent at the beginning of the year. The Fed kept interest rates on hold for three straight times from September to the year-end. Since March 2022, when the current rate hike cycle began, the Fed has raised its policy rate 11 times by a total of 525 bps, reaching the highest level since 2001. The December FOMC minutes showed that the Fed would maintain a restrictive policy stance for a period to ensure that inflation falls significantly, and rate cuts might start in the coming year. The dot plot of *Summary of Economic Projections* released at the December meeting showed that the median forecast by 18 members of the target range for the Fed Funds Rate would be 4.5-4.75 percent at the end of 2024, implying a 75-bp rate cut over the year. Meanwhile, the Fed reduced its holdings of Treasury securities and Mortgage-Backed Securities (MBS) as planned, with monthly reduction cap for Treasury securities and MBS being USD 60 billion and USD 35 billion, respectively, while the current pace of balance sheet reduction is to be sustained over time. By the end of 2023, the asset on Fed's balance sheet had registered USD 7.7 trillion, shrinking 14 percent from its March 2022 peak.

II. The European Central Bank

The European Central Bank (ECB) slowed its pace of tightening. In 2023, the ECB raised interest rates six times by a total of 200 bps, 50 bps each in February and March, 25 bps each in May, June, July and September, and has suspended rate hikes since October. At year-end, the interest rates on the main refinancing operations, the marginal lending facility and the deposit facility posted 4.5 percent, 4.75 percent and 4 percent, respectively. Meanwhile, the ECB has started to reduce its size of balance sheet since March 2023, with the shrinking pace amounting to EUR 15 billion per month on average until the end of June 2023. The ECB discontinued the reinvestment of principal payments from maturing securities under the Asset Purchase Programme (APP) as of July 2023, and planned to reduce the Pandemic Emergency Purchase Programme (PEPP) portfolio by EUR 7.5 billion per month on average over the second half of 2024, under which the ECB intended to discontinue reinvestment of principal payments of maturing securities at the end of 2024. Taking effect on May 1, 2023, the new ceiling for remuneration of euro area government deposits was set at the Euro Short-term Rate (€STR) minus 20 bps, from the lower of either the deposit facility rate or the €STR. Besides, the remuneration of minimum reserves was reduced to 0 from the deposit facility rate on September 20, so as to improve the transmission efficiency of monetary policy.

III. The Bank of Japan

The Bank of Japan (BOJ) maintained an accommodative monetary policy. In 2023, the BOJ maintained its short-term policy rate at minus 0.1 percent. The upper limits with which the BOJ would purchase Exchange-traded Funds (ETFs) and Japan Real Estate Investment Trusts (J-REITs) on annual paces were set at JPY 12 trillion and JPY 180 billion, respectively, staying unchanged. In addition, the BOJ continued to set no upper limits on the size of government bonds purchases to keep the yield of the 10-year Japan Government Bond (JGB) around 0, with an unchanged floating band of ±0.5 percent. However, the BOJ announced to increase the flexibility of the Yield Curve Control (YCC) on the July Monetary Policy Meeting, with the upper and lower bounds of the band being used as a reference rather than a strict restriction, allowing the yield of the 10-year JGB to fluctuate between 0.5 percent and 1 percent, and the daily purchases of the 10-year JGB would be carried out at a fixed interest rate of 1 percent.

IV. The Bank of England

The Bank of England (BOE) suspended its rate hike. In 2023, the BOE raised interest rates five times by a total of 175 bps, with 25 bps each in February, March and May, 50 bps in June, which surprised the market, before narrowing back to 25 bps in August. Since September, the BOE has suspended its rate hike, with the benchmark rate standing at 5.25 percent at year-end, the highest level in 15 years. Moreover, the BOE decided to gradually reduce the stock of gilts by GBP 100 billion from October 2023 to September 2024, so as to ultimately shrink the size of asset purchases to GBP 658 billion.

附录三 中国主要经济和金融指标
Appendix 3 China's Major Economic and Financial Indicators

一、经济发展与就业（Economic development and employment）
1.1 概览（Overview）

1978年以来中国经济增长与宏观经济政策
China's economic growth and macroeconomic policies since 1978

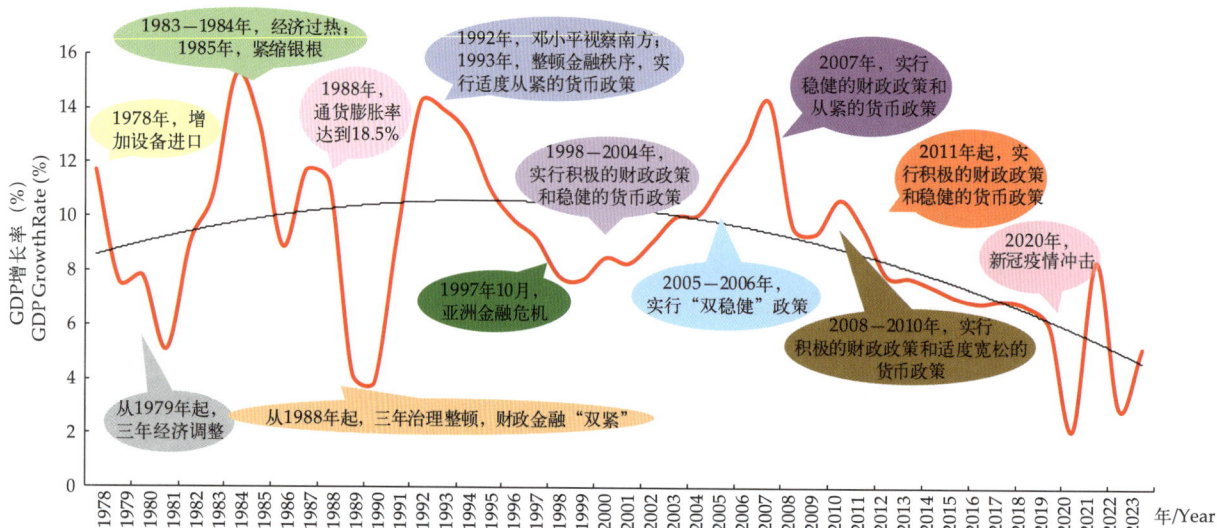

- Equipment import growth in 1978
- 3-year economic adjustment between 1979 and 1981
- Over-heated economy between 1983 and 1984, tight monetary policy in 1985
- Inflation of 18.5% in 1988
- 3-year rectification from 1988 to 1991, "double tightening" of fiscal and monetary policy
- Deng Xiaoping's remarks on economic reform during his 1992 trip to South China, rectification of financial order and adoption of appropriately tight monetary policy in 1993
- Asian financial crisis in October 1997
- Proactive fiscal policy and sound monetary policy from 1998 to 2004
- "Double sound" fiscal and monetary policy in 2005 and 2006
- Sound fiscal policy and tight monetary policy in 2007
- Proactive financial policy and moderately loose monetary policy in 2008 to 2010
- Proactive financial policy and sound monetary policy since 2011
- COVID-19 pandemic shock in 2020

人均国内生产总值
Per capita GDP

（图中数据根据国家统计局最新数据修订）
(Data are revised by National Bureau of Statistics of China)

1.2　国民经济核算（GDP）

1978年以来我国GDP及其增长率
GDP and its annual growth rate since 1978

年 Year	GDP（万亿元） GDP (RMB 1 trillion)	GDP 增长率 (%) GDP growth rate (%)
1978	0.4	11.7
1979	0.4	7.6
1980	0.5	7.8
1981	0.5	5.1
1982	0.5	9.0
1983	0.6	10.8
1984	0.7	15.2
1985	0.9	13.4
1986	1.0	8.9
1987	1.2	11.7
1988	1.5	11.2
1989	1.7	4.2
1990	1.9	3.9
1991	2.2	9.3
1992	2.7	14.2
1993	3.6	13.9
1994	4.9	13.0
1995	6.1	11.0
1996	7.2	9.9
1997	8.0	9.2
1998	8.5	7.8
1999	9.1	7.7
2000	10.0	8.5
2001	11.1	8.3
2002	12.2	9.1
2003	13.7	10.0
2004	16.2	10.1
2005	18.7	11.4
2006	21.9	12.7
2007	27.0	14.2
2008	31.9	9.7
2009	34.9	9.4
2010	41.2	10.6
2011	48.8	9.6
2012	53.9	7.9
2013	59.3	7.8
2014	64.4	7.4
2015	68.9	7.0
2016	74.6	6.9
2017	83.2	7.0
2018	91.9	6.8
2019	98.7	6.0
2020	101.4	2.2
2021	114.9	8.5
2022	120.5	3.0
2023	126.1	5.2

注：表中数据根据国家统计局最新数据修订。
Note: Data are revised by National Bureau of Statistics of China.

GDP及其增长率
GDP and its annual growth rate

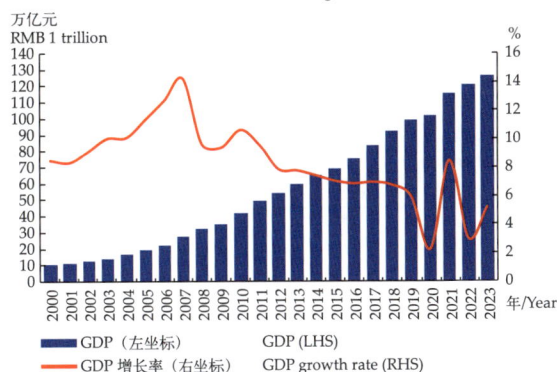

GDP（左坐标）　GDP (LHS)
GDP 增长率（右坐标）　GDP growth rate (RHS)

生产法现价GDP与支出法现价GDP及其增长率比较
Comparison between production-based GDP and expenditure-based GDP at current price

年 Year	(1) 生产法 GDP Production-based GDP		(2) 支出法 GDP Expenditure-based GDP		(1) - (2)	
	绝对量(亿元) Absolute value (RMB 100 million)	现价增速 (%) Growth rate at current price (%)	绝对量(亿元) Absolute value (RMB 100 million)	现价增速 (%) Growth rate at current price (%)	绝对量(亿元) Absolute value (RMB 100 million)	现价增速 (%) Growth rate at current price (%)
1991	22 006	16.6	21 997	16.0	8	0.60
1992	27 195	23.6	27 140	23.4	54	0.20
1993	35 673	31.2	35 576	31.1	97	0.10
1994	48 637	36.3	48 410	36.1	227	0.27
1995	61 340	26.1	61 050	26.1	290	0.01
1996	71 814	17.1	71 541	17.2	272	-0.11
1997	79 715	11.0	79 416	11.0	299	0.00
1998	85 196	6.9	84 791	6.8	405	0.11
1999	90 564	6.3	90 095	6.3	469	0.05
2000	100 280	10.7	99 799	10.8	481	-0.04
2001	110 863	10.6	110 388	10.6	475	-0.06
2002	121 717	9.8	121 327	9.9	391	-0.12
2003	137 422	12.9	137 147	13.0	275	-0.14
2004	161 840	17.8	161 356	17.7	485	0.12
2005	187 319	15.7	187 658	16.3	-339	-0.56
2006	219 438	17.1	219 598	17.0	-159	0.13
2007	270 092	23.1	270 499	23.2	-407	-0.10
2008	319 245	18.2	318 068	17.6	1 177	0.61
2009	348 518	9.2	347 650	9.3	867	-0.13
2010	412 119	18.2	408 505	17.5	3 614	0.74
2011	487 940	18.4	484 109	18.5	3 831	-0.11
2012	538 580	10.4	539 040	11.4	-460	-0.97
2013	592 963	10.1	596 344	10.6	-3 381	-0.53
2014	643 563	8.5	646 548	8.4	-2 985	0.11
2015	688 858	7.0	692 094	7.0	-3 235	0.00
2016	746 395	8.4	745 981	7.8	415	0.56
2017	832 036	11.5	828 983	11.1	3 053	0.34
2018	919 281	10.5	915 774	10.5	3 507	0.02
2019	986 515	7.3	990 708	8.2	-4 193	-0.87
2020	1 013 567	2.7	1 025 628	3.5	-12 061	-0.78
2021	1 149 237	13.4	1 145 283	11.7	3 954	1.72
2022	1 204 724	4.8	1 205 017	5.2	-293	-0.39
2023	1 260 582	4.6				

注：表中数据根据国家统计局最新数据修订。
Note: Data are revised by National Bureau of Statistics of China.

1.2.1 按生产法计算的国内生产总值（Production-based GDP）

按生产法计算的国内生产总值
Production-based gross domestic product

年 / 季度 Year/Quarter		国内生产总值 GDP		第一产业 Primary industry		第二产业 Secondary industry		第三产业 Tertiary industry	
		绝对值（亿元） Absolute value (RMB 100 million)	增长（%） Growth (%)	比重（%） Share (%)	增长（%） Growth (%)	比重（%） Share (%)	增长（%） Growth (%)	比重（%） Share (%)	增长（%） Growth (%)
2015	I	151 138	7.1	4.9	3.1	40.0	6.2	55.1	8.4
	I-II	319 688	7.1	6.0	3.4	41.1	6.0	52.9	8.7
	I-III	496 285	7.1	7.3	3.8	40.9	5.9	51.8	8.8
	I-IV	688 858	7.0	8.4	3.9	40.8	5.93	50.8	8.8
2016	I	162 410	6.9	5.1	2.9	37.6	5.8	57.3	8.0
	I-II	343 818	6.9	6.1	3.0	39.1	6.0	54.8	7.9
	I-III	534 829	6.9	7.2	3.5	39.3	6.0	53.6	8.0
	I-IV	746 395	6.9	8.1	3.3	39.6	6.03	52.4	8.1
2017	I	181 868	7.0	4.5	3.0	38.1	6.1	57.4	8.0
	I-II	383 818	7.0	5.4	3.5	39.5	6.2	55.1	8.0
	I-III	596 607	7.0	6.6	3.7	39.6	6.0	53.9	8.2
	I-IV	832 036	7.0	7.5	4.0	39.9	5.87	52.7	8.3
2018	I	202 036	6.9	4.2	3.2	37.9	6.2	57.8	7.8
	I-II	425 998	6.9	5.1	3.3	39.4	6.1	55.6	7.9
	I-III	660 472	6.8	6.0	3.4	39.5	5.8	54.5	8.1
	I-IV	919 281	6.8	7.0	3.5	39.7	5.79	53.3	8.0
2019	I	217 168	6.3	4.0	2.7	37.1	5.3	58.9	7.2
	I-II	458 671	6.1	5.1	3.1	38.5	5.0	56.5	7.2
	I-III	709 717	6.0	6.1	2.9	38.5	4.8	55.5	7.3
	I-IV	986 515	6.0	7.1	3.1	38.6	4.87	54.3	7.2
2020	I	205 245	−6.9	5.0	−3.1	35.3	−9.7	59.7	−5.4
	I-II	453 593	−1.7	5.8	1	37.5	−2.00	56.8	−1.7
	I-III	717 948	0.6	6.7	2.5	37.6	0.80	55.7	0.3
	I-IV	1 013 567	2.2	7.7	3.1	37.8	2.46	54.5	2.0
2021	I	249 200	18.7	4.6	8.1	37.1	24.90	58.3	15.9
	I-II	532 049	13.0	5.4	7.8	38.9	15.30	55.7	12.1
	I-III	823 338	10.1	6.3	7.5	38.9	11.10	54.8	9.8
	I-IV	1 149 237	8.5	7.2	7.1	39.3	8.67	53.5	8.5
2022	I	270 345	4.8	4.0	6.1	38.6	4.7	57.4	4.7
	I-II	562 791	2.5	5.2	5.1	39.9	2.1	54.9	2.5
	I-III	870 733	3.0	6.3	4.3	39.5	2.8	54.2	3.0
	I-IV	1 204 724	3.0	7.3	4.2	39.3	2.6	53.4	3.0
2023	I	284 423	4.5	4.1	3.7	37.3	3.3	58.6	5.4
	I-II	592 716	5.5	5.1	3.7	38.4	4.3	56.5	6.4
	I-III	912 692	5.2	6.2	4.0	38.2	4.4	55.6	6.0
	I-IV	1 260 582	5.2	7.1	4.1	38.3	4.7	54.6	5.8

注：1. 表中绝对数按当年价格计算，"比上年同期增长"按不变价格计算。
　　2. 表中数据根据国家统计局最新数据修订。

Notes: 1. Absolute figures in this table are calculated at current prices, and the year-on-year growth rates are calculated at constant prices.
　　2. Data are revised by National Bureau of Statistics of China.

GDP季度累计增长率
Quarterly accumulated GDP growth rate

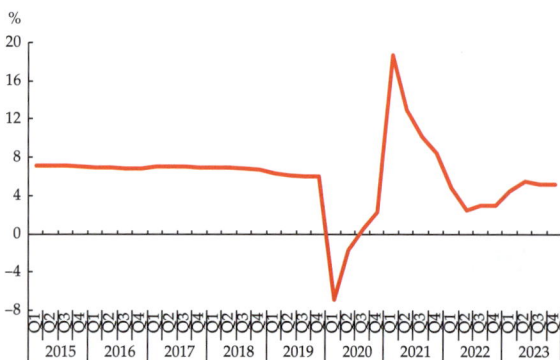

季度GDP三次产业所占的比重与增长率变化
Shares of industries in GDP and their growth rates on a quarterly basis

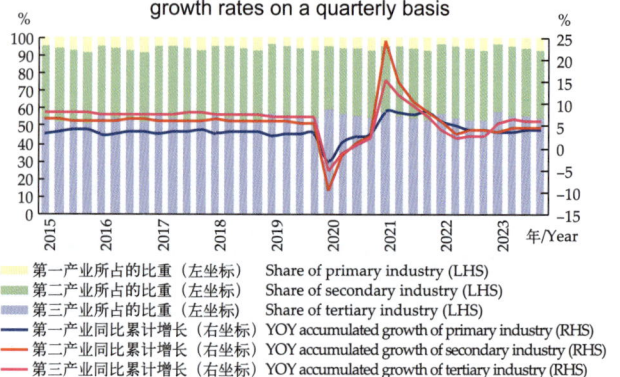

第一产业所占的比重（左坐标） Share of primary industry (LHS)
第二产业所占的比重（左坐标） Share of secondary industry (LHS)
第三产业所占的比重（左坐标） Share of tertiary industry (LHS)
第一产业同比累计增长（右坐标） YOY accumulated growth of primary industry (RHS)
第二产业同比累计增长（右坐标） YOY accumulated growth of secondary industry (RHS)
第三产业同比累计增长（右坐标） YOY accumulated growth of tertiary industry (RHS)

工业增加值当月同比增长率
Monthly growth rate (YOY) of value added of industry

单位：% Unit: %

年/月 Year/Month		工业增加值 Value added of industry	采矿业 Mining	制造业 Manufacturing	电力、热力、燃气 及水生产和供应业 Electricity, gas & water production and supply	国有及国有控股企业 State-owned and state-holding enterprises	股份制企业 Joint-stock enterprises	外商及港澳台投资企业 Enterprises with foreign, Hong Kong, Macao, and Taiwan investment	私营企业 Private enterprises
2021	1	—	—	—	—	—	—	—	—
	2	—	—	—	—	—	—	—	—
	3	14.1	2.9	15.2	13.9	10.9	13.4	17.4	16.8
	4	9.8	3.2	10.3	10.3	8.6	10.4	8.4	11.2
	5	8.8	3.2	9.0	11.0	7.7	8.9	8.5	9.1
	6	8.3	0.7	8.7	11.6	5.4	9.0	6.4	10.2
	7	6.4	0.6	6.2	13.2	7.2	7.1	3.8	6.1
	8	5.3	2.5	5.5	6.3	4.6	6.1	3.4	5.2
	9	3.1	3.2	2.4	9.7	4.5	4.0	0.4	2.8
	10	3.5	6.0	2.5	11.1	5.2	4.2	1.3	2.4
	11	3.8	6.2	2.9	11.1	3.6	4.5	1.9	3.9
	12	4.3	7.3	3.8	7.2	3.3	4.7	3.4	4.7
2022	1	—	—	—	—	—	—	—	—
	2	—	—	—	—	—	—	—	—
	3	5.0	12.2	4.4	4.6	3.3	6.9	−1.1	6.0
	4	−2.9	9.5	−4.6	1.5	−2.9	0.5	−16.1	−1.1
	5	0.7	7.0	0.1	0.2	0.7	2.3	−5.4	1.1
	6	3.9	8.7	3.4	3.3	3.1	4.0	3.6	3.0
	7	3.8	8.1	2.7	9.5	5.4	4.4	1.9	1.5
	8	4.2	5.3	3.1	13.6	5.6	4.1	4.0	1.1
	9	6.3	7.2	6.4	2.9	4.9	6.6	5.4	4.4
	10	5.0	4.0	5.2	4.0	4.4	5.9	2.0	3.1
	11	2.2	5.9	2.0	−1.5	2.2	4.0	−3.7	1.6
	12	1.3	4.9	0.2	7.0	1.9	3.5	−7.5	0.5
2023	1	—	—	—	—	—	—	—	—
	2	—	—	—	—	—	—	—	—
	3	3.9	0.9	4.2	5.2	4.4	4.4	1.4	2.0
	4	5.6	0.0	6.5	4.8	6.6	4.4	11.8	1.6
	5	3.5	−1.2	4.1	4.8	4.4	3.5	4.2	0.7
	6	4.4	1.5	4.8	4.9	5.4	5.9	−1.4	3.2
	7	3.7	1.3	3.9	4.1	3.4	5.0	−1.8	2.5
	8	4.5	2.3	5.4	0.2	5.2	5.7	0.8	3.4
	9	4.5	1.5	5.0	3.5	5.9	5.6	0.4	3.3
	10	4.6	2.9	5.1	1.5	4.9	5.6	0.9	3.9
	11	6.6	3.9	6.7	9.9	7.3	7.2	4.4	5.2
	12	6.8	4.7	7.1	7.3	7.3	7.2	6.9	5.4

工业增加值累计同比增长率
Accumulative growth rate (YOY) of value added of industry

单位：% Unit: %

年 / 月 Year/Month		工业增加值 Value added of industry	采矿业 Mining	制造业 Manufacturing	电力、热力、燃气及水生产和供应业 Electricity, gas & water production and supply	国有及国有控股企业 State-owned and state-holding enterprises	股份制企业 Joint-stock enterprises	外商及港澳台投资企业 Enterprises with foreign, Hong Kong, Macao, and Taiwan investment	私营企业 Private enterprises
2021	1~2	35.1	17.5	39.5	19.8	23.0	34.2	41.4	43.8
	1~3	24.5	10.1	27.3	15.9	16.9	23.7	29.2	29.7
	1~4	20.3	8.4	22.2	14.5	14.8	19.9	23.0	23.9
	1~5	17.8	7.4	19.3	13.8	13.4	17.5	19.7	20.4
	1~6	15.9	6.2	17.1	13.4	11.9	15.8	17.0	18.3
	1~7	14.4	5.3	15.4	13.4	11.2	14.4	14.9	16.3
	1~8	13.1	5.0	14.0	12.4	10.3	13.2	13.3	14.7
	1~9	11.8	4.7	12.5	12.0	9.6	12.0	11.6	13.1
	1~10	10.9	4.8	11.3	11.9	9.1	11.1	10.4	11.8
	1~11	10.1	5.1	10.4	11.9	8.5	10.4	9.5	10.9
	1~12	9.6	5.3	9.8	11.4	8.0	9.8	8.9	10.2
2022	1~2	7.5	9.8	7.3	6.8	5.9	8.4	4.2	8.7
	1~3	6.5	10.7	6.2	6.1	5.0	7.8	2.1	7.6
	1~4	4.0	10.4	3.2	5.0	3.1	5.8	−2.8	5.1
	1~5	3.3	9.6	2.6	4.1	2.6	5.0	−3.4	4.2
	1~6	3.4	9.5	2.8	3.9	2.7	4.8	−2.1	4.0
	1~7	3.5	9.3	2.7	4.8	3.1	4.7	−1.5	3.6
	1~8	3.6	8.7	2.7	6.0	3.4	4.6	−0.8	3.3
	1~9	3.9	8.5	3.2	5.6	3.6	4.9	−0.1	3.4
	1~10	4.0	7.9	3.4	5.5	3.7	5.0	0.1	3.4
	1~11	3.8	7.6	3.3	4.8	3.5	4.9	−0.3	3.2
	1~12	3.6	7.3	3.0	5.0	3.3	4.8	−1.0	2.9
2023	1~2	2.4	4.7	2.1	2.4	2.7	4.3	−5.2	2.0
	1~3	3.0	3.2	2.9	3.3	3.3	4.3	−2.7	2.0
	1~4	3.6	2.4	3.9	3.7	4.1	4.3	0.6	1.9
	1~5	3.6	1.7	4.0	3.9	4.2	4.1	1.3	1.6
	1~6	3.8	1.7	4.2	4.1	4.4	4.4	0.8	1.9
	1~7	3.8	1.7	4.2	4.1	4.3	4.5	0.4	2.0
	1~8	3.9	1.7	4.3	3.5	4.4	4.7	0.5	2.2
	1~9	4.0	1.7	4.4	3.5	4.6	4.8	0.5	2.3
	1~10	4.1	1.8	4.5	3.3	4.6	4.9	0.5	2.5
	1~11	4.3	2.1	4.7	3.9	4.8	5.1	0.9	2.8
	1~12	4.6	2.3	5.0	4.3	5.0	5.3	1.4	3.1

注：本表中"比上年同期增长"按可比价格计算。
Notes: The year-on-year changes in this table are calculated at comparable prices.

工业增加值及工业企业利润
Growth rate of industrial value added and profits of industrial companies

单位：% Unit: %

年 / 月 Year/Month		当月工业增加值同比增长 YOY growth of monthly industrial value added	工业增加值月度 累计同比增长 YOY growth of monthly accumulated industrial value added	工业企业利润累计同比增长 YOY growth of monthly profits of industrial companies
2021	1	—	—	—
	2	—	35.1	178.9
	3	14.1	24.5	137.3
	4	9.8	20.3	106.1
	5	8.8	17.8	83.4
	6	8.3	15.9	66.9
	7	6.4	14.4	57.3
	8	5.3	13.1	49.5
	9	3.1	11.8	44.7
	10	3.5	10.9	42.2
	11	3.8	10.1	38.0
	12	4.3	9.6	34.3
2022	1	—	—	—
	2	—	7.5	5.0
	3	5.0	6.5	8.5
	4	−2.9	4.0	3.5
	5	0.7	3.3	1.0
	6	3.9	3.4	1.0
	7	3.8	3.5	−1.1
	8	4.2	3.6	−2.1
	9	6.3	3.9	−2.3
	10	5.0	4.0	−3.0
	11	2.2	3.8	−3.6
	12	1.3	3.6	−4.0
2023	1	—	—	—
	2	—	2.4	−22.9
	3	3.9	3.0	−21.4
	4	5.6	3.6	−20.6
	5	3.5	3.6	−18.8
	6	4.4	3.8	−16.8
	7	3.7	3.8	−15.5
	8	4.5	3.9	−11.7
	9	4.5	4.0	−9.0
	10	4.6	4.1	−7.8
	11	6.6	4.3	−4.4
	12	6.8	4.6	−2.3

注：由于春节错位因素，1月不公布当月工业增加值同比增速，公布的2月数据为1~2月的合计数。

Note: The year-on-year growth rate of the added value of industries in January is not released, and the data released in February is the total from January to February.

工业增加值及工业企业利润
Growth rate of industrial value added and profits of industrial companies

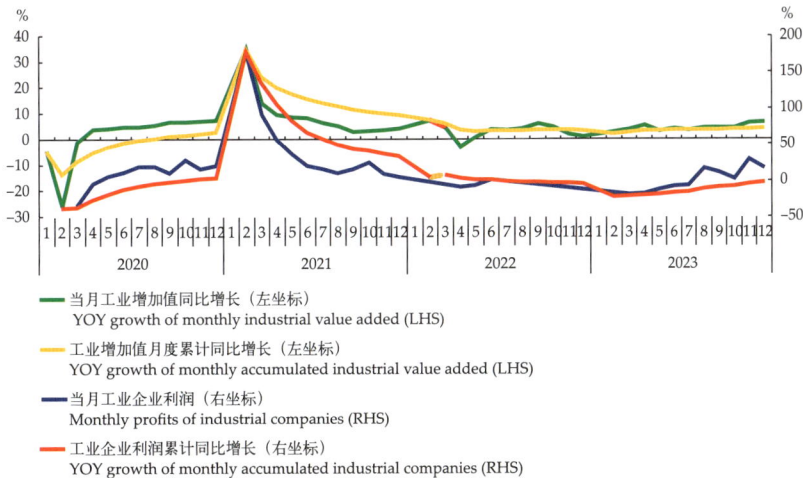

当月工业增加值同比增长（左坐标）
YOY growth of monthly industrial value added (LHS)

工业增加值月度累计同比增长（左坐标）
YOY growth of monthly accumulated industrial value added (LHS)

当月工业企业利润（右坐标）
Monthly profits of industrial companies (RHS)

工业企业利润累计同比增长（右坐标）
YOY growth of monthly accumulated industrial companies (RHS)

1.2.2　按支出法计算的国内生产总值（Expenditure-based GDP）

按支出法计算的国内生产总值及其构成
Expenditure-based GDP and its composition

年 Year	按支出法计算的国内生产总值　Expenditure-based GDP									
		最终消费　Final consumption					资本形成总额　Total capital formation			货物和服务净出口 Net exports of goods and services
			居民消费　Household consumption			政府消费 Government consumption		固定资本形成 Fixed capital formation	存货增加 Increased inventory	
				城镇居民 Urban	农村居民 Rural					
	绝对值（亿元）　Absolute value (RMB 100 million)									
2003	137 147	79 735	58 690	40 915	17 775	21 045	54 447	52 575	1 872	2 965
2004	161 356	89 394	65 725	46 492	19 233	23 670	67 726	63 975	3 751	4 236
2005	187 658	101 873	74 154	53 242	20 912	27 719	75 576	73 852	1 724	10 209
2006	219 598	115 364	82 842	60 203	22 640	32 522	87 579	84 979	2 600	16 655
2007	270 499	137 737	98 231	72 643	25 589	39 506	109 339	102 345	6 995	23 423
2008	318 068	158 899	112 655	84 414	28 241	46 245	134 942	124 701	10 241	24 227
2009	347 650	174 539	123 122	93 198	29 924	51 417	158 075	152 691	5 383	15 037
2010	408 505	201 581	141 466	108 909	32 556	60 116	191 867	181 041	10 826	15 057
2011	484 109	244 747	170 391	131 026	39 365	74 357	227 674	214 017	13 656	11 689
2012	539 040	275 444	190 585	147 770	42 815	84 859	248 960	238 321	10 639	14 636
2013	596 345	306 664	212 477	165 106	47 372	94 186	275 129	263 980	11 149	14 552
2014	646 548	338 031	236 239	183 605	52 633	101 793	294 906	282 242	12 664	13 611
2015	692 094	371 921	260 202	203 780	56 423	111 718	297 827	289 970	7 856	22 346
2016	745 981	410 806	288 668	226 960	61 708	122 138	318 198	310 145	8 054	16 976
2017	828 983	456 518	320 690	252 083	68 606	135 829	357 886	348 300	9 586	14 578
2018	915 774	506 135	354 124	277 365	76 759	152 011	402 585	393 848	8 737	7 054
2019	990 708	552 632	387 188	305 131	82 057	165 444	426 679	422 451	4 227	11 398
2020	1 025 628	560 811	387 186	304 086	83 100	173 625	439 550	430 625	8 925	25 267
2021	1 145 283	619 688	438 015	345 085	92 931	181 673	495 784	482 119	13 665	29 811
2022	1 205 017	641 633	447 910	—	—	193 723	523 890	507 958	15 933	39 494
	构成（%）　Composition (%)									
2003	100	58.1	42.8	29.8	13.0	15.3	39.7	38.3	1.4	2.2
2004	100	55.4	40.7	28.8	11.9	14.7	42.0	39.6	2.3	2.6
2005	100	54.3	39.5	28.4	11.1	14.8	40.3	39.4	0.9	5.4
2006	100	52.5	37.7	27.4	10.3	14.8	39.9	38.7	1.2	7.6
2007	100	50.9	36.3	26.9	9.5	14.6	40.4	37.8	2.6	8.7
2008	100	50.0	35.4	26.5	8.9	14.5	42.4	39.2	3.2	7.6
2009	100	50.2	35.4	26.8	8.6	14.8	45.5	43.9	1.5	4.3
2010	100	49.3	34.6	26.7	8.0	14.7	47.0	44.3	2.7	3.7
2011	100	50.6	35.2	27.1	8.1	15.4	47.0	44.2	2.8	2.4
2012	100	51.1	35.4	27.4	7.9	15.7	46.2	44.2	2.0	2.7
2013	100	51.4	35.6	27.7	7.9	15.8	46.1	44.3	1.9	2.4
2014	100	52.3	36.5	28.4	8.1	15.7	45.6	43.7	2.0	2.1
2015	100	53.7	37.6	29.4	8.2	16.1	43.0	41.9	1.1	3.2
2016	100	55.1	38.7	30.4	8.3	16.4	42.7	41.6	1.1	2.3
2017	100	55.1	38.7	30.4	8.3	16.4	43.2	42.0	1.2	1.8
2018	100	55.3	38.7	30.2	8.4	16.6	44.0	43.0	1.0	0.8
2019	100	55.8	39.1	30.8	8.3	16.7	43.1	42.6	0.4	1.2
2020	100	54.7	37.8	29.6	8.1	16.9	42.9	42.0	0.9	2.5
2021	100	54.1	38.2	30.1	8.1	15.9	43.3	42.1	1.2	2.6
2022	100	53.2	37.2	—	—	16.1	43.5	42.2	1.3	3.3

注：表中数据根据国家统计局最新数据修订。
Note: Data are revised by National Bureau of Statistics of China.

按支出法计算的国内生产总值构成变化
Changes in the composition of GDP (based on expenditures)

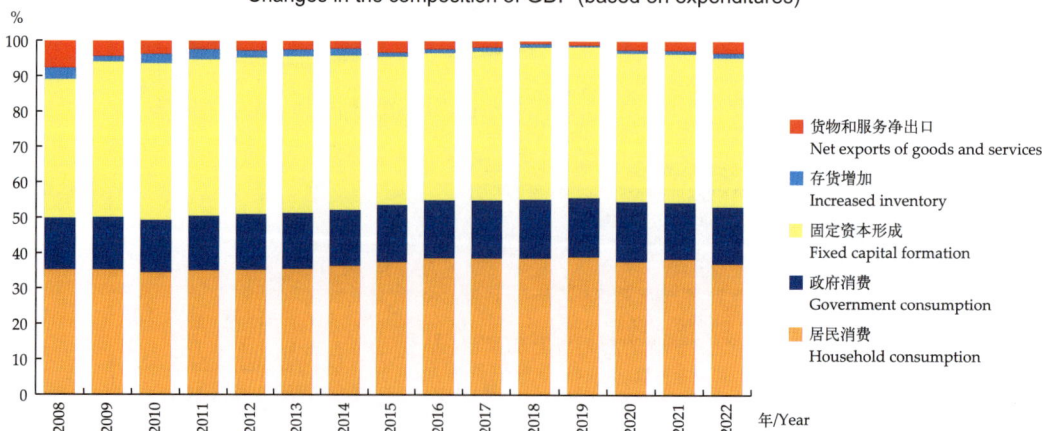

投资率和消费率
Investment ratio and consumption ratio

单位：% Unit: %

年 Year	资本形成率（投资率） Capital formation ratio (investment ratio)	最终消费率（消费率） Final consumption ratio (consumption ratio)
1986	37.7	64.8
1987	37.3	62.7
1988	39.0	62.0
1989	37.1	64.0
1990	34.0	63.3
1991	35.3	61.9
1992	39.2	59.8
1993	43.4	58.5
1994	40.2	58.5
1995	39.0	59.3
1996	37.7	60.3
1997	35.7	59.9
1998	35.0	60.7
1999	34.3	62.9
2000	33.7	63.9
2001	35.7	62.2
2002	36.3	61.2
2003	39.7	58.1
2004	42.0	55.4
2005	40.3	54.3
2006	39.9	52.5
2007	40.4	50.9
2008	42.4	50.0
2009	45.5	50.2
2010	47.0	49.4
2011	47.0	50.6
2012	46.2	51.1
2013	46.1	51.4
2014	45.6	52.3
2015	43.0	53.7
2016	42.7	55.1
2017	43.2	55.1
2018	44.0	55.3
2019	43.1	55.8
2020	42.9	54.7
2021	43.3	54.1
2022	43.5	53.2

注：表中数据根据国家统计局最新数据修订。
Note: Data are revised by National Bureau of Statistics of China.

主要经济指标环比增速
MOM growth rates of main economic indicators

单位：% Unit: %

年/季度 Year/ Quarter	国内生产总值 Gross domestic product	年/月 Year/ Month	规模以上工业增加值 Value added of industry	固定资产投资完成额 Completed investment in fixed assets	社会消费品零售总额 Retail sales of consumer goods
2021		2021 1	0.63	0.20	−0.52
		2	0.62	0.80	0.68
I	0.6	3	0.60	1.05	0.93
		4	0.52	3.16	0.02
		5	0.45	0.24	0.89
II	1.4	6	0.48	0.24	0.28
		7	0.21	0.32	−0.12
		8	0.30	1.16	0.52
III	0.6	9	0.05	0.86	0.21
		10	0.41	1.03	0.64
		11	0.38	1.74	−0.01
IV	1.6	12	0.40	0.49	−0.22
2022		2022 1	0.22	0.84	0.06
		2	0.38	0.62	0.49
I	0.6	3	0.51	1.89	−0.11
		4	0.16	−1.37	−0.02
		5	0.62	0.72	−0.05
II	−2.1	6	0.91	0.75	2.56
		7	0.35	0.59	1.82
		8	0.24	−0.50	−0.75
III	4.0	9	0.80	0.35	0.28
		10	0.18	−0.09	−0.58
		11	−0.24	−1.98	−0.27
IV	0.6	12	0.37	0.10	−0.15
2023		2023 1	0.64	1.54	0.72
		2	0.41	1.92	2.09
I	2.1	3	0.64	−0.67	0.41
		4	−0.18	−1.38	0.91
		5	0.77	0.69	0.45
II	0.6	6	0.76	−0.23	0.33
		7	0.13	0.01	−0.01
		8	0.61	0.18	1.30
III	1.5	9	0.40	0.13	0.18
		10	0.42	0.10	0.37
		11	0.87	0.21	0.09
IV	1.0	12	0.52	0.09	0.42

投资率和消费率
Investment ratio and consumption ratio

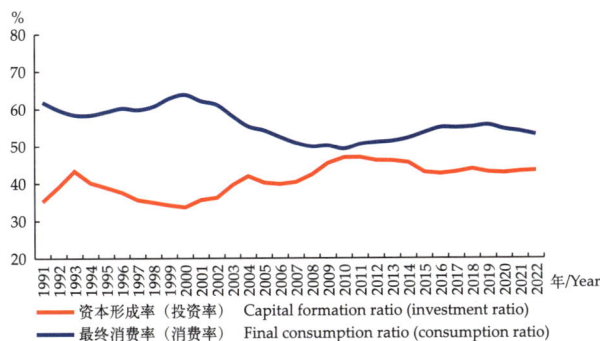

图例：
资本形成率（投资率）Capital formation ratio (investment ratio)
最终消费率（消费率）Final consumption ratio (consumption ratio)

社会消费品零售总额与最终消费增长率的比较
Comparison of growth rate at current prices between retail sales of consumer goods and final consumption expenditure

年 Year	社会消费品 零售总额 （万亿元） Retail sales of consumer goods (RMB 1 trillion)	最终消费 （万亿元） Final consumption (RMB 1 trillion)	社会消费品零售总额现 价增长率 (%) Growth rate at current prices of retail sales of consumer goods (%)	最终消费现价 增长率 (%) Growth rate at current prices of final consumption expenditure (%)
1991	0.94	1.36	13.4	13.4
1992	1.10	1.62	16.8	19.2
1993	1.43	2.08	29.8	28.2
1994	1.86	2.83	30.5	35.9
1995	2.36	3.62	26.8	28.0
1996	2.84	4.31	20.1	19.0
1997	3.13	4.75	10.2	10.3
1998	3.34	5.15	6.8	8.3
1999	3.56	5.67	6.8	10.0
2000	3.42	6.37	9.7	12.5
2001	3.76	6.87	10.1	7.7
2002	4.09	7.42	8.8	8.1
2003	4.58	7.97	9.1	7.4
2004	5.40	8.94	13.3	12.1
2005	6.72	10.19	12.9	14.0
2006	7.64	11.54	13.7	13.2
2007	8.92	13.77	16.8	19.4
2008	10.85	15.89	21.6	15.4
2009	12.53	17.45	15.9	9.8
2010	15.46	20.16	18.8	15.5
2011	18.12	24.47	18.5	21.4
2012	20.72	27.54	14.5	12.5
2013	23.44	30.67	13.1	11.3
2014	26.24	33.80	12.0	10.2
2015	30.09	37.19	10.7	10.0
2016	33.23	41.08	10.4	10.5
2017	36.63	45.65	10.2	11.1
2018	38.10	50.61	9.0	10.9
2019	41.16	55.26	8.0	9.2
2020	39.20	56.08	−3.9	1.5
2021	44.08	61.97	12.5	10.5
2022	43.97	64.16	−0.2	3.5
2023	47.15		7.2	—

注：表中数据根据国家统计局最新数据修订。
Note: Data are revised by National Bureau of Statistics of China.

社会消费品零售总额及最终消费增长趋势
Growth trend of retail sales of consumer goods and final consumption expenditure

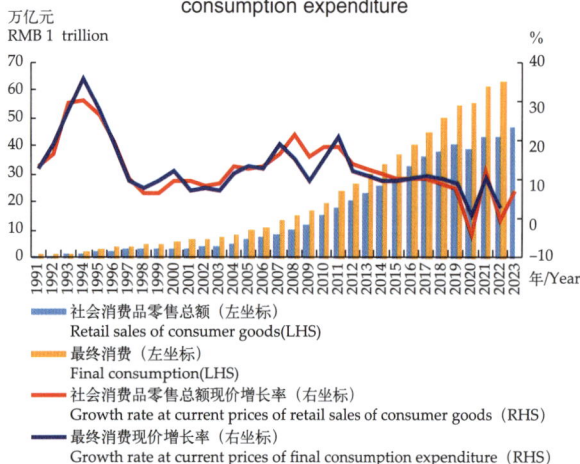

万亿元
RMB 1 trillion

社会消费品零售总额（左坐标）
Retail sales of consumer goods(LHS)
最终消费（左坐标）
Final consumption(LHS)
社会消费品零售总额现价增长率（右坐标）
Growth rate at current prices of retail sales of consumer goods（RHS）
最终消费现价增长率（右坐标）
Growth rate at current prices of final consumption expenditure（RHS）

社会消费品零售总额
Retail sales of consumer goods

年 / 月 Year/Month	当月社会消 费品零售总 额（亿元） Monthly retail sales of consumer goods (RMB 100 million)	当月同比 增长率 (%) Monthly growth rate (YOY)(%)	社会消费品 零售总额累 计（亿元） Accumulative retail sales of consumer goods (RMB 100 million)	累计同比 增长率 (%) Accumulative growth rate (YOY)(%)
2021.01	—	—		
2021.02	—	—	69 737	33.8
2021.03	35 484	34.2	105 221	33.9
2021.04	33 153	17.7	138 373	29.6
2021.05	35 945	12.4	174 319	25.7
2021.06	37 586	12.1	211 904	23.0
2021.07	34 925	8.5	246 829	20.7
2021.08	34 395	2.5	281 224	18.1
2021.09	36 833	4.4	318 057	16.4
2021.10	40 454	4.9	358 511	14.9
2021.11	41 043	3.9	399 554	13.7
2021.12	41 269	1.7	440 823	12.5
2022.01	—	—		
2022.02	—	—	74 426	6.7
2022.03	34 233	−3.5	108 659	3.3
2022.04	29 483	−11.1	138 142	−0.2
2022.05	33 547	−6.7	171 689	−1.5
2022.06	38 743	3.1	210 432	−0.7
2022.07	35 870	2.7	246 302	−0.2
2022.08	36 258	5.4	282 560	0.5
2022.09	37 745	2.5	320 305	0.7
2022.10	40 271	−0.5	360 575	0.6
2022.11	38 615	−5.9	399 190	−0.1
2022.12	40 542	−1.8	439 733	−0.2
2023.01	—	—		
2023.02	—	—	77 067	3.5
2023.03	37 855	10.6	114 922	5.8
2023.04	34 911	18.4	149 833	8.5
2023.05	37 803	12.7	187 636	9.3
2023.06	39 951	3.1	227 588	8.2
2023.07	36 761	2.5	264 348	7.3
2023.08	37 933	4.6	302 281	7.0
2023.09	39 826	5.5	342 107	6.8
2023.10	43 333	7.6	385 440	6.9
2023.11	42 505	10.1	427 945	7.2
2023.12	43 550	7.4	471 495	7.2

注：为消除春节日期不固定因素带来的影响，增强数据的可比性，按照国家统计制度，历年1~2月数据一起调查、一起发布。
Note: In order to eliminate the impact of the different date of "Spring Festival" of each year, and enhance the comparability of data, in accordance with the national statistical system,the data in January and February was investigated and released together.

当月社会消费品零售总额及其增长率
Monthly retail sales and growth rates of consumer goods

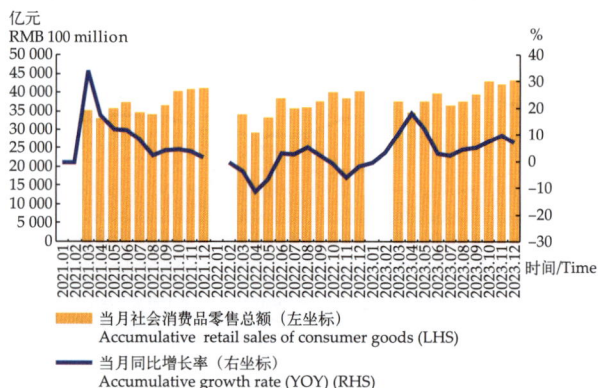

亿元
RMB 100 million

当月社会消费品零售总额（左坐标）
Accumulative retail sales of consumer goods (LHS)
当月同比增长率（右坐标）
Accumulative growth rate (YOY) (RHS)

固定资产投资完成额和固定资本形成总额的比较
Comparision of completed fixed-asset investment and gross capital formation

年 Year	全社会固定资产 投资完成额 （万亿元） Total completed fixed-asset investment (RMB 1 trillion)	固定资本 形成总额 （万亿元） Gross capital formation (RMB 1 trillion)	全社会固定资产投 资现价增长率 (%) Growth rate of total fixed-asset investment at current prices (%)	固定资本形成总额现 价增长率 (%) Growth rate of gross capital formation at current prices (%)
2000	3.29	3.37	10.3	9.0
2001	3.72	3.94	13.0	17.0
2002	4.35	4.40	16.9	11.7
2003	5.38	5.44	23.8	23.7
2004	6.62	6.77	23.0	24.4
2005	8.10	7.56	22.3	11.6
2006	9.76	8.76	20.5	15.9
2007	11.83	10.93	21.3	24.9
2008	14.46	13.49	22.2	23.4
2009	18.18	15.81	25.7	17.1
2010	19.88	19.19	20.4	21.4
2011	23.88	22.77	20.1	18.7
2012	28.17	24.90	18.0	9.4
2013	32.93	27.51	16.9	10.5
2014	37.36	29.49	13.5	7.2
2015	40.59	29.78	8.6	1.0
2016	43.44	31.82	7.0	6.8
2017	46.13	35.79	6.2	12.5
2018	48.85	40.26	5.9	12.5
2019	51.36	42.67	5.1	6.0
2020	52.73	43.96	2.7	3.0
2021	55.29	49.58	4.9	11.5
2022	57.96	52.39	4.9	5.7
2023	—	2.8	—	

注：表中数据根据国家统计局最新数据修订。
Note: Data are revised by National Bureau of Statistics of China.

固定资产投资完成额及增长率
Completed investment in fixed assets and growth rate

年／月 Year/Month		投资完成额 （万亿元） Investment completed (RMB 1 trillion)	增长率 (%) Growth rate (%)
2021	1~2	4.5	35.0
	1~3	9.6	25.6
	1~4	14.4	19.9
	1~5	19.4	15.4
	1~6	25.6	12.6
	1~7	30.3	10.3
	1~8	34.7	8.9
	1~9	39.8	7.3
	1~10	44.6	6.1
	1~11	49.4	5.2
	1~12	54.5	4.9
2022	1~2	5.1	12.2
	1~3	10.5	9.3
	1~4	15.4	6.8
	1~5	20.6	6.2
	1~6	27.1	6.1
	1~7	32.0	5.7
	1~8	36.7	5.8
	1~9	42.1	5.9
	1~10	47.2	5.8
	1~11	52.0	5.3
	1~12	57.2	5.1
2023	1~2	5.4	5.5
	1~3	10.7	5.1
	1~4	14.8	4.7
	1~5	18.9	4.0
	1~6	24.3	3.8
	1~7	28.6	3.4
	1~8	32.7	3.2
	1~9	37.5	3.1
	1~10	41.9	2.9
	1~11	46.1	2.9
	1~12	50.3	3.0

注：自2011年起，投资项目统计起点标准由原来的50万元调整为500万元，"固定资产投资（不含农户）"等于原口径的城镇固定资产投资加上农村企事业组织项目投资。
Note: Since 2011, investment indicators are calculated using new threshold criteria of RMB 5 million instead of RMB 500 thousand in the past. "Investment in fixed assets (excluding rural households)" equals to "investment in fixed assets in urban area" under the old criteria plus "investment of rural enterprises and institutions".

固定资产投资完成额和固定资本形成总额及其增长率
Completed fixed-asset investment and gross capital formation and growth rate

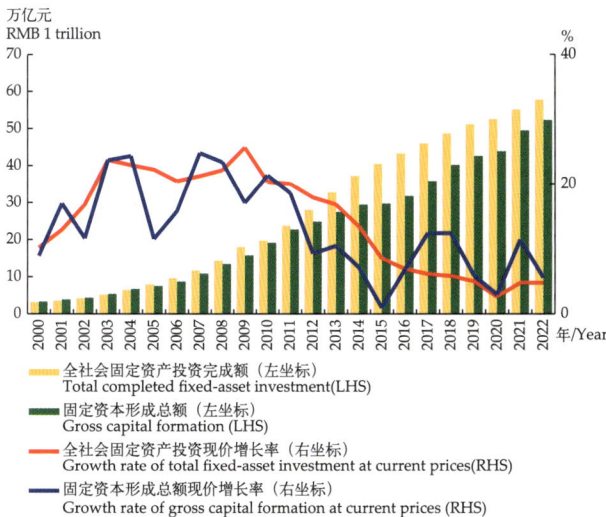

万亿元 RMB 1 trillion

全社会固定资产投资完成额（左坐标）
Total completed fixed-asset investment(LHS)

固定资本形成总额（左坐标）
Gross capital formation (LHS)

全社会固定资产投资现价增长率（右坐标）
Growth rate of total fixed-asset investment at current prices(RHS)

固定资本形成总额现价增长率（右坐标）
Growth rate of gross capital formation at current prices (RHS)

固定资产投资完成额及增长率
Completed investment in fixed assets and growth rate

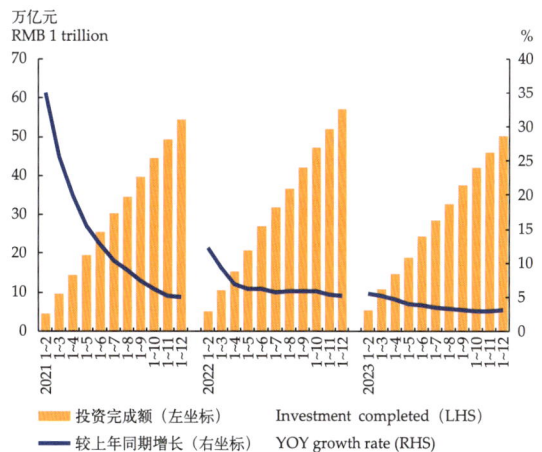

万亿元 RMB 1 trillion

投资完成额（左坐标）　Investment completed（LHS）

较上年同期增长（右坐标）　YOY growth rate (RHS)

固定资产投资完成额累计同比
Accumulated growth rates of completed investment in fixed assets

单位：%　Unit: %

年 / 月 Year/ Month	固定资产投资完成额累计同比 Accumulated growth rate of fixed-asset investment	制造业投资累计同比 Accumulated growth rate of investment in manufacturing industry	房地产投资累计同比 Accumulated growth rate of investment in real estate industry	基础设施建设投资累计同比 Accumulated growth rate of infrastructure investment
2021.02	35.0	37.3	36.8	35.0
2021.03	25.6	29.8	24.7	26.8
2021.04	19.9	23.8	21.2	16.9
2021.05	15.4	20.4	18.4	10.4
2021.06	12.6	19.2	14.7	7.2
2021.07	10.3	17.3	12.5	4.2
2021.08	8.9	15.7	10.8	2.6
2021.09	7.3	14.8	8.8	1.5
2021.10	6.1	14.2	7.4	0.7
2021.11	5.2	13.7	6.3	−0.2
2021.12	4.9	13.5	5.0	0.2
2022.02	12.2	20.9	4.7	8.6
2022.03	9.3	15.6	1.8	10.5
2022.04	6.8	12.2	−1.9	8.3
2022.05	6.2	10.6	−3.2	8.2
2022.06	6.1	10.4	−4.2	9.3
2022.07	5.7	9.9	−5.2	9.6
2022.08	5.8	10.0	−6.2	10.4
2022.09	5.9	10.1	−6.6	11.2
2022.10	5.8	9.7	−7.3	11.4
2022.11	5.3	9.3	−8.3	11.7
2022.12	5.1	9.1	−8.4	11.5
2023.02	5.5	8.1	−5.1	12.2
2023.03	5.1	7.0	−5.1	10.8
2023.04	4.7	6.4	−5.3	9.8
2023.05	4.0	6.0	−6.0	9.5
2023.06	3.8	6.0	−6.7	10.2
2023.07	3.4	5.7	−7.1	9.4
2023.08	3.2	5.9	−7.5	9.0
2023.09	3.1	6.2	−7.8	8.6
2023.10	2.9	6.2	−7.8	8.3
2023.11	2.9	6.3	−8.0	8.0
2023.12	3.0	6.5	−8.1	8.2

房地产开发投资及商品房销售
Real estate development investment completed and sales of commercial buildings

单位：亿元、万平方米
Unit: RMB 100 million, 10,000 square meters

年 / 月 Year/ Month	房地产开发投资完成额 Real estate development investment completed		商品房销售额 Accumulated sales volume of commercial buildings		商品房销售面积 Area sold of commercial buildings	
	绝对值 Absolute value	增长率 (%) Growth rate (%)	绝对值 Absolute value	同比增长 (%) YOY growth (%)	绝对值 Absolute value	同比增长 (%) YOY growth (%)
2021 1~2	13 986	38.3	19 151	133.4	17 363	104.9
1~3	27 576	25.6	38 378	88.5	36 007	63.8
1~4	40 240	21.6	53 609	68.2	50 305	48.1
1~5	54 318	18.3	70 534	52.4	66 383	36.3
1~6	72 179	15.0	92 931	38.9	88 635	27.7
1~7	84 895	12.7	106 430	30.7	101 648	21.5
1~8	98 060	10.9	119 047	22.8	114 193	15.9
1~9	112 568	8.8	134 795	16.6	130 332	11.3
1~10	124 934	7.2	147 185	11.8	143 041	7.3
1~11	137 314	6.0	161 667	8.5	158 131	4.8
1~12	147 602	4.4	181 930	4.8	179 433	1.9
2022 1~2	14 499	3.7	15 459	−19.3	15 703	−9.6
1~3	27 765	0.7	29 655	−22.7	31 046	−13.8
1~4	39 154	−2.7	37 789	−29.5	39 768	−20.9
1~5	52 134	−4.0	48 337	−31.5	50 738	−23.6
1~6	68 314	−5.4	66 072	−28.9	68 923	−22.2
1~7	79 462	−6.4	75 763	−28.8	78 178	−23.1
1~8	90 809	−7.4	85 870	−27.9	87 890	−23.0
1~9	103 559	−8.0	99 380	−26.3	101 422	−22.2
1~10	113 945	−8.8	108 832	−26.1	111 179	−22.3
1~11	123 863	−9.8	118 648	−26.6	121 250	−23.3
1~12	132 895	−10.0	133 308	−26.7	135 837	−24.3
2023 1~2	13 669	−5.7	15 449	−0.1	15 133	−3.6
1~3	25 974	−5.8	30 545	4.1	29 946	−1.8
1~4	35 514	−6.2	39 750	8.8	37 636	−0.4
1~5	45 701	−7.2	49 787	8.4	46 440	−0.9
1~6	58 550	−7.9	63 092	1.1	59 515	−5.3
1~7	67 717	−8.5	70 450	−1.5	66 563	−6.5
1~8	76 900	−8.8	78 158	−3.2	73 949	−7.1
1~9	87 269	−9.1	89 070	−4.6	84 806	−7.5
1~10	95 922	−9.3	97 161	−4.9	92 579	−7.8
1~11	104 045	−9.4	105 318	−5.2	100 509	−8.0
1~12	110 913	−9.6	116 622	−6.5	111 735	−8.5

固定资产投资完成额累计同比
Accumulated growth rates of completed investment in fixed assets

固定资产投资完成额累计同比
Accumulated growth rate of fixed-asset investment

制造业投资累计同比
Accumulated growth rate of investment in manufacturing industry

房地产投资累计同比
Accumulated growth rate of investment in real estate industry

基础设施建设投资累计同比
Accumulated growth rate of infrastructure

房地产开发投资及商品房销售
Real estate development investment completed and sales of commercial buildings

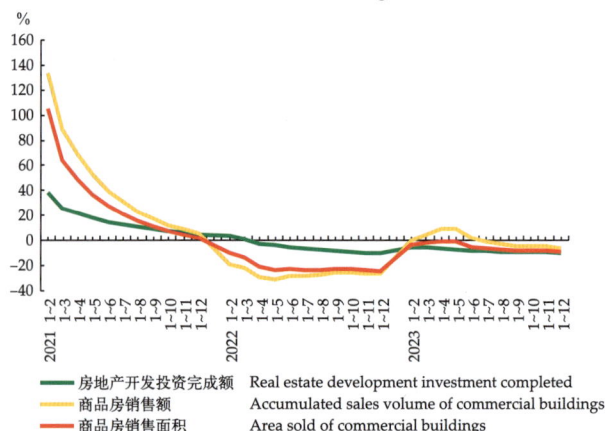

房地产开发投资完成额　Real estate development investment completed

商品房销售额　Accumulated sales volume of commercial buildings

商品房销售面积　Area sold of commercial buildings

商品房建筑情况
Construction of commercial buildings

单位：亿平方米
Unit: 100 million square meters

年 / 月 Year/Month		新开工面积 Area newly constructed	同比增长 (%) YOY growth (%)	施工面积 Area under construction	同比增长 (%) YOY growth (%)	竣工面积 Area completed	同比增长 (%) YOY growth (%)
2021	1~2	1.7	64.3	77.1	11.0	1.4	40.4
	1~3	3.6	28.2	79.8	11.2	1.9	22.9
	1~4	5.4	12.8	81.9	10.5	2.3	17.9
	1~5	7.4	6.9	84.0	10.1	2.8	16.4
	1~6	10.1	3.8	87.3	10.2	3.7	25.7
	1~7	11.9	−0.9	89.2	9.0	4.2	25.7
	1~8	13.6	−3.2	91.0	8.4	4.7	26.0
	1~9	15.3	−4.5	92.8	7.9	5.1	23.4
	1~10	16.7	−7.7	94.3	7.1	5.7	16.3
	1~11	18.3	−9.1	96.0	6.3	6.9	16.2
	1~12	19.9	−11.4	97.5	5.2	10.1	11.2
2022	1~2	1.5	−12.2	78.5	1.8	1.2	−9.8
	1~3	3.0	−17.5	80.6	1.0	1.7	−11.5
	1~4	4.0	−26.3	81.9	0.0	2.0	−11.9
	1~5	5.2	−30.6	83.2	−1.0	2.3	−15.3
	1~6	6.6	−34.4	84.9	−2.8	2.9	−21.5
	1~7	7.6	−36.1	85.9	−3.7	3.2	−23.3
	1~8	8.5	−37.2	86.9	−4.5	3.7	−21.1
	1~9	9.5	−38.0	87.9	−5.3	4.1	−19.9
	1~10	10.4	−37.8	88.9	−5.7	4.7	−18.7
	1~11	11.2	−38.9	89.7	−6.5	5.6	−19.0
	1~12	12.1	−39.4	90.5	−7.2	8.6	−15.0
2023	1~2	1.4	−9.4	75.0	−4.4	1.3	8.0
	1~3	2.4	−19.2	76.5	−5.2	1.9	14.7
	1~4	3.1	−21.2	77.1	−5.6	2.4	18.8
	1~5	4.0	−22.6	78.0	−6.2	2.8	19.6
	1~6	5.0	−24.3	79.2	−6.6	3.4	19.0
	1~7	5.7	−24.5	80.0	−6.8	3.8	20.5
	1~8	6.4	−24.4	80.6	−7.1	4.4	19.2
	1~9	7.2	−23.4	81.6	−7.1	4.9	19.8
	1~10	7.9	−23.2	82.3	−7.3	5.5	19.0
	1~11	8.8	−21.2	83.1	−7.2	6.5	17.9
	1~12	9.5	−20.4	83.8	−7.2	10.0	17.0

70个大中城市新建商品住宅价格指数当月同比
YOY growth rate of sales price of newly constructed commercial residential buildings in 70 large and medium-sized cities

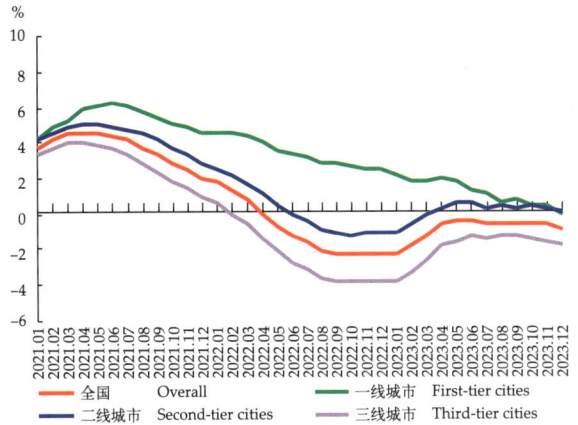

全国　Overall
一线城市　First-tier cities
二线城市　Second-tier cities
三线城市　Third-tier cities

70个大中城市二手住宅价格指数当月同比
YOY growth rate of sales price of second-handed residential buildings in 70 large and medium-sized cities

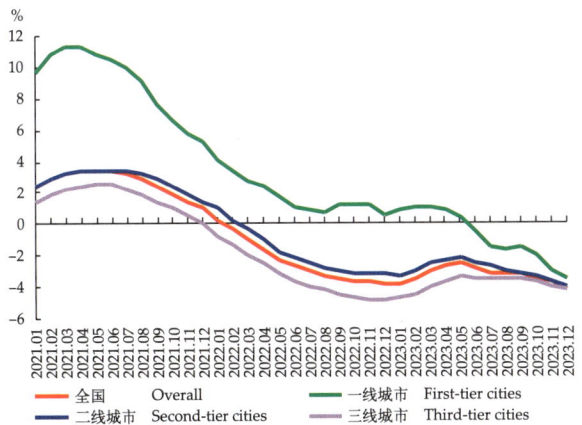

全国　Overall
一线城市　First-tier cities
二线城市　Second-tier cities
三线城市　Third-tier cities

商品房建筑情况
Construction of commercial buildings

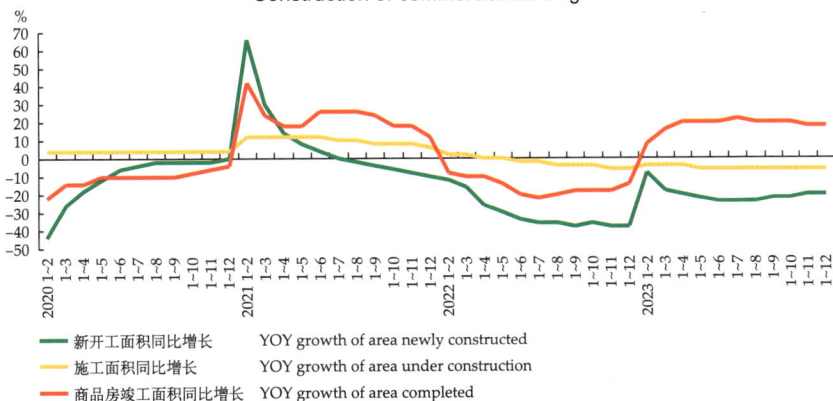

新开工面积同比增长　YOY growth of area newly constructed
施工面积同比增长　YOY growth of area under construction
商品房竣工面积同比增长　YOY growth of area completed

1.2.3　进出口与直接投资（Imports, exports and direct investments）

据世界贸易组织统计，2023年，中国货物贸易出口总值为3.36万亿美元，占世界货物贸易出口总值22.28万亿美元的15.1%，比上年上升0.7个百分点，在全球货物贸易出口中排名第一。2022年，中国货物贸易进口总值为2.72万亿美元，占世界货物贸易进口总值25.62万亿美元的10.6%，比上年下降1.3个百分点，在全球货物贸易进口中排名第二，位于美国之后。

According to WTO statistics, in 2023, China's export volume of goods totaled USD 3.36 trillion, accounting for 15.1 percent of the world total of USD 22.28 trillion, 0.7 percentage points higher than that in 2022. China's goods export ranked 1st in the world. China's import volume of goods reached USD 2.72 trillion, accounting for 10.6 percent of the world total of USD 25.62 trillion, 1.3 percentage points lower than that in 2021. China ranked 2nd in the world after the U.S. in terms of goods imports.

2023年世界货物贸易出口前十位排名
Top ten economies in the world in terms of goods exported in 2023

排名 Rank	经济体 Economy		出口（10亿美元） Exports (USD 1 billion)	比重（%） Share (%)
1	中　国	China	3 364	15.1
2	美　国	U.S.	1 755	7.9
3	德　国	Germany	1 632	7.3
4	荷　兰	Netherlands	836	3.8
5	日　本	Japan	756	3.4
6	中国香港	HK SAR of China	670	3.0
7	韩　国	Korea	644	2.9
8	意大利	Italy	610	2.7
9	法　国	France	585	2.6
10	比利时	Belgium	543	2.4
—	世　界	World total	22 284	100.0

2022年世界货物贸易进口前十位排名
Top ten economies in the world in terms of goods imported in 2022

排名 Rank	经济体 Economy		进口（10亿美元） Imports (USD 1 billion)	比重（%） Share (%)
1	美　国	U.S.	3 376	13.2
2	中　国	China	2 716	10.6
3	德　国	Germany	1 571	6.1
4	荷　兰	Netherlands	899	3.5
5	日　本	Japan	897	3.5
6	英　国	U.K.	824	3.2
7	法　国	France	818	3.2
8	韩　国	Korea	731	2.9
9	印　度	India	723	2.8
10	意大利	Italy	689	2.7
—	世　界	World total	25 621	100.0

我国出口总值、贸易总额与GDP之比
Total exports and total trade volume over GDP

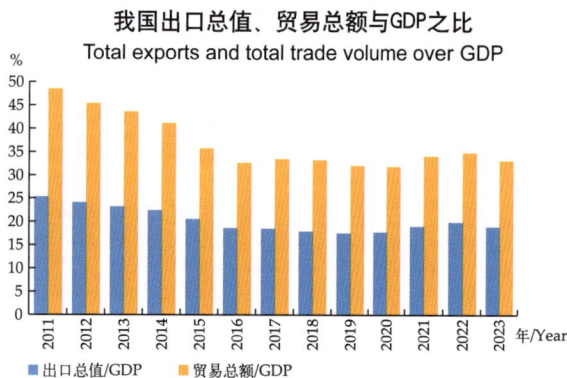

我国贸易总额及其增长趋势
Total trade volume and growth rate

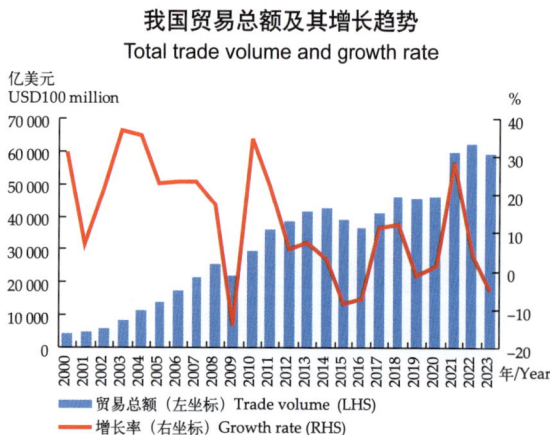

我国年度进出口额及其增长率
Annual imports & exports and growth rates

年 Year	进出口 Imports & Exports		出口 Exports		进口 Imports		进出口差额 （亿美元） Trade balance (USD 100 million)
	总额（亿美元） Total value (USD 100 million)	增长率（%） Growth rate (%)	总额（亿美元） Total value (USD 100 million)	增长率（%） Growth rate (%)	总额（亿美元） Total value (USD 100 million)	增长率（%） Growth rate (%)	
2000	4 743	31.5	2 492	27.8	2 251	35.8	241
2001	5 097	7.5	2 661	6.8	2 436	8.2	225
2002	6 208	21.8	3 256	22.4	2 952	21.2	304
2003	8 510	37.1	4 382	34.6	4 128	39.8	255
2004	11 546	35.7	5 933	35.4	5 612	36.0	321
2005	14 219	23.2	7 620	28.4	6 600	17.6	1 020
2006	17 604	23.8	9 690	27.2	7 915	19.9	1 775
2007	21 762	23.6	12 201	25.9	9 561	20.8	2 639
2008	25 633	17.8	14 307	17.3	11 326	18.5	2 981
2009	22 075	−13.9	12 016	−16.0	10 059	−11.2	1 957
2010	29 740	34.7	15 778	31.3	13 962	38.8	1 815
2011	36 419	22.5	18 984	20.3	17 435	24.9	1 549
2012	38 671	6.2	20 487	7.9	18 184	4.3	2 303
2013	41 590	7.5	22 090	7.8	19 500	7.2	2 590
2014	43 015	3.4	23 423	6.0	19 592	0.5	3 831
2015	39 530	−8.1	22 735	−2.9	16 796	−14.3	5 939
2016	36 856	−6.8	20 976	−7.7	15 879	−5.5	5 097
2017	41 071	11.4	22 633	7.9	18 438	16.1	4 196
2018	46 224	12.5	24 867	9.9	21 357	15.8	3 509
2019	45 779	−1.0	24 995	0.5	20 784	−2.7	4 211
2020	46 559	1.7	25 900	3.6	20 660	−0.6	5 240
2021	59 954	28.8	33 160	28.0	26 794	29.7	6 366
2022	62 509	4.3	35 444	6.9	27 065	1.0	8 379
2023	59 368	−5.0	33 800	−4.6	25 568	−5.5	8 232

注：表中数据根据海关总署最新数据修订。
Note: Data are revised by General Administration of Customs of the People's Republic of China.

当月进出口总值及其增长率
Total monthly imports, exports, and growth rates

年/月 Year/Month	出口总值（亿美元） Total exports (USD 100 million)	进口总值（亿美元） Total imports (USD 100 million)	出口同比增长率（%） Growth rate of exports (YOY)(%)	进口同比增长率（%） Growth rate of imports (YOY) (%)	当月差额（亿美元） Monthly trade balance (USD 100 million)
2020.12	2 819	2 038	18.1	6.5	782
2021.01	2 640	1 986	24.8	26.6	654
2021.02	2 049	1 670	154.9	17.3	379
2021.03	2 411	2 273	30.6	38.1	138
2021.04	2 639	2 211	32.3	43.1	429
2021.05	2 639	2 184	27.9	51.1	455
2021.06	2 814	2 299	32.2	36.7	515
2021.07	2 827	2 261	19.3	28.1	566
2021.08	2 943	2 360	25.6	33.1	583
2021.09	3 057	2 390	28.1	17.6	668
2021.10	3 002	2 157	27.1	20.6	845
2021.11	3 255	2 538	22.0	31.7	717
2021.12	3 405	2 460	20.9	19.5	945
2022.01	3 273	2 419	24.1	19.8	854
2022.02	2 174	1 868	6.2	10.4	306
2022.03	2 761	2 287	14.7	−0.1	474
2022.04	2 736	2 225	3.9	0.0	511
2022.05	3 082	2 295	16.9	4.1	788
2022.06	3 313	2 333	17.9	1.0	979
2022.07	3 330	2 317	18.0	2.3	1013
2022.08	3 149	2 355	7.1	0.3	794
2022.09	3 228	2 380	5.7	0.3	847
2022.10	2 984	2 132	−0.3	−0.7	852
2022.11	2 955	2 263	−8.7	−10.6	698
2022.12	3 061	2 281	−9.9	−7.5	780
2023.01	2 923	1 922	−12.0	−21.0	1001
2023.02	2 140	1 972	−1.3	4.2	168
2023.03	3 156	2 274	14.8	−1.4	882
2023.04	2 954	2 052	8.5	−7.9	902
2023.05	2 835	2 177	−7.5	−4.5	658
2023.06	2 853	2 147	−12.4	−6.8	706
2023.07	2 818	2 012	−14.5	−12.4	806
2023.08	2 848	2 166	−8.8	−7.3	682
2023.09	2 991	2 213	−6.2	−6.2	778
2023.10	2 748	2 183	−6.4	3.0	565
2023.11	2 919	2 235	0.5	−0.6	684
2023.12	3 036	2 283	2.3	0.2	753

当月进出口增长率及贸易差额
Total monthly imports, exports and growth rates

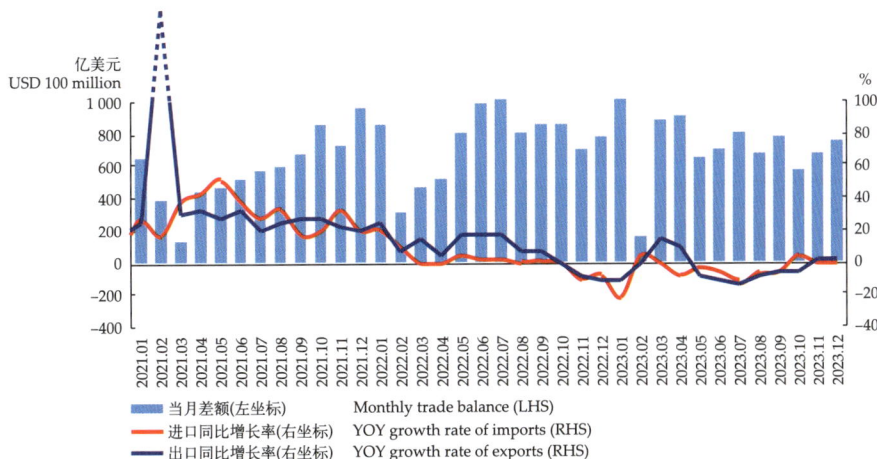

当月差额（左坐标）　Monthly trade balance (LHS)
进口同比增长率(右坐标)　YOY growth rate of imports (RHS)
出口同比增长率(右坐标)　YOY growth rate of exports (RHS)

中国对其他经济体出口金额累计同比
Accumulated growth rate of value of China's exports to other economies

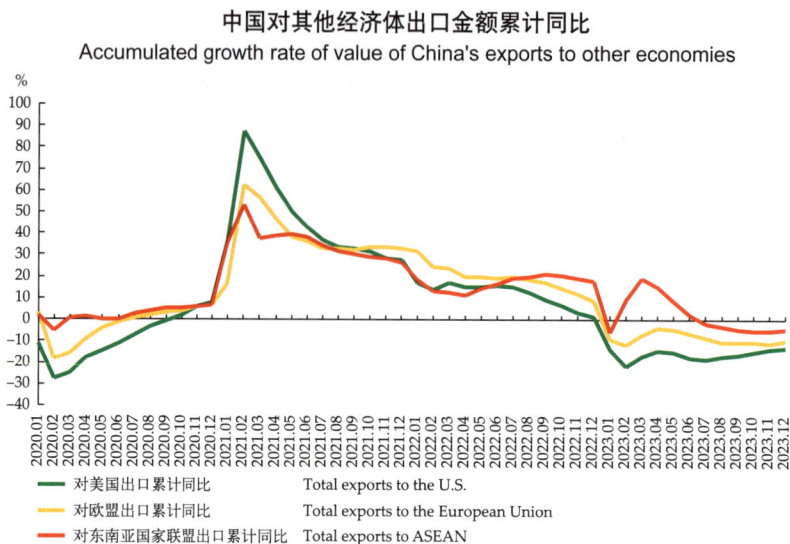

—— 对美国出口累计同比	Total exports to the U.S.
—— 对欧盟出口累计同比	Total exports to the European Union
—— 对东南亚国家联盟出口累计同比	Total exports to ASEAN

中国从其他经济体进口金额累计同比
Accumulated growth rate of value of China's imports from other economies

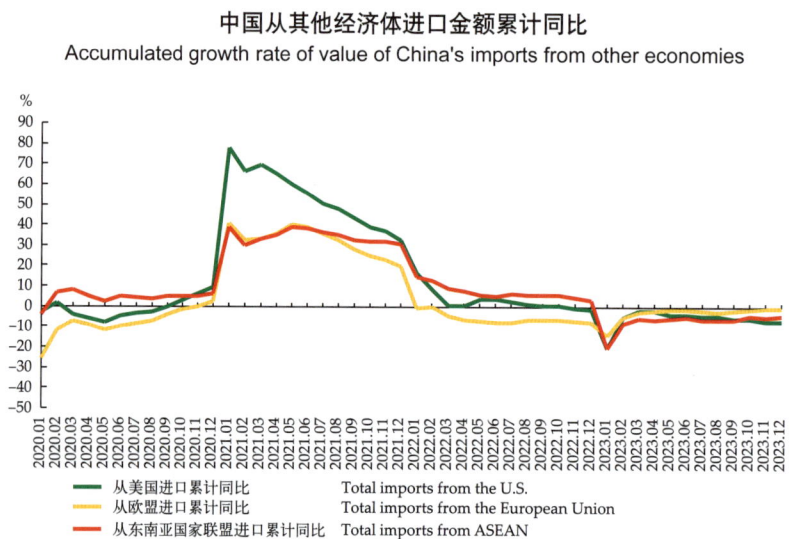

—— 从美国进口累计同比	Total imports from the U.S.
—— 从欧盟进口累计同比	Total imports from the European Union
—— 从东南亚国家联盟进口累计同比	Total imports from ASEAN

中国对其他经济体贸易差额
China's trade balance with other economies

亿美元
USD 100 million

■ 对东南亚国家联盟贸易差额当月值	Current month value of trade balance with ASEAN
■ 对欧盟贸易差额当月值	Current month value of trade balance with the European Union
■ 对美国贸易差额当月值	Current month value of trade balance with the U.S.

实际利用外商直接投资及其增长趋势
Actual utilized foreign direct investment and growth rate

年 Year	年度数（亿美元） Absolute value (USD 100 million)	同比增速（%） Growth rate（%）
2009	940.6	−13.2
2010	1 147.3	22.0
2011	1 239.9	8.1
2012	1 210.7	−2.4
2013	1 239.1	2.3
2014	1 285.0	3.7
2015	1 355.8	5.5
2016	1 337.1	−1.4
2017	1 363.2	2.0
2018	1 383.1	1.5
2019	1 412.2	2.1
2020	1 493.4	5.7
2021	1 809.6	21.2
2022	1 891.3	4.5
2023	1 632.5	−13.7

非金融类对外直接投资及其增长趋势
Non-financial outbound direct investment and growth rate

年 Year	年度数（亿美元） Absolute value (USD 100 million)	同比增速（%） Growth rate（%）
2008	406.5	63.6
2009	438.0	6.5
2010	590.0	36.3
2011	600.7	1.8
2012	772.2	28.6
2013	901.7	16.8
2014	1 028.9	14.1
2015	1 180.2	14.7
2016	1 701.1	44.1
2017	1 200.8	−29.4
2018	1 205.0	0.3
2019	1 106.0	−8.2
2020	1 101.5	−0.4
2021	1 136.4	3.2
2022	1 168.5	2.8
2023	1 301.3	11.4

实际利用外商直接投资及其增长趋势
Actual utilized foreign direct investment and growth rate

亿美元
USD 100 million

年度数（左坐标）　Absolute value (LHS)
同比增速（右坐标）　Growth rates (RHS)

非金融类对外直接投资及其增长趋势
Non-financial outbound direct investment and growth rate

亿美元
USD 100 million

年度数（左坐标）　Absolute value (LHS)
同比增速（右坐标）　Growth rates (RHS)

1.3 价格（Price）

主要价格指数

Main price indices

单位：% Unit: %

年 / 月 Year/Month		居民消费价格指数 Consumer price indices			工业生产者出厂价格指数 Producer price index for manufactured goods		进出口同比价格指数 Import-export price index (YOY)	
		月环比 MOM	当月同比 YOY	累计同比 Accumulated YOY	当月同比 YOY	累计同比 Accumulated YOY	出口 Exports	进口 Imports
2021	1	1.0	−0.3	−0.3	0.3	0.3	1.0	−4.1
	2	0.6	−0.2	−0.3	1.7	1.0	−2.1	1.2
	3	−0.5	0.4	0.0	4.4	2.1	−1.7	5.0
	4	−0.3	0.9	0.2	6.8	3.3	−2.2	10.4
	5	−0.2	1.3	0.4	9.0	4.4	−0.4	17.4
	6	−0.4	1.1	0.5	8.8	5.1	0.8	18.0
	7	0.3	1.0	0.6	9.0	5.7	2.6	17.2
	8	0.1	0.8	0.6	9.5	6.2	6.5	15.7
	9	0.0	0.7	0.6	10.7	6.7	10.6	16.4
	10	0.7	1.5	0.7	13.5	7.3	8.1	17.0
	11	0.4	2.3	0.9	12.9	7.9	7.5	17.6
	12	−0.3	1.5	0.9	10.3	8.1	9.3	16.5
2022	1	0.4	0.9	0.9	9.1	9.1	9.5	15.8
	2	0.6	0.9	0.9	8.8	8.9	11.7	11.9
	3	0.0	1.5	1.1	8.3	8.7	11.1	13.1
	4	0.4	2.1	1.4	8.0	8.5	8.9	17.1
	5	−0.2	2.1	1.5	6.4	8.1	9.6	12.7
	6	0.0	2.5	1.7	6.1	7.7	15.7	14.3
	7	0.5	2.7	1.8	4.2	7.2	14.3	15.6
	8	−0.1	2.5	1.9	2.3	6.6	12.7	10.5
	9	0.3	2.8	2.0	0.9	5.9	13.1	8.2
	10	0.1	2.1	2.0	−1.3	5.2	15.3	10.9
	11	−0.2	1.6	2.0	−1.3	4.6	13.2	6.4
	12	0.0	1.8	2.0	−0.7	4.1	13.1	7.1
2023	1	0.8	2.1	2.1	−0.8	−0.8	11.9	4.1
	2	−0.5	1.0	1.5	−1.4	−1.1	6.6	0.8
	3	−0.3	0.7	1.3	−2.5	−1.6	7.0	−0.4
	4	−0.1	0.1	1.0	−3.6	−2.1	5.3	−5.0
	5	−0.2	0.2	0.8	−4.6	−2.6	−0.5	−4.5
	6	−0.2	0.0	0.7	−5.4	−3.1	−6.7	−8.5
	7	0.2	−0.3	0.5	−4.4	−3.2	−5.5	−9.1
	8	0.3	0.1	0.5	−3.0	−3.2	−8.6	−6.5
	9	0.2	0.0	0.4	−2.5	−3.1	−7.9	−3.0
	10	−0.1	−0.2	0.4	−2.6	−3.1	−9.7	−2.7
	11	−0.5	−0.5	0.3	−3.0	−3.1	−9.2	0.0
	12	0.1	−0.3	0.2	−2.7	−3.0	−8.4	−2.0

CPI、PPI与进出口价格指数

CPI, PPI and Import-export price index (YOY)

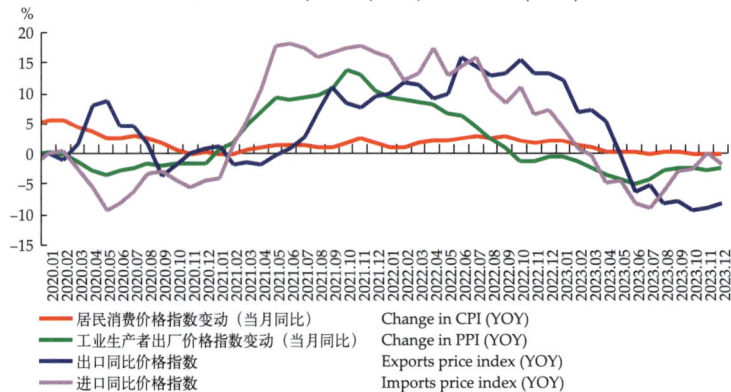

居民消费价格指数变动（当月同比）	Change in CPI (YOY)
工业生产者出厂价格指数变动（当月同比）	Change in PPI (YOY)
出口同比价格指数	Exports price index (YOY)
进口同比价格指数	Imports price index (YOY)

CPI同比指数变动
Change in CPI (YOY)

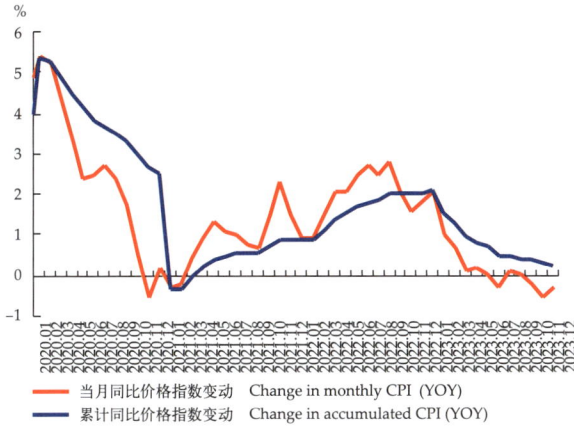

当月同比价格指数变动 Change in monthly CPI (YOY)
累计同比价格指数变动 Change in accumulated CPI (YOY)

PPI同比指数变动
Change in PPI (YOY)

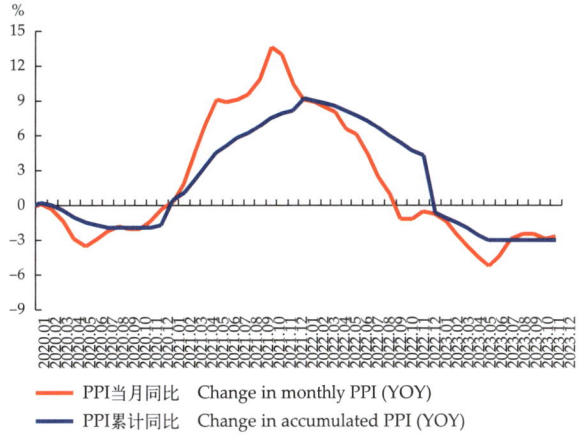

PPI当月同比 Change in monthly PPI (YOY)
PPI累计同比 Change in accumulated PPI (YOY)

CPI当月同比分类指数变动
Breakdown of changes in CPI (YOY)

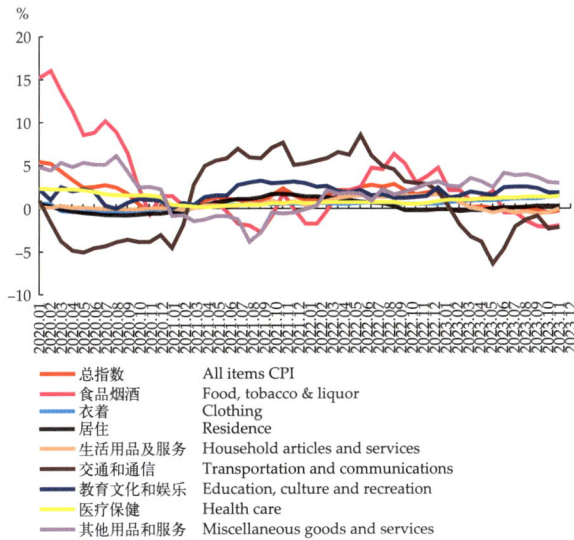

总指数 All items CPI
食品烟酒 Food, tobacco & liquor
衣着 Clothing
居住 Residence
生活用品及服务 Household articles and services
交通和通信 Transportation and communications
教育文化和娱乐 Education, culture and recreation
医疗保健 Health care
其他用品和服务 Miscellaneous goods and services

PPI当月同比分类指数变动
Breakdown of changes in PPI (YOY)

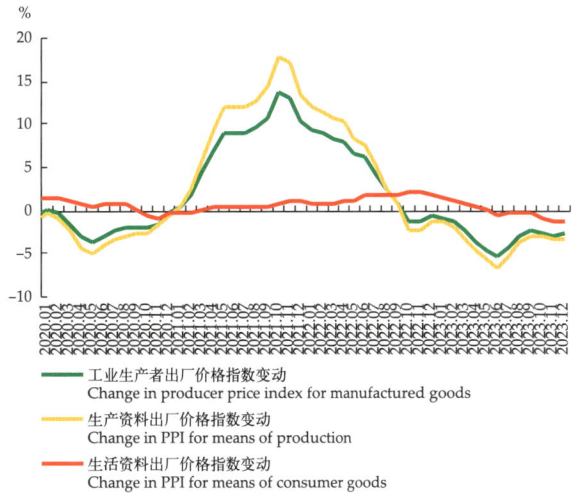

工业生产者出厂价格指数变动
Change in producer price index for manufactured goods
生产资料出厂价格指数变动
Change in PPI for means of production
生活资料出厂价格指数变动
Change in PPI for means of consumer goods

1.4 就业与居民收入 (Employment and household income)

人口与就业基本情况
Population and employment

年 Year	年底总人口（亿人） Population at the end of the year (100 million people)						15~64 岁 人口数（亿人） Population between 15~64 years of age (100 million people)	就业人员（亿人） Employment (100 million people)
		城镇 Urban	比重（%） Share (%)	乡村 Rural	比重（%） Share (%)			
2001	12.8	4.8	38	8.0	62		7.3
2002	12.8	5.0	39	7.8	61	9.0	7.3
2003	12.9	5.2	41	7.7	59	9.1	7.4
2004	13.0	5.4	42	7.6	58	9.2	7.4
2005	13.1	5.6	43	7.5	57	9.4	7.5
2006	13.1	5.8	44	7.3	56	9.5	7.5
2007	13.2	6.1	46	7.1	54	9.6	7.5
2008	13.3	6.2	47	7.0	53	9.7	7.6
2009	13.3	6.5	48	6.9	52	9.7	7.6
2010	13.4	6.7	50	6.7	50	10.0	7.6
2011	13.5	7.0	52	6.5	48	10.0	7.6
2012	13.6	7.2	53	6.4	47	10.1	7.6
2013	13.7	7.5	54	6.2	46	10.1	7.6
2014	13.8	7.7	56	6.1	44	10.1	7.6
2015	13.8	7.9	57	5.9	43	10.1	7.6
2016	13.9	8.2	59	5.7	41	10.1	7.6
2017	14.0	8.4	60	5.6	40	10.1	7.6
2018	14.1	8.6	62	5.4	38	10.0	7.6
2019	14.1	8.8	63	5.3	37	10.0	7.5
2020	14.1	9.0	64	5.1	36	9.7	7.5
2021	14.1	9.1	65	5.0	35	9.7	7.5
2022	14.1	9.2	65	4.9	35	9.6	7.3
2023	14.1	9.3	66	4.8	34		

注：表中数据根据第七次人口普查数据修订。
Note: Data are revised according to the 7th National Population Census.

就业人员按城乡和产业分类
Employment in urban and rural areas and in industries

年 Year	就业人员（亿人）Employment (100 million people)											
		按城乡分 Urban & rural				按产业分 Industries						
		城镇 Urban	比重（%） Share (%)	乡村 Rural	比重（%） Share (%)	第一产业 Primary industry	比重（%） Share (%)	第二产业 Secondary industry	比重（%） Share (%)	第三产业 Tertiary industry	比重（%） Share (%)
2001	7.28	2.41	33.1	4.87	66.9	3.64	50.0	1.62	22.3	2.02	27.7
2002	7.33	2.52	34.3	4.81	65.7	3.66	50.0	1.57	21.4	2.10	28.6
2003	7.37	2.62	35.6	4.75	64.4	3.62	49.1	1.59	21.6	2.16	29.3
2004	7.43	2.73	36.8	4.70	63.2	3.48	46.9	1.67	22.5	2.27	30.6
2005	7.46	2.84	38.0	4.63	62.0	3.34	44.8	1.78	23.8	2.34	31.4
2006	7.50	2.96	39.5	4.53	60.5	3.19	42.6	1.89	25.2	2.41	32.2
2007	7.53	3.10	41.1	4.44	58.9	3.07	40.8	2.02	26.8	2.44	32.4
2008	7.56	3.21	42.5	4.35	57.5	2.99	39.6	2.06	27.2	2.51	33.2
2009	7.58	3.33	43.9	4.25	56.1	2.89	38.1	2.11	27.8	2.59	34.1
2010	7.61	3.47	45.6	4.14	54.4	2.79	36.7	2.18	28.7	2.63	34.6
2011	7.62	3.60	47.3	4.02	52.7	2.65	34.7	2.25	29.6	2.72	35.7
2012	7.63	3.73	48.9	3.90	51.1	2.55	33.5	2.32	30.5	2.75	36.1
2013	7.63	3.85	50.5	3.78	49.5	2.38	31.2	2.31	30.3	2.93	38.4
2014	7.63	3.97	52.0	3.66	48.0	2.24	29.3	2.31	30.2	3.09	40.5
2015	7.63	4.09	53.6	3.54	46.4	2.14	28.1	2.26	29.7	3.23	42.3
2016	7.62	4.21	55.2	3.42	44.8	2.09	27.4	2.23	29.2	3.30	43.3
2017	7.61	4.32	56.8	3.29	43.2	2.03	26.7	2.18	28.6	3.40	44.7
2018	7.58	4.43	58.4	3.15	41.6	1.95	25.8	2.14	28.2	3.49	46.1
2019	7.54	4.52	60.0	3.02	40.0	1.87	24.7	2.12	28.1	3.56	47.1
2020	7.51	4.63	61.6	2.88	38.4	1.77	23.6	2.15	28.7	3.58	47.7
2021	7.47	4.68	62.7	2.79	37.3	1.71	22.9	2.17	29.1	3.59	48.0
2022	7.34	4.59	62.6	2.74	37.4	1.77	24.1	2.11	28.8	3.46	47.1
2023	7.40	4.70	63.5	2.70	36.5						

注：表中数据根据第七次人口普查数据重新修订。
Note: Data are revised according to the 7th National Population Census.

城镇失业人数和失业率
Unemployed urban population and unemployment rate

年 / 季度末 Year/End of quarter	城镇登记失业人数 （万人） Registered unemployment in urban areas (10 000 people)	城镇登记失业率 (%) Registered unemployment rate in urban areas (%)	城镇调查失业率 (%) Surveyed unemployment rate in urban areas (%)
2018　I	971	3.9	5.1
II	969	3.8	4.8
III	975	3.8	4.9
IV	974	3.8	4.9
2019　I	959	3.7	5.2
II	947	3.6	5.1
III	948	3.6	5.2
IV	945	3.6	5.2
2020　I	957	3.7	5.9
II	1 005	3.8	5.7
III	1 126	4.2	5.4
IV	1 160	4.2	5.2
2021　I	1 060	3.9	5.3
II	1 042	3.9	5.0
III	1 016	3.9	4.9
IV	1 040	4.0	5.1
2022　I	1 102	—	5.8
II	1 281	—	5.5
III	—	—	5.5
IV	—	—	5.5
2023　I	—	—	5.3
II	—	—	5.2
III	—	—	5.0
IV	—	—	5.1

居民人均可支配收入
Per capita disposable income

年 / 季度 Year/ Quarter	农村居民人均可支配收入 Per capita disposable income in rural area		城镇居民人均可支配收入 Per capita disposable income in urban area	
	绝对值（元） Absolute value (RMB)	同比实际增长 (%) Growth in real terms (YOY) (%)	绝对值（元） Absolute value (RMB)	同比实际增长 (%) Growth in real terms (YOY) (%)
2018　I	4 226	6.8	10 781	5.7
I~II	7 142	6.8	19 770	5.8
I~III	10 645	6.8	29 599	5.7
I~IV	14 617	6.6	39 251	5.6
2019　I	4 600	6.9	11 633	5.9
I~II	7 778	6.6	21 342	5.7
I~III	11 622	6.4	31 939	5.4
I~IV	16 021	6.2	42 359	5.0
2020　I	4 641	−4.7	11 691	−3.9
I~II	8 069	−1.0	21 655	−2.0
I~III	12 297	1.6	32 821	−0.3
I~IV	17 131	3.8	43 834	1.2
2021　I	5 398	16.3	13 120	12.3
I~II	9 248	14.1	24 125	10.7
I~III	13 726	11.2	35 946	8.7
I~IV	18 931	9.7	47 412	7.1
2022　I	5 778	6.3	13 832	4.2
I~II	9 787	4.2	25 003	1.9
I~III	14 600	4.3	37 482	2.3
I~IV	20 133	4.2	49 283	1.9
2023　I	6 131	4.8	14 388	2.7
I~II	10 551	7.2	26 357	4.7
I~III	15 705	7.3	39 428	4.7
I~IV	21 691	7.6	51 821	4.8

城镇调查失业率
Unemployment rate

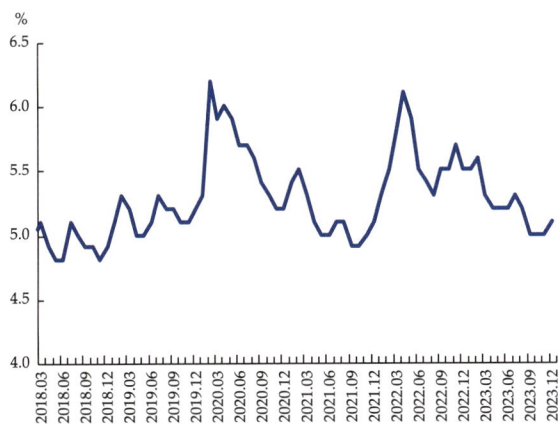

人均可支配收入变化率
Growth rate of per capita disposable income of residents

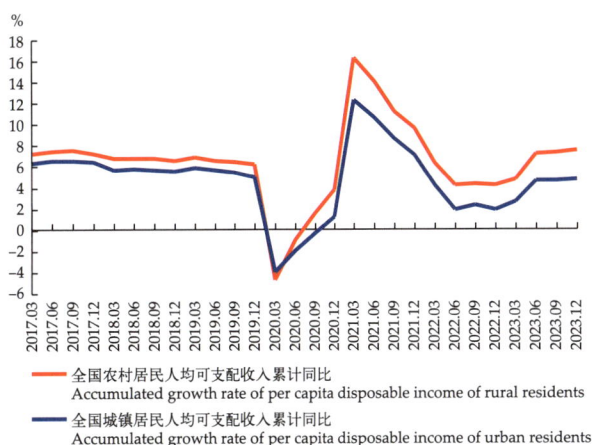

全国农村居民人均可支配收入累计同比
Accumulated growth rate of per capita disposable income of rural residents

全国城镇居民人均可支配收入累计同比
Accumulated growth rate of per capita disposable income of urban residents

二、货币与存贷款（Money, deposits and loans）

2.1 基础货币与中央银行资产负债表
（Monetary base and balance sheet of central banks）

基础货币余额及其增长趋势
Monetary base and its growth

单位：万亿元
Unit: RMB 1 trillion

年 / 月 Year/Month	余额 Outstanding amounts	同比增长率（%） Growth rate (YOY) (%)
2020.12	33.04	1.9
2021.01	31.68	−1.5
2021.02	32.16	4.2
2021.03	32.70	2.9
2021.04	31.87	2.2
2021.05	32.07	3.9
2021.06	32.45	5.2
2021.07	31.06	4.5
2021.08	30.74	3.1
2021.09	32.43	2.8
2021.10	31.50	4.2
2021.11	31.78	1.0
2021.12	32.95	−0.3
2022.01	33.12	4.5
2022.02	32.86	2.2
2022.03	33.55	2.6
2022.04	32.68	2.6
2022.05	32.51	1.4
2022.06	33.43	3.0
2022.07	32.42	4.4
2022.08	32.56	5.9
2022.09	34.18	5.4
2022.10	33.30	5.7
2022.11	33.48	5.4
2022.12	36.10	9.6
2023.01	35.89	8.4
2023.02	35.04	6.6
2023.03	36.41	8.5
2023.04	35.17	7.6
2023.05	34.42	5.9
2023.06	36.52	9.3
2023.07	34.78	7.3
2023.08	35.36	8.6
2023.09	36.39	6.5
2023.10	35.07	5.3
2023.11	36.32	8.5
2023.12	38.90	7.8

基础货币构成
Composition of monetary base

单位：亿元
Unit: RMB 100 million

年 / 季度 Year/Quarter	货币发行 Currency issue	金融机构存款 Deposits of depository corporations
2020Q4	89 823	222 906
2021Q1	92 459	216 683
2021Q2	89 614	216 321
2021Q3	92 427	212 047
2021Q4	96 165	212 393
2022Q1	100 738	215 232
2022Q2	101 229	212 469
2022Q3	104 051	216 254
2022Q4	110 013	227 877
2023Q1	110 937	230 383
2023Q2	110 311	231 389
2023Q3	114 478	224 685
2023Q4	118 661	245 687

金融机构准备金账户存款和超额准备金率
Deposit in reserve account and excess reserve ratio of financial institutions

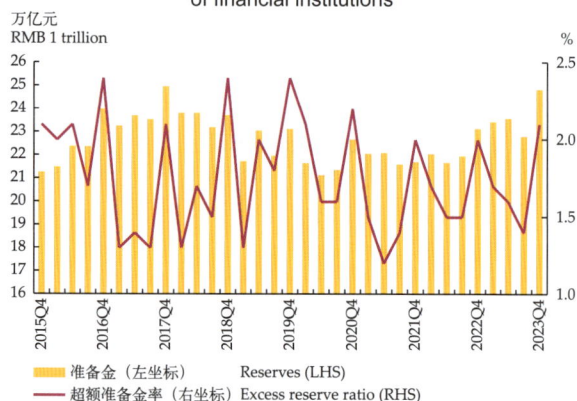

万亿元
RMB 1 trillion

准备金（左坐标）　Reserves (LHS)
超额准备金率（右坐标）Excess reserve ratio (RHS)

基础货币余额及其增长趋势
Monetary base and its growth

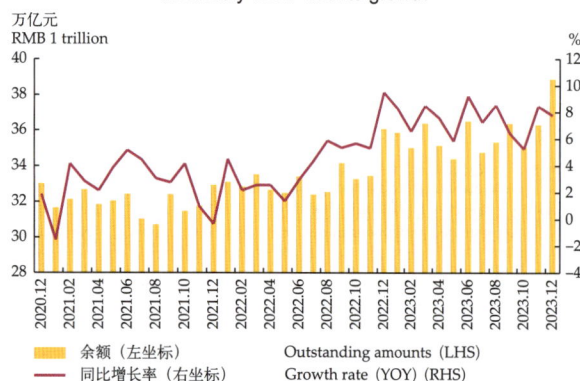

万亿元
RMB 1 trillion

余额（左坐标）　Outstanding amounts (LHS)
同比增长率（右坐标）Growth rate (YOY) (RHS)

金融机构法定人民币存款准备金率

Official RMB reserve requirement ratios of financial institutions

单位：%
Unit: %

日期 Date	中资全国性大型银行^① Chinese-funded large banks operating nationwide[1]	中型银行^② Medium-sized banks[2]	小型银行^③ Small banks[3]
2003.09.21	7.0	7.0	6.0
2004.04.25	7.5	7.5	6.0
2006.07.05	8.0	8.0	6.0
2006.08.15	8.5	8.5	6.0
2006.11.15	9.0	9.0	6.5
2007.01.15	9.5	9.5	7.0
2007.02.25	10.0	10.0	7.5
2007.04.16	10.5	10.5	8.0
2007.05.15	11.0	11.0	8.5
2007.06.05	11.5	11.5	9.0
2007.08.15	12.0	12.0	9.5
2007.09.25	12.5	12.5	10.0
2007.10.25	13.0	13.0	10.5
2007.11.26	13.5	13.5	11.0
2007.12.25	14.5	14.5	12.0
2008.01.25	15.0	15.0	12.5
2008.03.25	15.5	15.5	13.0
2008.04.25	16.0	16.0	13.5
2008.05.20	16.5	16.5	14.0
2008.06.15	17.0	17.0	14.5
2008.06.25	17.5	17.5	15.0
2008.09.25	17.5	16.5	14.0
2008.10.15	17.0	16.0	13.5
2008.12.05	16.0	14.0	11.5
2008.12.25	15.5	13.5	11.0
2010.01.18	16.0	14.0	11.0
2010.02.25	16.5	14.5	11.0
2010.05.10	17.0	15.0	11.0
2010.11.16	17.5	15.5	11.5
2010.11.29	18.0	16.0	12.0
2010.12.20	18.5	16.5	12.5
2011.01.20	19.0	17.0	13.0
2011.02.24	19.5	17.5	13.5
2011.03.25	20.0	18.0	14.0
2011.04.21	20.5	18.5	14.5
2011.05.18	21.0	19.0	15.0
2011.06.20	21.5	19.5	15.5
2011.12.05	21.0	19.0	15.0
2012.02.24	20.5	18.5	14.5
2012.05.18	20.0	18.0	14.0
2015.02.05	19.5	17.5	13.5
2015.04.20	18.5	16.5	11.5
2015.09.06	18.0	16.0	10.5
2015.10.24	17.5	15.5	9.5
2016.03.01	17.0	15.0	9.0
2018.04.25	16.0	14.0	9.0
2018.07.05	15.5	13.5	9.0
2018.10.15	14.5	12.5	9.0
2019.01.15	14.0	12.0	8.5
2019.01.25	13.5	11.5	8.0
2019.09.16	13.0	11.0	7.5
2020.01.06	12.5	10.5	7.0
2020.04.15	12.5	10.5	6.5
2020.05.15	12.5	10.5	6.0
2021.07.15	12.0	10.0	5.5
2021.12.15	10.0	8.0	5.0
2022.04.25	9.75	7.75	5.0
2022.12.05	9.5	7.5	5.0
2023.03.17	9.25	7.25	5.0
2023.09.15	9.0	7.0	5.0

注：①包括中国工商银行、中国农业银行、中国银行、中国建设银行、交通银行和中国邮政储蓄银行。
　　②包括股份制商业银行等。
　　③包括农村商业银行、农村合作银行、农村信用社和村镇银行。服务县域的农村商业银行在2019年5月降准后执行与农村信用社相同档次的存款准备金率。
　　④表中数据为基准档存款准备金率。

Notes: 1. Including Industrial and Commercial Bank of China, Agricultural Bank of China, Bank of China, China Construction Bank, Bank of Communications, Postal Savings Bank of China.
　　2. Including joint-stock commercial banks, etc.
　　3. Including rural commercial banks, rural cooperative banks, rural credit cooperatives and township and village banks. Rural commercial banks serving counties implemented the same level of deposit reserve ratio as rural credit cooperatives after the RRR reduction in May 2019.
　　4. Statistics in the table are baseline required reserve ratio.

中国人民银行资产负债表
Balance sheet of the PBOC

单位：亿元
Unit: RMB 100 million

年/月 Year/ Month	总资产 Total Assets	国外资产 Foreign Assets	对政府债权 Claims on government	对其他存款性公司债权 Claims on other depository corporations	对其他金融性公司债权 Claims on other financial corporations	对非金融性公司债权 Claims on non-financial corporations	其他资产 Other assets	总负债 Total liabilities	储备货币（基础货币） Reserve money	货币发行 Currency issue	金融性公司存款 Deposits of financial corporations	非金融机构存款 Deposits of non-financial corporations	不计入储备货币的金融性公司存款 Deposits of financial corporations excluded from reserve money	发行债券 Bond issue	国外负债 Foreign liabilities	政府存款 Deposits of government	自有资金 Own capital	其他负债 Other liabilities
2021.12	395 702	225 103	15 241	128 645	4 125		22 588	395 702	329 487	96 165	212 393	20 930	6 053	950	998	42 932	220	15 062
2022.01	403 125	225 696	15 241	134 700	4 112		23 376	403 125	331 197	111 877	194 280	25 041	6 041	950	1 036	49 781	220	13 900
2022.02	406 229	225 836	15 241	137 638	4 114		23 399	406 229	328 649	104 182	204 313	20 153	6 918	950	1 634	54 659	220	13 199
2022.03	398 726	226 202	15 241	129 349	4 118		23 816	398 726	335 458	100 738	215 232	19 489	7 090	950	1 188	42 003	220	11 817
2022.04	389 336	226 268	15 241	120 160	4 119		23 548	389 336	326 823	100 857	206 134	19 832	7 321	950	1 187	43 330	220	9 505
2022.05	385 320	225 478	15 241	119 481	1 771		23 350	385 320	325 085	100 710	204 606	19 769	6 447	950	1 294	46 414	220	4 911
2022.06	392 555	225 366	15 241	126 805	1 744		23 399	392 555	334 252	101 229	212 469	20 554	6 441	950	1 313	45 748	220	3 631
2022.07	385 627	225 615	15 241	119 635	1 743		23 394	385 627	324 197	101 513	202 093	20 591	6 026	950	1 554	50 123	220	2 557
2022.08	384 642	225 576	15 241	117 690	1 746		24 390	384 642	325 624	102 296	202 149	21 180	6 274	950	1 538	47 048	220	2 989
2022.09	397 402	224 440	15 241	128 811	1 755		27 156	397 402	341 832	104 051	216 254	21 527	5 316	950	1 466	43 738	220	3 881
2022.10	398 871	224 737	15 241	129 060	1 569		28 265	398 871	332 954	103 576	208 543	20 835	4 964	950	1 686	53 510	220	4 588
2022.11	401 528	225 813	15 241	129 031	1 556		29 887	401 528	334 806	104 836	208 722	21 248	5 164	950	1 718	52 363	220	6 307
2022.12	416 784	226 907	15 241	143 132	1 557		29 947	416 784	360 956	110 013	227 877	23 067	5 208	950	1 574	41 273	220	6 602
2023.01	422 065	228 514	15 241	148 167	1 549		28 595	422 065	358 911	122 673	209 148	27 089	5 229	950	1 925	47 737	220	7 094
2023.02	417 679	229 062	15 241	143 390	1 551		28 435	417 679	350 384	113 860	213 457	23 067	5 963	950	1 572	51 300	220	7 291
2023.03	421 007	230 941	15 241	146 628	1 565		26 632	421 007	364 072	110 937	230 383	22 752	6 105	950	1 653	41 318	220	6 691
2023.04	412 654	231 338	15 241	137 902	1 563		26 610	412 654	351 669	110 903	217 623	23 143	6 493	1 000	1 504	44 985	220	6 784
2023.05	406 421	231 469	15 241	131 712	1 566		26 434	406 421	344 207	109 771	211 438	22 997	6 409	950	1 944	46 017	220	6 675
2023.06	418 063	231 574	15 241	143 450	1 559		26 239	418 063	365 235	110 311	231 389	23 535	6 781	950	1 458	36 874	220	6 544
2023.07	408 092	231 737	15 241	135 784	1 363		23 968	408 092	347 844	111 061	213 841	22 942	6 372	950	1 487	45 155	220	6 064
2023.08	416 840	231 576	15 241	146 836	1 360		21 828	416 840	353 555	111 438	218 103	24 014	6 917	1 050	1 855	44 706	220	8 537
2023.09	427 355	230 939	15 241	158 157	1 341		21 677	427 355	363 921	114 478	224 685	24 758	5 771	1 150	3 540	43 979	220	8 774
2023.10	433 260	232 046	15 241	163 238	1 331		21 404	433 260	350 659	113 544	213 552	23 563	6 368	1 250	4 459	60 560	220	9 844
2023.11	440 655	232 797	15 241	169 885	1 335		21 397	440 655	363 160	115 073	224 099	23 988	5 733	1 250	4 403	55 036	220	10 853
2023.12	456 944	233 549	15 241	185 561	1 311		21 283	456 944	389 037	118 661	245 687	24 689	6 038	1 250	3 062	46 292	220	11 045

主要经济体央行资产负债表规模
Balance sheet size of major central banks

折合亿美元
Equivalent USD 100 million

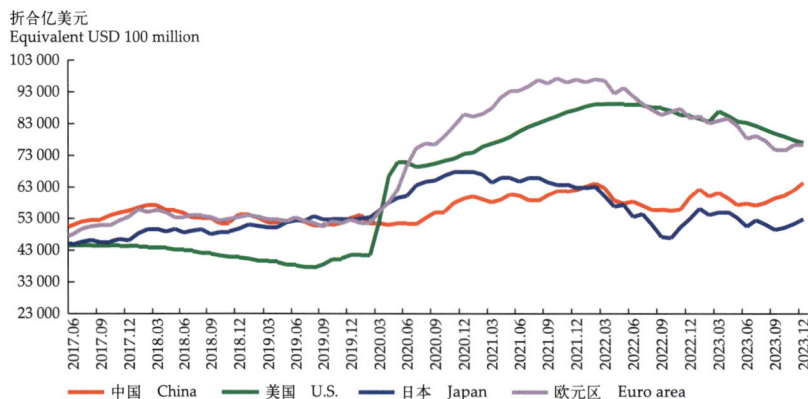

（数据来源：各经济体中央银行官方统计网站、Wind）
(Source: Official statistical websites of the major central banks, Wind)

2.2 货币供应量（Money supply）

货币供应量构成
Composition of money supply

年 / 月 Year/Month	广义货币 (亿元) Money & quasi-money (M2) (RMB 100 million)	M2 同比 增长率 (%) Growth rate of M2 (YOY)(%)	货币 (亿元) Money (M1) (RMB 100 million)	M1 同比 增长率 (%) Growth rate of M1 (YOY)(%)	流通中现金 (亿元) Currency in circulation (M0) (RMB 100 million)	M0 同比增 长率 (%) Growth rate of M0 (YOY)(%)	单位活期存款 (亿元) Corporate demand deposits (RMB 100 million)	准货币 (亿元) Quasi-money (RMB 100 million)	单位定期存款 (亿元) Corporate time deposits (RMB 100 million)	个人存款 (亿元) Personal deposits (RMB 100 million)	其他存款 (亿元) Other deposits (RMB 100 million)
2021.12	2 382 900	9.0	647 443	3.5	90 825	7.7	556 618	1 735 456	412 952	1 032 441	290 063
2022.01	2 431 023	9.8	613 859	−1.9	106 189	18.5	507 670	1 817 163	437 385	1 086 711	293 068
2022.02	2 441 489	9.2	621 612	4.7	97 228	5.8	524 384	1 819 877	432 729	1 083 800	303 348
2022.03	2 497 688	9.7	645 064	4.7	95 142	9.9	549 922	1 852 625	440 627	1 110 997	301 000
2022.04	2 499 711	10.5	636 139	5.1	95 626	11.4	540 513	1 863 572	449 669	1 103 942	309 961
2022.05	2 527 026	11.1	645 108	4.6	95 547	13.5	549 561	1 881 919	454 597	1 111 383	315 939
2022.06	2 581 451	11.4	674 375	5.8	96 011	13.8	578 364	1 907 076	457 184	1 136 280	313 612
2022.07	2 578 079	12.0	661 832	6.7	96 509	13.9	565 323	1 916 246	459 427	1 132 832	323 987
2022.08	2 595 068	12.2	664 605	6.1	97 231	14.3	567 374	1 930 463	467 432	1 141 166	321 865
2022.09	2 626 601	12.1	664 535	6.4	98 672	13.6	565 863	1 962 066	477 618	1 165 283	319 165
2022.10	2 612 915	11.8	662 141	5.8	98 417	14.4	563 724	1 950 774	469 458	1 160 137	321 178
2022.11	2 647 008	12.4	667 043	4.6	99 740	14.1	567 302	1 979 966	468 412	1 182 823	328 731
2022.12	2 664 321	11.8	671 675	3.7	104 706	15.3	566 969	1 992 646	462 002	1 211 693	318 952
2023.01	2 738 072	12.6	655 214	6.7	114 601	7.9	540 613	2 082 858	473 131	1 273 792	335 935
2023.02	2 755 249	12.9	657 939	5.8	107 603	10.6	550 336	2 097 310	488 057	1 281 773	327 481
2023.03	2 814 566	12.7	678 060	5.1	105 591	11.0	572 468	2 136 507	498 891	1 311 044	326 571
2023.04	2 808 469	12.4	669 762	5.3	105 904	10.7	563 857	2 138 708	507 413	1 298 936	332 359
2023.05	2 820 505	11.6	675 253	4.7	104 757	9.6	570 496	2 145 252	503 708	1 304 289	337 255
2023.06	2 873 024	11.3	695 595	3.1	105 419	9.8	590 176	2 177 428	507 503	1 331 169	338 757
2023.07	2 854 032	10.7	677 219	2.3	106 130	9.9	571 089	2 176 813	511 062	1 322 953	342 797
2023.08	2 869 343	10.6	679 588	2.2	106 515	9.5	573 073	2 189 755	519 227	1 330 847	339 681
2023.09	2 896 659	10.3	678 444	2.1	109 253	10.7	569 190	2 218 215	526 044	1 356 228	335 943
2023.10	2 882 276	10.3	674 696	1.9	108 565	10.2	566 131	2 207 580	523 057	1 349 790	334 733
2023.11	2 912 014	10.0	675 903	1.3	110 225	10.4	565 678	2 236 111	526 663	1 358 833	350 615
2023.12	2 922 713	9.7	680 543	1.3	113 445	8.3	567 098	2 242 171	520 996	1 378 567	342 608

2023年12月末货币供应量构成
Composition of money supply at the end of December, 2023

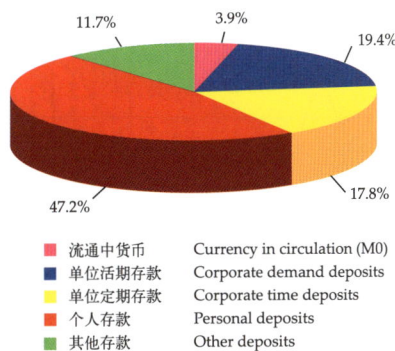

11.7%　3.9%　19.4%　17.8%　47.2%

	流通中货币	Currency in circulation (M0)
	单位活期存款	Corporate demand deposits
	单位定期存款	Corporate time deposits
	个人存款	Personal deposits
	其他存款	Other deposits

年度M0、M1、M2及其变化趋势
Annual M0, M1, and M2 and their changes

年 Year	M0 （万亿元， RMB 1 trillion）	M1 （万亿元， RMB 1 trillion）	M2 （万亿元， RMB 1 trillion）	M0 同比 增长率 (%) Growth rate of M0 (YOY)(%)	M1 同比 增长率 (%) Growth rate of M1 (YOY) (%)	M2 同比 增长率 (%) Growth rate of M2 (YOY) (%)
2000	1.5	5.3	13.8	8.9	16.0	14.0
2001	1.6	6.0	15.8	7.1	12.7	14.4
2002	1.7	7.1	18.5	10.1	16.8	16.8
2003	2.0	8.4	22.1	14.3	18.7	19.6
2004	2.1	9.6	25.3	8.7	13.6	14.6
2005	2.4	10.7	29.9	11.9	11.8	17.6
2006	2.7	12.6	34.6	12.7	17.5	16.9
2007	3.0	15.3	40.3	12.2	21.0	16.7
2008	3.4	16.6	47.5	12.7	9.1	17.8
2009	3.8	22.1	61.0	11.8	33.2	28.5
2010	4.5	26.7	72.6	16.7	21.2	19.7
2011	5.1	29.0	85.2	13.8	7.9	13.6
2012	5.5	30.9	97.4	7.7	6.5	13.8
2013	5.9	33.7	110.7	7.2	9.3	13.6
2014	6.0	34.8	122.8	2.9	3.2	12.2
2015	6.3	40.1	139.2	4.9	15.2	13.3
2016	6.8	48.7	155.0	8.1	21.4	11.3
2017	7.1	54.4	169.0	3.4	11.8	8.1
2018	7.3	55.2	182.7	3.6	1.5	8.1
2019	7.7	57.6	198.6	5.4	4.4	8.7
2020	8.4	62.6	218.7	9.2	8.6	10.1
2021	9.1	64.7	238.3	7.7	3.5	9.0
2022	10.5	67.2	266.4	15.3	3.7	11.8
2023	11.3	68.1	292.3	8.3	1.3	9.7

月度M0、M1、M2及其变化趋势
Monthly M0, M1, and M2 and their changes

年/月 Year/ Month	M0 （万亿元， RMB 1 trillion）	M1 （万亿元， RMB 1 trillion）	M2 （万亿元， RMB 1 trillion）	M0 同比 增长率 (%) Growth rate of M0 (YOY)(%)	M1 同比 增长率 (%) Growth rate of M1 (YOY)(%)	M2 同比 增长率 (%) Growth rate of M2 (YOY)(%)
2021.12	9.1	64.7	238.3	7.7	3.5	9.0
2022.01	10.6	61.4	243.1	18.5	−1.9	9.8
2022.02	9.7	62.2	244.1	5.8	4.7	9.2
2022.03	9.5	64.5	249.8	9.9	4.7	9.7
2022.04	9.6	63.6	250.0	11.4	5.1	10.5
2022.05	9.6	64.5	252.7	13.5	4.6	11.1
2022.06	9.6	67.4	258.1	13.8	5.8	11.4
2022.07	9.7	66.2	257.8	13.9	6.7	12.0
2022.08	9.7	66.5	259.5	14.3	6.1	12.2
2022.09	9.9	66.5	262.7	13.6	6.4	12.1
2022.10	9.8	66.2	261.3	14.4	5.8	11.8
2022.11	10.0	66.7	264.7	14.1	4.6	12.4
2022.12	10.5	67.2	266.4	15.3	3.7	11.8
2023.01	11.5	65.5	273.8	7.9	6.7	12.6
2023.02	10.8	65.8	275.5	10.6	5.8	12.9
2023.03	10.6	67.8	281.5	11.0	5.1	12.7
2023.04	10.6	67.0	280.8	10.7	5.3	12.4
2023.05	10.5	67.5	282.1	9.6	4.7	11.6
2023.06	10.5	69.6	287.3	9.8	3.1	11.3
2023.07	10.6	67.7	285.4	9.9	2.3	10.7
2023.08	10.7	68.0	286.9	9.5	2.2	10.6
2023.09	10.9	67.8	289.7	10.7	2.1	10.3
2023.10	10.9	67.5	288.2	10.2	1.9	10.3
2023.11	11.0	67.6	291.2	10.4	1.3	10.0
2023.12	11.3	68.1	292.3	8.3	1.3	9.7

年度M0、M1、M2及其变化趋势
Annual M0, M1, and M2 and their changes

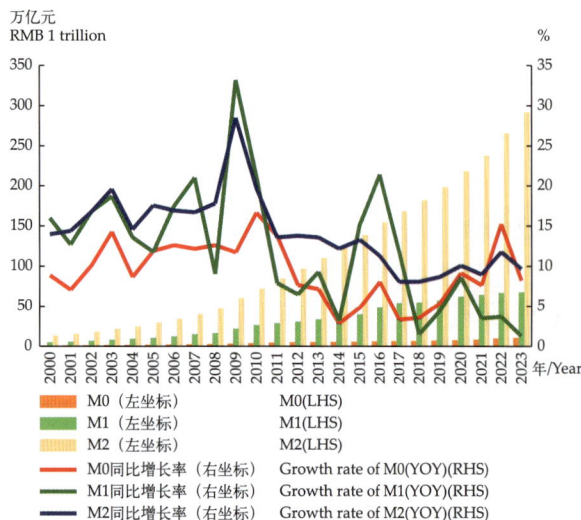

月度M0、M1、M2及其变化趋势
Monthly M0, M1, and M2 and their changes

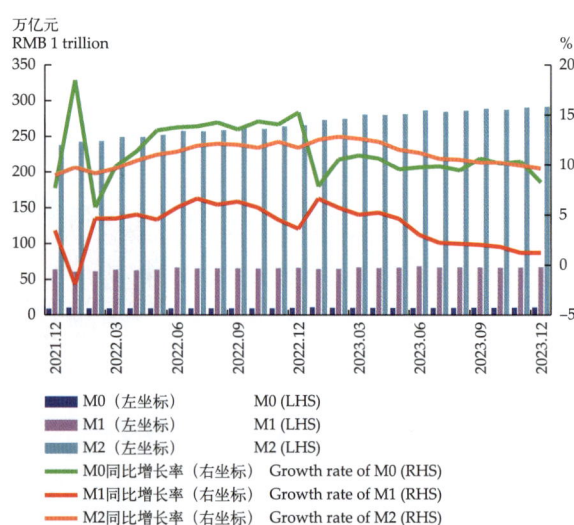

存款性公司概览
Depository corporations survey

单位：万亿元
Unit: RMB 1 trillion

年/月 Year/ Month	国外净资产 Net foreign assets	国内信贷 Domestic credits	对政府债权 （净） Claims on government (net)	对非金融部门债权 Claims on non- financial sectors	对其他金融部门债权 Claims on other financial sectors	货币和准货币 Money & quasi money	货币 Money	准货币 Quasi money	不纳入广义货币的存款 Deposits excluded from broad money	债券 Bonds	实收资本 Paid-in capital	其他（净） Other items (net)
2020.12	26.95	244.00	34.02	185.35	24.63	218.68	62.56	156.12	5.35	31.22	7.36	8.35
2021.01	27.07	245.83	32.77	189.21	23.85	221.30	62.56	158.75	5.64	31.30	7.36	7.30
2021.02	27.32	248.53	33.95	190.49	24.08	223.60	59.35	164.25	5.77	31.41	7.36	7.71
2021.03	27.58	253.15	34.77	193.23	25.15	227.65	61.61	166.04	5.82	32.07	7.38	7.80
2021.04	27.74	252.30	34.25	194.25	23.80	226.21	60.54	165.67	6.02	32.20	7.48	8.13
2021.05	27.79	254.05	34.42	195.42	24.22	227.55	61.68	165.87	6.00	32.51	7.53	8.24
2021.06	27.99	257.61	35.05	197.36	25.21	231.78	63.75	168.03	6.11	32.64	7.68	7.40
2021.07	28.02	256.87	34.67	197.97	24.23	230.22	62.04	168.18	5.97	33.07	7.70	7.94
2021.08	28.36	258.90	35.27	199.01	24.62	231.23	62.67	168.56	5.99	33.57	7.79	8.69
2021.09	28.48	261.91	36.43	200.91	24.57	234.28	62.46	171.82	5.97	33.86	7.85	8.43
2021.10	28.53	261.90	35.96	201.64	24.30	233.62	62.61	171.01	6.04	34.21	7.91	8.64
2021.11	28.39	264.36	36.75	202.77	24.83	235.60	63.75	171.85	6.07	34.86	8.04	8.17
2021.12	28.30	267.34	38.52	203.72	25.10	238.29	64.74	173.55	5.94	35.06	8.14	8.22
2022.01	28.54	271.77	38.49	208.05	25.23	243.10	61.39	181.72	6.14	35.08	8.19	7.81
2022.02	28.67	272.38	38.35	208.96	25.07	244.15	62.16	181.99	6.26	35.71	8.24	6.71
2022.03	28.79	278.35	40.21	212.23	25.91	249.77	64.51	185.26	6.23	36.11	8.24	6.79
2022.04	28.95	278.56	40.44	212.70	25.41	249.97	63.61	186.36	6.19	35.99	8.31	7.05
2022.05	29.03	281.12	40.99	214.23	25.90	252.70	64.51	188.19	6.16	36.21	8.33	6.75
2022.06	29.02	285.83	42.68	217.11	26.04	258.15	67.44	190.71	6.20	36.88	8.35	5.27
2022.07	28.79	285.74	42.39	217.26	26.09	257.81	66.18	191.62	6.05	36.78	8.39	5.51
2022.08	28.81	287.69	42.75	218.89	26.05	259.51	66.46	193.05	5.90	37.09	8.44	5.56
2022.09	28.82	291.55	43.50	222.08	25.97	262.66	66.45	196.21	5.90	37.79	8.43	5.60
2022.10	28.80	290.69	42.93	222.72	25.04	261.29	66.21	195.08	5.83	38.00	8.43	5.93
2022.11	28.81	292.53	43.67	223.44	25.42	264.70	66.70	198.00	5.83	37.88	8.46	4.48
2022.12	28.91	294.95	44.99	224.33	25.63	266.43	67.17	199.26	5.61	38.25	8.47	5.09
2023.01	29.05	300.18	45.00	229.22	25.96	273.81	65.52	208.29	5.65	38.05	5.54	6.18
2023.02	29.10	302.41	45.39	231.15	25.87	275.52	65.79	209.73	5.77	38.53	5.55	6.14
2023.03	29.32	308.89	46.77	234.97	27.14	281.46	67.81	213.65	5.88	39.03	5.59	6.24
2023.04	29.21	309.08	46.81	235.27	27.00	280.85	66.98	213.87	5.73	39.45	5.60	6.66
2023.05	29.22	311.28	47.22	236.39	27.67	282.05	67.53	214.53	5.66	39.90	5.61	7.28
2023.06	29.48	316.66	48.51	239.75	28.39	287.30	69.56	217.74	5.65	40.49	5.63	7.07
2023.07	29.48	315.19	48.15	239.24	27.80	285.40	67.72	217.68	5.48	41.35	5.63	6.81
2023.08	29.43	317.38	49.00	240.63	27.75	286.93	67.96	218.98	5.31	41.23	5.62	7.72
2023.09	29.03	320.66	49.93	243.10	27.63	289.67	67.84	221.82	5.19	41.35	5.64	7.84
2023.10	28.91	319.63	49.62	243.53	26.48	288.23	67.47	220.76	52206.09	41.50	5.68	7.90
2023.11	28.92	323.04	50.80	244.46	27.79	291.20	67.59	223.61	52163.11	41.84	5.69	8.01
2023.12	29.29	325.79	52.29	245.40	28.10	292.27	68.05	224.22	52672.94	42.16	5.74	9.65

2.3　存贷款（Deposits and loans）

金融机构人民币各项存贷款余额及其增长趋势
Outstanding amounts of total deposits & loans and their growth in financial institutions

年／月 Year/Month	各项存款（万亿元） Total deposits (RMB 1 trillion)	各项贷款（万亿元） Total loans (RMB 1 trillion)	各项存款同比增长率（%） Growth rate of deposits (YOY) (%)	各项贷款同比增长率（%） Growth rate of loans (YOY) (%)
2021.12	232.3	192.7	9.3	11.6
2022.01	236.1	196.7	9.2	11.5
2022.02	238.6	197.9	9.8	11.4
2022.03	243.1	201.0	10.0	11.4
2022.04	243.2	201.7	10.4	10.9
2022.05	246.2	203.5	10.5	11.0
2022.06	251.1	206.4	10.8	11.2
2022.07	251.1	207.0	11.4	11.0
2022.08	252.4	208.3	11.3	10.9
2022.09	255.0	210.8	11.3	11.2
2022.10	254.8	211.4	10.8	11.1
2022.11	257.8	212.6	11.6	11.0
2022.12	258.5	214.0	11.3	11.1
2023.01	265.4	219.7	12.4	11.3
2023.02	268.2	221.6	12.4	11.6
2023.03	273.9	225.4	12.7	11.8
2023.04	273.4	226.2	12.4	11.8
2023.05	274.9	227.5	11.6	11.4
2023.06	278.6	230.6	11.0	11.3
2023.07	277.5	230.9	10.5	11.1
2023.08	278.8	232.3	10.5	11.1
2023.09	281.0	234.6	10.2	10.9
2023.10	281.6	235.3	10.5	10.9
2023.11	284.2	236.4	10.2	10.8
2023.12	284.3	237.6	10.0	10.6

金融机构人民币各项存贷款余额及其增长趋势
Outstanding amounts of total deposits & loans and their growth in financial institutions

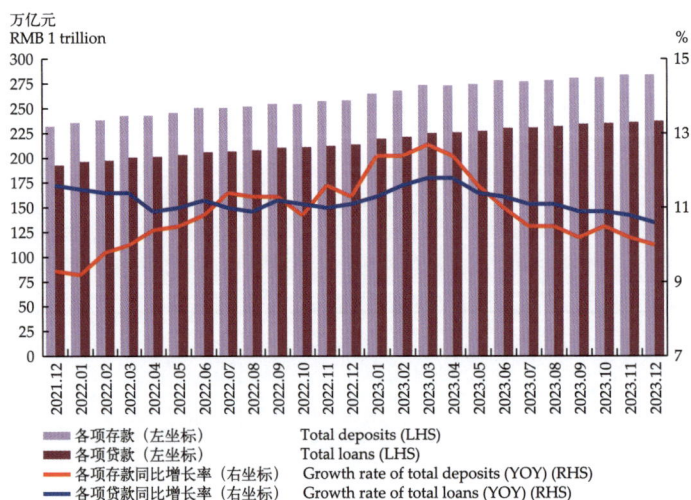

住户存款和非金融企业存款余额
Outstanding amounts of household deposits and non-financial corporate deposits

单位：亿元
Unit: RMB 100 million

年 / 月 Year/Month	住户存款 Deposits of households	活期及临时性存款 Demand & temporary deposits	定期及保证性存款 Time & marginal deposits	非金融企业存款 Deposits of non-financial enterprises	活期及临时性存款 Demand & temporary deposits	定期及保证性存款 Time & marginal deposits
2021.12	1 025 012	342 904	682 108	696 695	255 117	441 578
2022.01	1 079 150	366 449	712 701	681 644	229 654	451 991
2022.02	1 076 227	345 201	731 026	683 033	235 551	447 482
2022.03	1 103 202	351 188	752 014	709 618	249 725	459 892
2022.04	1 096 170	341 103	755 068	708 407	242 058	466 349
2022.05	1 103 564	342 458	761 105	719 456	245 635	473 821
2022.06	1 128 280	355 958	772 322	748 704	261 328	487 376
2022.07	1 124 900	349 029	775 871	738 286	251 815	486 471
2022.08	1 133 186	350 840	782 346	747 837	255 422	492 414
2022.09	1 157 130	361 207	795 923	755 441	254 772	500 669
2022.10	1 152 027	354 605	797 422	743 785	251 698	492 086
2022.11	1 174 574	365 579	808 996	745 760	252 144	493 617
2022.12	1 203 387	383 900	819 487	746 574	254 651	491 923
2023.01	1 265 275	396 349	868 926	738 366	240 331	498 036
2023.02	1 273 201	379 554	893 647	751 236	245 104	506 132
2023.03	1 302 280	386 220	916 060	777 323	257 099	520 224
2023.04	1 290 294	371 355	918 938	775 915	250 140	525 775
2023.05	1 295 658	370 076	925 582	774 522	247 729	526 793
2023.06	1 322 387	384 261	938 125	795 171	259 403	535 768
2023.07	1 314 294	375 019	939 274	779 849	248 648	531 201
2023.08	1 322 171	373 901	948 270	788 739	248 978	539 760
2023.09	1 347 449	383 736	963 714	790 706	245 137	545 569
2023.10	1 341 080	377 405	963 675	782 054	244 100	537 953
2023.11	1 350 169	380 040	970 129	784 541	244 853	539 688
2023.12	1 369 895	390 266	979 629	787 756	248 676	539 080

2023年12月末人民币存款余额
Outstanding amounts of RMB deposits at the end of December, 2023

单位：亿元
Unit: RMB 100 million

项目 Item	余额 Outstanding amount
各项存款 **Total deposits**	**2 842 623**
境内存款 Domestic deposits	2 824 093
住户存款 Deposits of households	1 369 895
非金融企业存款 Deposits of non-financial enterprises	787 756
机关团体存款 Deposits of government departments & organizations	353 261
财政性存款 Fiscal deposits	57 937
非银行业金融机构存款 Deposits of non-banking financial institutions	255 244
境外存款 Overseas deposits	18 531

2023年12月末人民币存款余额
Outstanding amounts of RMB deposits at the end of December, 2023

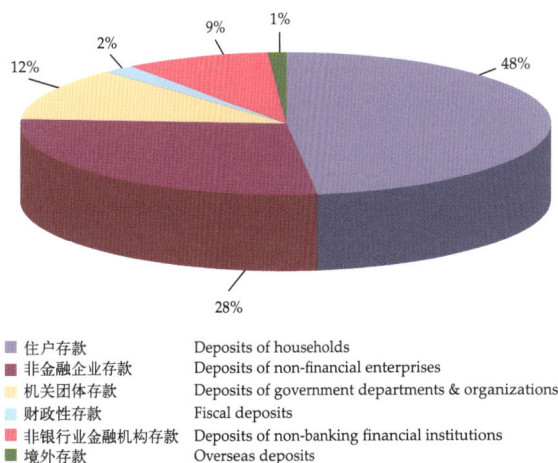

- 住户存款　Deposits of households — 48%
- 非金融企业存款　Deposits of non-financial enterprises — 28%
- 机关团体存款　Deposits of government departments & organizations — 12%
- 财政性存款　Fiscal deposits — 2%
- 非银行业金融机构存款　Deposits of non-banking financial institutions — 9%
- 境外存款　Overseas deposits — 1%

2023年12月末人民币贷款余额
RMB loans issued by the end of December 2023 by sectors

单位：亿元
Unit: RMB 100 million

项目 Item	余额 Outstanding amounts	较上年末增加 Increase from the end of last year
各项贷款 **Total loans**	2 375 905	236 053
境内贷款 Domestic loans	2 362 901	232 841
住户贷款 Loans to households	800 921	51 598
短期贷款 Short-term loans	207 034	23 052
中长期贷款 Mid & long-term loans	593 887	28 546
企（事）业单位贷款 Loans to non-financial enterprises and government departments & organizations	1 554 232	179 024
短期贷款 Short-term loans	398 388	38 602
中长期贷款 Mid & long-term loans	991 853	136 169
票据融资 Paper financing	131 500	3 410
融资租赁 Financial leases	30 824	1 349
各项垫款 Total advances	1 666	−506
非银行业金融机构贷款 Loans to non-banking financial institutions	7 748	2 219
境外贷款 Overseas loans	13 005	3 212

绿色贷款余额
Outstanding amount of green loans

单位：亿元
Unit: RMB 100 million

年 / 季度 Year/Quarter	绿色贷款余额 Outstanding amount of green loans
2019Q4	102 200
2020Q1	104 600
2020Q2	110 100
2020Q3	115 500
2020Q4	119 500
2021Q1	130 300
2021Q2	139 200
2021Q3	147 800
2021Q4	159 000
2022Q1	180 700
2022Q2	195 500
2022Q3	209 000
2022Q4	220 300
2023Q1	249 900
2023Q2	270 500
2023Q3	285 800
2023Q4	300 800

当月新增住户贷款
New loans to households by month

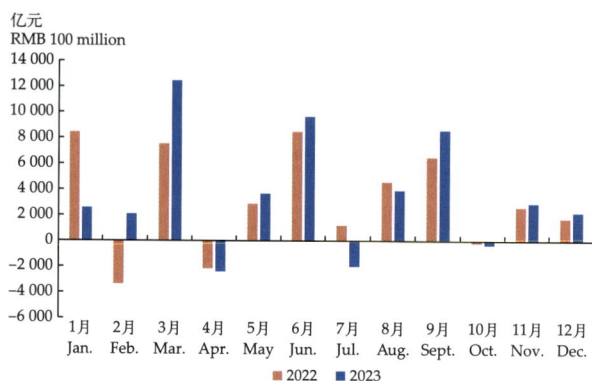

当月新增非金融企业及机关团体贷款
New loans to non-financial institutions and other sectors by month

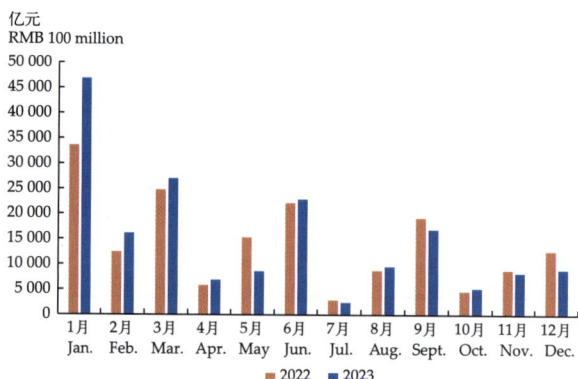

绿色贷款余额
Outstanding amount of green loans

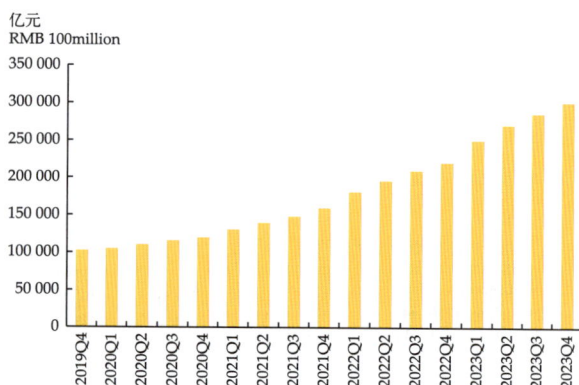

2.4 社会融资规模（Aggregate financing to the real economy, AFRE）

社会融资规模增量统计表
Aggregate financing to the real economy (flow)

单位：亿元
Unit: RMB 100 million

年/月 Year/Month	社会融资规模增量 AFRE (flow)	其中 Of which									
		人民币贷款 RMB loans	外币贷款（折合人民币）Foreign currency-denominated loans (RMB equivalent)	委托贷款 Entrusted loans	信托贷款 Trust loans	未贴现银行承兑汇票 Undiscounted bankers' acceptances	企业债券 Net financing of corporate bonds	政府债券 Government bonds	非金融企业境内股票融资 Equity financing on the domestic stock market by non-financial enterprises	存款类金融机构资产支持证券 Asset-backed securities of depository financial institutions	贷款核销 Loans written off
2023.01	59 954	49 314	−131	584	−62	2 963	1 638	4 140	964	−333	312
2023.02	31 605	18 184	310	−77	66	−69	3 662	8 138	571	−279	367
2023.03	53 860	39 487	427	175	−45	1 792	3 357	6 015	614	−150	1 235
2023.04	12 240	4 431	−319	83	119	−1 345	2 940	4 548	993	−376	448
2023.05	15 540	12 219	−338	35	303	−1 795	−2 154	5 571	753	−349	516
2023.06	42 265	32 413	−191	−56	−154	−691	2 246	5 371	700	−26	1 776
2023.07	5 366	364	−339	8	230	−1 963	1 290	4 109	786	−296	402
2023.08	31 279	13 412	−201	97	−221	1 129	2 788	11 759	1 036	−135	596
2023.09	41 326	25 369	−583	208	402	2 397	650	9 920	326	−172	1 799
2023.10	18 441	4 837	152	−429	393	−2 536	1 178	15 638	321	−2 530	427
2023.11	24 554	11 120	−357	−386	197	202	1 388	11 512	359	−1 355	742
2023.12	19 326	11 092	−635	−43	347	−1 865	−2 741	9 324	508	−278	2 347

注：1. 社会融资规模增量是指一定时期内实体经济从金融体系获得的资金额。数据来源于中国人民银行、中国银行保险监督管理委员会、中国证券监督管理委员会、中央国债登记结算有限责任公司和银行间市场交易商协会等部门。

2. 2019年12月起，人民银行进一步完善社会融资规模统计，将"国债"和"地方政府一般债券"纳入社会融资规模统计，与原有"地方政府专项债券"合并为"政府债券"指标。指标数值为托管机构的托管面值。

3. 2019年9月起，人民银行完善"社会融资规模"中的"企业债券"统计，将"交易所企业资产支持证券"纳入"企业债券"指标。

4. 2018年9月起，人民银行将"地方政府专项债券"纳入社会融资规模统计。

5. 2018年7月起，人民银行完善社会融资规模统计方法，将"存款类金融机构资产支持证券"和"贷款核销"纳入社会融资规模统计，在"其他融资"项下单独列示。

Notes: 1. AFRE (flow) refers to the total volume of financing provided by the financial system to the real economy during a certain period of time. In the calculation of AFRE, data are from the PBC, CBIRC, CSRC, CCDC and NAFMII.

2. Since December 2019, the People's Bank of China made further efforts to improve the statistical method of AFRE. "Treasury Bonds" and "Local Government General Bonds" were newly introduced into AFRE and merged with "Local Government Special Bonds" into "Government Bonds", which is recorded at face value at depositories.

3. Since September 2019, the People's Bank of China improved the statistics of "Net Financing of Corporate Bonds" in AFRE, and incorporated "Asset-backed Securities of Non-Financial Enterprises" into "Net Financing of Corporate Bonds".

4. Since September 2018, the People's Bank of China incorporated "Local Government Special Bonds" into AFRE.

5. Since July 2018, the People's Bank of China improved the statistical method of AFRE, and incorporated "Asset-backed Securities of Depository Financial Institutions" and "Loans Written off" into AFRE, which is reflected as a sub-item of "Other Financing".

社会融资规模存量统计表
Aggregate financing to the real economy (stock)

单位：万亿元
Unit: RMB 1 trillion

项目 Item	2023.01		2023.02		2023.03		2023.04		2023.05		2023.06	
	存量 Stock	增速 (%) Growth rate (%)	存量 Stock	增速 (%) Growth rate (%)	存量 Stock	增速 (%) Growth rate (%)	存量 Stock	增速 (%) Growth rate (%)	存量 Stock	增速 (%) Growth rate (%)	存量 Stock	增速 (%) Growth rate (%)
社会融资规模存量 AFRE (stock)	350.9	9.4	354.0	9.9	359.0	10.0	360.0	10.0	361.4	9.5	365.5	9.0
人民币贷款 RMB loans	218.2	11.1	220.0	11.5	224.0	11.7	224.4	11.7	225.6	11.3	228.9	11.2
外币贷款（折合人民币） Foreign currency-denominated loans (RMB equivalent)	1.8	−21.6	1.9	−19.0	1.9	−19.3	1.9	−20.8	1.9	−20.1	1.9	−18.9
委托贷款 Entrusted loans	11.3	3.5	11.3	3.5	11.3	3.5	11.3	3.6	11.3	3.8	11.3	4.1
信托贷款 Trust loans	3.7	−12.6	3.8	−10.9	3.7	−10.4	3.8	−8.8	3.8	−6.7	3.8	−5.1
未贴现银行承兑汇票 Undiscounted bankers' acceptances	3.0	−14.9	3.0	−3.3	3.1	1.6	3.0	6.0	2.8	3.6	2.8	−2.8
企业债券 Net financing of corporate bonds	31.0	1.9	31.3	1.8	31.4	1.2	31.5	0.6	31.2	−0.1	31.3	−0.4
政府债券 Government bonds	60.6	12.9	61.4	13.9	62.0	13.5	62.5	13.5	63.0	12.4	63.6	10.1
非金融企业境内股票 Equity financing on the domestic stock market by non-financial enterprises	10.7	11.7	10.8	11.7	10.9	11.2	11.0	10.9	11.0	11.3	11.1	11.4
存款类金融机构资产支持证券 Asset-backed securities of depository financial institutions	2.0	−9.2	1.9	−10.3	1.9	−10.6	1.9	−11.4	1.8	−12.3	1.8	−12.3
贷款核销 Loans written off	7.5	16.6	7.6	16.7	7.7	15.7	7.8	15.5	7.8	15.4	8.0	14.9

项目 Item	2023.07		2023.08		2023.09		2023.10		2023.11		2023.12	
	存量 Stock	增速 (%) Growth rate (%)	存量 Stock	增速 (%) Growth rate (%)	存量 Stock	增速 (%) Growth rate (%)	存量 Stock	增速 (%) Growth rate (%)	存量 Stock	增速 (%) Growth rate (%)	存量 Stock	增速 (%) Growth rate (%)
社会融资规模存量 AFRE (stock)	365.8	8.9	368.6	9.0	372.5	9.0	374.2	9.3	376.4	9.4	378.1	9.5
人民币贷款 RMB loans	228.9	11.0	230.2	10.9	232.8	10.7	233.3	10.7	234.4	10.7	235.5	10.4
外币贷款（折合人民币） Foreign currency-denominated loans (RMB equivalent)	1.8	−17.8	1.8	−16.8	1.8	−19.3	1.8	−16.7	1.7	−16.7	1.7	−10.2
委托贷款 Entrusted loans	11.3	4.0	11.3	2.4	11.4	1.3	11.3	0.5	11.3	0.2	11.3	0.2
信托贷款 Trust loans	3.8	−3.6	3.8	−2.9	3.8	−1.4	3.9	−0.3	3.9	1.2	3.9	4.2
未贴现银行承兑汇票 Undiscounted bankers' acceptances	2.6	0.0	2.7	−8.2	2.9	−0.3	2.7	−1.8	2.7	−1.7	2.5	−6.7
企业债券 Net financing of corporate bonds	31.4	−0.4	31.5	−0.2	31.4	−0.3	31.4	−0.7	31.5	−0.4	31.1	0.3
政府债券 Government bonds	64.0	10.1	65.2	11.5	66.1	12.2	67.7	14.3	68.9	14.9	69.8	16.0
非金融企业境内股票 Equity financing on the domestic stock market by non-financial enterprises	11.2	10.6	11.3	10.2	11.3	9.4	11.3	8.9	11.4	8.4	11.4	7.5
存款类金融机构资产支持证券 Asset-backed securities of depository financial institutions	1.8	−12.2	1.8	−12.9	1.8	−12.9	1.5	−24.8	1.4	−30.7	1.4	−31.6
贷款核销 Loans written off	8.0	13.8	8.1	13.6	8.3	13.6	8.3	13.6	8.4	13.6	8.6	14.6

注：1. 社会融资规模存量是指一定时期末（月末、季末或年末）实体经济从金融体系获得的资金余额。数据来源于中国人民银行、中国银行保险监督管理委员会、中国证券监督管理委员会、中央国债登记结算有限责任公司和银行间市场交易商协会等部门。

2. 2019年12月起，人民银行进一步完善社会融资规模统计，将"国债"和"地方政府一般债券"纳入社会融资规模统计，与原有"地方政府专项债券"合并为"政府债券"指标。指标数值为托管机构的托管面值。

3. 2019年9月起，人民银行完善"社会融资规模"中的"企业债券"统计，将"交易所企业资产支持证券"纳入"企业债券"指标。

4. 2018年9月起，人民银行将"地方政府专项债券"纳入社会融资规模统计。

5. 2018年7月起，人民银行完善社会融资规模统计方法，将"存款类金融机构资产支持证券"和"贷款核销"纳入社会融资规模统计，在"其他融资"项下单独列示。

Notes: 1. AFRE(stock) refers to the outstanding of financing provided by the financial system to the real economy at the end of a period(monthly/quarterly/annual). In the calculation of AFRE, data are from the PBC, CBIRC, CSRC, CCDC and NAFMII.

2. Since December 2019, the People's Bank of China made further efforts to improve the statistical method of AFRE. "Treasury Bonds" and "Local Government General Bonds" were newly introduced into AFRE and merged with "Local Government Special Bonds" into "Government Bonds", which is recorded at face value at depositories.

3. Since September 2019, the People's Bank of China improved the statistics of "Net Financing of Corporate Bonds" in AFRE, and incorporated "Asset-backed Securities of Non-Financial Enterprises" into "Net Financing of Corporate Bonds".

4. Since September 2018, the People's Bank of China incorporated "Local Government Special Bonds" into AFRE.

5. Since July 2018, the People's Bank of China improved the statistical method of AFRE, and incorporated "Asset-backed Securities of Depository Financial Institutions" and "Loans Written off" into AFRE, which is reflected as a sub-item of "Other Financing".

2.5　宏观杠杆率（Macro leverage ratio）

中国、美国、欧元区、日本宏观杠杆率
Leverage ratio of China, the U.S., Euro area and Japan

单位：%
Unit: %

年／月 Year/Month	中国 China	美国 The U.S.	欧元区 Euro area	日本 Japan
2020.09	294.1	290.2	283.2	416.6
2020.12	294.1	293.5	286.0	420.9
2021.03	291.5	290.1	287.3	419.8
2021.06	288.7	285.3	279.6	415.3
2021.09	287.6	280.2	277	413.1
2021.12	285.0	279.6	272.5	414.2
2022.03	289.8	273.5	265.6	416.7
2022.06	294.0	265.6	256.9	417.4
2022.09	295.9	259.3	251.9	415.6
2022.12	297.4	257.9	245.3	413.0
2023.03	306.3	257.0	242.4	413.9
2023.06	308.4	255.4	239.6	410.1
2023.09	310.7	253.3	235.8	399.8

数据来源：国际清算银行。
Source: BIS.

中国分部门宏观杠杆率
Leverage ratio of different sectors in China

单位：%
Unit: %

年／月 Year/Month	居民 Resident	企业 Corporation	政府 Government
2019.12	65.6	152.2	38.6
2020.03	67.8	162	40.8
2020.06	70.0	165.2	42.7
2020.09	72.2	164.7	45.1
2020.12	73.1	161.7	45.9
2021.03	72.7	160.9	44.6
2021.06	72.6	158.3	44.9
2021.09	72.8	156.2	45.7
2021.12	72.4	152.8	46.8
2022.03	72.0	157	47.3
2022.06	72.1	159.3	49.6
2022.09	72.1	159.6	49.7
2022.12	72.3	160.1	50.6
2023.03	72.9	166.3	51.7
2023.06	72.9	166.8	52.1
2023.09	73.0	167.3	53.9
2023.12	72.3	166.3	56.1

数据来源：中国人民银行。
Source: PBOC.

中国、美国、欧元区、日本宏观杠杆率
Leverage ratio of China, the U.S., Euro area and Japan

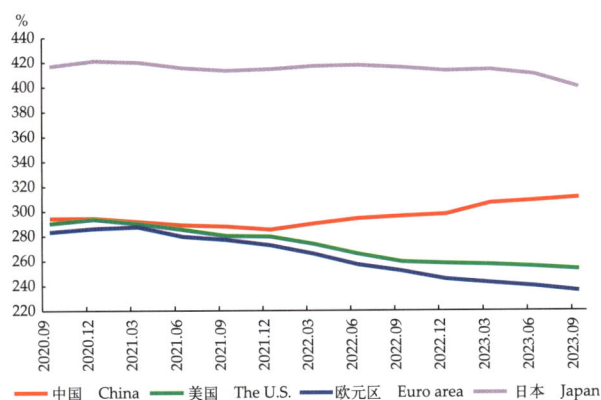

（数据来源：国际清算银行）
(Source: BIS)

中国分部门宏观杠杆率
Leverage ratio of different sectors in China

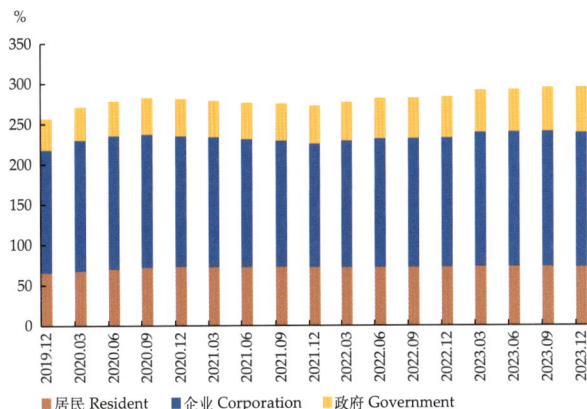

（数据来源：中国人民银行）
(Source: PBOC)

三、利率与汇率（Interest rates and exchange rates）

3.1　中央银行政策利率体系（Central bank's policy rates）

中央银行政策利率体系

Central bank policy rate system

单位：%
Unit: %

年 / 月 Year/Month	公开市场 7 天期逆回购利率 OMO 7-day repo rate	中期借贷便利 1 年期利率 1-year MLF rate
2022.01	2.16	2.85
2022.02	2.10	2.85
2022.03	2.10	2.85
2022.04	2.10	2.85
2022.05	2.10	2.85
2022.06	2.10	2.85
2022.07	2.10	2.85
2022.08	2.00	2.75
2022.09	2.00	2.75
2022.10	2.00	2.75
2022.11	2.00	2.75
2022.12	2.00	2.75
2023.01	2.00	2.75
2023.02	2.00	2.75
2023.03	2.00	2.75
2023.04	2.00	2.75
2023.05	2.00	2.75
2023.06	1.90	2.65
2023.07	1.90	2.65
2023.08	1.80	2.50
2023.09	1.80	2.50
2023.10	1.80	2.50
2023.11	1.80	2.50
2023.12	1.80	2.50

注：上述利率均为当月最后一次操作的利率水平。

Note: Above data were the interest rates of last operation in each month.

中央银行短期政策利率与DR007

Central bank short-term policy rate and DR007

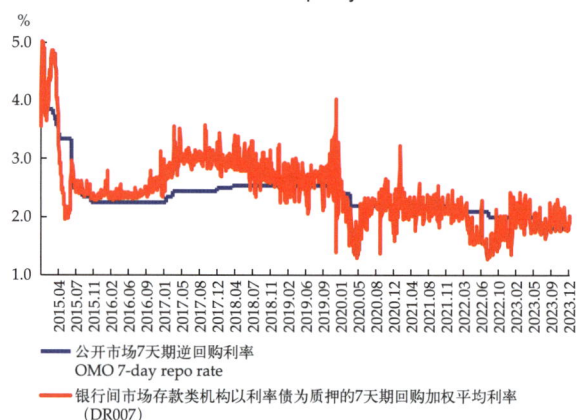

公开市场7天期逆回购利率
OMO 7-day repo rate

银行间市场存款类机构以利率债为质押的7天期回购加权平均利率
（DR007）

中央银行政策利率体系

Central bank policy rate system

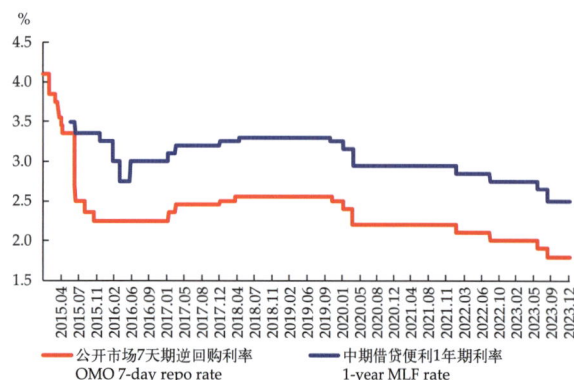

公开市场7天期逆回购利率
OMO 7-day repo rate
中期借贷便利1年期利率
1-year MLF rate

中央银行中期政策利率与贷款市场报价利率

Central bank median-term policy rate and LPR

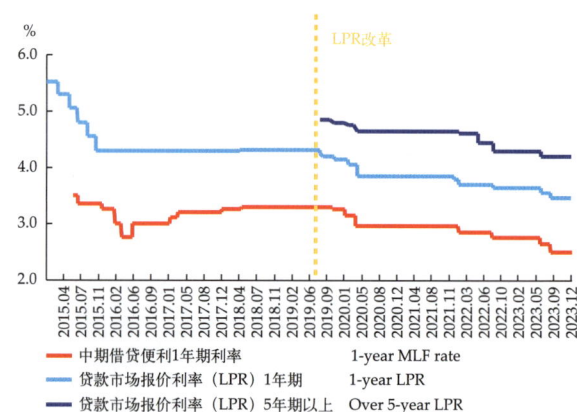

中期借贷便利1年期利率　　　　1-year MLF rate
贷款市场报价利率（LPR）1年期　1-year LPR
贷款市场报价利率（LPR）5年期以上　Over 5-year LPR

3.2　中央银行公开市场操作（Central bank open market operations）

中央银行公开市场操作
Central bank open market operations

日期 Date		操作工具 Mode of transaction	招标方式 Mode of bidding	期限品种（天） Maturity (Day)	招标数量（亿元） Bidding amount (RMB 100 million)	中标量（亿元） Transaction volume (RMB 100 million)	中标利率（%） Interest rate of successful bidding (%)
2023.01.03	周二 Tuesday	逆回购 Reverse Repo	利率招标 Interest rate bidding	7 天 7-day	500	500	2.00
2023.01.04	周三 Wednesday	逆回购 Reverse Repo	利率招标 Interest rate bidding	7 天 7-day	30	30	2.00
2023.01.05	周四 Thursday	逆回购 Reverse Repo	利率招标 Interest rate bidding	7 天 7-day	20	20	2.00
2023.01.06	周五 Friday	逆回购 Reverse Repo	利率招标 Interest rate bidding	7 天 7-day	20	20	2.00
2023.01.09	周一 Monday	逆回购 Reverse Repo	利率招标 Interest rate bidding	7 天 7-day	20	20	2.00
2023.01.10	周二 Tuesday	逆回购 Reverse Repo	利率招标 Interest rate bidding	7 天 7-day	20	20	2.00
2023.01.11	周三 Wednesday	逆回购 Reverse Repo	利率招标 Interest rate bidding	14 天 14-day	220	220	2.15
2023.01.11	周三 Wednesday	逆回购 Reverse Repo	利率招标 Interest rate bidding	7 天 7-day	650	650	2.00
2023.01.12	周四 Thursday	逆回购 Reverse Repo	利率招标 Interest rate bidding	14 天 14-day	520	520	2.15
2023.01.12	周四 Thursday	逆回购 Reverse Repo	利率招标 Interest rate bidding	7 天 7-day	650	650	2.00
2023.01.13	周五 Friday	逆回购 Reverse Repo	利率招标 Interest rate bidding	7 天 7-day	550	550	2.00
2023.01.13	周五 Friday	逆回购 Reverse Repo	利率招标 Interest rate bidding	14 天 14-day	770	770	2.15
2023.01.16	周一 Monday	逆回购 Reverse Repo	利率招标 Interest rate bidding	14 天 14-day	740	740	2.15
2023.01.16	周一 Monday	逆回购 Reverse Repo	利率招标 Interest rate bidding	7 天 7-day	820	820	2.00
2023.01.17	周二 Tuesday	逆回购 Reverse Repo	利率招标 Interest rate bidding	14 天 14-day	3 010	3 010	2.15
2023.01.17	周二 Tuesday	逆回购 Reverse Repo	利率招标 Interest rate bidding	7 天 7-day	2 050	2 050	2.00
2023.01.18	周三 Wednesday	逆回购 Reverse Repo	利率招标 Interest rate bidding	14 天 14-day	4 470	4 470	2.15
2023.01.18	周三 Wednesday	逆回购 Reverse Repo	利率招标 Interest rate bidding	7 天 7-day	1 330	1 330	2.00
2023.01.19	周四 Thursday	逆回购 Reverse Repo	利率招标 Interest rate bidding	14 天 14-day	4 670	4 670	2.15
2023.01.19	周四 Thursday	逆回购 Reverse Repo	利率招标 Interest rate bidding	7 天 7-day	650	650	2.00
2023.01.20	周五 Friday	逆回购 Reverse Repo	利率招标 Interest rate bidding	7 天 7-day	620	620	2.00
2023.01.20	周五 Friday	逆回购 Reverse Repo	利率招标 Interest rate bidding	14 天 14-day	3 190	3 190	2.15
2023.01.28	周六 Saturday	逆回购 Reverse Repo	利率招标 Interest rate bidding	7 天 7-day	2 220	2 220	2.00
2023.01.29	周日 Sunday	逆回购 Reverse Repo	利率招标 Interest rate bidding	7 天 7-day	1 280	1 280	2.00
2023.01.30	周一 Monday	逆回购 Reverse Repo	利率招标 Interest rate bidding	7 天 7-day	1 730	1 730	2.00
2023.01.31	周二 Tuesday	逆回购 Reverse Repo	利率招标 Interest rate bidding	7 天 7-day	4 710	4 710	2.00

续表

日期 Date		操作工具 Mode of transaction	招标方式 Mode of bidding	期限品种（天） Maturity (Day)	招标数量（亿元） Bidding amount (RMB 100 million)	中标量（亿元） Transaction volume (RMB 100 million)	中标利率（%） Interest rate of successful bidding (%)
2023.02.01	周三 Wednesday	逆回购 Reverse Repo	利率招标 Interest rate bidding	7 天 7-day	1 550	1 550	2.00
2023.02.02	周四 Thursday	逆回购 Reverse Repo	利率招标 Interest rate bidding	7 天 7-day	660	660	2.00
2023.02.03	周五 Friday	逆回购 Reverse Repo	利率招标 Interest rate bidding	7 天 7-day	230	230	2.00
2023.02.06	周一 Monday	逆回购 Reverse Repo	利率招标 Interest rate bidding	7 天 7-day	1 500	1 500	2.00
2023.02.07	周二 Tuesday	逆回购 Reverse Repo	利率招标 Interest rate bidding	7 天 7-day	3 930	3 930	2.00
2023.02.08	周三 Wednesday	逆回购 Reverse Repo	利率招标 Interest rate bidding	7 天 7-day	6 410	6 410	2.00
2023.02.09	周四 Thursday	逆回购 Reverse Repo	利率招标 Interest rate bidding	7 天 7-day	4 530	4 530	2.00
2023.02.10	周五 Friday	逆回购 Reverse Repo	利率招标 Interest rate bidding	7 天 7-day	2 030	2 030	2.00
2023.02.13	周一 Monday	逆回购 Reverse Repo	利率招标 Interest rate bidding	7 天 7-day	460	460	2.00
2023.02.14	周二 Tuesday	逆回购 Reverse Repo	利率招标 Interest rate bidding	7 天 7-day	910	910	2.00
2023.02.15	周三 Wednesday	逆回购 Reverse Repo	利率招标 Interest rate bidding	7 天 7-day	2 030	2 030	2.00
2023.02.16	周四 Thursday	逆回购 Reverse Repo	利率招标 Interest rate bidding	7 天 7-day	4 870	4 870	2.00
2023.02.17	周五 Friday	逆回购 Reverse Repo	利率招标 Interest rate bidding	7 天 7-day	8 350	8 350	2.00
2023.02.20	周一 Monday	逆回购 Reverse Repo	利率招标 Interest rate bidding	7 天 7-day	2 700	2 700	2.00
2023.02.21	周二 Tuesday	逆回购 Reverse Repo	利率招标 Interest rate bidding	7 天 7-day	1 500	1 500	2.00
2023.02.22	周三 Wednesday	逆回购 Reverse Repo	利率招标 Interest rate bidding	7 天 7-day	3 000	3 000	2.00
2023.02.23	周四 Thursday	逆回购 Reverse Repo	利率招标 Interest rate bidding	7 天 7-day	3 000	3 000	2.00
2023.02.24	周五 Friday	逆回购 Reverse Repo	利率招标 Interest rate bidding	7 天 7-day	4 700	4 700	2.00
2023.02.27	周一 Monday	逆回购 Reverse Repo	利率招标 Interest rate bidding	7 天 7-day	3 360	3 360	2.00
2023.02.28	周二 Tuesday	逆回购 Reverse Repo	利率招标 Interest rate bidding	7 天 7-day	4 810	4 810	2.00
2023.03.01	周三 Wednesday	逆回购 Reverse Repo	利率招标 Interest rate bidding	7 天 7-day	1 070	1 070	2.00
2023.03.02	周四 Thursday	逆回购 Reverse Repo	利率招标 Interest rate bidding	7 天 7-day	730	730	2.00
2023.03.03	周五 Friday	逆回购 Reverse Repo	利率招标 Interest rate bidding	7 天 7-day	180	180	2.00
2023.03.06	周一 Monday	逆回购 Reverse Repo	利率招标 Interest rate bidding	7 天 7-day	70	70	2.00
2023.03.07	周二 Tuesday	逆回购 Reverse Repo	利率招标 Interest rate bidding	7 天 7-day	30	30	2.00
2023.03.08	周三 Wednesday	逆回购 Reverse Repo	利率招标 Interest rate bidding	7 天 7-day	40	40	2.00
2023.03.09	周四 Thursday	逆回购 Reverse Repo	利率招标 Interest rate bidding	7 天 7-day	30	30	2.00
2023.03.10	周五 Friday	逆回购 Reverse Repo	利率招标 Interest rate bidding	7 天 7-day	150	150	2.00

续表

日期 Date		操作工具 Mode of transaction	招标方式 Mode of bidding	期限品种（天） Maturity (Day)	招标数量（亿元） Bidding amount (RMB 100 million)	中标量（亿元） Transaction volume (RMB 100 million)	中标利率（%） Interest rate of successful bidding (%)
2023.03.13	周一 Monday	逆回购 Reverse Repo	利率招标 Interest rate bidding	7 天 7-day	410	410	2.00
2023.03.14	周二 Tuesday	逆回购 Reverse Repo	利率招标 Interest rate bidding	7 天 7-day	290	290	2.00
2023.03.15	周三 Wednesday	逆回购 Reverse Repo	利率招标 Interest rate bidding	7 天 7-day	1 040	1 040	2.00
2023.03.16	周四 Thursday	逆回购 Reverse Repo	利率招标 Interest rate bidding	7 天 7-day	1 090	1 090	2.00
2023.03.17	周五 Friday	逆回购 Reverse Repo	利率招标 Interest rate bidding	7 天 7-day	1 800	1 800	2.00
2023.03.20	周一 Monday	逆回购 Reverse Repo	利率招标 Interest rate bidding	7 天 7-day	300	300	2.00
2023.03.21	周二 Tuesday	逆回购 Reverse Repo	利率招标 Interest rate bidding	7 天 7-day	1 820	1 820	2.00
2023.03.22	周三 Wednesday	逆回购 Reverse Repo	利率招标 Interest rate bidding	7 天 7-day	670	670	2.00
2023.03.23	周四 Thursday	逆回购 Reverse Repo	利率招标 Interest rate bidding	7 天 7-day	640	640	2.00
2023.03.24	周五 Friday	逆回购 Reverse Repo	利率招标 Interest rate bidding	7 天 7-day	70	70	2.00
2023.03.27	周一 Monday	逆回购 Reverse Repo	利率招标 Interest rate bidding	7 天 7-day	2 550	2 550	2.00
2023.03.28	周二 Tuesday	逆回购 Reverse Repo	利率招标 Interest rate bidding	7 天 7-day	2 780	2 780	2.00
2023.03.29	周三 Wednesday	逆回购 Reverse Repo	利率招标 Interest rate bidding	7 天 7-day	2 000	2 000	2.00
2023.03.30	周四 Thursday	逆回购 Reverse Repo	利率招标 Interest rate bidding	7 天 7-day	2 390	2 390	2.00
2023.03.31	周五 Friday	逆回购 Reverse Repo	利率招标 Interest rate bidding	7 天 7-day	1 890	1 890	2.00
2023.04.03	周一 Monday	逆回购 Reverse Repo	利率招标 Interest rate bidding	7 天 7-day	20	20	2.00
2023.04.04	周二 Tuesday	逆回购 Reverse Repo	利率招标 Interest rate bidding	7 天 7-day	20	20	2.00
2023.04.06	周四 Thursday	逆回购 Reverse Repo	利率招标 Interest rate bidding	7 天 7-day	80	80	2.00
2023.04.07	周五 Friday	逆回购 Reverse Repo	利率招标 Interest rate bidding	7 天 7-day	170	170	2.00
2023.04.10	周一 Monday	逆回购 Reverse Repo	利率招标 Interest rate bidding	7 天 7-day	180	180	2.00
2023.04.11	周二 Tuesday	逆回购 Reverse Repo	利率招标 Interest rate bidding	7 天 7-day	50	50	2.00
2023.04.12	周三 Wednesday	逆回购 Reverse Repo	利率招标 Interest rate bidding	7 天 7-day	70	70	2.00
2023.04.13	周四 Thursday	逆回购 Reverse Repo	利率招标 Interest rate bidding	7 天 7-day	90	90	2.00
2023.04.14	周五 Friday	逆回购 Reverse Repo	利率招标 Interest rate bidding	7 天 7-day	150	150	2.00
2023.04.17	周一 Monday	逆回购 Reverse Repo	利率招标 Interest rate bidding	7 天 7-day	200	200	2.00
2023.04.18	周二 Tuesday	逆回购 Reverse Repo	利率招标 Interest rate bidding	7 天 7-day	380	380	2.00
2023.04.19	周三 Wednesday	逆回购 Reverse Repo	利率招标 Interest rate bidding	7 天 7-day	320	320	2.00
2023.04.20	周四 Thursday	逆回购 Reverse Repo	利率招标 Interest rate bidding	7 天 7-day	340	340	2.00

续表

日期 Date		操作工具 Mode of transaction	招标方式 Mode of bidding	期限品种（天） Maturity (Day)	招标数量（亿元） Bidding amount (RMB 100 million)	中标量（亿元） Transaction volume (RMB 100 million)	中标利率（%） Interest rate of successful bidding (%)
2023.04.21	周五 Friday	逆回购 Reverse Repo	利率招标 Interest rate bidding	7 天 7-day	880	880	2.00
2023.04.23	周日 Sunday	逆回购 Reverse Repo	利率招标 Interest rate bidding	7 天 7-day	890	890	2.00
2023.04.24	周一 Monday	逆回购 Reverse Repo	利率招标 Interest rate bidding	7 天 7-day	1 150	1 150	2.00
2023.04.25	周二 Tuesday	逆回购 Reverse Repo	利率招标 Interest rate bidding	7 天 7-day	1 700	1 700	2.00
2023.04.25	周二 Tuesday	中央银行票据 Central bank bills	利率招标 Interest rate bidding	3 个月 3-month	50	50	2.35
2023.04.26	周三 Wednesday	逆回购 Reverse Repo	利率招标 Interest rate bidding	7 天 7-day	950	950	2.00
2023.04.27	周四 Thursday	逆回购 Reverse Repo	利率招标 Interest rate bidding	7 天 7-day	930	930	2.00
2023.04.28	周五 Friday	逆回购 Reverse Repo	利率招标 Interest rate bidding	7 天 7-day	1 650	1 650	2.00
2023.05.04	周四 Thursday	逆回购 Reverse Repo	利率招标 Interest rate bidding	7 天 7-day	330	330	2.00
2023.05.05	周五 Friday	逆回购 Reverse Repo	利率招标 Interest rate bidding	7 天 7-day	30	30	2.00
2023.05.06	周六 Saturday	逆回购 Reverse Repo	利率招标 Interest rate bidding	7 天 7-day	20	20	2.00
2023.05.08	周一 Monday	逆回购 Reverse Repo	利率招标 Interest rate bidding	7 天 7-day	20	20	2.00
2023.05.09	周二 Tuesday	逆回购 Reverse Repo	利率招标 Interest rate bidding	7 天 7-day	20	20	2.00
2023.05.10	周三 Wednesday	逆回购 Reverse Repo	利率招标 Interest rate bidding	7 天 7-day	20	20	2.00
2023.05.11	周四 Thursday	逆回购 Reverse Repo	利率招标 Interest rate bidding	7 天 7-day	20	20	2.00
2023.05.12	周五 Friday	逆回购 Reverse Repo	利率招标 Interest rate bidding	7 天 7-day	20	20	2.00
2023.05.15	周一 Monday	逆回购 Reverse Repo	利率招标 Interest rate bidding	7 天 7-day	20	20	2.00
2023.05.16	周二 Tuesday	逆回购 Reverse Repo	利率招标 Interest rate bidding	7 天 7-day	20	20	2.00
2023.05.17	周三 Wednesday	逆回购 Reverse Repo	利率招标 Interest rate bidding	7 天 7-day	20	20	2.00
2023.05.18	周四 Thursday	逆回购 Reverse Repo	利率招标 Interest rate bidding	7 天 7-day	20	20	2.00
2023.05.19	周五 Friday	逆回购 Reverse Repo	利率招标 Interest rate bidding	7 天 7-day	20	20	2.00
2023.05.22	周一 Monday	逆回购 Reverse Repo	利率招标 Interest rate bidding	7 天 7-day	20	20	2.00
2023.05.23	周二 Tuesday	逆回购 Reverse Repo	利率招标 Interest rate bidding	7 天 7-day	20	20	2.00
2023.05.24	周三 Wednesday	逆回购 Reverse Repo	利率招标 Interest rate bidding	7 天 7-day	20	20	2.00
2023.05.25	周四 Thursday	逆回购 Reverse Repo	利率招标 Interest rate bidding	7 天 7-day	70	70	2.00
2023.05.26	周五 Friday	逆回购 Reverse Repo	利率招标 Interest rate bidding	7 天 7-day	50	50	2.00
2023.05.29	周一 Monday	逆回购 Reverse Repo	利率招标 Interest rate bidding	7 天 7-day	250	250	2.00
2023.05.29	周一 Monday	中央银行票据 Central bank bills	利率招标 Interest rate bidding	3 个月 3-month	50	50	2.35

续表

日期 Date		操作工具 Mode of transaction	招标方式 Mode of bidding	期限品种（天） Maturity (Day)	招标数量（亿元） Bidding amount (RMB 100 million)	中标量（亿元） Transaction volume (RMB 100 million)	中标利率（%） Interest rate of successful bidding (%)
2023.05.30	周二 Tuesday	逆回购 Reverse Repo	利率招标 Interest rate bidding	7 天 7-day	370	370	2.00
2023.05.31	周三 Wednesday	逆回购 Reverse Repo	利率招标 Interest rate bidding	7 天 7-day	130	130	2.00
2023.06.01	周四 Thursday	逆回购 Reverse Repo	利率招标 Interest rate bidding	7 天 7-day	20	20	2.00
2023.06.02	周五 Friday	逆回购 Reverse Repo	利率招标 Interest rate bidding	7 天 7-day	20	20	2.00
2023.06.05	周一 Monday	逆回购 Reverse Repo	利率招标 Interest rate bidding	7 天 7-day	20	20	2.00
2023.06.06	周二 Tuesday	逆回购 Reverse Repo	利率招标 Interest rate bidding	7 天 7-day	20	20	2.00
2023.06.07	周三 Wednesday	逆回购 Reverse Repo	利率招标 Interest rate bidding	7 天 7-day	20	20	2.00
2023.06.08	周四 Thursday	逆回购 Reverse Repo	利率招标 Interest rate bidding	7 天 7-day	20	20	2.00
2023.06.09	周五 Friday	逆回购 Reverse Repo	利率招标 Interest rate bidding	7 天 7-day	20	20	2.00
2023.06.12	周一 Monday	逆回购 Reverse Repo	利率招标 Interest rate bidding	7 天 7-day	20	20	2.00
2023.06.13	周二 Tuesday	逆回购 Reverse Repo	利率招标 Interest rate bidding	7 天 7-day	20	20	1.90
2023.06.14	周三 Wednesday	逆回购 Reverse Repo	利率招标 Interest rate bidding	7 天 7-day	20	20	1.90
2023.06.15	周四 Thursday	逆回购 Reverse Repo	利率招标 Interest rate bidding	7 天 7-day	20	20	1.90
2023.06.16	周五 Friday	逆回购 Reverse Repo	利率招标 Interest rate bidding	7 天 7-day	420	420	1.90
2023.06.19	周一 Monday	逆回购 Reverse Repo	利率招标 Interest rate bidding	7 天 7-day	890	890	1.90
2023.06.20	周二 Tuesday	逆回购 Reverse Repo	利率招标 Interest rate bidding	7 天 7-day	1 820	1 820	1.90
2023.06.21	周三 Wednesday	逆回购 Reverse Repo	利率招标 Interest rate bidding	7 天 7-day	1 450	1 450	1.90
2023.06.25	周日 Sunday	逆回购 Reverse Repo	利率招标 Interest rate bidding	7 天 7-day	1 960	1 960	1.90
2023.06.26	周一 Monday	逆回购 Reverse Repo	利率招标 Interest rate bidding	7 天 7-day	2 440	2 440	1.90
2023.06.27	周二 Tuesday	逆回购 Reverse Repo	利率招标 Interest rate bidding	7 天 7-day	2 190	2 190	1.90
2023.06.27	周二 Tuesday	中央银行票据 Central bank bills	利率招标 Interest rate bidding	3 个月 3-month	50	50	2.35
2023.06.28	周三 Wednesday	逆回购 Reverse Repo	利率招标 Interest rate bidding	7 天 7-day	2 140	2 140	1.90
2023.06.29	周四 Thursday	逆回购 Reverse Repo	利率招标 Interest rate bidding	7 天 7-day	1 930	1 930	1.90
2023.06.30	周五 Friday	逆回购 Reverse Repo	利率招标 Interest rate bidding	7 天 7-day	1 030	1 030	1.90
2023.07.03	周一 Monday	逆回购 Reverse Repo	利率招标 Interest rate bidding	7 天 7-day	50	50	1.90
2023.07.04	周二 Tuesday	逆回购 Reverse Repo	利率招标 Interest rate bidding	7 天 7-day	20	20	1.90
2023.07.05	周三 Wednesday	逆回购 Reverse Repo	利率招标 Interest rate bidding	7 天 7-day	20	20	1.90
2023.07.06	周四 Thursday	逆回购 Reverse Repo	利率招标 Interest rate bidding	7 天 7-day	20	20	1.90

续表

日期 Date		操作工具 Mode of transaction	招标方式 Mode of bidding	期限品种（天） Maturity (Day)	招标数量（亿元） Bidding amount (RMB 100 million)	中标量（亿元） Transaction volume (RMB 100 million)	中标利率（%） Interest rate of successful bidding (%)
2023.07.07	周五 Friday	逆回购 Reverse Repo	利率招标 Interest rate bidding	7 天 7-day	20	20	1.90
2023.07.10	周一 Monday	逆回购 Reverse Repo	利率招标 Interest rate bidding	7 天 7-day	20	20	1.90
2023.07.11	周二 Tuesday	逆回购 Reverse Repo	利率招标 Interest rate bidding	7 天 7-day	20	20	1.90
2023.07.12	周三 Wednesday	逆回购 Reverse Repo	利率招标 Interest rate bidding	7 天 7-day	20	20	1.90
2023.07.13	周四 Thursday	逆回购 Reverse Repo	利率招标 Interest rate bidding	7 天 7-day	50	50	1.90
2023.07.14	周五 Friday	逆回购 Reverse Repo	利率招标 Interest rate bidding	7 天 7-day	200	200	1.90
2023.07.17	周一 Monday	逆回购 Reverse Repo	利率招标 Interest rate bidding	7 天 7-day	330	330	1.90
2023.07.18	周二 Tuesday	逆回购 Reverse Repo	利率招标 Interest rate bidding	7 天 7-day	150	150	1.90
2023.07.19	周三 Wednesday	逆回购 Reverse Repo	利率招标 Interest rate bidding	7 天 7-day	250	250	1.90
2023.07.20	周四 Thursday	逆回购 Reverse Repo	利率招标 Interest rate bidding	7 天 7-day	260	260	1.90
2023.07.21	周五 Friday	逆回购 Reverse Repo	利率招标 Interest rate bidding	7 天 7-day	130	130	1.90
2023.07.24	周一 Monday	逆回购 Reverse Repo	利率招标 Interest rate bidding	7 天 7-day	140	140	1.90
2023.07.25	周二 Tuesday	逆回购 Reverse Repo	利率招标 Interest rate bidding	7 天 7-day	440	440	1.90
2023.07.25	周二 Tuesday	中央银行票据 Central bank bills	利率招标 Interest rate bidding	3 个月 3-month	50	50	2.35
2023.07.26	周三 Wednesday	逆回购 Reverse Repo	利率招标 Interest rate bidding	7 天 7-day	1 040	1 040	1.90
2023.07.27	周四 Thursday	逆回购 Reverse Repo	利率招标 Interest rate bidding	7 天 7-day	1 140	1 140	1.90
2023.07.28	周五 Friday	逆回购 Reverse Repo	利率招标 Interest rate bidding	7 天 7-day	650	650	1.90
2023.07.31	周一 Monday	逆回购 Reverse Repo	利率招标 Interest rate bidding	7 天 7-day	310	310	1.90
2023.08.01	周二 Tuesday	逆回购 Reverse Repo	利率招标 Interest rate bidding	7 天 7-day	80	80	1.90
2023.08.02	周三 Wednesday	逆回购 Reverse Repo	利率招标 Interest rate bidding	7 天 7-day	90	90	1.90
2023.08.03	周四 Thursday	逆回购 Reverse Repo	利率招标 Interest rate bidding	7 天 7-day	30	30	1.90
2023.08.04	周五 Friday	逆回购 Reverse Repo	利率招标 Interest rate bidding	7 天 7-day	20	20	1.90
2023.08.07	周一 Monday	逆回购 Reverse Repo	利率招标 Interest rate bidding	7 天 7-day	30	30	1.90
2023.08.08	周二 Tuesday	逆回购 Reverse Repo	利率招标 Interest rate bidding	7 天 7-day	60	60	1.90
2023.08.09	周三 Wednesday	逆回购 Reverse Repo	利率招标 Interest rate bidding	7 天 7-day	20	20	1.90
2023.08.10	周四 Thursday	逆回购 Reverse Repo	利率招标 Interest rate bidding	7 天 7-day	50	50	1.90
2023.08.11	周五 Friday	逆回购 Reverse Repo	利率招标 Interest rate bidding	7 天 7-day	20	20	1.90
2023.08.14	周一 Monday	逆回购 Reverse Repo	利率招标 Interest rate bidding	7 天 7-day	60	60	1.90

续表

日期 Date		操作工具 Mode of transaction	招标方式 Mode of bidding	期限品种（天） Maturity (Day)	招标数量（亿元） Bidding amount (RMB 100 million)	中标量（亿元） Transaction volume (RMB 100 million)	中标利率（%） Interest rate of successful bidding (%)
2023.08.15	周二 Tuesday	逆回购 Reverse Repo	利率招标 Interest rate bidding	7 天 7-day	2 040	2 040	1.80
2023.08.16	周三 Wednesday	逆回购 Reverse Repo	利率招标 Interest rate bidding	7 天 7-day	2 990	2 990	1.80
2023.08.17	周四 Thursday	逆回购 Reverse Repo	利率招标 Interest rate bidding	7 天 7-day	1 680	1 680	1.80
2023.08.18	周五 Friday	逆回购 Reverse Repo	利率招标 Interest rate bidding	7 天 7-day	980	980	1.80
2023.08.21	周一 Monday	逆回购 Reverse Repo	利率招标 Interest rate bidding	7 天 7-day	340	340	1.80
2023.08.22	周二 Tuesday	逆回购 Reverse Repo	利率招标 Interest rate bidding	7 天 7-day	1 110	1 110	1.80
2023.08.23	周三 Wednesday	逆回购 Reverse Repo	利率招标 Interest rate bidding	7 天 7-day	3 010	3 010	1.80
2023.08.24	周四 Thursday	逆回购 Reverse Repo	利率招标 Interest rate bidding	7 天 7-day	610	610	1.80
2023.08.25	周五 Friday	逆回购 Reverse Repo	利率招标 Interest rate bidding	7 天 7-day	2 210	2 210	1.80
2023.08.28	周一 Monday	逆回购 Reverse Repo	利率招标 Interest rate bidding	7 天 7-day	3 320	3 320	1.80
2023.08.29	周二 Tuesday	逆回购 Reverse Repo	利率招标 Interest rate bidding	7 天 7-day	3 850	3 850	1.80
2023.08.29	周二 Tuesday	中央银行票据 Central bank bills	利率招标 Interest rate bidding	3 个月 3-month	50	50	2.35
2023.08.30	周三 Wednesday	逆回购 Reverse Repo	利率招标 Interest rate bidding	7 天 7-day	3 820	3 820	1.80
2023.08.31	周四 Thursday	逆回购 Reverse Repo	利率招标 Interest rate bidding	7 天 7-day	2 090	2 090	1.80
2023.09.01	周五 Friday	逆回购 Reverse Repo	利率招标 Interest rate bidding	7 天 7-day	1 010	1 010	1.80
2023.09.04	周一 Monday	逆回购 Reverse Repo	利率招标 Interest rate bidding	7 天 7-day	120	120	1.80
2023.09.05	周二 Tuesday	逆回购 Reverse Repo	利率招标 Interest rate bidding	7 天 7-day	140	140	1.80
2023.09.06	周三 Wednesday	逆回购 Reverse Repo	利率招标 Interest rate bidding	7 天 7-day	260	260	1.80
2023.09.07	周四 Thursday	逆回购 Reverse Repo	利率招标 Interest rate bidding	7 天 7-day	3 300	3 300	1.80
2023.09.08	周五 Friday	逆回购 Reverse Repo	利率招标 Interest rate bidding	7 天 7-day	3 630	3 630	1.80
2023.09.11	周一 Monday	逆回购 Reverse Repo	利率招标 Interest rate bidding	7 天 7-day	2 150	2 150	1.80
2023.09.12	周二 Tuesday	逆回购 Reverse Repo	利率招标 Interest rate bidding	7 天 7-day	2 090	2 090	1.80
2023.09.13	周三 Wednesday	逆回购 Reverse Repo	利率招标 Interest rate bidding	7 天 7-day	650	650	1.80
2023.09.14	周四 Thursday	逆回购 Reverse Repo	利率招标 Interest rate bidding	7 天 7-day	1 100	1 100	1.80
2023.09.15	周五 Friday	逆回购 Reverse Repo	利率招标 Interest rate bidding	7 天 7-day	1 050	1 050	1.80
2023.09.15	周五 Friday	逆回购 Reverse Repo	利率招标 Interest rate bidding	14 天 14-day	340	340	1.95
2023.09.18	周一 Monday	逆回购 Reverse Repo	利率招标 Interest rate bidding	7 天 7-day	1 840	1 840	1.80
2023.09.18	周一 Monday	逆回购 Reverse Repo	利率招标 Interest rate bidding	14 天 14-day	600	600	1.95

续表

日期 Date		操作工具 Mode of transaction	招标方式 Mode of bidding	期限品种（天） Maturity (Day)	招标数量（亿元） Bidding amount (RMB 100 million)	中标量（亿元） Transaction volume (RMB 100 million)	中标利率（%） Interest rate of successful bidding (%)
2023.09.19	周二 Tuesday	逆回购 Reverse Repo	利率招标 Interest rate bidding	14 天 14-day	600	600	1.95
2023.09.19	周二 Tuesday	逆回购 Reverse Repo	利率招标 Interest rate bidding	7 天 7-day	2 080	2 080	1.80
2023.09.20	周三 Wednesday	逆回购 Reverse Repo	利率招标 Interest rate bidding	7 天 7-day	2 050	2 050	1.80
2023.09.20	周三 Wednesday	逆回购 Reverse Repo	利率招标 Interest rate bidding	14 天 14-day	860	860	1.95
2023.09.21	周四 Thursday	逆回购 Reverse Repo	利率招标 Interest rate bidding	14 天 14-day	820	820	1.95
2023.09.21	周四 Thursday	逆回购 Reverse Repo	利率招标 Interest rate bidding	7 天 7-day	1 690	1 690	1.80
2023.09.22	周五 Friday	逆回购 Reverse Repo	利率招标 Interest rate bidding	14 天 14-day	2 020	2 020	1.95
2023.09.25	周一 Monday	逆回购 Reverse Repo	利率招标 Interest rate bidding	14 天 14-day	3 190	3 190	1.95
2023.09.26	周二 Tuesday	逆回购 Reverse Repo	利率招标 Interest rate bidding	14 天 14-day	3 780	3 780	1.95
2023.09.27	周三 Wednesday	逆回购 Reverse Repo	利率招标 Interest rate bidding	14 天 14-day	4 170	4 170	1.95
2023.09.27	周三 Wednesday	中央银行票据 Central bank bills	利率招标 Interest rate bidding	3 个月 3-month	50	50	2.35
2023.09.27	周三 Wednesday	逆回购 Reverse Repo	利率招标 Interest rate bidding	7 天 7-day	2 000	2 000	1.80
2023.09.28	周四 Thursday	逆回购 Reverse Repo	利率招标 Interest rate bidding	14 天 14-day	5 080	5 080	1.95
2023.09.28	周四 Thursday	逆回购 Reverse Repo	利率招标 Interest rate bidding	7 天 7-day	1 010	1 010	1.80
2023.10.07	周六 Saturday	逆回购 Reverse Repo	利率招标 Interest rate bidding	7 天 7-day	2 000	2 000	1.80
2023.10.08	周日 Sunday	逆回购 Reverse Repo	利率招标 Interest rate bidding	7 天 7-day	200	200	1.80
2023.10.09	周一 Monday	逆回购 Reverse Repo	利率招标 Interest rate bidding	7 天 7-day	200	200	1.80
2023.10.10	周二 Tuesday	逆回购 Reverse Repo	利率招标 Interest rate bidding	7 天 7-day	670	670	1.80
2023.10.11	周三 Wednesday	逆回购 Reverse Repo	利率招标 Interest rate bidding	7 天 7-day	1 020	1 020	1.80
2023.10.12	周四 Thursday	逆回购 Reverse Repo	利率招标 Interest rate bidding	7 天 7-day	1 620	1 620	1.80
2023.10.13	周五 Friday	逆回购 Reverse Repo	利率招标 Interest rate bidding	7 天 7-day	950	950	1.80
2023.10.16	周一 Monday	逆回购 Reverse Repo	利率招标 Interest rate bidding	7 天 7-day	1 060	1 060	1.80
2023.10.17	周二 Tuesday	逆回购 Reverse Repo	利率招标 Interest rate bidding	7 天 7-day	710	710	1.80
2023.10.18	周三 Wednesday	逆回购 Reverse Repo	利率招标 Interest rate bidding	7 天 7-day	1 050	1 050	1.80
2023.10.19	周四 Thursday	逆回购 Reverse Repo	利率招标 Interest rate bidding	7 天 7-day	3 440	3 440	1.80
2023.10.20	周五 Friday	逆回购 Reverse Repo	利率招标 Interest rate bidding	7 天 7-day	8 280	8 280	1.80
2023.10.23	周一 Monday	逆回购 Reverse Repo	利率招标 Interest rate bidding	7 天 7-day	8 080	8 080	1.80
2023.10.24	周二 Tuesday	逆回购 Reverse Repo	利率招标 Interest rate bidding	7 天 7-day	5 930	5 930	1.80

续表

日期 Date		操作工具 Mode of transaction	招标方式 Mode of bidding	期限品种（天） Maturity (Day)	招标数量（亿元） Bidding amount (RMB 100 million)	中标量（亿元） Transaction volume (RMB 100 million)	中标利率（%） Interest rate of successful bidding (%)
2023.10.25	周三 Wednesday	逆回购 Reverse Repo	利率招标 Interest rate bidding	7 天 7-day	5 000	5 000	1.80
2023.10.25	周三 Wednesday	中央银行票据 Central bank bills	利率招标 Interest rate bidding	3 个月 3-month	50	50	2.35
2023.10.26	周四 Thursday	逆回购 Reverse Repo	利率招标 Interest rate bidding	7 天 7-day	4 240	4 240	1.80
2023.10.27	周五 Friday	逆回购 Reverse Repo	利率招标 Interest rate bidding	7 天 7-day	4 990	4 990	1.80
2023.10.30	周一 Monday	逆回购 Reverse Repo	利率招标 Interest rate bidding	7 天 7-day	6 580	6 580	1.80
2023.10.31	周二 Tuesday	逆回购 Reverse Repo	利率招标 Interest rate bidding	7 天 7-day	6 120	6 120	1.80
2023.11.01	周三 Wednesday	逆回购 Reverse Repo	利率招标 Interest rate bidding	7 天 7-day	3 910	3 910	1.80
2023.11.02	周四 Thursday	逆回购 Reverse Repo	利率招标 Interest rate bidding	7 天 7-day	1 940	1 940	1.80
2023.11.03	周五 Friday	逆回购 Reverse Repo	利率招标 Interest rate bidding	7 天 7-day	430	430	1.80
2023.11.06	周一 Monday	逆回购 Reverse Repo	利率招标 Interest rate bidding	7 天 7-day	180	180	1.80
2023.11.07	周二 Tuesday	逆回购 Reverse Repo	利率招标 Interest rate bidding	7 天 7-day	3 530	3 530	1.80
2023.11.08	周三 Wednesday	逆回购 Reverse Repo	利率招标 Interest rate bidding	7 天 7-day	4 740	4 740	1.80
2023.11.09	周四 Thursday	逆回购 Reverse Repo	利率招标 Interest rate bidding	7 天 7-day	2 020	2 020	1.80
2023.11.10	周五 Friday	逆回购 Reverse Repo	利率招标 Interest rate bidding	7 天 7-day	2 030	2 030	1.80
2023.11.13	周一 Monday	逆回购 Reverse Repo	利率招标 Interest rate bidding	7 天 7-day	1 130	1 130	1.80
2023.11.14	周二 Tuesday	逆回购 Reverse Repo	利率招标 Interest rate bidding	7 天 7-day	4 240	4 240	1.80
2023.11.15	周三 Wednesday	逆回购 Reverse Repo	利率招标 Interest rate bidding	7 天 7-day	4 950	4 950	1.80
2023.11.16	周四 Thursday	逆回购 Reverse Repo	利率招标 Interest rate bidding	7 天 7-day	3 770	3 770	1.80
2023.11.17	周五 Friday	逆回购 Reverse Repo	利率招标 Interest rate bidding	7 天 7-day	3 520	3 520	1.80
2023.11.20	周一 Monday	逆回购 Reverse Repo	利率招标 Interest rate bidding	7 天 7-day	2 050	2 050	1.80
2023.11.21	周二 Tuesday	逆回购 Reverse Repo	利率招标 Interest rate bidding	7 天 7-day	3 190	3 190	1.80
2023.11.22	周三 Wednesday	逆回购 Reverse Repo	利率招标 Interest rate bidding	7 天 7-day	4 600	4 600	1.80
2023.11.23	周四 Thursday	逆回购 Reverse Repo	利率招标 Interest rate bidding	7 天 7-day	5 190	5 190	1.80
2023.11.24	周五 Friday	逆回购 Reverse Repo	利率招标 Interest rate bidding	7 天 7-day	6 640	6 640	1.80
2023.11.27	周一 Monday	逆回购 Reverse Repo	利率招标 Interest rate bidding	7 天 7-day	5 010	5 010	1.80
2023.11.28	周二 Tuesday	中央银行票据 Central bank bills	利率招标 Interest rate bidding	3 个月 3-month	50	50	2.35
2023.11.28	周二 Tuesday	逆回购 Reverse Repo	利率招标 Interest rate bidding	7 天 7-day	4 150	4 150	1.80
2023.11.29	周三 Wednesday	逆回购 Reverse Repo	利率招标 Interest rate bidding	7 天 7-day	4 380	4 380	1.80

续表

日期 Date		操作工具 Mode of transaction	招标方式 Mode of bidding	期限品种（天） Maturity (Day)	招标数量（亿元） Bidding amount (RMB 100 million)	中标量（亿元） Transaction volume (RMB 100 million)	中标利率（%） Interest rate of successful bidding (%)
2023.11.30	周四 Thursday	逆回购 Reverse Repo	利率招标 Interest rate bidding	7 天 7-day	6 630	6 630	1.80
2023.12.01	周五 Friday	逆回购 Reverse Repo	利率招标 Interest rate bidding	7 天 7-day	1 190	1 190	1.80
2023.12.04	周一 Monday	逆回购 Reverse Repo	利率招标 Interest rate bidding	7 天 7-day	670	670	1.80
2023.12.05	周二 Tuesday	逆回购 Reverse Repo	利率招标 Interest rate bidding	7 天 7-day	2 100	2 100	1.80
2023.12.06	周三 Wednesday	逆回购 Reverse Repo	利率招标 Interest rate bidding	7 天 7-day	2 400	2 400	1.80
2023.12.07	周四 Thursday	逆回购 Reverse Repo	利率招标 Interest rate bidding	7 天 7-day	3 630	3 630	1.80
2023.12.08	周五 Friday	逆回购 Reverse Repo	利率招标 Interest rate bidding	7 天 7-day	1 970	1 970	1.80
2023.12.11	周一 Monday	逆回购 Reverse Repo	利率招标 Interest rate bidding	7 天 7-day	2 850	2 850	1.80
2023.12.12	周二 Tuesday	逆回购 Reverse Repo	利率招标 Interest rate bidding	7 天 7-day	4 140	4 140	1.80
2023.12.13	周三 Wednesday	逆回购 Reverse Repo	利率招标 Interest rate bidding	7 天 7-day	2 650	2 650	1.80
2023.12.14	周四 Thursday	逆回购 Reverse Repo	利率招标 Interest rate bidding	7 天 7-day	2 620	2 620	1.80
2023.12.15	周五 Friday	逆回购 Reverse Repo	利率招标 Interest rate bidding	7 天 7-day	500	500	1.80
2023.12.18	周一 Monday	逆回购 Reverse Repo	利率招标 Interest rate bidding	7 天 7-day	1 840	1 840	1.80
2023.12.18	周一 Monday	逆回购 Reverse Repo	利率招标 Interest rate bidding	14 天 14-day	600	600	1.95
2023.12.19	周二 Tuesday	逆回购 Reverse Repo	利率招标 Interest rate bidding	14 天 14-day	1 820	1 820	1.95
2023.12.19	周二 Tuesday	逆回购 Reverse Repo	利率招标 Interest rate bidding	7 天 7-day	1 190	1 190	1.80
2023.12.20	周三 Wednesday	逆回购 Reverse Repo	利率招标 Interest rate bidding	14 天 14-day	1 510	1 510	1.95
2023.12.20	周三 Wednesday	逆回购 Reverse Repo	利率招标 Interest rate bidding	7 天 7-day	1 340	1 340	1.80
2023.12.21	周四 Thursday	逆回购 Reverse Repo	利率招标 Interest rate bidding	14 天 14-day	2 260	2 260	1.95
2023.12.21	周四 Thursday	逆回购 Reverse Repo	利率招标 Interest rate bidding	7 天 7-day	1 950	1 950	1.80
2023.12.22	周五 Friday	逆回购 Reverse Repo	利率招标 Interest rate bidding	7 天 7-day	400	400	1.80
2023.12.22	周五 Friday	逆回购 Reverse Repo	利率招标 Interest rate bidding	14 天 14-day	2 910	2 910	1.95
2023.12.25	周一 Monday	逆回购 Reverse Repo	利率招标 Interest rate bidding	14 天 14-day	900	900	1.95
2023.12.25	周一 Monday	逆回购 Reverse Repo	利率招标 Interest rate bidding	7 天 7-day	3 810	3 810	1.80
2023.12.26	周二 Tuesday	逆回购 Reverse Repo	利率招标 Interest rate bidding	14 天 14-day	850	850	1.95
2023.12.26	周二 Tuesday	逆回购 Reverse Repo	利率招标 Interest rate bidding	7 天 7-day	3 830	3 830	1.80
2023.12.26	周二 Tuesday	中央银行票据 Central bank bills	利率招标 Interest rate bidding	3 个月 3-month	50	50	2.35
2023.12.27	周三 Wednesday	逆回购 Reverse Repo	利率招标 Interest rate bidding	7 天 7-day	4 210	4 210	1.80
2023.12.28	周四 Thursday	逆回购 Reverse Repo	利率招标 Interest rate bidding	7 天 7-day	3 740	3 740	1.80
2023.12.29	周五 Friday	逆回购 Reverse Repo	利率招标 Interest rate bidding	7 天 7-day	1 950	1 950	1.80

3.3　中央银行对金融机构存贷款利率（Central bank's interest rates to financial institutions）

中央银行对金融机构存贷款利率
Central bank interest rates

单位：%（年利率）
Unit: % (annual interest rate)

日期 Date	法定存款 准备金 Required reserves	超额存款 准备金 Excess reserves	常备借贷便利 SLF			再贴现 Rediscount
			隔夜 Overnight	7 天 7-day	1 个月 1-month	
1996.05.01	8.82	8.82	—	—	—	*
1996.08.23	8.28	7.92	—	—	—	*
1997.10.23	7.56	7.02	—	—	—	*
1998.03.25	5.22	—	—	—	—	6.03
1998.07.01	3.51	—	—	—	—	4.32
1998.12.07	3.24	—	—	—	—	3.96
1999.06.10	2.07	—	—	—	—	2.16
2001.09.11	—	—	—	—	—	2.97
2002.02.21	1.89	—	—	—	—	2.97
2003.12.20	—	1.62	—	—	—	—
2004.03.25	—	—	—	—	—	3.24
2005.03.17	—	0.99	—	—	—	—
2008.01.01	—	—	—	—	—	4.32
2008.11.27	1.62	0.72	—	—	—	2.97
2008.12.23	—	—	—	—	—	1.80
2010.12.26	—	—	—	—	—	2.25
2014.01.20	—	—	5.00	7.00	—	—
2015.03.04	—	—	4.50	5.50	—	—
2015.11.05	—	—	—	—	—	2.25
2015.11.20	—	—	2.75	3.25	—	—
2016.02.01	—	—	—	—	3.60	—
2017.02.03	—	—	3.10	3.35	3.70	—
2017.03.16	—	—	3.30	3.45	3.80	—
2017.12.14	—	—	3.35	3.50	3.85	—
2018.03.22	—	—	3.40	3.55	3.90	—
2019.12.31	—	—	3.35	3.50	3.85	—
2020.04.07	—	0.35	—	—	—	—
2020.04.10	—	—	3.05	3.20	3.55	—
2020.07.01	—	—	—	—	—	2.00
2022.01.17	—	—	2.95	3.10	3.45	—
2022.08.15	—	—	2.85	3.00	3.35	—
2023.06.13	—	—	2.75	2.90	3.25	—
2023.08.15	—	—	2.65	2.80	3.15	—

注：1.1998年3月法定准备金和超额准备金两个账户合并为准备金账户。
　　2.*按同档次中央银行贷款利率下浮5%～10%。

Notes: 1. The required reserves account and excess reserves account were merged into the reserves account in March 1998.
　　2. *The interest rate is 5%-10% below that of the central bank lending rate of the same tranche.

法定和超额存款准备金利率
Required reserves interest rates and rediscount interest rates

常备借贷便利利率
SLF interest rates

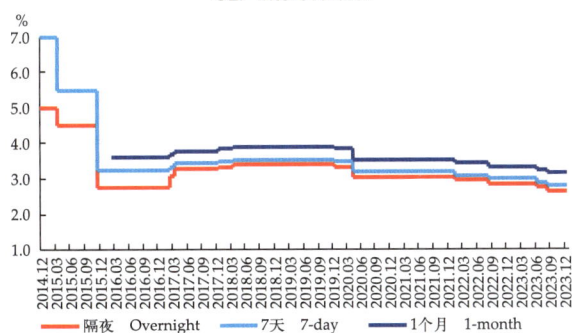

3.4 金融机构对客户存贷款利率 (Interest rates in financial institutions)

人民币存款基准利率

RMB deposit benchmark interest rates

单位：%（年利率）
Unit: % (annual interest rate)

日期 Date	活期 Demand deposits	定期 Time deposits					
		3 个月 3-month	6 个月 6-month	1 年 1-year	2 年 2-year	3 年 3-year	5 年 5-year
1990.04.15	2.88	6.30	7.74	10.08	10.98	11.88	13.68
1990.08.21	2.16	4.32	6.48	8.64	9.36	10.08	11.52
1991.04.21	1.80	3.24	5.40	7.56	7.92	8.28	9.00
1993.05.15	2.16	4.86	7.20	9.18	9.90	10.80	12.06
1993.07.11	3.15	6.66	9.00	10.98	11.70	12.24	13.86
1996.05.01	2.97	4.86	7.20	9.18	9.90	10.80	12.06
1996.08.23	1.98	3.33	5.40	7.47	7.92	8.28	9.00
1997.10.23	1.71	2.88	4.14	5.67	5.94	6.21	6.66
1998.03.25	1.71	2.88	4.14	5.22	5.58	6.21	6.66
1998.07.01	1.44	2.79	3.96	4.77	4.86	4.95	5.22
1998.12.07	1.44	2.79	3.33	3.78	3.96	4.14	4.50
1999.06.10	0.99	1.98	2.16	2.25	2.43	2.70	2.88
2002.02.21	0.72	1.71	1.89	1.98	2.25	2.52	2.79
2004.10.29	0.72	1.71	2.07	2.25	2.70	3.24	3.60
2006.08.19	0.72	1.80	2.25	2.52	3.06	3.69	4.14
2007.03.18	0.72	1.98	2.43	2.79	3.33	3.96	4.41
2007.05.19	0.72	2.07	2.61	3.06	3.69	4.41	4.95
2007.07.21	0.81	2.34	2.88	3.33	3.96	4.68	5.22
2007.08.22	0.81	2.61	3.15	3.60	4.23	4.95	5.49
2007.09.15	0.81	2.88	3.42	3.87	4.50	5.22	5.76
2007.12.21	0.72	3.33	3.78	4.14	4.68	5.40	5.85
2008.10.09	0.72	3.15	3.51	3.87	4.41	5.13	5.58
2008.10.30	0.72	2.88	3.24	3.60	4.14	4.77	5.13
2008.11.27	0.36	1.98	2.25	2.52	3.06	3.60	3.87
2008.12.23	0.36	1.71	1.98	2.25	2.79	3.33	3.60
2010.10.20	0.36	1.91	2.20	2.50	3.25	3.85	4.20
2010.12.26	0.36	2.25	2.50	2.75	3.55	4.15	4.55
2011.02.09	0.40	2.60	2.80	3.00	3.90	4.50	5.00
2011.04.06	0.50	2.85	3.05	3.25	4.15	4.75	5.25
2011.07.07	0.50	3.10	3.30	3.50	4.40	5.00	5.50
2012.06.08	0.40	2.85	3.05	3.25	4.10	4.65	5.10
2012.07.06	0.35	2.60	2.80	3.00	3.75	4.25	4.75
2014.11.22	0.35	2.35	2.55	2.75	3.35	4.00	—
2015.03.01	0.35	2.10	2.30	2.50	3.10	3.75	—
2015.05.11	0.35	1.85	2.05	2.25	2.85	3.50	—
2015.06.28	0.35	1.60	1.80	2.00	2.60	3.25	—
2015.08.26	0.35	1.35	1.55	1.75	2.35	3.00	—
2015.10.24	0.35	1.10	1.30	1.50	2.10	2.75	—

注：从2014年11月起，中国人民银行不再公布人民币5年期定期存款基准利率。
Note: Since November, 2014, the PBC stopped publishing the benchmark interest rate for 5-year RMB deposits.

人民币存款基准利率

RMB deposit benchmark interest rates

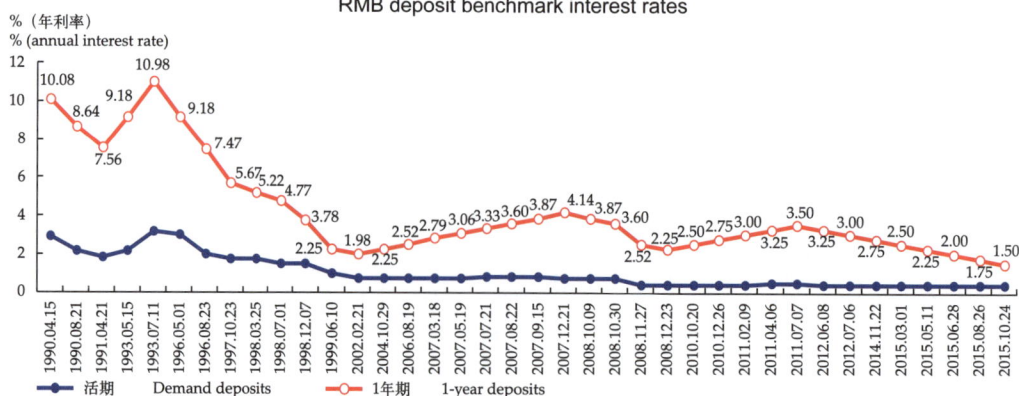

贷款市场报价利率
Loan prime rate

单位：%（年利率）
Unit: % (annual interest rate)

日期 Date	1年期 1-year	5年期以上 Over 5-year
2022.01.20	3.70	4.60
2022.02.21	3.70	4.60
2022.03.21	3.70	4.60
2022.04.20	3.70	4.60
2022.05.20	3.70	4.45
2022.06.20	3.70	4.45
2022.07.20	3.70	4.45
2022.08.22	3.65	4.30
2022.09.20	3.65	4.30
2022.10.20	3.65	4.30
2022.11.21	3.65	4.30
2022.12.20	3.65	4.30
2023.01.20	3.65	4.30
2023.02.20	3.65	4.30
2023.03.20	3.65	4.30
2023.04.20	3.65	4.30
2023.05.22	3.65	4.30
2023.06.20	3.55	4.20
2023.07.20	3.55	4.20
2023.08.21	3.45	4.20
2023.09.20	3.45	4.20
2023.10.20	3.45	4.20
2023.11.20	3.45	4.20
2023.12.20	3.45	4.20

贷款市场报价利率
Loan prime rate

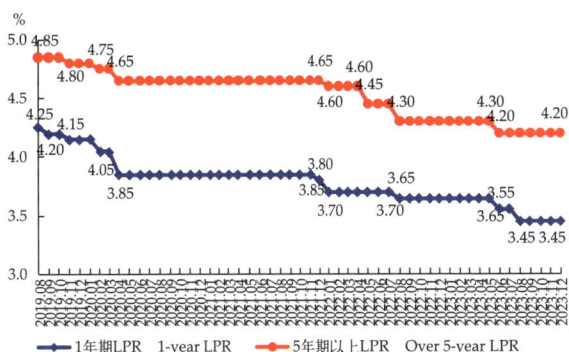

1年期LPR　1-year LPR　　5年期以上LPR　Over 5-year LPR

金融机构新发放贷款加权平均利率
Weighted interest rates on new loans

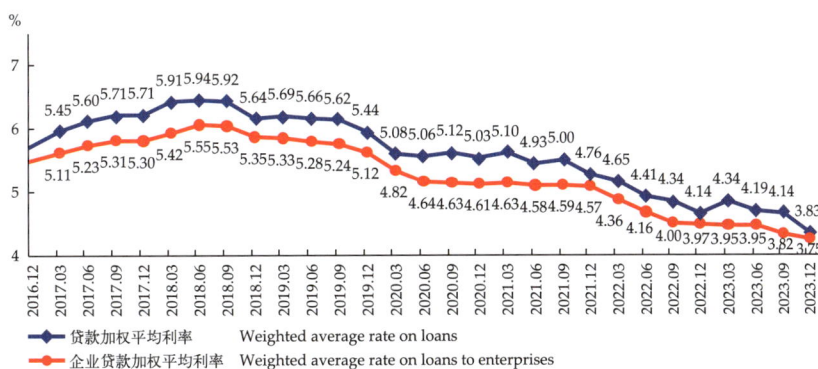

贷款加权平均利率　Weighted average rate on loans
企业贷款加权平均利率　Weighted average rate on loans to enterprises

金融机构人民币贷款各利率区间占比

Share of loans with floating rates in various ranges

单位：% Unit: %

年/月 Year/Month	LPR 减点 LPR-bps	LPR	LPR 加点　LPR+bps					
			小计 Subtotal	(LPR, LPR+0.5%)	[LPR+0.5%, LPR+1.5%)	[LPR+1.5%, LPR+3%)	[LPR+3%, LPR+5%)	LPR+5% 及以上 Above LPR+5%
2022.01	24.15	6.72	69.14	18.20	23.88	12.90	7.74	6.41
2022.02	27.19	6.79	66.02	16.55	21.39	11.76	7.72	8.61
2022.03	25.42	7.63	66.95	17.18	22.95	13.24	7.40	6.18
2022.04	24.79	6.89	68.31	15.92	22.44	13.66	8.37	7.92
2022.05	28.40	6.60	65.00	16.07	21.24	12.75	7.63	7.32
2022.06	29.80	7.82	62.39	17.15	20.98	12.10	6.64	5.52
2022.07	30.37	6.21	63.41	15.95	19.96	12.38	7.54	7.58
2022.08	30.55	5.16	64.29	17.60	19.57	12.08	7.76	7.27
2022.09	34.03	5.22	60.75	17.85	19.32	11.21	6.76	5.60
2022.10	34.23	4.79	60.97	16.06	18.39	11.37	7.68	7.46
2022.11	34.32	5.40	60.28	16.31	18.71	11.54	7.36	6.35
2022.12	38.27	5.52	56.21	14.98	18.05	11.18	6.66	5.33
2023.01	37.38	6.28	56.34	16.65	19.06	10.22	5.70	4.72
2023.02	37.60	6.02	56.38	16.32	16.84	10.28	6.54	6.40
2023.03	36.96	6.88	56.16	17.10	17.57	10.57	6.18	4.74
2023.04	36.62	6.20	57.18	15.54	17.18	11.14	7.08	6.24
2023.05	36.28	5.52	58.20	13.98	16.79	11.71	7.98	7.74
2023.06	37.74	5.59	56.67	17.79	17.31	10.81	6.09	4.68
2023.07	37.05	5.13	57.82	16.60	16.43	10.44	7.12	7.23
2023.08	35.76	4.92	59.32	17.08	16.40	10.75	7.57	7.51
2023.09	37.37	5.62	57.11	16.70	16.88	10.62	6.71	6.19
2023.10	37.34	5.15	57.51	14.92	15.83	11.43	7.43	7.90
2023.11	38.43	5.77	55.80	14.60	16.39	11.37	7.01	6.44
2023.12	41.89	5.64	52.48	13.70	16.15	10.97	6.34	5.33

注：1. 2019年8月17日，中国人民银行宣布改革完善LPR形成机制，金融机构主要参考LPR进行贷款定价，贷款利率区间占比情况也相应调整为按LPR加减点方式统计。

2. 2019年7月及之前的下浮和上浮是指在贷款基准利率的基础上浮动一定倍数，2019年8月及之后的加点和减点是指贷款利率在LPR的基础上加减一定的百分点。

Notes: 1. On August 17, 2019, the People's Bank of China announced the reform and improvement of the LPR formation mechanism. Financial institutions mainly refer to LPR for loan pricing, and the proportion of the loan interest rate range is also adjusted as LPR plus or minus points.

2. The floating down and floating up in July 2019 and before refer to the floating of a certain multiple on the basis of the benchmark lending rate, while the floating up and down in August 2019 and after refer to the addition and subtraction of a certain percentage point on the basis of LPR.

2023年第四季度金融机构人民币贷款各利率区间占比

Share of loans with rates floating at various ranges in the forth quarter of 2023

单位：% Unit: %

机构类型 Type of institution	低于 LPR Lower than LPR	LPR	高于 LPR　Higher than LPR					
			小计 Subtotal	(LPR, LPR+0.5%)	[LPR+0.5%, LPR+1.5%)	[LPR+1.5%, LPR+3%)	[LPR+3%, LPR+5%)	LPR+5% 及以上 Above LPR+5%
四大国有商业银行 Four state-owned commercial banks	62.15	8.66	29.19	18.03	10.53	0.60	0.03	0.00
股份制商业银行 Joint-stock commercial banks	42.89	4.88	52.22	18.19	20.28	8.64	2.49	2.62
外资商业银行 Foreign commercial banks	50.27	2.94	46.79	15.27	15.10	5.41	2.10	8.91
城市商业银行 City commercial banks	12.51	2.40	85.09	9.05	19.00	21.72	14.04	21.28
农村合作金融机构 Rural cooperative financial institutions	7.34	3.05	89.61	12.22	23.38	26.20	20.02	7.78
政策性银行 Policy banks	59.32	5.00	35.68	20.22	1.76	9.24	1.80	8.82
合计 Total	39.62	5.55	54.82	14.30	16.14	11.21	6.83	6.34

大额美元存款与美元贷款平均利率
Average interest rates of large-value dollar deposits and loans

单位：% Unit: %

年 / 月 Year/Month	大额存款 Large-value deposits						贷款 Loans				
	活期 Demand	3个月以内 Within 3 months	3（含）~6个月 3-6 months (including 3 months)	6（含）~12个月 6-12 months (including 6 months)	1 年 1 year	1年以上 Above 1 year	3个月以内 Within 3 months	3（含）~6个月 3-6 months (including 3 months)	6（含）~12个月 6-12 months (including 6 months)	1 年 1 year	1年以上 Above 1 year
2020.12	0.16	0.59	0.79	0.86	1.09	1.19	1.22	1.36	1.25	1.30	2.10
2021.01	0.14	0.65	0.88	0.92	1.10	1.17	1.25	1.12	1.06	1.04	1.94
2021.02	0.14	0.61	0.72	0.90	1.05	1.04	1.23	1.17	1.05	1.16	2.37
2021.03	0.14	0.55	0.77	0.91	1.09	0.99	1.23	1.09	1.01	0.90	2.14
2021.04	0.12	0.51	0.77	0.81	0.99	1.07	1.32	1.15	1.16	1.03	1.93
2021.05	0.11	0.46	0.69	0.73	0.92	0.84	1.31	1.11	0.86	0.90	2.20
2021.06	0.10	0.43	0.62	0.77	0.91	0.90	1.15	0.99	0.90	0.78	2.22
2021.07	0.11	0.43	0.65	0.70	0.93	0.59	1.14	1.03	0.93	0.86	1.93
2021.08	0.09	0.41	0.64	0.69	0.99	0.88	1.25	1.05	0.94	0.90	2.24
2021.09	0.10	0.40	0.55	0.71	0.85	0.80	1.11	1.05	1.10	0.93	2.16
2021.10	0.11	0.41	0.55	0.76	0.85	1.02	1.16	1.15	1.11	0.96	1.32
2021.11	0.11	0.42	0.68	0.72	0.85	1.00	1.20	1.01	1.02	1.06	2.03
2021.12	0.10	0.31	0.65	0.78	0.97	0.96	1.11	1.11	0.98	1.09	2.00
2022.01	0.12	0.31	0.59	0.91	1.01	1.28	1.04	1.11	1.04	1.14	2.09
2022.02	0.11	0.31	0.67	0.97	1.31	1.62	1.17	1.29	1.37	1.47	2.10
2022.03	0.12	0.53	1.00	1.41	1.52	1.44	1.40	1.54	1.70	1.60	2.20
2022.04	0.13	0.70	1.19	1.85	2.10	1.67	1.69	1.95	2.02	1.87	3.10
2022.05	0.18	1.01	1.65	2.15	2.49	2.34	1.99	2.25	2.33	2.25	3.14
2022.06	0.28	1.49	2.07	2.85	3.19	3.28	2.34	2.58	2.79	3.00	3.81
2022.07	0.27	1.78	2.77	3.22	3.59	2.94	2.99	3.25	3.46	3.42	4.54
2022.08	0.43	2.21	3.10	3.60	3.69	3.61	3.33	3.60	3.72	3.85	4.28
2022.09	0.60	2.59	3.36	4.17	4.13	4.14	3.64	3.78	4.18	4.15	4.18
2022.10	0.73	3.06	3.61	4.84	4.46	4.98	4.27	4.59	4.99	4.69	4.78
2022.11	0.94	3.38	4.41	5.23	5.20	5.40	4.95	5.09	5.38	4.82	5.10
2022.12	1.20	3.66	4.84	5.22	5.49	5.34	5.03	4.99	5.28	5.18	5.67
2023.01	1.25	3.99	4.62	5.34	5.46	4.96	4.91	5.12	5.10	5.53	5.99
2023.02	1.42	4.18	5.10	5.51	5.50	5.44	5.08	5.23	5.39	5.46	5.58
2023.03	1.64	4.23	5.02	5.53	5.67	5.54	5.25	5.33	5.11	5.34	5.86
2023.04	1.76	4.50	5.29	5.49	4.91	5.72	5.39	5.47	5.49	5.64	5.62
2023.05	1.78	4.63	4.65	5.68	5.63	5.64	5.55	5.46	5.52	5.39	5.98
2023.06	1.65	4.46	5.29	5.63	5.47	5.75	5.68	5.63	5.46	5.41	5.71
2023.07	2.13	4.44	5.12	5.50	5.52	5.28	5.68	5.66	5.59	5.31	5.65
2023.08	2.19	4.37	4.57	5.45	5.45	5.25	5.72	5.14	5.30	5.34	5.46
2023.09	2.26	4.50	5.20	5.34	5.58	5.39	5.88	5.49	5.45	5.42	6.34
2023.10	2.29	4.56	5.34	5.42	4.76	5.46	5.99	5.73	5.60	5.44	5.79
2023.11	2.19	4.61	4.69	4.75	4.85	5.37	5.85	5.80	5.59	5.51	6.34
2023.12	2.23	4.70	5.33	5.49	5.39	5.30	5.81	5.80	5.51	5.82	6.36

3.5 人民币汇率（RMB exchange rates）

世界主要货币兑人民币期末汇率
Exchange rate of the RMB against major foreign currencies at the end of the period

人民币元/单位外币
RMB per unit of foreign currency

美元　USD　　100日元　JPY100　　欧元　EUR　　英镑　GBP

CFETS人民币汇率指数
CFETS RMB exchange rate index

%

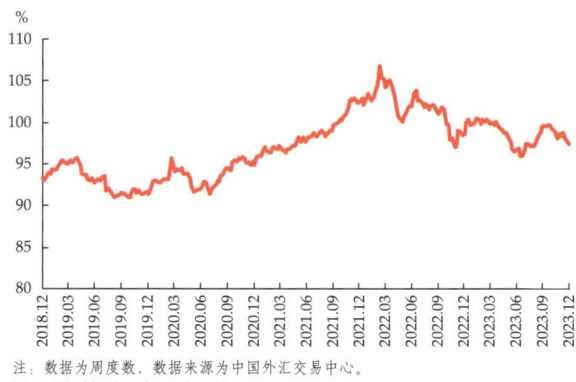

注：数据为周度数，数据来源为中国外汇交易中心。
Note: Weekly data from CFETS.

人民币／美元中间价
（2005年至2023年12月）
Central parity of the RMB against the USD
(From 2005 to Dec. 2023)

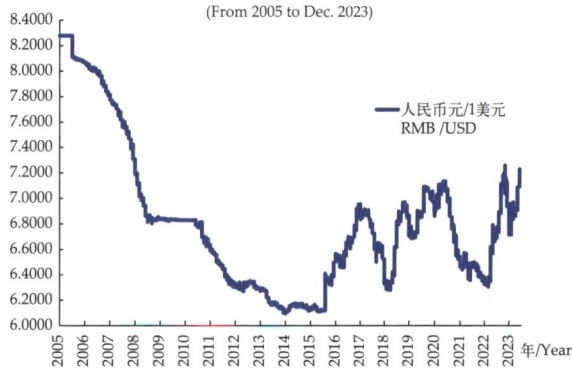

人民币元/1美元
RMB /USD

人民币／欧元中间价
（2005年至2023年12月）
Central parity of the RMB against the EUR
(From 2005 to Dec. 2023)

人民币元/1欧元
RMB/EUR

人民币／日元中间价
（2005年至2023年12月）
Central parity of the RMB against the JPY
(From 2005 to Dec. 2023)

人民币元/100日元
RMB/JPY 100

人民币／英镑中间价
（2005年至2023年12月）
Central parity of the RMB against the GBP
(From 2005 to Dec. 2023)

人民币元/1英镑
RMB/GBP

世界主要货币兑人民币月平均汇率
Monthly average exchange rate of the RMB against major foreign currencies

年 / 月 Year/Month	人民币 / 美元 RMB/USD	人民币 / 欧元 RMB/EUR	人民币 / 英镑 RMB/GBP	人民币 /100 日元 RMB/JPY 100
2021.12	6.3700	7.1991	8.4737	5.5926
2022.01	6.3588	7.2042	8.6277	5.5362
2022.02	6.3470	7.1990	8.5890	5.5024
2022.03	6.3457	6.9900	8.3575	5.3561
2022.04	6.4280	6.9456	8.3182	5.0833
2022.05	6.7071	7.0977	8.3454	5.2136
2022.06	6.6991	7.0791	8.2557	4.9980
2022.07	6.7324	6.8628	8.0782	4.9222
2022.08	6.7949	6.8831	8.1518	5.0299
2022.09	6.9621	6.9160	7.9202	4.8921
2022.10	7.1287	7.0284	8.0857	4.8396
2022.11	7.1628	7.2948	8.3997	5.0263
2022.12	6.9833	7.3872	8.4985	5.1684
2023.01	6.7976	7.3025	8.2842	5.2130
2023.02	6.8296	7.3189	8.2590	5.1434
2023.03	6.8982	7.3847	8.3693	5.1578
2023.04	6.8852	7.5439	8.5620	5.1648
2023.05	6.9912	7.5931	8.7256	5.0994
2023.06	7.1492	7.7418	9.0214	5.0733
2023.07	7.1619	7.9461	9.2575	5.0977
2023.08	7.1733	7.8908	9.1932	5.0078
2023.09	7.1839	7.7405	8.9947	4.9187
2023.10	7.1786	7.6281	8.7897	4.8336
2023.11	7.1544	7.7528	8.9043	4.7942
2023.12	7.1039	7.7612	9.0034	4.9394

CFETS人民币汇率指数月末值
Month end value of CFETS RMB exchange rate index

日期 Date	CFETS 人民币汇率指数 CFETS RMB exchange rate index
2021.12.31	102.47
2022.01.28	103.43
2022.02.28	104.41
2022.03.31	104.28
2022.04.30	103.24
2022.05.31	100.80
2022.06.30	102.01
2022.07.29	102.62
2022.08.31	101.62
2022.09.30	101.03
2022.10.31	99.86
2022.11.30	97.00
2022.12.30	98.67
2023.01.31	99.83
2023.02.28	99.83
2023.03.31	99.80
2023.04.28	99.52
2023.05.31	98.46
2023.06.30	96.74
2023.07.31	96.81
2023.08.31	97.14
2023.09.28	99.55
2023.10.31	99.31
2023.11.30	98.29
2023.12.29	97.42

2023年1月3日以来人民币汇率中间价
Central parity of RMB against major foreign currencies
Since January 3, 2023

日期 Date	人民币 / 美元 RMB/USD	人民币/欧元 RMB/EUR	人民币/100 日元 RMB/JPY 100	人民币 / 英镑 RMB/GBP	日期 Date	人民币 / 美元 RMB/USD	人民币/欧元 RMB/EUR	人民币/100 日元 RMB/JPY 100	人民币 / 英镑 RMB/GBP
2023.01.03	6.9475	7.4133	5.3080	8.3777	2023.02.21	6.8557	7.3265	5.1062	8.2547
2023.01.04	6.9131	7.2921	5.2677	8.2748	2023.02.22	6.8759	7.3229	5.0975	8.3289
2023.01.05	6.8926	7.3160	5.2136	8.3123	2023.02.23	6.9028	7.3214	5.1174	8.3163
2023.01.06	6.8912	7.2535	5.1665	8.2071	2023.02.24	6.8942	7.3070	5.1267	8.2864
2023.01.09	6.8265	7.2718	5.1703	8.2607	2023.02.27	6.9572	7.3406	5.1040	8.3143
2023.01.10	6.7611	7.2549	5.1297	8.2355	2023.02.28	6.9519	7.3747	5.1024	8.3885
2023.01.11	6.7756	7.2746	5.1273	8.2327	2023.03.01	6.9400	7.3416	5.0926	8.3513
2023.01.12	6.7680	7.2877	5.1340	8.2307	2023.03.02	6.8808	7.3417	5.0576	8.2765
2023.01.13	6.7292	7.3067	5.2080	8.2217	2023.03.03	6.9117	7.3267	5.0576	8.2601
2023.01.16	6.7135	7.2709	5.2431	8.2099	2023.03.06	6.8951	7.3280	5.0718	8.2970
2023.01.17	6.7222	7.2792	5.2395	8.2025	2023.03.07	6.9156	7.3854	5.0874	8.3120
2023.01.18	6.7602	7.2913	5.2693	8.3028	2023.03.08	6.9525	7.3363	5.0652	8.2232
2023.01.19	6.7674	7.3044	5.2658	8.3538	2023.03.09	6.9666	7.3483	5.0762	8.2542
2023.01.20	6.7702	7.3361	5.2729	8.3915	2023.03.10	6.9655	7.3738	5.1145	8.3029
2023.01.30	6.7626	7.3517	5.2089	8.3854	2023.03.13	6.9375	7.4156	5.1534	8.3892
2023.01.31	6.7604	7.3354	5.1840	8.3483	2023.03.14	6.8949	7.3952	5.1744	8.3891
2023.02.01	6.7492	7.3318	5.1895	8.3094	2023.03.15	6.8680	7.3703	5.1090	8.3462
2023.02.02	6.7130	7.3935	5.2211	8.3205	2023.03.16	6.9149	7.3194	5.1987	8.3443
2023.02.03	6.7382	7.3497	5.2348	8.2357	2023.03.17	6.9052	7.3301	5.1753	8.3617
2023.02.06	6.7737	7.3101	5.1434	8.1606	2023.03.20	6.8694	7.3380	5.1968	8.3735
2023.02.07	6.7967	7.2901	5.1234	8.1722	2023.03.21	6.8763	7.3703	5.2353	8.4421
2023.02.08	6.7752	7.2682	5.1677	8.1631	2023.03.22	6.8715	7.4012	5.1937	8.3982
2023.02.09	6.7905	7.2753	5.1697	8.1960	2023.03.23	6.8709	7.4675	5.2349	8.4340
2023.02.10	6.7884	7.2886	5.1636	8.2263	2023.03.24	6.8374	7.4069	5.2286	8.3977
2023.02.13	6.8151	7.2737	5.1773	8.2112	2023.03.27	6.8714	7.4038	5.2554	8.4141
2023.02.14	6.8136	7.3087	5.1493	8.2730	2023.03.28	6.8749	7.4303	5.2371	8.4544
2023.02.15	6.8183	7.3204	5.1270	8.3019	2023.03.29	6.8771	7.4551	5.2484	8.4804
2023.02.16	6.8519	7.3228	5.1171	8.2438	2023.03.30	6.8886	7.4680	5.1956	8.4797
2023.02.17	6.8659	7.3193	5.1189	8.2199	2023.03.31	6.8717	7.4945	5.1693	8.5127
2023.02.20	6.8643	7.3330	5.1102	8.2569					

续表

日期 Date	人民币/美元 RMB/USD	人民币/欧元 RMB/EUR	人民币/100日元 RMB/JPY 100	人民币/英镑 RMB/GBP	日期 Date	人民币/美元 RMB/USD	人民币/欧元 RMB/EUR	人民币/100日元 RMB/JPY 100	人民币/英镑 RMB/GBP
2023.04.03	6.8805	7.4381	5.1660	8.4614	2023.05.19	7.0356	7.5829	5.0790	8.7349
2023.04.04	6.8699	7.4930	5.1955	8.5356	2023.05.22	7.0157	7.5911	5.0942	8.7392
2023.04.06	6.8747	7.4986	5.2532	8.5689	2023.05.23	7.0326	7.6031	5.0713	8.7454
2023.04.07	6.8838	7.5149	5.2253	8.5616	2023.05.24	7.0560	7.6002	5.0928	8.7629
2023.04.10	6.8764	7.5008	5.2045	8.5432	2023.05.25	7.0529	7.5843	5.0614	8.7207
2023.04.11	6.8882	7.4859	5.1581	8.5343	2023.05.26	7.0760	7.5888	5.0566	8.7186
2023.04.12	6.8854	7.5158	5.1528	8.5575	2023.05.29	7.0575	7.5679	5.0133	8.7135
2023.04.13	6.8658	7.5504	5.1631	8.5772	2023.05.30	7.0818	7.5836	5.0419	8.7479
2023.04.14	6.8606	7.5819	5.1759	8.5928	2023.05.31	7.0821	7.6016	5.0652	8.7899
2023.04.17	6.8679	7.5451	5.1288	8.5187	2023.06.01	7.0965	7.5887	5.1047	8.8326
2023.04.18	6.8814	7.5178	5.1190	8.5144	2023.06.02	7.0939	7.6321	5.1094	8.8854
2023.04.19	6.8731	7.5436	5.1290	8.5414	2023.06.05	7.0904	7.5854	5.0572	8.8130
2023.04.20	6.8987	7.5537	5.1206	8.5731	2023.06.06	7.1075	7.6115	5.0971	8.8353
2023.04.21	6.8752	7.5400	5.1271	8.5512	2023.06.07	7.1196	7.6144	5.1004	8.8465
2023.04.24	6.8835	7.5648	5.1382	8.5674	2023.06.08	7.1280	7.6269	5.0910	8.8668
2023.04.25	6.8847	7.6109	5.1357	8.6039	2023.06.09	7.1115	7.6692	5.1216	8.9326
2023.04.26	6.9237	7.5999	5.1803	8.5941	2023.06.12	7.1212	7.6540	5.1101	8.9572
2023.04.27	6.9207	7.6435	5.1859	8.6308	2023.06.13	7.1498	7.6953	5.1264	8.9471
2023.04.28	6.9240	7.6361	5.1723	8.6504	2023.06.14	7.1566	7.7214	5.1050	9.0209
2023.05.04	6.9054	7.6458	5.1335	8.6810	2023.06.15	7.1489	7.7486	5.1057	9.0552
2023.05.05	6.9114	7.6189	5.1491	8.6967	2023.06.16	7.1289	7.8042	5.0851	9.1161
2023.05.08	6.9158	7.6217	5.1163	8.7345	2023.06.19	7.1201	7.7895	5.0176	9.1332
2023.05.09	6.9255	7.6135	5.1260	8.7328	2023.06.20	7.1596	7.8226	5.0467	9.1638
2023.05.10	6.9299	7.6004	5.1241	8.7501	2023.06.21	7.1795	7.8396	5.0795	9.1627
2023.05.11	6.9101	7.5911	5.1539	8.7270	2023.06.26	7.2056	7.8618	5.0260	9.1774
2023.05.12	6.9481	7.5850	5.1672	8.6936	2023.06.27	7.2098	7.8773	5.0357	9.1788
2023.05.15	6.9654	7.5583	5.1293	8.6708	2023.06.28	7.2101	7.8999	5.0118	9.1903
2023.05.16	6.9506	7.5593	5.1116	8.7066	2023.06.29	7.2208	7.9167	5.0247	9.1692
2023.05.17	6.9748	7.5778	5.1133	8.7069	2023.06.30	7.2258	7.8771	5.0094	9.1432
2023.05.18	6.9967	7.5858	5.0870	8.7389					

续表

日期 Date	人民币／美元 RMB/USD	人民币／欧元 RMB/EUR	人民币/100 日元 RMB/JPY 100	人民币／英镑 RMB/GBP	日期 Date	人民币／美元 RMB/USD	人民币/欧元 RMB/EUR	人民币/100 日元 RMB/JPY 100	人民币／英镑 RMB/GBP
2023.07.03	7.2157	7.8992	5.0171	9.1965	2023.08.16	7.1986	7.9205	5.0053	9.2318
2023.07.04	7.2046	7.8934	5.0026	9.1824	2023.08.17	7.2076	7.9151	4.9896	9.2688
2023.07.05	7.1968	7.8501	4.9944	9.1737	2023.08.18	7.2006	7.9087	5.0139	9.2907
2023.07.06	7.2098	7.8641	5.0176	9.2035	2023.08.21	7.1987	7.9051	5.0164	9.2650
2023.07.07	7.2054	7.8869	5.0303	9.2266	2023.08.22	7.1992	7.9350	4.9955	9.2941
2023.07.10	7.1926	7.9034	5.0669	9.2521	2023.08.23	7.1988	7.8965	5.0081	9.2688
2023.07.11	7.1886	7.9381	5.1070	9.2822	2023.08.24	7.1886	7.8864	5.0312	9.2322
2023.07.12	7.1765	7.9198	5.1321	9.3028	2023.08.25	7.1883	7.8510	4.9928	9.1559
2023.07.13	7.1527	7.9739	5.1769	9.3035	2023.08.28	7.1856	7.8437	4.9711	9.1438
2023.07.14	7.1318	8.0169	5.1800	9.3770	2023.08.29	7.1851	7.8602	4.9760	9.1576
2023.07.17	7.1326	8.0150	5.1467	9.3454	2023.08.30	7.1816	7.8966	4.9870	9.1690
2023.07.18	7.1453	8.0550	5.1687	9.3692	2023.08.31	7.1811	7.9271	4.9847	9.2252
2023.07.19	7.1486	8.0558	5.1625	9.3517	2023.09.01	7.1788	7.8815	5.0112	9.2125
2023.07.20	7.1466	8.0879	5.1724	9.3360	2023.09.04	7.1786	7.8144	4.9782	9.1344
2023.07.21	7.1456	8.0041	5.1399	9.2556	2023.09.05	7.1783	7.8127	4.9629	9.1538
2023.07.24	7.1451	7.9880	5.0670	9.2284	2023.09.06	7.1969	7.8120	4.9579	9.1593
2023.07.25	7.1406	7.9636	5.0882	9.2263	2023.09.07	7.1986	7.8120	4.9501	9.1070
2023.07.26	7.1295	7.8850	5.0629	9.2005	2023.09.08	7.2150	7.8069	4.9753	9.1040
2023.07.27	7.1265	7.9208	5.0895	9.2390	2023.09.11	7.2148	7.8140	4.9710	9.1054
2023.07.28	7.1338	7.8627	5.1491	9.1606	2023.09.12	7.1986	7.7952	4.9573	9.0706
2023.07.31	7.1305	7.8836	5.0802	9.1955	2023.09.13	7.1894	7.7919	4.9356	9.0491
2023.08.01	7.1283	7.8579	5.0207	9.1706	2023.09.14	7.1874	7.7611	4.9174	9.0323
2023.08.02	7.1368	7.8835	5.0167	9.1613	2023.09.15	7.1786	7.6865	4.9064	8.9732
2023.08.03	7.1495	7.8614	5.0199	9.1374	2023.09.18	7.1736	7.6994	4.8848	8.9471
2023.08.04	7.1418	7.8563	5.0310	9.1237	2023.09.19	7.1733	7.7179	4.8907	8.9390
2023.08.07	7.1380	7.8784	5.0515	9.1299	2023.09.20	7.1732	7.7107	4.8897	8.9414
2023.08.08	7.1565	7.8933	5.0443	9.1736	2023.09.21	7.1730	7.6863	4.8722	8.9043
2023.08.09	7.1588	7.8984	5.0389	9.1887	2023.09.22	7.1729	7.6881	4.8935	8.8741
2023.08.10	7.1576	7.8963	5.0135	9.1517	2023.09.25	7.1727	7.6776	4.8729	8.8285
2023.08.11	7.1587	7.9171	4.9842	9.1375	2023.09.26	7.1727	7.6281	4.8560	8.8184
2023.08.14	7.1686	7.8988	4.9992	9.1756	2023.09.27	7.1717	7.6288	4.8507	8.7738
2023.08.15	7.1768	7.9013	4.9890	9.1909	2023.09.28	7.1798	7.5849	4.8398	8.7667

续表

日期 Date	人民币／美元 RMB/USD	人民币/欧元 RMB/EUR	人民币/100日元 RMB/JPY 100	人民币／英镑 RMB/GBP	日期 Date	人民币／美元 RMB/USD	人民币/欧元 RMB/EUR	人民币/100日元 RMB/JPY 100	人民币／英镑 RMB/GBP
2023.10.09	7.1789	7.6229	4.8515	8.8159	2023.11.20	7.1612	7.8340	4.8001	8.9465
2023.10.10	7.1781	7.6171	4.8673	8.8208	2023.11.21	7.1406	7.8349	4.8257	8.9481
2023.10.11	7.1779	7.6443	4.8583	8.8582	2023.11.22	7.1254	7.7946	4.8203	8.9545
2023.10.12	7.1776	7.6561	4.8449	8.8701	2023.11.23	7.1212	7.7738	4.7785	8.9220
2023.10.13	7.1775	7.6045	4.8258	8.7990	2023.11.24	7.1151	7.7708	4.7657	8.9314
2023.10.16	7.1798	7.5920	4.8320	8.7720	2023.11.27	7.1159	7.7873	4.7645	8.9672
2023.10.17	7.1796	7.5944	4.8314	8.8046	2023.11.28	7.1132	7.7989	4.7996	8.9891
2023.10.18	7.1795	7.6259	4.8287	8.7863	2023.11.29	7.1031	7.8225	4.8322	9.0314
2023.10.19	7.1795	7.6082	4.8278	8.7713	2023.11.30	7.1018	7.8045	4.8362	9.0290
2023.10.20	7.1793	7.6275	4.8232	8.7510	2023.12.01	7.1104	7.7586	4.8116	8.9996
2023.10.23	7.1792	7.6378	4.8234	8.7696	2023.12.04	7.1011	7.7382	4.8583	9.0375
2023.10.24	7.1786	7.6899	4.8265	8.8271	2023.12.05	7.1127	7.7167	4.8401	8.9998
2023.10.25	7.1785	7.6449	4.8268	8.7812	2023.12.06	7.1140	7.6937	4.8440	8.9797
2023.10.26	7.1784	7.6272	4.8212	8.7400	2023.12.07	7.1176	7.6746	4.8442	8.9537
2023.10.27	7.1782	7.6180	4.8094	8.7536	2023.12.08	7.1123	7.6792	4.9431	8.9492
2023.10.30	7.1781	7.6198	4.8301	8.7400	2023.12.11	7.1163	7.6737	4.9166	8.9464
2023.10.31	7.1779	7.6480	4.8433	8.7639	2023.12.12	7.1174	7.6812	4.8853	8.9590
2023.11.01	7.1778	7.6399	4.7861	8.7814	2023.12.13	7.1126	7.6933	4.9062	8.9545
2023.11.02	7.1797	7.6332	4.7994	8.7798	2023.12.14	7.1090	7.7356	4.9908	8.9748
2023.11.03	7.1796	7.6612	4.8037	8.7904	2023.12.15	7.0957	7.7988	4.9897	9.0542
2023.11.06	7.1780	7.7262	4.8303	8.9077	2023.12.18	7.0933	7.7414	4.9930	9.0034
2023.11.07	7.1776	7.7230	4.8118	8.8949	2023.12.19	7.0982	7.7584	4.9819	8.9850
2023.11.08	7.1773	7.7133	4.8051	8.8672	2023.12.20	7.0966	7.7975	4.9383	9.0414
2023.11.09	7.1772	7.7143	4.7843	8.8514	2023.12.21	7.1012	7.7775	4.9553	8.9858
2023.11.10	7.1771	7.6917	4.7744	8.8153	2023.12.22	7.0953	7.8160	4.9988	9.0070
2023.11.13	7.1769	7.7042	4.7693	8.8163	2023.12.25	7.1010	7.8238	4.9926	9.0344
2023.11.14	7.1768	7.7102	4.7629	8.8490	2023.12.26	7.0965	7.8335	5.0019	9.0324
2023.11.15	7.1752	7.8152	4.7840	8.9747	2023.12.27	7.1002	7.8452	4.9951	9.0436
2023.11.16	7.1724	7.8027	4.7586	8.9303	2023.12.28	7.0974	7.8901	5.0201	9.0886
2023.11.17	7.1728	7.8057	4.7801	8.9178	2023.12.29	7.0827	7.8592	5.0213	9.0411

四、金融市场（Financial market）

4.1 货币市场与债券市场（Money market and bond market）

银行间市场交易量
Transaction volume in the interbank market

单位：万亿元
Unit: RMB 1 trillion

年 Year	债券回购 Repurchasing	同业拆借 Interbank borrowing	现券买卖 Outright transactions
2001	4.0	0.8	0.1
2002	10.2	1.2	0.4
2003	11.7	2.4	3.1
2004	9.4	1.5	2.5
2005	15.9	1.3	6.0
2006	26.6	2.2	10.2
2007	44.8	10.6	15.6
2008	58.1	15.0	37.1
2009	70.3	19.4	47.3
2010	87.6	27.9	64.0
2011	99.5	33.4	63.6
2012	141.7	46.7	75.2
2013	158.2	35.5	41.6
2014	224.4	37.7	40.4
2015	457.8	64.2	86.7
2016	601.3	95.9	127.1
2017	616.4	79.0	102.8
2018	722.7	139.3	150.7
2019	819.6	151.6	213.7
2020	959.8	147.1	232.8
2021	1045.2	118.8	214.4
2022	1380.2	146.8	271.2
2023	1674.2	142.9	307.3

债券回购交易成交金额
Turnover of repurchasing

单位：亿元
Unit: RMB 100 million

年 / 月 Year/Month	银行间债券市场 Interbank bond market	交易所 Stock exchanges
2022.01	1 004 824	316 735
2022.02	800 347	270 840
2022.03	1 073 395	377 946
2022.04	1 042 211	308 121
2022.05	1 118 521	308 295
2022.06	1 260 593	345 690
2022.07	1 318 609	328 775
2022.08	1 526 047	370 265
2022.09	1 331 465	350 493
2022.10	974 857	277 955
2022.11	1 183 613	382 640
2022.12	1 167 064	396 934
2023.01	971 230	305 573
2023.02	1 109 644	382 244
2023.03	1 449 734	442 730
2023.04	1 321 294	357 713
2023.05	1 555 866	378 700
2023.06	1 556 425	384 687
2023.07	1 676 699	394 706
2023.08	1 703 259	407 195
2023.09	1 367 693	365 475
2023.10	1 171 202	331 853
2023.11	1 420 362	420 303
2023.12	1 438 851	404 424

银行间市场交易量
Transaction volume in the interbank market

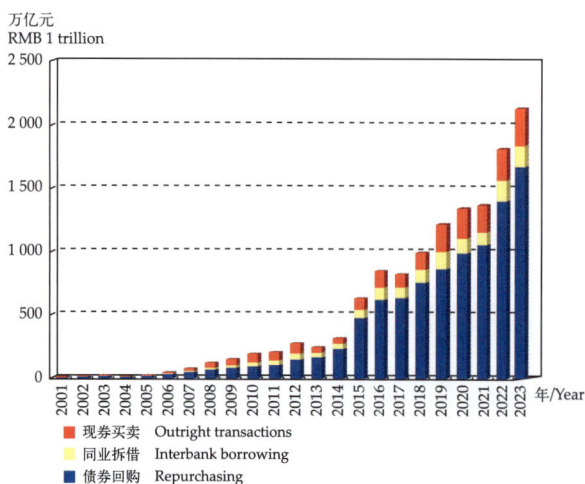

万亿元
RMB 1 trillion

- 现券买卖 Outright transactions
- 同业拆借 Interbank borrowing
- 债券回购 Repurchasing

债券回购交易成交金额
Turnover of repurchasing

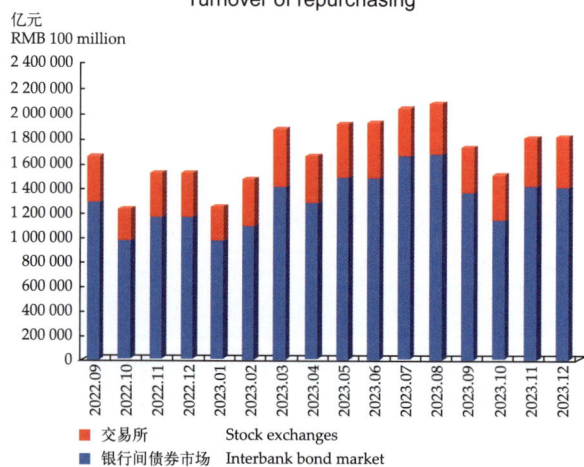

亿元
RMB 100 million

- 交易所 Stock exchanges
- 银行间债券市场 Interbank bond market

银行间市场月加权平均利率
Monthly weighted average interest rates in the interbank market

单位：%
Unit:%

年 / 月 Year/Month	同业拆借市场 Interbank borrowing market	质押式债券回购 Bond-pledged repurchasing
2022.01	2.01	2.04
2022.02	2.06	2.06
2022.03	2.07	2.08
2022.04	1.62	1.61
2022.05	1.50	1.47
2022.06	1.56	1.57
2022.07	1.35	1.33
2022.08	1.23	1.24
2022.09	1.41	1.46
2022.10	1.41	1.46
2022.11	1.55	1.61
2022.12	1.26	1.41
2023.01	1.44	1.56
2023.02	1.92	2.07
2023.03	1.70	1.85
2023.04	1.69	1.77
2023.05	1.50	1.55
2023.06	1.57	1.67
2023.07	1.49	1.53
2023.08	1.71	1.76
2023.09	1.87	1.96
2023.10	1.92	2.06
2023.11	1.89	1.98
2023.12	1.78	1.90

债券现券交易成交金额
Turnover of outright transactions

单位：亿元
Unit: RMB 100 million

年 / 月 Year/Month	银行间债券市场 Interbank bond market	交易所 Stock exchanges
2022.01	208 810	23 144
2022.02	173 195	20 389
2022.03	235 330	36 201
2022.04	202 747	31 992
2022.05	197 908	38 483
2022.06	225 397	47 213
2022.07	235 323	36 825
2022.08	282 502	31 451
2022.09	247 152	23 061
2022.10	196 277	19 756
2022.11	286 295	34 869
2022.12	221 299	35 654
2023.01	159 590	21 136
2023.02	216 717	30 482
2023.03	284 535	35 854
2023.04	244 280	32 062
2023.05	261 641	33 522
2023.06	270 397	39 349
2023.07	273 712	44 551
2023.08	306 273	57 000
2023.09	273 549	43 881
2023.10	216 630	35 533
2023.11	283 579	49 078
2023.12	282 146	43 915

银行间市场月加权平均利率
Monthly weighted average interest rates in the interbank market

同业拆借市场　Interbank borrowing market
质押式债券回购　Bond-pledged repurchasing

债券现券交易成交金额
Turnover of outright transactions

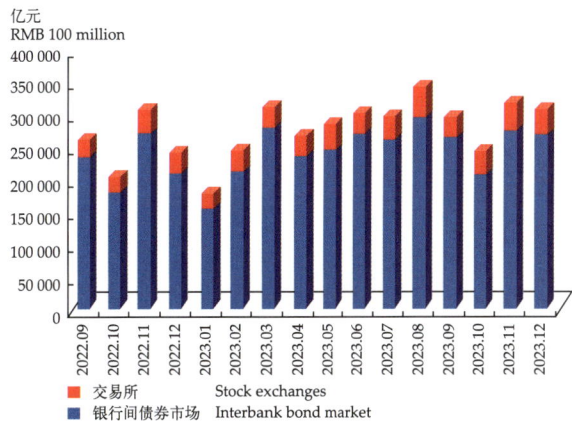

交易所　Stock exchanges
银行间债券市场　Interbank bond market

主要货币市场利率品种走势
Trend chart of major money market interest rates

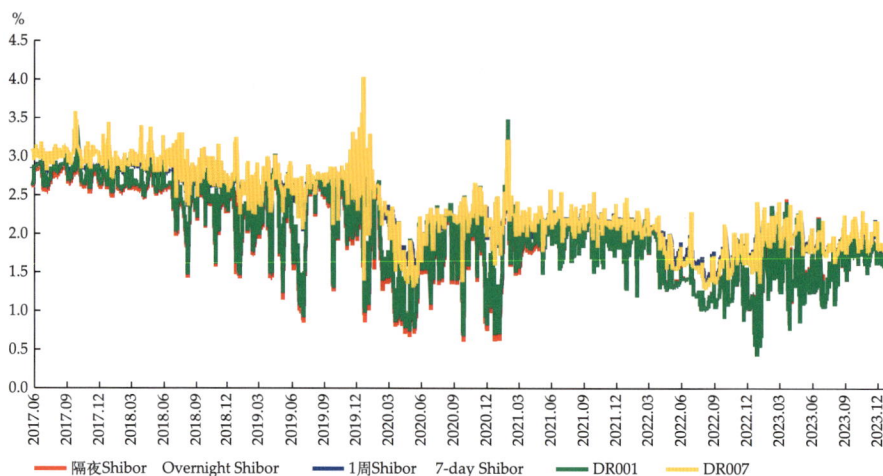

隔夜Shibor Overnight Shibor　1周Shibor 7-day Shibor　DR001　DR007

全国银行间同业拆借各期限当月交易量及月加权平均利率
Monthly transaction volume and monthly weighted average interest rates of interbank borrowing with different maturities

单位：亿元、%
Unit: RMB 100 million, %

年 / 月 Year/Month	1天 1 day		7天 7 days		14天 14 days		21天 21 days		1个月 1 month		2个月 2 months		3个月 3 months		4个月 4 months		6个月 6 months		9个月 9 months		1年 1 year	
	交易量 Volume	利率 Rate	交易量 Volume	利率 Rate	交易量 Volume	利率 Rate	交易量 Volume	利率 Rate	交易量 Volume	利率 Rate	交易量 Volume	利率 Rate	交易量 Volume	利率 Rate	交易量 Volume	利率 Rate	交易量 Volume	利率 Rate	交易量 Volume	利率 Rate	交易量 Volume	利率 Rate
2022.01	97 045	1.94	9 439	2.42	2527	2.43	192	2.52	496	2.63	481	2.59	519	3.32	34	3.70	64	3.50	22	3.44	54	3.72
2022.02	77 621	2.01	7 770	2.39	437	2.25	102	2.28	337	2.54	147	2.85	485	3.20	65	3.72	30	3.17	16	3.42	24	3.49
2022.03	91 871	2.01	11 631	2.37	970	2.35	112	2.38	566	2.51	142	2.90	714	3.17	9	3.07	40	3.26	20	3.31	40	3.39
2022.04	94 813	1.54	12 421	2.06	979	2.03	150	2.27	229	2.58	160	2.68	565	2.99	15	3.24	53	3.23	23	3.36	24	3.45
2022.05	107 234	1.44	11 626	1.89	801	1.84	107	1.89	278	2.32	130	2.42	574	2.81	7	2.70	38	2.93	11	3.15	30	3.25
2022.06	125 798	1.51	10 779	1.98	707	1.87	142	1.89	206	2.14	261	2.15	596	2.76	12	2.80	43	3.16	11	3.32	43	3.06
2022.07	133 486	1.30	11 223	1.80	596	1.77	97	1.85	197	2.04	99	2.00	512	2.79	22	2.49	52	2.85	21	3.15	57	3.09
2022.08	160 258	1.19	11 793	1.67	711	1.54	57	1.53	287	1.72	54	1.85	417	2.50	13	2.24	40	2.84	5	2.75	36	3.02
2022.09	134 353	1.35	10 765	1.90	2616	2.04	347	1.85	251	1.98	376	1.87	535	2.36	26	2.77	30	2.65	7	2.72	21	2.70
2022.10	95 837	1.33	10 370	1.97	955	1.83	187	1.75	368	2.02	102	2.10	525	2.43	6	2.37	25	2.76	3	2.40	20	2.88
2022.11	91 389	1.49	10 869	1.98	671	2.01	139	2.05	231	2.09	141	2.43	570	2.68	9	3.14	22	2.92	14	2.84	32	2.98
2022.12	99 601	1.13	11 536	2.10	889	2.41	103	2.43	331	2.06	218	2.58	673	2.79	42	3.16	35	3.04	5	3.21	48	3.40
2023.01	89 057	1.32	8 935	2.15	1330	2.46	536	2.47	897	2.24	285	2.44	562	2.90	101	2.38	215	2.45	23	3.15	58	3.41
2023.02	86 407	1.87	7 965	2.37	374	2.38	44	2.53	233	2.48	168	2.80	608	2.94	80	3.03	36	2.97	22	3.02	49	3.09
2023.03	121 294	1.64	9 066	2.36	417	2.50	120	2.50	169	2.72	65	2.95	631	3.05	12	3.15	32	2.96	14	3.07	55	3.37
2023.04	108 312	1.62	10 942	2.30	596	2.26	42	2.68	173	2.58	73	2.59	578	2.89	5	3.19	21	2.90	21	3.02	31	3.39
2023.05	138 223	1.44	11 635	2.05	499	2.04	78	2.34	293	2.51	113	2.67	555	2.98	4	2.66	32	2.85	16	2.90	46	3.13
2023.06	125 453	1.50	11 528	2.15	440	2.19	89	2.19	227	2.37	257	2.30	722	2.81	6	2.70	29	2.81	5	3.01	36	3.29
2023.07	131 477	1.43	12 080	2.00	363	2.04	43	2.11	333	2.36	68	2.32	613	2.57	15	2.53	29	2.79	8	2.72	37	3.05
2023.08	117 508	1.67	11 240	2.04	698	1.98	60	1.98	298	2.16	83	2.32	546	2.63	9	2.63	31	2.69	14	2.86	26	2.71
2023.09	88 969	1.80	9 000	2.28	1072	2.67	142	2.61	325	2.48	155	2.64	710	2.64	11	2.85	17	2.58	1	2.64	18	2.77
2023.10	74 323	1.87	9 573	2.24	502	2.33	41	2.37	375	2.58	95	2.55	546	2.73	5	2.60	26	2.80	3	2.89	29	3.01
2023.11	96 291	1.84	10 918	2.27	373	2.37	80	2.45	317	2.69	110	2.74	626	2.88	12	2.95	23	3.04	1	3.05	41	3.14
2023.12	102 640	1.71	13 486	2.12	746	2.45	94	2.89	453	2.94	121	2.91	690	3.02	10	2.94	91	2.76	3	3.34	57	3.23

政府债券发行、兑付、期末余额

Issue and redemption values and end-period balance of government bonds

单位：亿元
Unit: RMB 100 million

年 / 月 Year/Month	发行额 Issue value	兑付额 Redemption value	期末余额 End-period balance
2022.01	11 649	4 670	538 770
2022.02	9 871	6 332	541 492
2022.03	12 786	6 817	548 566
2022.04	10 502	7 027	552 613
2022.05	17 693	5 638	563 195
2022.06	24 377	7 325	579 411
2022.07	14 599	11 381	583 409
2022.08	14 290	11 802	586 754
2022.09	12 316	7 376	592 337
2022.10	14 959	9 936	595 129
2022.11	12 002	7 226	601 662
2022.12	15 676	13 446	604 602
2023.01	10 620	6 488	608 742
2023.02	14 015	5 866	616 880
2023.03	16 013	9 859	623 034
2023.04	15 013	9 683	628 386
2023.05	15 391	9 551	634 222
2023.06	15 829	10 134	639 673
2023.07	16 396	12 493	643 836
2023.08	21 799	9 932	655 726
2023.09	19 863	9 985	665 646
2023.10	26 591	10 956	681 284
2023.11	19 773	7 985	693 077
2023.12	12 909	3 222	702 779

5年期与10年期国债收益率

5-year and 10-year government bond yield

单位：%
Unit: %

年 / 月 Year/Month	5 年期国债收益率 5-year government bond yield	10 年期国债收益率 10-year government bond yield
2022.01	2.36	2.70
2022.02	2.51	2.78
2022.03	2.57	2.79
2022.04	2.61	2.84
2022.05	2.55	2.74
2022.06	2.65	2.82
2022.07	2.51	2.76
2022.08	2.41	2.62
2022.09	2.58	2.76
2022.10	2.43	2.64
2022.11	2.69	2.89
2022.12	2.64	2.84
2023.01	2.70	2.90
2023.02	2.74	2.90
2023.03	2.68	2.85
2023.04	2.61	2.78
2023.05	2.46	2.69
2023.06	2.42	2.64
2023.07	2.45	2.66
2023.08	2.40	2.56
2023.09	2.53	2.68
2023.10	2.53	2.69
2023.11	2.57	2.67
2023.12	2.40	2.56

政府债券发行与兑付

Issue and redemption values of government bonds

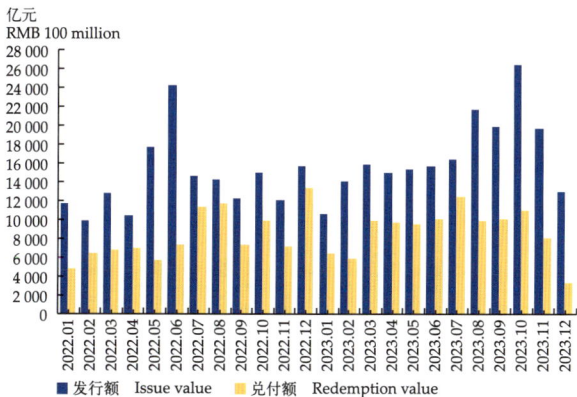

国债收益率曲线

Government bond yield curve

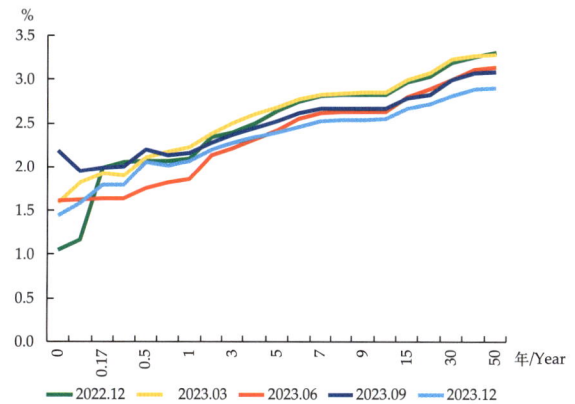

4.2 票据市场 （Commercial paper market）

票据市场交易额与期末余额
Transactions and outstanding balance of commercial paper market

单位：亿元
Unit: RMB 100 million

年 / 月 Year/Month	商业汇票 Drafts	贴现 Discount bills	再贴现 Rediscount bills
发生额 Transactions during the period			
2022.01	29 190	46 043	1 517
2022.02	13 819	33 542	1 374
2022.03	26 627	54 678	1 664
2022.04	20 536	52 295	1 297
2022.05	25 089	55 506	1 225
2022.06	25 379	46 624	1 544
2022.07	21 134	44 168	1 275
2022.08	22 017	43 521	1 122
2022.09	20 536	36 564	1 252
2022.10	16 883	34 720	1 062
2022.11	21 679	39 927	1 292
2022.12	30 999	51 408	1 526
2023.01	21 662	36 475	1 268
2023.02	15 238	28 669	1 567
2023.03	21 801	42 911	1 788
2023.04	18 596	49 175	1 598
2023.05	23 201	53 243	1 275
2023.06	23 756	45 660	1 518
2023.07	30 242	70 447	1 507
2023.08	29 715	61 238	1 207
2023.09	26 920	44 126	1 529
2023.10	26 970	57 420	1 303
2023.11	35 077	65 459	1 592
2023.12	40 301	71 582	1 924
期末余额 Outstanding balance at the end of the period			
2022.01	156 564	100 301	5 790
2022.02	154 791	103 353	6 039
2022.03	157 504	106 540	6 247
2022.04	159 156	111 688	6 112
2022.05	165 070	118 817	6 033
2022.06	166 325	119 600	6 145
2022.07	165 720	122 736	5 890
2022.08	171 248	124 327	5 669
2022.09	170 320	123 516	5 449
2022.10	169 829	125 421	5 258
2022.11	171 326	126 970	5 284
2022.12	173 755	128 090	5 583
2023.01	171 019	123 964	5 281
2023.02	169 604	122 975	5 594
2023.03	166 704	118 288	6 061
2023.04	165 640	119 568	6 219
2023.05	164 753	119 988	6 128
2023.06	162 672	119 167	5 950
2023.07	163 197	122 764	5 714
2023.08	167 913	126 236	5 283
2023.09	166 434	124 734	5 289
2023.10	169 296	127 912	5 172
2023.11	171 779	130 004	5 245
2023.12	171 373	131 500	5 920

注：中国人民银行于2019年第三季度调整了商业汇票、贴现口径，与以前数据不可比。

Note: Since Q3 2019, the PBOC has improved the statistics of drafts and discount bills, the data is not comparable to previous.

商业汇票交易情况
Draft transactions

亿元 RMB 100 million （left） 亿元 RMB 100 million （right）

■ 发生额（左坐标）
Transactions during the period (LHS)
— 期末未到期金额（右坐标）
Outstanding balance at the end of the period (RHS)

贴现情况
Discount bills

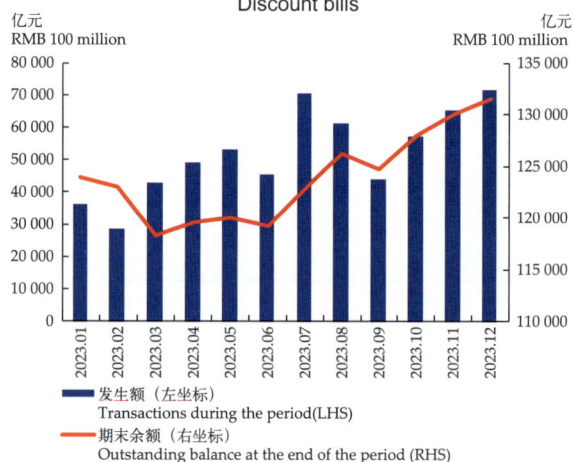

亿元 RMB 100 million （left） 亿元 RMB 100 million （right）

■ 发生额（左坐标）
Transactions during the period(LHS)
— 期末余额（右坐标）
Outstanding balance at the end of the period (RHS)

再贴现情况
Rediscount bills

亿元 RMB 100 million （left） 亿元 RMB 100 million （right）

■ 发生额（左坐标）
Transactions during the period (LHS)
— 期末余额（右坐标）
Outstanding balance at the end of the period (RHS)

4.3 股票市场（Stock market）

股票指数
Stock market index

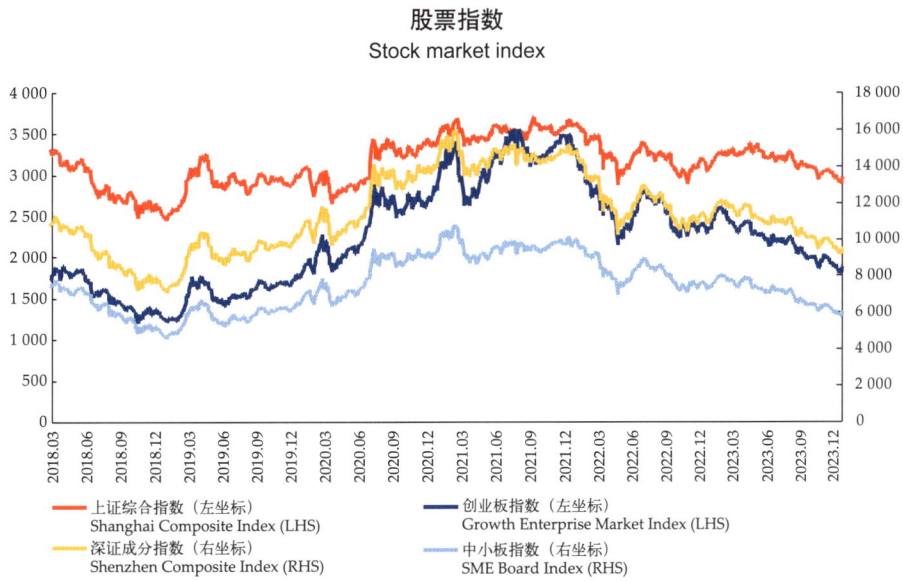

上证综合指数（左坐标）
Shanghai Composite Index (LHS)

深证成分指数（右坐标）
Shenzhen Composite Index (RHS)

创业板指数（左坐标）
Growth Enterprise Market Index (LHS)

中小板指数（右坐标）
SME Board Index (RHS)

股票成交金额
Turnover of stock trading

亿元
RMB 100 million

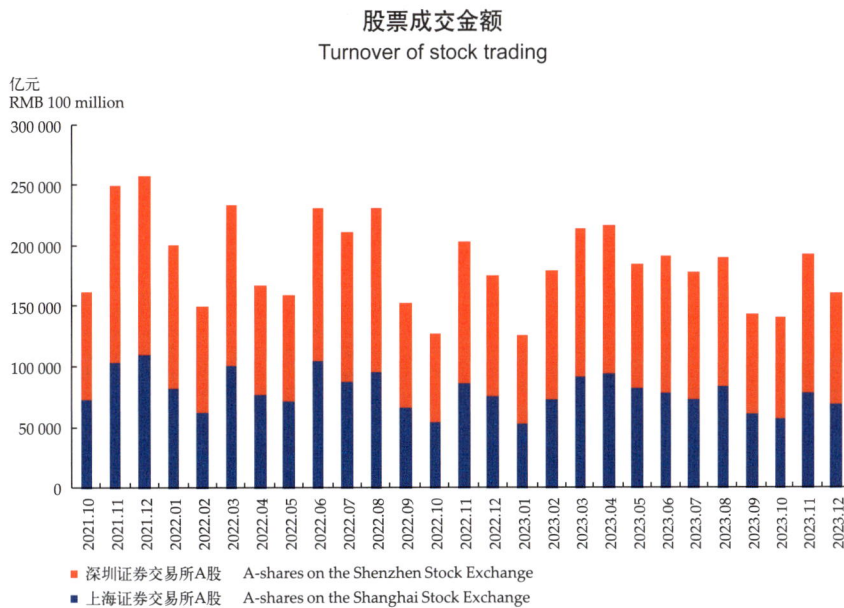

■ 深圳证券交易所A股　A-shares on the Shenzhen Stock Exchange

■ 上海证券交易所A股　A-shares on the Shanghai Stock Exchange

股票成交、发行筹资额
Turnover of stock trading and funds raised in the stock market

单位：亿元
Unit: RMB 100 million

年 Year	成交金额 Turnover of stock trading		A 股筹资 A-shares capital raised			H 股筹资 H-shares capital raised	
	上海证券交易所 A 股 A-shares on the Shanghai Stock Exchange	深圳证券交易所 A 股 A-shares on the Shenzhen Stock Exchange	首次发行金额 Initial public offering	增发 Additional offering	配股 Rights issues	首次发行金额 Initial public offering	再筹资金额 Refinancing
2011	236 809	183 530	2 825	1 797	422	78	33
2012	164 047	149 668	1 034	1 972	121	80	35
2013	228 919	237 713	0	2 327	669	113	84
2014	375 150	366 228	669	4 050	138	129	213
2015	1 323 231	1 223 607	1 767	6 709	42	236	227
2016	496 880	775 478	1 634	16 978	299	1079	529
2017	507 215	616 433	2 186	12 871	157	487	1342
2018	401 575	499 528	1 375	8 421	228	902	305
2019	543 464	730 108	2 490	7 365	134	956	182
2020	839 470	1 228 162	4 742	8 779	434	739	248
2021	1 139 595	1 439 455	5 351	9 556	493	306	872
2022	962 081	1 282 331	5 711	6 166	615	542	—
2023	893 350	1 228 332	3 716	5 067	150	245	—

月末加权平均市盈率
Weighted average price-earnings ratio at month-end

年 / 月 Year/Month	上海证券交易所 A 股 A-shares on the Shanghai Stock Exchange	深圳证券交易所 A 股 A-shares on the Shenzhen Stock Exchange	科创板 SSE STAR Market
2022.01	16.6	29.7	66.7
2022.02	17.2	30.3	61.2
2022.03	16.1	26.0	59.1
2022.04	15.1	21.6	51.2
2022.05	12.9	23.6	38.3
2022.06	13.8	26.2	43.8
2022.07	13.3	25.7	45.7
2022.08	13.2	24.8	49.3
2022.09	12.5	22.7	46.4
2022.10	12.0	22.3	45.3
2022.11	13.0	23.9	48.0
2022.12	12.8	23.5	45.3
2023.01	13.6	25.6	46.6
2023.02	13.7	25.7	48.5
2023.03	13.7	24.3	47.8
2023.04	14.0	24.3	50.3
2023.05	12.8	23.6	39.4
2023.06	12.8	24.1	39.9
2023.07	13.1	24.3	38.9
2023.08	12.5	23.0	36.2
2023.09	12.5	22.5	35.7
2023.10	12.1	22.1	34.8
2023.11	12.1	22.1	36.2
2023.12	12.0	21.7	35.2

月末加权平均市盈率
Weighted average price-earnings ratio at month-end

上海证券交易所A股　A-Shares on the Shanghai Stock Exchange
深圳证券交易所A股　A-Shares on the Shenzhen Stock Exchange
科创板　　　　　　　SSE STAR Market

五、国际收支（Balance of payments）

2023年第四季度国际收支平衡表简表
BOP sheet in 2023 Q4

单位：亿美元
Unit: USD 100 million

项目 Items		金额 Amounts
一、经常账户 Current account		562
	贷方 credit	9 885
	借方 debit	−9 324
1.1 货物和服务 Goods and services		944
	贷方 credit	9 287
	借方 debit	−8 343
1.1.1 货物 Goods		1 511
	贷方 credit	8 432
	借方 debit	−6 921
1.1.2 服务 Services		−567
	贷方 credit	855
	借方 debit	−1 422
1.2 初次收入 Primary income		−426
	贷方 credit	501
	借方 debit	−928
1.3 二次收入 Secondary income		44
	贷方 credit	97
	借方 debit	−53
二、资本和金融账户 Capital and financial account		−466
2.1 资本账户 Capital account		−1
	贷方 credit	0
	借方 debit	−1
2.2 金融账户 Financial account		−466
资产 Assets		−899
负债 Liabilities		434
2.2.1 非储备性质的金融账户 Financial account excluding reserve assets		−340
2.2.1.1 直接投资 Direct investment		−259
资产 Assets		−436
负债 Liabilities		177
2.2.1.2 证券投资 Portfolio investment		348
资产 Assets		−111
负债 Liabilities		458
2.2.1.3 金融衍生工具 Financial derivatives		−5
资产 Assets		9
负债 Liabilities		−14
2.2.1.4 其他投资 Other investment		−424
资产 Assets		−237
负债 Liabilities		−187
2.2.2 储备资产 Reserve assets		−125
三、净误差与遗漏 Net errors and omissions		−96

注：根据《国际收支和国际投资头寸手册》（第六版）编制，为初步数。
Note: Compiled in accordance with the sixth edition of *Balance of Payments and International Investment Postion Manual* (BPM6). The Data are preliminary.

中国国际收支变化趋势
Movement of China's balance of payments

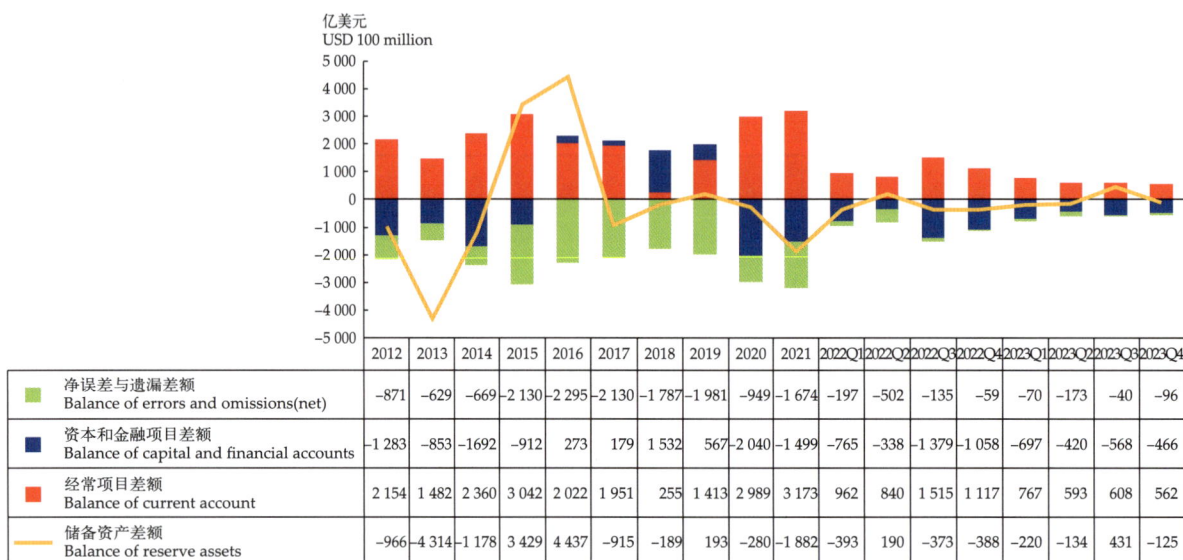

亿美元
USD 100 million

	2012	2013	2014	2015	2016	2017	2018	2019	2020	2021	2022Q1	2022Q2	2022Q3	2022Q4	2023Q1	2023Q2	2023Q3	2023Q4
净误差与遗漏差额 Balance of errors and omissions(net)	−871	−629	−669	−2 130	−2 295	−2 130	−1 787	−1 981	−949	−1 674	−197	−502	−135	−59	−70	−173	−40	−96
资本和金融项目差额 Balance of capital and financial accounts	−1 283	−853	−1692	−912	273	179	1 532	567	−2 040	−1 499	−765	−338	−1 379	−1 058	−697	−420	−568	−466
经常项目差额 Balance of current account	2 154	1 482	2 360	3 042	2 022	1 951	255	1 413	2 989	3 173	962	840	1 515	1 117	767	593	608	562
储备资产差额 Balance of reserve assets	−966	−4 314	−1 178	3 429	4 437	−915	−189	193	−280	−1 882	−393	190	−373	−388	−220	−134	431	−125

2023年12月末外债结构
External debt structure at the end of 2023Q4

短期外债余额占比为56%
Balance of short-term external debt accounted for 56 percent

中长期外债余额占比为44%
Balance of medium- and long-term external debt accounted for 44 percent

2023年12月末，中国外债余额为24 475亿美元，其中，中长期外债余额为10 847亿美元，占外债余额的44%；短期外债余额为13 628亿美元，占外债余额的56%。

China's outstanding balance of external debt was USD 2,447.5 billion at the end of 2023Q4 among which USD 1,084.7 billion or 44 percent was medium- and long-term debt, and USD 1,362.8 billion or 56 percent was short-term debt.

2023年12月末外债数据
External debt balance at the end of 2023 Q4

项目 Item	外债余额 Outstanding external debt	广义政府债务 General government debt	中央银行债务 Monetary authority debt	其他接受存款公司 Other deposit receiving companies debt	其他部门债务 Other sectors debt	直接投资：公司间贷款 Direct investment: intercompany lending
债务余额（亿美元） Debt balance (USD 100 million)	24 475	4 345	1 072	10 093	6 007	2 958
比重（%） Share (%)	100.00	17.75	4.38	41.24	24.54	12.08

注：2014年末，国家外汇管理局按照国际货币基金组织"数据公布特殊标准"（SDDS）的分类标准公布我国外币外债数据，机构部门的分类相应进行了调整。

Note: At the end of 2014, State Administration of Foreign Exchange (SAFE) started to publish the data of China's external debts denominated in foreign currencies according to IMF's SDDS classification standards. The classification of sectors and departments were also adjusted accordingly.

外币外债余额与负债率
Balance and ratio of external debt to GDP

（图中数据根据国家外汇管理局最新数据修订）
(Data are revised by State Administration of Foreign Exchange)

外汇储备及其增长率
Foreign exchange reserves and growth rate

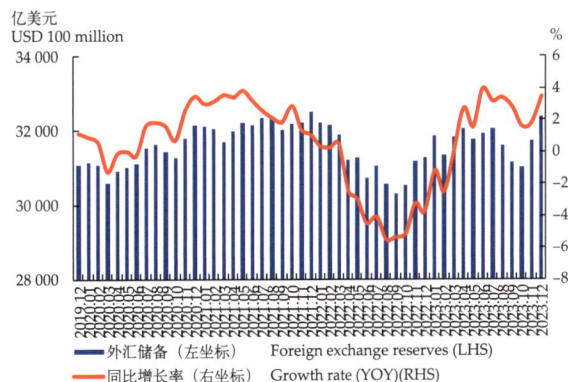

六、财政收支
（Fiscal revenue and expenditure）

年度财政收入、财政支出及其增长趋势
Annual budgetary revenue, budgetary expenditure,
and their growth

年 Year	财政收入（亿元）Budgetary revenue (RMB 100 million)	财政支出（亿元）Budgetary expenditure (RMB 100 million)	财政收入同比增长率（%）Growth rate of budgetary revenue (YOY) (%)	财政支出同比增长率（%）Growth rate of budgetary expenditure (YOY) (%)
2003	19 774	24 650	19.9	11.8
2004	26 396	28 487	21.6	15.6
2005	31 649	33 930	19.9	19.1
2006	38 760	40 423	22.5	19.1
2007	51 322	49 781	32.4	23.2
2008	61 317	62 427	19.5	25.4
2009	68 477	75 874	11.7	21.2
2010	83 080	89 575	21.3	17.4
2011	103 740	108 930	24.8	21.2
2012	117 210	125 712	12.8	15.1
2013	129 143	139 744	10.1	10.9
2014	140 350	151 662	8.6	8.2
2015	152 217	175 768	8.4	15.8
2016	159 552	187 841	4.5	6.4
2017	172 567	203 330	7.4	7.7
2018	183 352	220 906	6.2	8.7
2019	190 382	238 874	3.8	8.1
2020	182 895	245 588	-3.9	2.8
2021	202 539	246 322	10.7	0.3
2022	203 703	260 609	0.6	6.1
2023	216 784	274 574	6.4	5.4

注：表中数据根据财政部最新数据修订。
Note: Data are revised by Ministry of Finance.

月度累计财政收支增长率与收支差额
Monthly growth rates and balance of accumulated fiscal revenue and expenditure

年 / 月 Year/Month	财政收入累计同比增长率（%）Growth rate of accumulated fiscal revenue (YOY) (%)	财政支出累计同比增长率（%）Growth rate of accumulated fiscal expenditure (YOY) (%)	累计财政收支总量差额（亿元）Balance of accumulated fiscal revenue and expenditure (RMB 100 million)
2021.01	—	—	
2021.02	18.7	10.5	6 072
2021.03	24.2	6.2	-1 588
2021.04	25.5	3.8	1 612
2021.05	24.2	3.6	2 901
2021.06	21.8	4.5	-4 560
2021.07	20.0	3.3	-212
2021.08	18.4	3.6	-5 283
2021.09	16.3	2.3	-15 273
2021.10	14.5	2.4	-12 435
2021.11	12.8	2.9	-22 672
2021.12	10.7	0.3	-43 783
2022.01	—	—	
2022.02	10.5	7.0	7 976
2022.03	8.6	8.3	-1 550
2022.04	-4.8	5.9	-6 640
2022.05	-10.1	5.9	-12 320
2022.06	-10.2	5.9	-23 666
2022.07	-9.2	6.4	-21 770
2022.08	-8.0	6.3	-27 134
2022.09	-6.6	6.2	-37 238
2022.10	-4.5	6.4	-32 937
2022.11	-3.0	6.2	-41 737
2022.12	0.6	6.1	-56 906
2023.01	—	—	
2023.02	-1.2	7.0	4 744
2023.03	0.5	6.8	-5 574
2023.04	11.9	6.8	-3 247
2023.05	14.9	5.8	-5 129
2023.06	13.3	3.9	-14 690
2023.07	11.5	3.3	-12 289
2023.08	10.0	3.8	-19 586
2023.09	8.9	3.9	-31 184
2023.10	8.1	4.6	-28 240
2023.11	7.9	4.9	-38 331
2023.12	6.4	5.4	-57 790

注：表中数据根据财政部最新数据修订。
Note: Data are revised by Ministry of Finance.

年度财政收入、财政支出及其增长趋势
Annual budgetary revenue, budgetary expenditure, and their growth

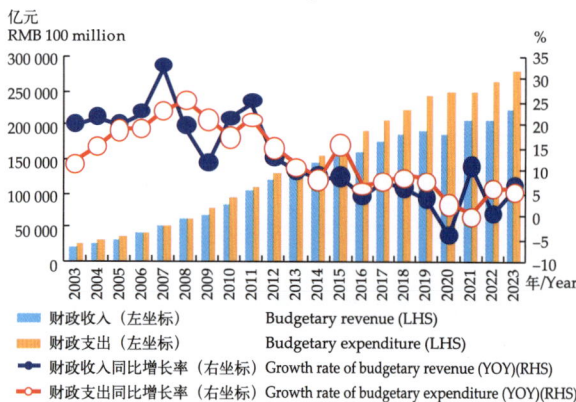

财政收入（左坐标） Budgetary revenue (LHS)
财政支出（左坐标） Budgetary expenditure (LHS)
财政收入同比增长率（右坐标） Growth rate of budgetary revenue (YOY)(RHS)
财政支出同比增长率（右坐标） Growth rate of budgetary expenditure (YOY)(RHS)

月度累计财政收支增长率与收支差额
Monthly growth rates and balance of accumulated fiscal revenue and expenditure

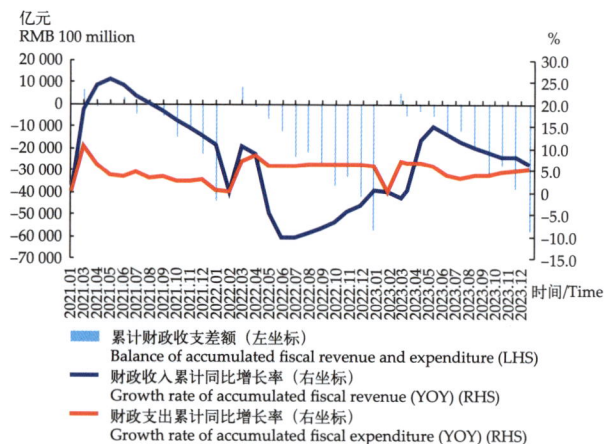

累计财政收支差额（左坐标）
Balance of accumulated fiscal revenue and expenditure (LHS)
财政收入累计同比增长率（右坐标）
Growth rate of accumulated fiscal revenue (YOY) (RHS)
财政支出累计同比增长率（右坐标）
Growth rate of accumulated fiscal expenditure (YOY) (RHS)

一、经济增长率（Economic growth rate）

世界经济增长率
World economic growth rate

单位：% Unit: %

年 Year	国际货币基金组织按购买力平价方法计算的实际 GDP 增长率 Real GDP growth rate based on PPP (IMF)	世界银行按市场汇率法计算的实际 GDP 增长率 Real GDP growth rate based on market exchange rate（WB）
2006	5.4	4.4
2007	5.6	4.3
2008	3.1	1.9
2009	−0.1	−1.7
2010	5.4	4.3
2011	4.3	3.1
2012	3.5	2.5
2013	3.4	2.5
2014	3.5	2.6
2015	3.4	2.8
2016	3.3	2.4
2017	3.8	3.0
2018	3.6	3.2
2019	2.8	2.6
2020	−2.8	−3.1
2021	6.3	6.2
2022	3.5	3.0
2023*	3.1	2.6
2024*	3.1	2.4

数据来源：国际货币基金组织、世界银行、Wind。
注：*为预测数。
Source: IMF, The World Bank, Wind.
Note: *Projection.

主要经济体GDP增长率
Annual GDP growth rate of major economies

单位：% Unit: %

年 Year	美国 U.S.	日本 Japan	欧元区 Euro Area	英国 U.K.
2006	2.8	1.4	3.2	2.2
2007	2.0	1.5	3.0	2.6
2008	0.1	−1.2	0.4	−0.2
2009	−2.6	−5.7	−4.5	−4.5
2010	2.7	4.1	2.1	2.4
2011	1.6	0.0	1.7	1.1
2012	2.3	1.4	−0.9	1.4
2013	1.8	2.0	−0.2	1.8
2014	2.3	0.3	1.4	3.2
2015	2.7	1.6	2.0	2.4
2016	1.7	0.8	1.9	2.2
2017	2.2	1.7	2.6	2.4
2018	2.9	0.6	1.8	1.7
2019	2.3	−0.4	1.6	1.6
2020	−2.8	−4.3	−6.1	−11.0
2021	5.9	2.2	5.3	7.6
2022	1.9	1.0	3.4	4.3
2023	2.5	1.9	0.5	0.5
2024*	2.1	0.9	0.9	0.6

数据来源：国际货币基金组织、世界银行、Wind。
注：*为预测数。
Source: IMF, The World Bank, Wind.
Note: *Projection.

世界经济增长率
World economic growth rate

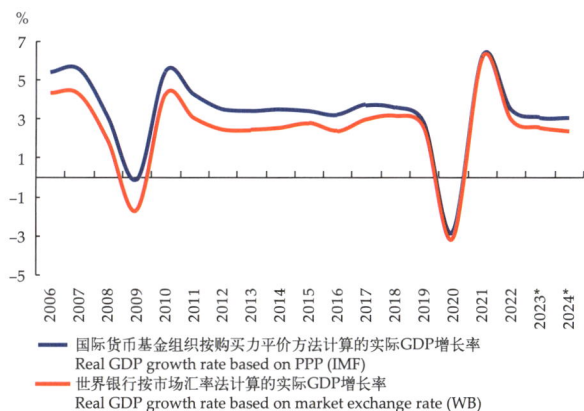

国际货币基金组织按购买力平价方法计算的实际GDP增长率
Real GDP growth rate based on PPP (IMF)
世界银行按市场汇率法计算的实际GDP增长率
Real GDP growth rate based on market exchange rate (WB)

主要经济体GDP增长率
Annual GDP growth rate of major economies

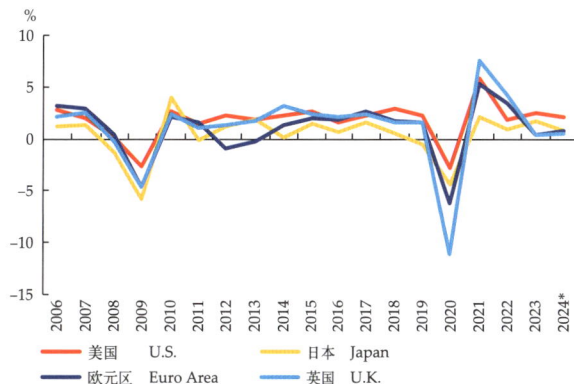

美国　U.S.　　日本　Japan
欧元区　Euro Area　　英国　U.K.

GDP季度同比增长率
Year-on-year quarterly growth rate of GDP

单位：% Unit: %

年 / 季度 Year/Quarter	美国 U.S.	日本 Japan	欧元区 Euro Area	英国 U.K.
2020Q1	1.2	−1.7	−2.9	−1.7
2020Q2	−7.5	−9.7	−14.1	−21.9
2020Q3	−1.5	−5.0	−3.9	−9.5
2020Q4	−1.1	−0.4	−4.0	−8.3
2021Q1	1.6	−0.6	−0.2	−6.7
2021Q2	12.0	8.0	14.8	25.7
2021Q3	4.7	2.1	4.6	9.5
2021Q4	5.4	1.3	5.2	9.7
2022Q1	3.6	0.3	5.4	11.4
2022Q2	1.9	1.5	4.1	3.9
2022Q3	1.7	1.5	2.4	2.1
2022Q4	0.7	0.5	1.8	0.6
2023Q1	1.7	2.6	1.8	0.3
2023Q2	2.4	2.3	1.1	0.3
2023Q3	2.9	1.7	0.5	0.2
2023Q4	3.1	1.0	0.7	−0.2

数据来源：各经济体官方统计网站、Wind。
Sources: Official statistical websites of the economies, Wind.

GDP季度环比折年率
Quarter-on-quarter annualized growth rate of GDP

单位：% Unit: %

年 / 季度 Year/Quarter	美国 U.S.	日本 Japan	欧元区 Euro Area	英国 U.K.
2020Q1	−5.3	2.1	−13.0	−9.7
2020Q2	−28.0	−27.7	−38.0	−57.9
2020Q3	34.8	23.9	57.7	91.2
2020Q4	4.2	7.8	−0.3	6.1
2021Q1	5.2	1.0	1.8	−4.1
2021Q2	6.2	1.5	8.6	29.2
2021Q3	3.3	−1.9	8.6	7.1
2021Q4	7.0	5.0	2.0	6.2
2022Q1	−2.0	−2.7	2.6	2.5
2022Q2	−0.6	4.6	3.3	0.2
2022Q3	2.7	−0.8	1.9	−0.4
2022Q4	2.6	1.7	−0.4	0.5
2023Q1	2.2	4.4	0.4	0.6
2023Q2	2.1	4.0	0.5	0.0
2023Q3	4.9	−3.3	−0.5	0.0
2023Q4	3.3	−0.4	0.2	

数据来源：各经济体官方统计网站、Wind。
Sources: Official statistical websites of the economies, Wind.

GDP季度同比增长率
Year-on-year quarterly growth rate of GDP

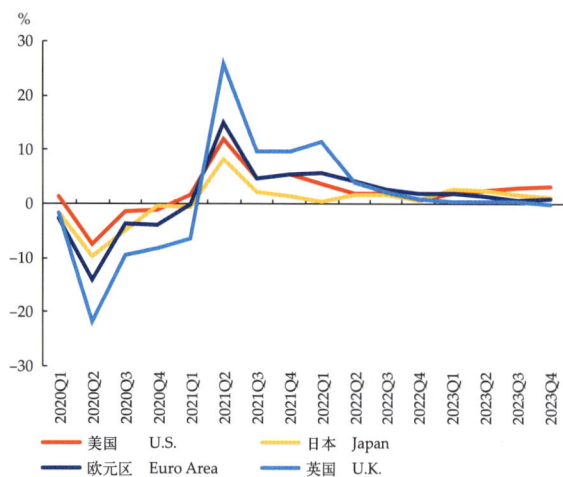

GDP季度环比折年率
Quarter-on-quarter annualized growth rate of GDP

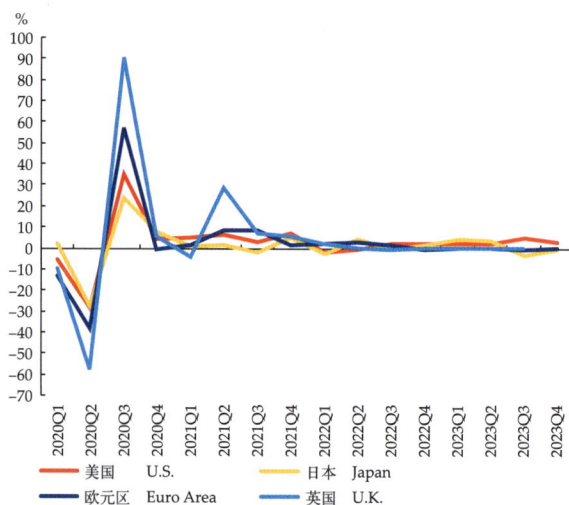

二、消费价格指数（CPI）

消费价格当月同比指数
Monthly CPI (YOY)

单位：% Unit: %

年 / 月 Year/Month	美国 U.S.	日本 Japan	欧元区 Euro Area	英国 U.K.
2022.01	7.5	0.5	5.1	5.5
2022.02	7.9	0.9	5.9	6.2
2022.03	8.5	1.2	7.4	7.0
2022.04	8.3	2.5	7.4	9.0
2022.05	8.6	2.5	8.1	9.1
2022.06	9.1	2.4	8.6	9.4
2022.07	8.5	2.6	8.9	10.1
2022.08	8.3	3.0	9.1	9.9
2022.09	8.2	3.0	9.9	10.1
2022.10	7.7	3.7	10.6	11.1
2022.11	7.1	3.8	10.1	10.7
2022.12	6.5	4.0	9.2	10.5
2023.01	6.4	4.3	8.6	10.1
2023.02	6.0	3.3	8.5	10.4
2023.03	5.0	3.2	6.9	10.1
2023.04	4.9	3.5	7.0	8.7
2023.05	4.0	3.2	6.1	8.7
2023.06	3.0	3.3	5.5	7.9
2023.07	3.2	3.3	5.3	6.8
2023.08	3.7	3.2	5.2	6.7
2023.09	3.7	3.0	4.3	6.7
2023.10	3.2	3.3	2.9	4.6
2023.11	3.1	2.8	2.4	3.9
2023.12	3.4	2.6	2.9	4.0

数据来源：各经济体官方统计网站、Wind。
Sources: Official statistical websites of the economies, Wind.

三、失业率（Unemployment rate）

失业率（季节调整后）
Unemployment rate (after seasonal adjustment)

单位：% Unit: %

年 / 月 Year/Month	美国 U.S.	日本 Japan	欧元区 Euro Area	英国 U.K.
2022.01	4.0	2.7	6.9	4.6
2022.02	3.8	2.6	6.8	4.4
2022.03	3.6	2.6	6.8	4.2
2022.04	3.7	2.7	6.7	4.1
2022.05	3.6	2.8	6.7	4.0
2022.06	3.6	2.7	6.7	3.9
2022.07	3.5	2.5	6.7	3.9
2022.08	3.6	2.6	6.7	3.9
2022.09	3.5	2.7	6.7	3.9
2022.10	3.6	2.6	6.6	3.9
2022.11	3.6	2.4	6.7	3.9
2022.12	3.5	2.3	6.7	3.9
2023.01	3.4	2.4	6.7	3.9
2023.02	3.6	2.5	6.6	3.8
2023.03	3.5	2.8	6.5	3.9
2023.04	3.4	2.7	6.5	3.9
2023.05	3.7	2.7	6.5	3.9
2023.06	3.6	2.6	6.4	3.9
2023.07	3.5	2.6	6.5	4.0
2023.08	3.8	2.7	6.5	3.9
2023.09	3.8	2.6	6.5	4.0
2023.10	3.8	2.5	6.5	4.0
2023.11	3.7	2.4	6.4	4.0
2023.12	3.7	2.3	6.4	4.0

数据来源：各经济体官方统计网站、Wind。
Sources: Official statistical websites of the economies, Wind.

消费价格当月同比增速
Monthly CPI (YOY)

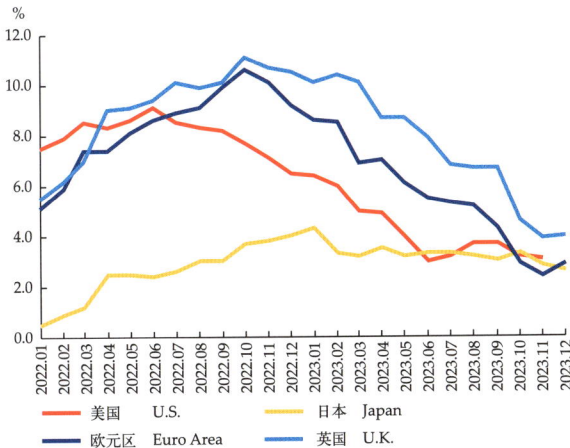

失业率（季节调整后）
Unemployment rate (after seasonal adjustment)

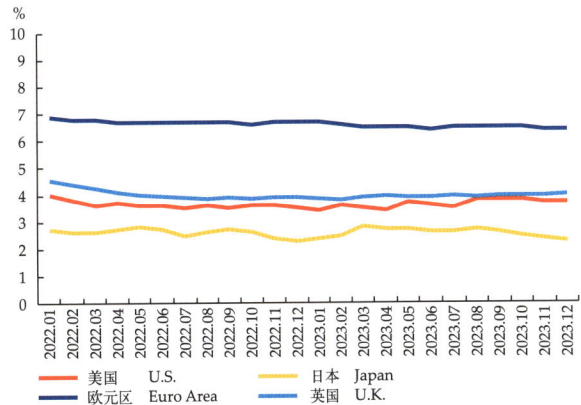

四、国际收支（BOP）

单位：10亿
Unit: billion

年 / 季度 Year/Quarter	美国/美元 U.S./USD			日本/日元 Japan/JPY			欧元区/欧元 Euro Area/EUR			英国/英镑 U.K./GBP		
	经常项目 Current account	资本与金融项目 Capital and financial account	净误差与遗漏 Net errors and omissions	经常项目 Current account	资本与金融项目 Capital and financial account	净误差与遗漏 Net errors and omissions	经常项目 Current account	资本与金融项目 Capital and financial account	净误差与遗漏 Net errors and omissions	经常项目 Current account	资本与金融项目 Capital and financial account	净误差与遗漏 Net errors and omissions
2020Q1	−100.45	156.95	−56.51	5 293.90	−4 738.70	−555.20	9.89	24.04		−11.34	−15.10	−7.87
2020Q2	−149.23	70.65	78.58	892.90	−1 691.80	798.80	32.49	−0.44		−7.74	−3.44	6.19
2020Q3	−167.26	168.00	−0.73	4 897.40	−4 468.00	−429.50	65.71	−94.52		−10.33	−12.83	3.98
2020Q4	−180.20	267.73	−87.52	4 907.40	−3 433.90	−1 473.60	91.54	−128.45		−30.97	−45.25	−12.52
2021Q1	−175.55	175.89	−0.34	6 248.10	−3 930.50	−2 317.60	108.78	−114.48		−4.54	−3.59	0.27
2021Q2	−200.22	219.77	−19.56	5 545.70	−4 288.20	−1 257.60	100.92	−115.62		5.81	6.95	2.41
2021Q3	−226.73	215.80	10.93	6 086.20	−6 682.90	596.70	89.00	−82.84		−14.09	−9.37	8.77
2021Q4	−228.95	174.86	54.09	3 605.10	−2 308.10	−1 296.90	46.91	−46.28		2.01	−13.43	−15.61
2022Q1	−283.90	266.74	17.16	4 858.60	−5 124.90	266.30	18.27	3.50		−45.70	−35.34	11.72
2022Q2	−248.78	129.75	119.03	2 087.10	163.00	−2 250.10	−26.61	75.07		−23.75	−28.23	−1.87
2022Q3	−222.76	220.55	2.20	2 136.00	−1 238.10	−897.90	−66.38	28.86		−11.86	−16.02	−0.46
2022Q4	−216.15	183.14	33.02	1 632.80	317.00	−1 949.80	−7.78	−35.90		4.10	16.38	10.88
2023Q1	−214.47	344.15	−129.67	2 412.30	−7 517.40	5 105.20	32.64	−34.67		−15.70	−4.72	14.97
2023Q2	−216.81	137.65	79.15	5 192.30	−4 181.00	−1 011.20	66.99	−45.61		−23.97	−27.02	3.86
2023Q3	−200.30	136.49	63.82	7 772.40	−7 760.20	−12.20	76.85	−89.61		−17.18	−21.63	8.07
2023Q4	—	—	—	5 252.70	−3 668.10	−1 584.60	83.07	−123.15		—	—	—

数据来源：各经济体官方统计网站、Wind。
Source: Official statistical websites of the economies, Wind.

美国国际收支
BOP of U.S.

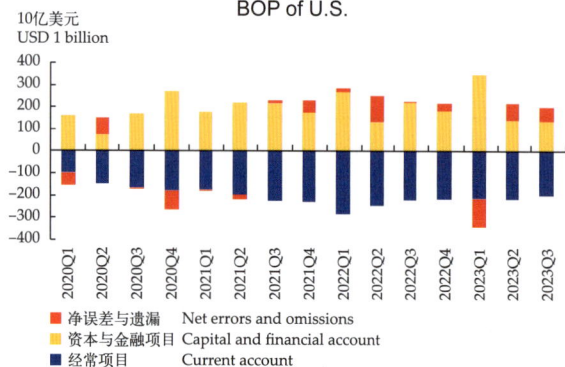

欧元区国际收支
BOP of Euro area

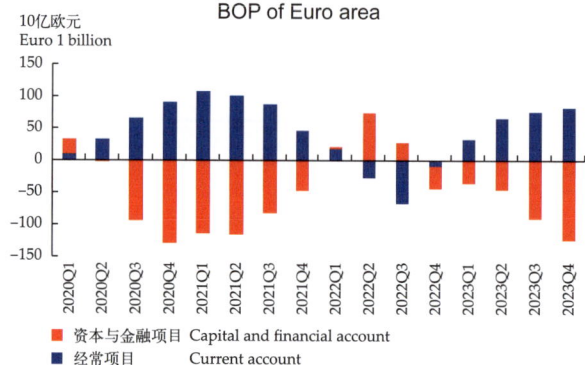

日本国际收支
BOP of Japan

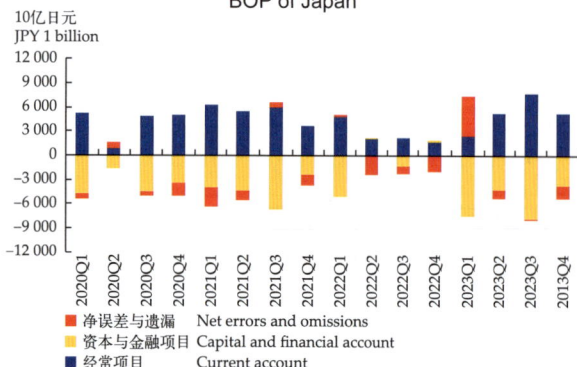

英国国际收支
BOP of U.K.

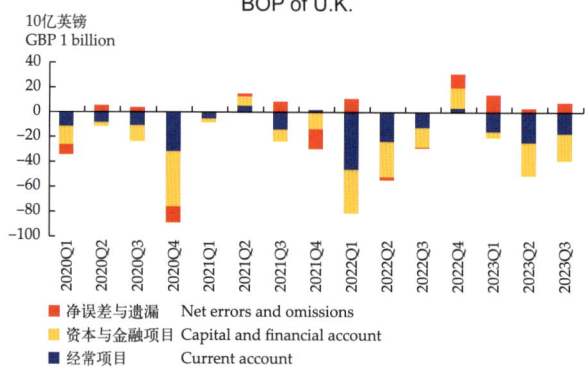

五、利率（Interest rate）

5.1 中央银行政策利率（Central bank policy rates）

中央银行政策利率
Central bank policy rates

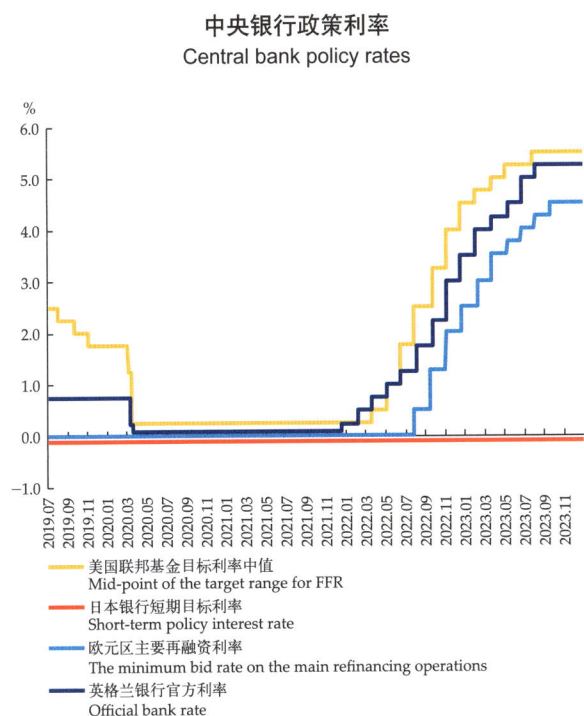

中央银行政策利率图例：
- 美国联邦基金目标利率中值
  Mid-point of the target range for FFR
- 日本银行短期目标利率
  Short-term policy interest rate
- 欧元区主要再融资利率
  The minimum bid rate on the main refinancing operations
- 英格兰银行官方利率
  Official bank rate

5.2 市场利率（Market interest rates）

隔夜基准利率
Overnight benchmark rates

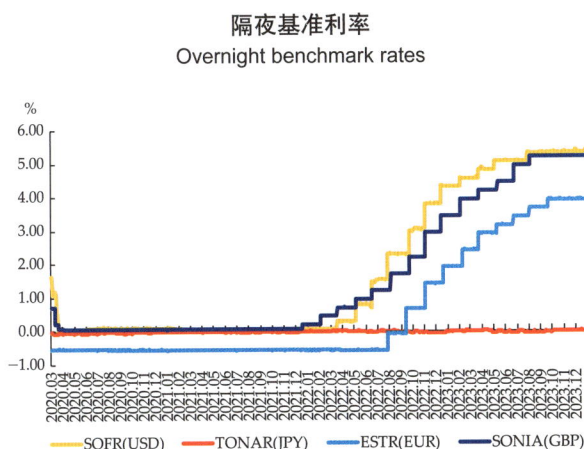

SOFR(USD)　TONAR(JPY)　ESTR(EUR)　SONIA(GBP)

10年期国债收益率
（年率，月平均）
10-year government bond yield
(annualized, monthly average)

单位：% Unit: %

年 / 月 Year/Month	美元 USD	日元 JPY	欧元 EUR	英镑 GBP
2022.01	1.76	0.14	−0.06	1.21
2022.02	1.93	0.21	0.24	1.49
2022.03	2.13	0.21	0.36	1.55
2022.04	2.75	0.24	0.82	1.84
2022.05	2.90	0.24	1.06	1.91
2022.06	3.14	0.25	1.58	2.38
2022.07	2.90	0.23	1.23	2.15
2022.08	2.90	0.21	1.17	2.33
2022.09	3.52	0.27	1.86	3.50
2022.10	3.98	0.26	2.30	4.11
2022.11	3.89	0.27	2.17	3.42
2022.12	3.62	0.36	2.17	3.50
2023.01	3.53	0.48	2.27	3.51
2023.02	3.75	0.52	2.46	3.56
2023.03	3.66	0.40	2.47	3.56
2023.04	3.46	0.47	2.47	3.65
2023.05	3.57	0.42	2.45	3.96
2023.06	3.75	0.42	2.48	4.37
2023.07	3.90	0.46	2.56	4.44
2023.08	4.17	0.64	2.65	4.53
2023.09	4.38	0.71	2.76	4.42
2023.10	4.80	0.82	2.91	4.57
2023.11	4.50	0.81	2.67	4.27
2023.12	4.02	0.69	2.20	3.86

数据来源：各经济体官方统计网站、Wind。
Sources: Official statistical websites of the economies, Wind.

10年期国债收益率（年率，月平均）
10-year government bond yield (annualized, monthly average)

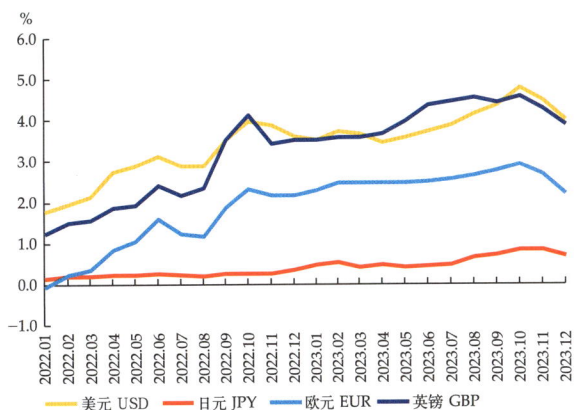

美元 USD　日元 JPY　欧元 EUR　英镑 GBP

六、汇率（Exchange rates）

汇率（月平均）
Exchange rates (monthly average)

年 / 月 Year/Month	美元 / 欧元 USD/EUR	美元 / 英镑 USD/GBP	日元 / 美元 JPY/USD
2022.01	1.1317	1.3555	114.83
2022.02	1.1349	1.3540	115.28
2022.03	1.1019	1.3168	118.58
2022.04	1.0803	1.2933	126.37
2022.05	1.0567	1.2438	128.85
2022.06	1.0567	1.2320	133.96
2022.07	1.0168	1.1987	136.71
2022.08	1.0129	1.1983	135.28
2022.09	0.9899	1.1320	143.28
2022.10	0.9853	1.1332	147.05
2022.11	1.0192	1.1727	142.45
2022.12	1.0591	1.2180	134.91
2023.01	1.0777	1.2237	130.45
2023.02	1.0702	1.2084	133.05
2023.03	1.0711	1.2138	133.66
2023.04	1.0962	1.2446	133.47
2023.05	1.0867	1.2484	137.05
2023.06	1.0840	1.2627	141.36
2023.07	1.1067	1.2893	140.94
2023.08	1.0910	1.2706	144.78
2023.09	1.0672	1.2381	147.85
2023.10	1.0565	1.2175	149.59
2023.11	1.0819	1.2437	149.68
2023.12	1.0909	1.2657	143.98

数据来源：各经济体官方统计网站、Wind。
Sources: Official statistical websites of the economies, Wind.

实际有效汇率（月平均，2010年＝100）
Real effective exchange rates (monthly average, year 2010=100)

年 / 月 Year/Month	美元 USD	欧元 EUR	日元 JPY	英镑 GBP
2022.01	100.9	97.6	86.7	105.6
2022.02	100.8	97.8	85.9	105.2
2022.03	102.4	98.6	84.0	104.1
2022.04	103.2	96.5	79.3	105.2
2022.05	106.2	96.6	79.4	103.4
2022.06	107.4	96.8	76.0	102.6
2022.07	109.2	94.8	75.7	102.6
2022.08	108.7	94.6	77.0	103.0
2022.09	111.3	95.5	74.6	99.3
2022.10	113.0	97.1	73.7	101.3
2022.11	110.2	98.2	75.2	103.0
2022.12	107.4	99.1	77.7	104.4
2023.01	105.7	98.3	78.9	101.9
2023.02	106.2	98.5	77.2	102.2
2023.03	106.8	99.5	77.5	103.1
2023.04	106.0	101.1	77.5	105.0
2023.05	106.8	100.7	76.0	106.9
2023.06	107.3	101.5	74.3	108.9
2023.07	106.2	102.6	74.4	109.2
2023.08	107.7	102.6	73.1	108.8
2023.09	109.1	102.0	72.3	108.1
2023.10	110.5	101.6	72.5	106.9
2023.11	108.4	101.6	71.5	107.2
2023.12	106.7	101.4	73.4	108.4

数据来源：各经济体官方统计网站、Wind。
Sources: Official statistical websites of the economies, Wind.

汇率（月平均）
Exchange rates (monthly average)

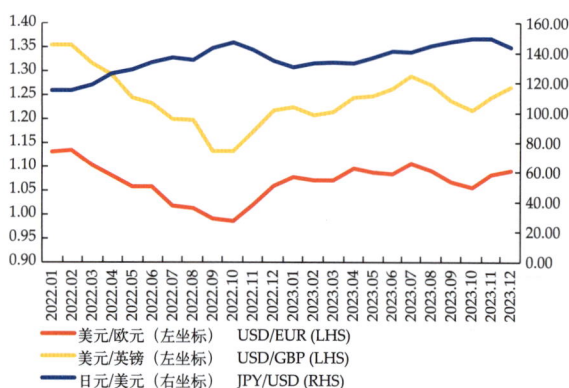

美元/欧元（左坐标）　USD/EUR (LHS)
美元/英镑（左坐标）　USD/GBP (LHS)
日元/美元（右坐标）　JPY/USD (RHS)

实际有效汇率（月平均，2010年＝100）
Real effective exchange rates (monthly average, year 2010=100)

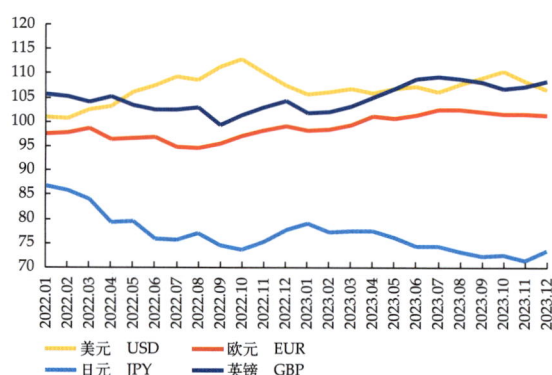

美元　USD　　欧元　EUR
日元　JPY　　英镑　GBP

七、股票市场指数（Stock market indices）

主要股票市场指数（期末）
Major stock market indices (end-period)

年 / 月 Year/Month	美国道琼斯工业平均指数 Dow Jones 30	纳斯达克综合指数 NASDAQ	日本日经 225 种股票平均 价格指数 Nikkei 225	道琼斯欧元区 STOXX 50 股票指数 Dow Jones EURO STOXX 50
2022.01	35 132	14 240	27 002	4 175
2022.02	33 893	13 751	26 527	3 924
2022.03	34 678	14 221	27 821	3 903
2022.04	32 977	12 335	26 848	3 803
2022.05	32 990	12 081	27 280	3 789
2022.06	30 775	11 029	26 393	3 455
2022.07	32 845	12 391	27 802	3 708
2022.08	31 510	11 816	28 092	3 517
2022.09	28 726	10 576	25 937	3 318
2022.10	32 733	10 988	27 587	3 618
2022.11	34 590	11 468	27 969	3 965
2022.12	33 147	10 466	26 095	3 794
2023.01	34 086	11 585	27 327	4 163
2023.02	32 657	11 456	27 446	4 238
2023.03	33 274	12 222	28 041	4 315
2023.04	34 098	12 227	28 856	4 359
2023.05	32 908	12 935	30 888	4 218
2023.06	34 408	13 788	33 189	4 399
2023.07	35 560	14 346	33 172	4 471
2023.08	34 722	14 035	32 619	4 297
2023.09	33 508	13 219	31 858	4 175
2023.10	33 053	12 851	30 859	4 061
2023.11	35 951	14 226	33 487	4 382
2023.12	37 690	15 011	33 464	4 522

数据来源：Wind。
Source: Wind.

主要股票市场指数（期末）
Major stock market indices (end-period)

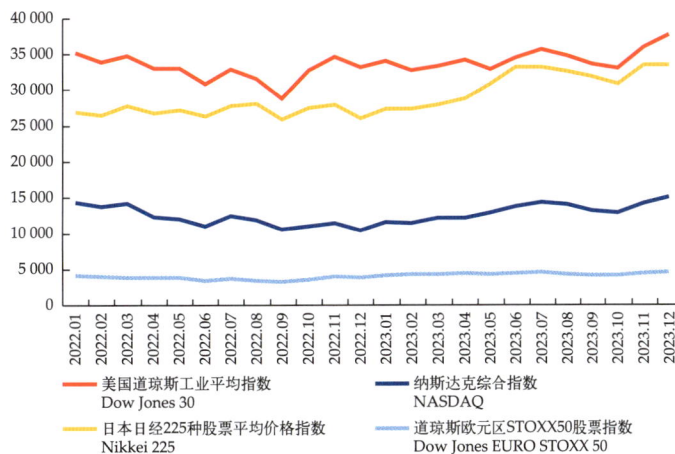

美国道琼斯工业平均指数 Dow Jones 30　纳斯达克综合指数 NASDAQ　日本日经225种股票平均价格指数 Nikkei 225　道琼斯欧元区STOXX50股票指数 Dow Jones EURO STOXX 50